CONCEPTS AND TECHNIQUES IN URBAN ANALYSIS

CROOM HELM SERIES IN GEOGRAPHY AND ENVIRONMENT
Edited by Alan Wilson, Nigel Thrift and Michael Bradford

Concepts and Techniques in Urban Analysis

'Bola Ayeni

CROOM HELM LONDON

© 1979 'Bola Ayeni
Croom Helm Ltd, 2–10 St John's Road, London SW11

British Library Calaloguing in Publication Data

Ayeni, Bola
    Concepts and techniques in urban
    analysis. – (Croom Helm geography series).
    1. Cities and towns – Mathematical models
    2. Systems analysis
    I. Title
    301.36   HT153

    ISBN 0-85664-557-5
    ISBN 0-85664-832-9 Pbk

Printed in Great Britain by offset lithography by
Billing & Sons Ltd, Guildford, London and Worcester

79 000212

CONTENTS

FIGURES

TABLES

ACKNOWLEDGEMENTS

I would like to thank the editors and publishers of the following journals for permission to use and revise previously published materials: the *Nigerian Journal for Quantitative Economics* for material in Chapter 3; the *Nigerian Geographical Journal* for material in Chapter 4; *Urban Ecology* for material in Chapters 7 and 10; the *Annals of Regional Science* for some material in Chapter 11; and *Environment and Planning A* for material in Chapters 3 and 13. The material in Chapter 5 was modified from a paper read at a conference on Nigerian youth in 1976. I would like to thank Dr A.O. Sanda of the Department of Sociology of the University of Ibadan for permission to use this work.

I also want to thank the following authors and publishers for permission to quote from copyright material: R. Park, E. Burgess and R. McKenzie and the University of Chicago Press for Figure 1.2.1; the Editor and Publisher of the *Annals of the American Academy of Political and Social Science* for Figure 1.2.2; W. Shevky and W. Bell and Stanford University Press for Table 1.3.1; B.J.L. Berry and P. Rees and Prentice-Hall for Figures 1.3.1, 2.3.1 and 2.3.2; W. Alonso and Harvard University Press for Figures 1.4.1 and 1.4.2; L. Wingo and Resources for the Future Inc. for Figure 1.4.3; and Alan Wilson and Pion for Figure 2.3.2.

PREFACE

This is a book on urban analysis. It is written with the conviction that geography, as well as other social sciences, has developed over the years some concepts, tools and techniques that are crucial to the understanding of man's greatest artefact: cities and metropolitan areas. Its principal emphasis is spatial. It regards urban studies as man-centred and investigates how man's interactions give rise to urban spatial structure. It also emphasises man's preoccupation with decision-making and problem solving in an urban system.

The interest in urban analysis is only recent, dating back to the quantitative revolution that swept through the social sciences in the 1940s and 1950s. The contents of the book are therefore recent and represent a collection and synthesis of major developments in the field. It is inevitably based on the accumulated knowledge of students, researchers and all those interested in the city. The extensive list of references and bibliographical material at the end of each chapter is a testimony of my indebtedness to colleagues in this field. These authors, to whom I am most grateful for permission to quote from published material, are in no way responsible for errors of omission or commission that may be in the book. Space limitations prevent me from cataloguing their names.

None the less, I must express my appreciation for help rendered by Akin Mabogunje and Alan Wilson of the Departments of Geography at the Universities of Ibadan and Leeds respectively. Their individual scholarship is instrumental to the evolution of my approach to urban analysis. Furthermore, many of the analyses reported in the book were carried out under the supervision of Akin Mabogunje.

I appreciate the financial support of the University of Ibadan which has enabled me to pursue the researches that culminate in this book. I also appreciate the support of Ken Duecker and the Institute of Urban and Regional Research of the University of Iowa towards the preparation of the book.

I have written this book in the hope that it will contribute to the understanding of the nature of the city and its problems. I also hope it will stimulate further researches of both a conceptual and analytical nature that will lead to the development of useful and versatile planning mechanisms.

'Bola Ayeni
Iowa City

INTRODUCTION

Social scientists have shown increasing interest not only in finding solutions to the numerous problems resulting from urbanisation but also in the distribution, organisation and interaction of activities within an urban system as well as in the development of both theoretical and quantitative preoccupations that could be evaluative of policies that affect the urban system. Consequently a number of concepts and techniques have evolved in the attempt to understand and articulate the nature of cities. Such concepts and techniques, which range from methods of descriptive statistics to the construction of mathematical models, could be described as tools of urban analysis.

Urban analysis was defined by Catanese as 'the *breakdown* of urban systems into their physical, political, economic and social parts in order to *understand* them, *determine* their problems and *seek* solutions to these problems' (Catanese, 1972, p. 2, my emphasis). Therefore in urban analysis, understanding is the key word and it involves the description and explanation of the component parts into which an urban system may be divided. Description and explanation are not separable, as one involves statements arising from close examination of a phenomenon while the other involves 'the reduction of an unexpected outcome to an expected outcome' (Harvey, 1969, p. 11). Understanding therefore furnishes us with the reasons for, and the means of, the growth and development of the phenomenon of interest. Consequently, it is conceivable to expect the goals of urban analysis to bear close affinities with those of scientific enquiry, the aims and purposes of which are 'to provide systematic and responsibly supported explanations . . . for individual occurrences, for recurring processes, or for invariable as well as statistical regularities' (Nagel, 1961, p. 15).

Urbanisation and its consequences are world-wide phenomena, and their origins and causes show not only recurring processes but also a large variety of statistical regularities. Yet understanding, planning and controlling the mechanisms of the twentieth-century city remain one of the greatest challenges of all times. Consequently, urban analysts should be concerned not only with the grouping and classification of these cities but also with providing explanations for their temporal as well as spatial organisation. It might also be expected that these would be precursors to the much-needed explanation and articulation of the problems generated by urban centres all over the world. Furthermore, the city is a functional unit, and its conceptualisation as an organic entity with interactions should be a primary focus for urban analysts. Thus, like geography itself, urban analysis should attempt

> to acquire knowledge of the world in which we live, both facts and relationships, which shall be as objective and accurate as possible. It [should] seek to present that knowledge in the form of concepts, relationships and principles that shall, as far as possible, apply to all parts of the world. Finally, it [should] seek to organize the dependable knowledge so obtained in logical systems, reduced by mutual connections into as small a number of independent systems as possible (Hartshorne, 1939, p. 375; slightly modified).

Our view therefore is that the analysis of urbanisation, as well as its consequences, should involve both the use of quantitative techniques and the use of models, theories and the search for laws in the spatial as well as temporal manifestations of our phenomena of interest. To this extent, we share the view of Harvey (1969, p. 130) that the search for laws in geography could proceed along two levels — the development of theory from some abstract calculi or through some model-building approach. However, we shall in this book concentrate on the explanation of our phenomenon, using old concepts and generating new ones as well as putting these within a modelling framework that recognises the complexities of the urban system. It is believed that such an approach is likely to lead to the identification of the gaps which exist in our knowledge and understanding and hence in how to control and monitor the urban system. This view, when based on a strong empirical backcloth also conforms with the views of Nagel and Hartshorne on scientific enquiry and geography respectively.

It is not my intention to make the book a compendium of all that has been done in urban studies. Besides the fact that this is almost an impossible task, neither my interests nor my ability lie that way. My intention is to describe and interpret some of the more important techniques that are used in evaluating the single city or metropolitan area as opposed to those used in evaluating a system of cities. Thus such concepts as the central place theory, theories of urban regional growth and the growth pole concept will not be considered in this book. Instead, much space will be given to the development of theories, models, concepts and techniques that deal with the single city, and in which I have been personally involved. While this could be a personal bias, I believe it enables me to emphasise and demonstrate their utility in urban analysis.

This book is a direct outcome of my researches at the Department of Geography of the University of Ibadan since 1972, although much of the material had been taught to both undergraduate and graduate students in geography and planning science since 1974. The comments, criticisms and ideas of these students have been crucial to the clarification of subject contents as well as the general arrangement of the book. In fact, my plan to write the book arose from the felt need for collection, interpretation and illustration of a number of concepts, models and techniques which have varied utilisation in geography and planning, but which at present are either inaccessible to students or are scattered in numerous journals or monographs. Consequently, the book is aimed at both undergraduate and graduate students, researchers and practitioners who are concerned not only with methodological developments in urban geography, but are also interested in exploring the extent to which concepts and techniques become applicable to practical problems that face the spatial analyst of urban centres.

1. An Outline of the Book

The book is organised into two sections dealing with methods of urban analysis and techniques of urban simulation modelling respectively. This dichotomy is arbitrary, as both sections overlap, since many concepts discussed in the first section are used in the section of simulation modelling. These sections correspond roughly with the descriptive-explanatory and analytical-predictive aspects of the understanding process. These two aspects are considered crucial to the manipulation and control of an urban system, in such a way as to meet the goals, aims and objectives of society.

The first section contains six chapters, the first of which, 'The Nature of Cities', deals with such varied topics as the classical models of urban spatial structure, its reformulation in terms of factorial ecology and social area analysis and the earlier micro-economic approaches to urban structure. This chapter provides most of the theoretical framework of this section as well as for some of the second section. The second chapter examines the spatial and socio-economic characteristics of urban populations as well as emphasising the role of migration *vis-à-vis* natural growth in analysing aggregate rates of the growth of urban population.

The third chapter, dealing with urban economic activity from an analytical point of view, examines three widely used techniques of the urban economic base, input-output analysis and the shift and share technique within both a descriptive and a forecasting framework. This is related to empirical work based on the author's researches in Jos and Lagos in Nigeria. The fourth chapter recognises the role of spatial inter-action in an urban system. It uses two interrelated approaches of micro- and macro-level behaviour and stresses the need to relate micro-level behaviour (social processes) to macro-level patterns. The fifth chapter picks up the theme of spatial interaction and links it with the location and utilisation of intra-city service facilities. On the other hand, Chapter 6 provides an aggregate description of urban spatial interaction patterns in terms of the functional association of land uses; and links these with the formal spatial structure through the technique of canonical correlation.

Throughout this book, and especially in this section, numerous statistical techniques are used in testing concepts and generating new hypotheses. Unlike many books on urban analysis, these techniques were not seen as the end in themselves, but rather as a means to an end: the understanding of the urban system. Consequently, only minimum descriptions of the mathematics and inferential properties of these techniques were provided, since a fuller description would unnecessarily lengthen the book, and these techniques are well documented in standard textbooks (Blalock, 1960; Draper and Smith, 1966; Winer, 1962; Anderson, 1958; Morrison, 1967) and many books on statistical geography (King, 1969; Gregory, 1963).

The second section deals with simulation modelling techniques in urban analysis and covers the next seven chapters. Chapter 7 examines the basis and role of simulation modelling and thus provides the rationale and the conceptual framework for the subsequent chapters. Although the techniques covered could in no way claim to be exhaustive of all the approaches to urban simulation modelling, they represent the major developments in the field. Chapter 8 examines the probability or stochastic approaches to model construction through the Monte Carlo and Markov chain techniques while Chapter 9 examines optimisation models as normative frameworks for the analysis of the urban form. These two approaches represent opposite views to the study of urban analysis as the first recognises not only the complexities of the urban phenomenon and man's inability to comprehend this fully, while the latter, on the other hand, assumes that a perfect knowledge of this phenomenon is possible.

Chapter 10 introduces the rather controversial concept of entropy maximisation in urban modelling and illustrates a use of the two approaches offered by the origins of the concept of entropy. It also posits that the two origins, though different, are not irreconcilable, as one could be seen as a special case of the other. The entropy-maximising framework is one of the most recent of the approaches to urban modelling and it is one that justifies a characterisation of simulation on the basis of its hypothesis-testing capability as an experimental technique for the solution of mathematical problems where analytical solutions are either difficult or impossible. Chapter 11 uses this theme to derive a disaggregated residential location model while in Chapter 12 a general model of metropolis is developed. The entropy-maximising framework is also flexible. It allows hypothesis generation and it is easily extended into a predictive framework. In Chapter 13, therefore, we develop a predictive model of urban stock and activity incorporating many of the earlier developments as well as other new ideas and concepts of dynamic modelling.

An important objective of the book is simplicity, expressed in the level of complexity of each chapter as well as in the arrangement of the chapters. For instance, each chapter moves from the simple to the complex, reflecting not only the level of research into urban analysis but also the continuing development of sophisticated theoretical and methodological approaches to the subject. In many cases, these techniques are first developed and illustrated by simple examples before examples of wider geographical interest are discussed. Such an approach leaves little room for technicalities, which are either left out or briefly discussed, although a rather extensive list of references is given at the end of each chapter for the more ambitious and enquiring student.

In the same way, the fourteen chapters of the book represent a graded synthesis. For instance, the book moves from the descriptive analysis of urban spatial structure by means of the classical models in Chapter 7, through the more demanding multivariate techniques of principal components and canonical correlation analyses in Chapter 6. From Chapter 7 onwards the contents of the chapters take on a more complicated level with extensive use of mathematics and mathematical symbols that culminate in the predictive model of urban stock and activity in Chapter 13. Although many of the chapters could be independent, a better perspective of the aims and purposes of the book is achieved by carefully reading both sections separately or together. Not more than high school or first year university mathematics is required for a full understanding of the book. The book by Wilson and Kirkby (1975) may be a useful background.

The final chapter is a reflection on the wide gap that exists in our knowledge of the urban system as well as on some of the ways, the concepts, techniques and models discussed in this book can be used in planning analysis. For urban analysis to provide the much-needed input into the monitoring, manipulation and control of the urban system, it is argued that there is a need for a planning process which recognises the aims, goals and objectives of a society and which at the same time provides the necessary institutional framework.

References

Anderson, T.W. 1958. *Introduction to Multivariate Statistical Analysis*. New York: John Wiley

Blalock, H.M. 1960. *Social Statistics*. New York: McGraw-Hill

Catanese, A.J. 1972. *Scientific Methods of Urban Analysis*. Urbana, Illinois: University of Illinois Press

Draper, N.R. and Smith H. 1966. *Applied Regression Analysis*. New York: Wiley

Gregory, S. 1963. *Statistical Methods and the Geographer*. London: Longmans, Green and Co.

Hartshone, R. 1939. *The Nature of Geography*. Chicago: University of Chicago Press

Harvey, D. 1969. *Explanation in Geography*. London: Arnold

King, L.J. 1969. *Statistical Analysis in Geography*. Englewood Cliffs, New Jersey: Prentice-Hall

Morrison, D.F. 1967. *Multivariate Statistical Methods*. New York: McGraw-Hill

Nagel, E. 1961. *The Structure of Science*. London: Routledge

Wilson, A.G. and Kirkby, M.J. 1975. *Mathematics for Geographers and Planners*. Oxford: Oxford University Press

Winer, B.J. 1962. *Statistical Principles in Experimental Design*. New York: McGraw-Hill

Part One:

CONCEPTS AND METHODS IN URBAN ANALYSIS

1 THE NATURE OF CITIES

1. Introduction

Urban analysis at the level of the individual city has seen, within the past few decades, a number of theories and models purporting to explain the internal spatial structure. Generally, these models have proceeded along three lines of investigation. The first line, characterised by the classical theories of urban spatial structure, strives to explain ecological patterns of land-use organisation through three major models, namely: the concentric zone (Burgess, 1927); the sector (Hoyt, 1939); and the multiple-nuclei (Harris and Ullman, 1945). The second, on the other hand, strives to explain the determinants of the social areas existing within the city. Two principal techniques for achieving this have been through the use of social area analysis, developed by Shevky and Bell (1955), and factorial ecology (Berry and Horton, 1970). In many cases factorial ecology has not only confirmed some of the findings of social area analysis but has also identified the complexity of the urban ecological field.

The third major approach to understand urban spatial structure is based on micro-economic considerations of household behaviour. In this regard, it has been argued that the urban land-use pattern is determined by the urban land-rent mechanism, which provides the theoretically perfect site in terms of the trade-off between site rentals and the cost of overcoming the friction of distance. Micro-economic theory of urban spatial structure pioneered by Wingo (1961) and Alonso (1964) has been very valuable in terms of researches generated both on theoretical and empirical fronts as well as in the general orientation of urban research. None the less, it is generally recognised that while these models and theories are laudible, they have not succeeded in totally explaining urban spatial form.

In this chapter, therefore, we shall provide a synthesis of the major tenets of these traditional approaches and in particular attempt a critical evaluation of the assumptions and hypotheses that underlie their formulation. We believe this is the only way to examine the applicability of these 'North American' models to cities in other parts of the world, where there may be cross-cultural differences as well as differences in societal value systems. Furthermore, it is expected that our synthesis will generate a suitable conceptual framework for much of the development of methods and techniques in the rest of the book.

2. Classical Models of Urban Spatial Structure

(i) The Concentric Zone Model

The concentric zone model, developed by Burgess (Park *et al.*, 1925), is really the first set of ideas towards the theoretical understanding of the city. It postulates that urban land use is arranged around a single centre, the central business district (CBD), in concentric zones made up of the zone in transition, the zone of the independent working men's homes, the zone of better residences and the commuters' zone (see Figure 1.2.1). The central business district is the hub of all urban activities, including financial, economic, social and recreational functions. In may also have some light manufacturing activities towards its outer fringes. The second zone comprises areas of residential deterioration as a result of the encroachment of business and industrial activities from the first zone and it is usually occupied by first-stage migrants. The third zone, the zone of independent working men's homes, comprises largely the residences of second-generation migrants into the city, while the fourth zone contains the residences of the middle class and is occupied by managers, clerks, salesmen and professional people. The last zone, the commuter's zone, is a ring of encircling small cities, towns and hamlets which serve as dormitory suburbs for the wealthier city-dwellers (see Figure 1.2.1).

Furthermore, it was argued that the zones are not static, as each tends to extend its area by the ecological process of 'invasion and succession'. Although it was not explicity stated in the formulation of the model, the operation of the urban rent mechanism was implicit, as it underlies the process of invasion and succession of land uses.

The generalisations contained in this concentric zone model of urban land-use organisations were based on empirical studies on the growth of Chicago. Consequently, the model has been criticised as not being the prototype of all American cities, especially since it can be shown that not all cities grow concentrically around a single centre. None the less, the fundamental assumptions of this model remain unchallenged (Davies, 1937; Quinn, 1940; Murphy, 1966, pp. 207–10) and few of the critics of Burgess provided alternative explanations. One who did was Homer Hoyt.

(ii) The Sector Model

The second model of urban spatial structure, though developed by Homer Hoyt, had its origins in the works of Hurd (1924) who described urban expansion as 'axial growth, pushing out from the centre along transportation lines'. However, Hoyt's formulation was based on

Figure 1.2.1: The Concentric Model of Urban Structure
Figure 1.2.2a: The Sector Model of Urban Structure
Figure 1.2.2b: The Multiple-nuclei Model of Urban Structure

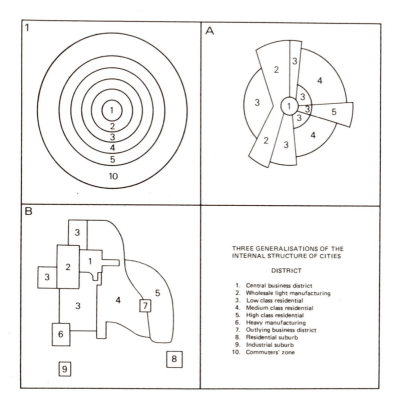

THREE GENERALISATIONS OF THE
INTERNAL STRUCTURE OF CITIES

DISTRICT

1. Central business district
2. Wholesale light manufacturing
3. Low class residential
4. Medium class residential
5. High class residential
6. Heavy manufacturing
7. Outlying business district
8. Residential suburb
9. Industrial suburb
10. Commuters' zone

extensive empirical investigation of rent differentials and the ability of urban functions to bid for city lands. According to him,

> rent in American cities tends to conform to a pattern of sectors rather than of concentric circles. The highest rent areas tend to be located in one or more sectors of the city ... There is a gradation of rentals downward from these high rental areas in all directions. Intermediate rental areas ... adjoin the high rent area in one or more sides and tend to be located in the same sectors as the high rental areas. Low rent areas occupy other entire sectors of the city from the centre to the periphery (Hoyt, 1939, p. 70).

Consequently Hoyt's model was meant to be an alternative to that of Burgess. The effect of land pricing leads to the occupation of the central zones by CBD functions alone as it is the only group of functions that could afford the rent. On the other hand, the major lines of transportation constitute lines of least resistance for growth in addition to their being important arteries along which similar types of land use are situated. The result is the emergence of a star-shaped pattern of city growth in which different types of land use radiate from the CBD along particular sectors towards the periphery of the city (Figure 1.2.2a).

The sector model did not go unchallenged (Firey, 1947, 1950; Rodwin, 1950), in spite of its extensive empirical background. However, in a recent appraisal by Hoyt (1966) it was maintained that residential land use in American cities still follows the sector pattern modified to a large extent by the influence of the automobile. Perhaps the one single important criticism of the sector model as well as the concentric model was the assumption of a monocentric urban area, a fact hardly borne out in any part of the world. This is probably one of the reasons why the multiple-nuclei model was proposed by Harris and Ullman.

(iii) The Multiple-nuclei Model

This model had its origins in the works of Mackenzie, a contemporary of Burgess, although it was formally set out by Harris and Ullman in 1945. It was formulated to forestall one of the criticisms of the earlier two models that visualised urban growth as originating from one single centre. According to Harris and Ullman (1965), the land use of a city is built around several discrete nuclei rather than one single nucleus as postulated by the sector and concentric models. Such a nucleus may be residential, industrial, commercial, etc., or even political as in the classical example of London, which has political and administrative centres. Of course other nuclei may arise from different requirements of urban activities as in the antagonising requirements of heavy industrial and high-class residential activities (see Figure 1.2.2b). The number of nuclei would vary greatly from city to city, although it is usual to expect this to vary with size of cities. Once a nucleus has been formed, the other types of land use are expected to develop around it. Consequently, it is valid to assume the existence of a single nucleus as suggested by the models of Burgess and Hoyt.

In a recent article, Ullman (1962) took another look into the American urban scene he had proposed in conjunction with Harris. In particular, the effect of automobiles on increasing decentralisation of the city as well as the increasing dependence of the city on commuters was used as another reason why the central business district would become just one of the many nuclei from which the city could grow.

In a sense, the multiple-nuclei model is both an amalgamation and a generalisation of earlier models. It is very adaptable to situations in the modern urban scene both in the developing and developed countries of the world. As a result it has been least criticised.

As methods of urban analysis at the very elementary stages, these models can be very useful, but the researcher should well note that they more or less deal with different aspects of the city. For example, the sector model concerns only residential use while the concentric model is more general. In this way, it has been argued (Mabogunje, 1968, pp. 117–8) that the models deal with different types of growth. Using this premise, Mabogunje argues that the first two models deal with what may be defined as 'natural growth process' of human population involving the slow, almost imperceptible change in the character and extent of function-areas in the city. On the other hand, the multiple-nuclei model assumes a relatively more dramatic growth, sometimes divergent, but infinitely more impressive in terms of its effect on the city's size and structure. The modern urban scene is characterised by these two features, a slow imperceptible natural growth and a dramatic and impressive growth that result from policy decisions and sometimes the whims and caprices of urban administrators.

Another important point about these models concerns their applicability in countries outside America where they were developed. It could be contended that where conditions are similar to those that obtain in North America, each or all of the models could be found applicable. However, the situation in many developing countries, especially areas where there was a fairly long history of urbanisation, could be slightly different. This is because urban centres in these areas show in the main characteristics of European pre-industrial urbanisation as well as features of modern industrial urbanisation. Thus the homogeneity of land uses found in Burgess's concentric zones would not be applicable since land uses in many African cities are less differentiated by function and area. In the same way, Hoyt's assumption of an economic system where people and business compete for land and in which the highest bidder wins is susceptible to very strong criticisms. Most cities in areas of pre-industrial urbanisation show evidence of deliberate allocation of particular areas of the city to certain uses, the rationale of which is in no way economic. Furthermore, the level of economic development is generally so low that until very recently there has been hardly any separation of businesses and residences, implying that there had never been any serious competition for land. Moreover, the influence of modern transportation on land uses has been hardly discernible until recently.

Consequently, a detailed analysis of the nature of Nigerian cities (Mabogunje, 1968, p. 184) concludes that

> while modern technology has served to transform medieval European cities into modern European cities, its effect in Nigeria so far has been to create twin cities – one traditional and one modern . . . The interaction between these two provides the really existing basis for understanding the emerging urban forms and functions in Nigeria. The larger the traditional urban mass, the clearer and more comprehensive is the nature of the interaction.

This is the origin of the dual-centre model of the growth of colonial cities (Johnson, 1972, p. 185). The dual-centre model is a form of the multiple-nuclei model whereby the two centres result from the interaction between two histories of urbanisation, a precolonial and pre-industrial urbanisation; and a colonial quasi-industrial urbanisation.

In a way, the three models can be judiciously used to provide some basis for the analysis of the city. However, such an analysis may be general and susceptible to the criticism that the models are largely descriptive and devoid of all mathematical rigour and analysis, in addition to saying very little about the processes that cause these changes in land-use patterns. Factorial ecology, to some extent, and micro-economic theories, to a larger extent, provide answers to some of the criticisms.

Figure 1.3.1: Social Area Analysis, Broadly Defined

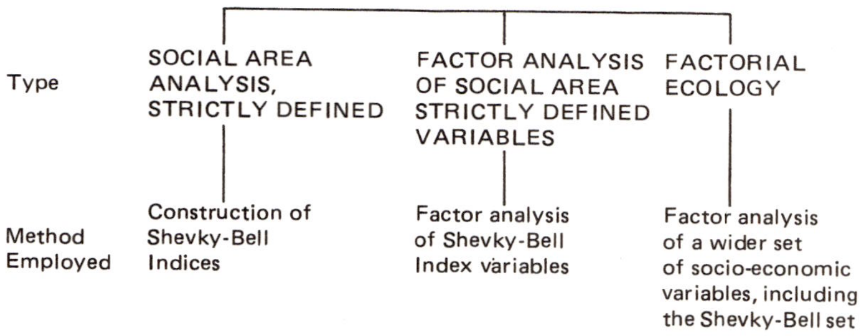

Type	SOCIAL AREA ANALYSIS, STRICTLY DEFINED	FACTOR ANALYSIS OF SOCIAL AREA STRICTLY DEFINED VARIABLES	FACTORIAL ECOLOGY
Method Employed	Construction of Shevky-Bell Indices	Factor analysis of Shevky-Bell Index variables	Factor analysis of a wider set of socio-economic variables, including the Shevky-Bell set

Table 1.3.1: Typology of Social Area Analysis

Shevky and Bell's Steps to Construct Formation and Index Construction

Postulates Concerning Industrial Society (Aspects of Increasing Scale) (1)	Statistics of Trends (2)	Changes in the Structure of a Given Social System (3)	Constructs (4)	Sample Statistics Related to the Constructs (5)	Derived Measures (from Col.5) (6)
Change in the range and intensity of relations	→ Changing Direction of skills: Lessening importance of manual productive operations — growing importance of clerical, supervisory, management operations	→ Changes in the arrangement of occupations based on function	→ Social Rank (economic status)	→ Years of schooling Employment status Class of worker Major occupation group Value of home Rent by dwelling unit Plumbing and repair Persons per room Heating and refrigeration	→ Occupation Schooling Rent → Index I

Table 1.3.1—cont.

Differentiation of function	→ Changing structure of productive activity: Lessening importance of primary production—growing importance of relations centered in cities — lessening importance of the household as economic unit	→ Changes in the ways of living—movement of women into urban occupations—spread of alternative family patterns	→ Urbanisation (family status)	→ Age and sex Owner or tenant House structure Persons in household	→ Fertility Women at work Single-family dwelling units	Index II
Complexity of organisation	→ Changing composition of population: Increasing movement—alterations in age and sex distribution — increasing diversity	→ Redistribution in space-changes in the proportion of supporting and dependent population—isolation and segregation of groups	→ Segregation (ethnic status)	→ Race and Nativity Country of birth Citizenship	→ Racial and national groups in relative isolation	Index III

Source: Shevky and Bell (1955), Table II—1, by permission of Stanford Univeristy Press.

3. Social Area Analysis and Factorial Ecology

We have seen in the last section that there are discussions about the relative merits of the classical models of urban spatial structure. It was suggested that the models might be regarded as affording independent, additive contributions to the total socio-economic structuring of the city. Such a view is fostered by social area analysis and factorial ecology. The term social area analysis, strictly speaking, applies to the mode of analysis developed by Shevky, Williams and Bell in their studies of Los Angeles and San Francisco (Shevky and Bell, 1951). On the other hand, factorial ecology is the use of the multivariate techniques of factor analysis to study the dimensions of the spatial variation of socio-economic characteristics. In effect, the two techniques achieve the same purpose, except that while the second represents a more objective approach to the analysis of urban form, it is inductive and thus compares poorly with the deductive approach of social area analysis. A typology of social area analysis and factorial ecology is summarised in Figure 1.3.1, as well as Table 1.3.1.

(i) Social Area Analysis

As developed by Shevky, Williams and Bell, this technique involves the derivation, from theoretical postulates concerning an industrial society, of a number of constructs about the ways urban populations in this society are differentiated. The first of these postulates concerns the changes in the range and intensity of relations, especially as typified by changes in the distribution of skills (lessening importance of manual productive operations and growing importance of clerical, supervising and managerial operations) and changes reflected in the social system, also reflected in the arrangement of occupations based on functions. Second, there is the differentiation of function resulting from the changing structure of productive activity (lessening importance of primary production and of the household on the economic unit) leading to changes in ways of living, especially the movement of women into urban occupations and the spread of alternative family patterns. Third, there is the changing composition of population (increasing movement, alterations in age and sex distribution and increasing diversity). This changing complexity often leads to a redistribution of population in space and the isolation and segregation of groups.

From the three postulates described above, three constructs called social rank or economic status, urbanisation or family status, and segregation or ethnic status were derived. The first construct could be measured by such variables as years of schooling, employment status, class of worker, major occupation group, value of home, rent per dwelling unit, persons per room, etc. On the other hand, the second construct, urbanisation or family status, may be measured by the age and sex, the ownership of the dwelling unit, the home structure and the number of persons in a household, while the segregation or ethnic status could be measured by race and nativity; the country of birth and citizenship.

The most important contribution by these authors was the derivation of the measurements for each of the constructs to ensure three indexes of the urban spatial form. The method of construction is now probably important only from a historical context. Basically, it combined the most important of the variables of each construct to produce the particular index. Thus, the first index emerged from a combination of the occupation, schooling and rent variables, the second index from the fertility, women at work, and single family dwelling units variables, while the third index was derived from a combination of the racial and national groups in relative location.

Such a heuristic way of developing indexes cannot go unchallenged (Hawley and Duncan, 1957). Indeed both the theory and the empirical dimensioning of the constructs were subjects of severe criticism; and in a test of the model by Bell (1955) on ten cities, only six yielded acceptable results. The emerging issues were a re-examination of the adequacy of the constructs and the development of a more objective technique of dimensioning the constructs. It was in order to meet the second criticism that more socio-economic variables were used in a factor analytic model. This is factorial ecology.

(ii) Factorial Ecology

Factorial ecology uses the multivariate techniques of factor analysis to dimension a larger group of socio-economic characteristics of people over small areas (wards, enumeration areas, etc.) of the urban space. Factor analysis, simply defined, is a technique that reduces a matrix of n tracts (or small areas) by m variables (usually socio-economic) to one of n tracts and r dimensions or factors where $r \leqslant m$. The r factors account for most of the variability in the data and hence provide useful summaries of the behaviour of each of the tracts. It is therefore an objective way of dimensioning the socio-economic variables of urban spatial form. The method of dimensioning is described in standard textbooks such as Harman (1960) and Rummell (1970) on factor analysis.

A very important result of social area analysis and factorial ecology is the pattern of variation exhibited over space by the three constructs or dimensions of social rank; urbanisation or family status; and ethnic status. The first one is said to vary by sectors of the urban space while the second one varies concentrically and the third is said to isolate pockets or clusters within the city. The fact that these patterns of variation are similar to those identified by the three classical models has led to a conclusion that the classical models are not competitive but rather constitute additive components of the urban spatial structure (Rees, 1970).

Studies in many parts of the world using the approach of factorial ecology have produced interesting results. Most studies in America and Western Europe usually isolate at least these three dimensions or constructs, while many studies from Eastern Europe have failed to identify the ethnic status dimension. The evidence from studies on cities in developing countries is that family and socio-economic status are not only weakly independent variables but also that the socio-economic status is the more important criterion for segregating households. Additional determinants such as migrant status, ethnic status in areas of powerful poly-ethnic hinterland and caste and religion, especially in India, have been suggested (Friedman and Wulff, 1972).

Social area analysis might be totally irrelevant and hence unapplicable to cities in the developing countries on account of the fact that these cities do not meet the criteria of cities in industrialised societies. On the other hand, factorial ecology lacks the theoretical postulates of social area analysis as basically it is a data reduction technique. None the less, if social area analysis is used to guide variable selection, one could conceive factorial ecology as an operationalising technique of social area analysis. It is within considerations of this nature that factor analysis of urban data matrices in cities in developing countries must be viewed.

4. Micro-economic Theories of Urban Land Values

Economic theories of land values date back to Ricardo and Von Thunen. Von Thunen, for instance, was essentially concerned with the location of agricultural activities, but his ideas came to be applied to the location of urban activities first by Hurd (1903), and later by Haig (1926).Two concepts which featured prominently in their formulations are those of urban land rent and transportation accessibility. Although these two concepts were not new, the fact that they were seen as complementary was new. This complementarity was aptly described by Haig (1926) as follows:

> while transportation overcomes friction, site rentals and trans-
> portation costs represent the cost of what friction remains . . . The
> theoretically perfect site for the activity is that which furnishes
> the desired degree of accessibility at the lowest cost of friction . . .
> The layout of the metropolis . . . tends to be determined by a
> principle which may be termed minimizing of the cost of friction.

The earliest contributions of micro-economic theory to the analysis
of urban form are set out in the works of Alonso (1964), Wingo (1961),
Kain (1961) and Muth (1969). The major assumptions of these writers
were threefold. First, a household or firm determines its location in
the city according to its total budget which enables it to pay the cost
of a 'market basket' comprising a unique combination of residential transportation and all other commodities consumed. Second, in locational
choice, there is a set of 'market baskets' among which each household
is indifferent. And third, the household or firm optimises by selecting
a 'market basket' from all conceivable sets which help to maximise its
savings. Both Alonso and Wingo produce explicit models based on these
premises.

(i) Alonso's Model

The development of a model of urban form by Alonso proceeds at the
household or firm level. According to him, the individual household or
firm has a budget constraint on the type of goods he can buy and
consequently would spend his income in such a way that how much
space he consumes, commuting costs and other expenditure are in
equilibrium, viz.

$$y = p_z z + P(x)q + k(x) \tag{1}$$

Where y is the income, p_z is the price of the composite good, z is the
quantity of the goods, $P(x)$ the price of land at distance (x) from the
centre, q the amount of land purchased and $k(x)$ are commuting
costs. Furthermore, the household satisfaction is defined through a
utility equation of the form

$$u = u(z, q, x) \tag{2}$$

This utility function plus the budget constraint equation 1 defines the locational choice of the household or firm in the city. In determining this choice, Alonso offered two methods of solution, graphical and mathematical.

The graphical method proceeds by obtaining a three-dimensional surface that represents all of the alternatives open to the consumer. This surface, called the locus of opportunities, is such that every point on it is a possible alternative for the household while every point not on it is not. This surface is a generalisation from two dimensions into three of the well-known budget line. Different cross-sections of this surface may be obtained by holding one of the three variables constant. However, the three-dimensional surface is shown in Figure 1.4.1, where $0q$, $0z$, and $0x$ are perpendicular axes. Note in essence that this is a graphical representation of equation 1.

Let us now proceed to examine the preferences of individual households. This again may be mapped through indifference surfaces which are sets of combinations of quantity of land, q; composite goods, z; and distance, x; such that the individual household will be equally satisfied by any of the combination (see Figures 1.4.2a and 1.4.2b). For every household, the point of equilibrium is given by that point where the locus of opportunities surface touches the highest point of

Figure 1.4.1: Locus of Opportunities Surface

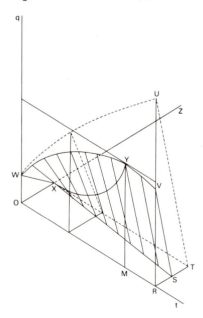

Figure 1.4.2a: An Indifference Surface

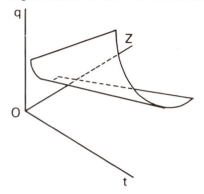

Figure 1.4.2b: Sections through an Indifference Surface

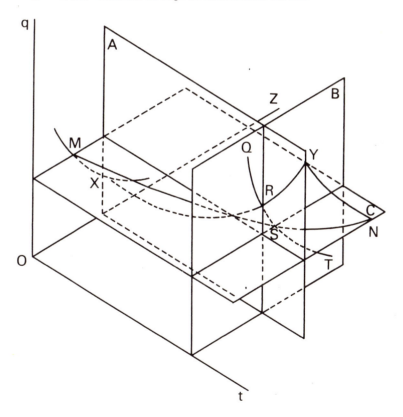

the indifference surface. Through an analysis of the nature of the indifference surface it is possible to show that the point of equilibrium must lie within the portion of the locus of opportunities bounded by the curves WX, XY and YZ. Since the two curves are smooth curves it might be expected that this tangential point always exists.

The mathematical solution is neater and is obtained by the method of differential calculus. It is based on the notion that when the household is at equilibrium, marginal utility is equal to marginal expenditure. Thus at this point,

$$dy = y_z \, dz + y_q dq + y_p dP + y_k dk = 0 \tag{3}$$

and

$$du = u_z dz + u_q dq + u_x dx = 0 \tag{4}$$

where y_z, y_q, y_p and y_k are the partial derivatives of the income y with respect to the composite goods z, the quantity of space q, the price of land P and commuter cost k. Similarly u_z, u_q and u_x are partial derivatives of the utility function. Since y is a constant $dy = 0$, and using equation 1, we can find the partial derivatives given by y_z, y_q, y_P and y_k. These are

$$y_z = P_z; \quad y_q = P(x); \quad y_P = q \text{ and } y_k = 1$$

Thus it is possible to express equation 3 as

$$dy = p_z dz + P(x) \, dq + q dP + dk = 0 \tag{5}$$

If equation 4 is expressed in terms of the marginal rates of substitution between distance x and composite good z on the one hand, and quantity q and composite good z on the other, i.e. in terms of

$$\frac{u_x}{u_z} \text{ and } \frac{u_q}{u_z} \text{ and solved we have}$$

$$\frac{u_x}{u_z} = -\frac{dz}{dx} \tag{6}$$

and

$$\frac{u_q}{u_z} = -\frac{dz}{dq} \tag{7}$$

Similarly, if equation 3 is solved for z and x respectively, then

$$\frac{P(x)}{P_z} = -\frac{dz}{dq} \tag{8}$$

$$\frac{q\dfrac{dP}{dx} + \dfrac{dk}{dx}}{P_z} = -\frac{dz}{dx} \tag{9}$$

Equations 8 and 9 constitute the mathematical solution of Alonso's model as they express the marginal rate of substitution between land and the composite goods on the one hand in terms of their marginal costs; while on the other, they express the marginal rate of substitution between distance and goods in terms of the sum of the rates of the marginal rates of substitution between distance and price; distance and commuter costs and the rates of the price of the composite good. The solution of these two equations in addition to the specification of the household's bid price curve, i.e. the set of prices for land which the individual is willing to pay at various distances while deriving a constant level of satisfaction therefore constitute the behaviour of the household in an urban area.

Alonso's model is not only applicable to residential land use but also the behaviour of firms within the urban setting. It is to this extent a general model of urban land use. It has potential applications, therefore, in understanding urban spatial structure and its market equilibrium. None the less, and in spite of the model's theoretical elegance, there are a number of biting criticisms. First, there are those that deal with the assumptions of the model. These assumptions which include the view of the urban landscape as featureless with equal transportation in all directions as well as the existence of one single employment centre in the city, are unrealistic. In addition, there is the notion that households or firms maximise some utility function subject to budgetary constraints. Studies have shown that intra-city residential location is more complex than this and it seems that households are satisficers rather than maximisers. Second, the model as formulated is not easy to operationalise. This is because the derivation of macro-models from micro-behaviour is faced with the thorny problem of aggregation, which is both analytically and operationally difficult. None the less Alonso's model represents a major break through in urban land-use analysis, as he shows clearly the relationship between some of the determinants of the urban spatial structure and thus provides a frame of analysis for numerous other researchers (Muth, 1969). Furthermore, the theoretical conceptualisation of this model has been used by Herbert and Stevens to derive an operational residential location model using a linear programming methodology (Herbert and Stevens, 1960; see also Chapter 9).

(ii) Wingo's Model

Both Alonso and Wingo developed their models at about the same time, although their thoughts were independent. Wingo's contribution considers the technology of transportation very explicitly and separates preferences for accessibility and living space. He emphasised the complementary between rent and transportation. The major postulates have been summarised by Wingo himself as follows:

> The model concentrates on how labor services are organized in space, given the spatial arrangement of production, the nature of the labor force and the institution by which the labor force is articulated with the processes of production ... The arrangement of workshifts, the journey to work and the degree of labor orientation of industry are behavioural characteristics which are important in the model. The technology of the transportation system enters the model through its effects on transportation costs of the journey to work (Wingo, 1961 pp. 21–2).

The formulation of the model begins with the definition of the costs of transport in terms of a number of characteristics of the transportation system, for example velocity, system capacity, number of carriers, etc. The journey to work is seen as the technological link between the labour force and the production processes. Assuming that the cost of the journey to work is borne by the firm and not by the individual and that the daily wage is equal to the product of the hours worked and the hourly wage rate, we can define the mean labour value as a 'curve expressing the wage rate necessary to induce the worker to give up one additional hour of leisure daily' as $p_o(u)$. The value of the cost of the journey to work $p_o(x)$ at distance x is then given by

$$p_o(x_o) = p_o(u + x_o) - \bar{p}_o(u) \tag{10}$$

Wingo argues further that as a result of the differential characteristics of urban space whereby some residences have an economic advantage over others, workers will compete with all others to capture this advantage. The price of any individual location will be bid up to

Figure 1.4.3: The Spatial Structure of Position Rents

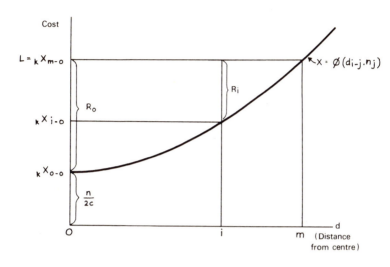

the point where all workers but one are excluded. This means that the individual finds his greatest utility, with the result that all or part of the value of the locational advantage is absorbed. In this way a unique set of locational rents is generated.

The conditions for an equilibrium distribution of workers' residences result from the effects of position rent, location cost and transportation costs, namely

$$_kR_i = L - {_kX_{i\text{-}o}} = {_kX_{m\text{-}o}} - {_kX_{i\text{-}o}} \tag{11}$$

where L is location cost, $_kR_i$ is position rent at a point i, $_kX_{i\text{-}o}$ the transportation costs between central city and any point i for household k and $_kX_{m\text{-}o}$ is the transportation cost to the margin point m from the city centre for household k (Figure 1.4.3). In such a scheme, no household could increase its net returns by changing location, and no location could increase its returns by changing occupants.

The demand for space by households is elastic with respect to price and if we assume that there is a margin point m which establishes the position rent structure for the urban area, and if the space demand function R is constant among households and log linear in shape, then

$$R = rq \tag{12}$$

where r is rent and q the quantity of space consumed.

Also, per each household,

$$q_i = \frac{\lambda^{1/\eta}}{r_i} \qquad \eta > 1 \tag{13}$$

where q_i is the quantity of land consumed per household at point i, r_i is the unit value of space at i and λ and η are parameters of the demand function. By manipulating equations 11 and 12, we may relate the density directly to position rent as

$$q^{-1} = \frac{R}{\lambda}^{1/\eta-1} \tag{14}$$

The density gradient is then related to the given population by finding the limits on integration necessary for a negatively sloped function rotated about an axis to describe a specified volume of population P in Euclidean space. This is given by

$$P = 2\pi \int_o^m sq^{-1}\, ds = \int_o^m \sigma q^{-1}\, ds \tag{15}$$

where σ is a transformation of the Euclidean space into an appropriate demand space. As described, the model relates the movement of the margin point to changes in population and hence is suggestive of the rate at which rural lands are converted to urban use.

Wingo's model, like Alonso's, is subject to similar criticisms. Nevertheless, these models constitute a totally radical departure from the ecological models, particularly in the sense that they are framed in mathematical terms and also because they are fairly abstract. Their influences in later researches have been immense and beneficial and they are therefore major breakthroughs in urban analysis.

5. Conclusion

This chapter has provided three major views on the nature of cities. The first two, which study the city from an ecological point of view, describing either the urban spatial structure or the determinants of its social areas, are purely descriptive while the third, which utilises economic theory to derive the urban spatial configuration, is mathematical and could be highly abstract in understanding urban macro-behaviour. None the less, it is feasible to regard these models as complementary as they virtually describe different aspects of the city. It is perhaps more important to remember that these models are based on the American urban experience and it might seem worth while to comment further here on their wholesale application to the situation in other parts of the world, especially in the developing countries.

Social area analysis, factorial ecology, and the classical models provide useful experience for re-examining the utility of these models. In the application of factorial ecology to cities in developing countries, it is claimed that the reason why the three constructs are not identifiable is a result of the enclave (even within the city) industrial structure which exhibits little socio-economic differentiation. It is further argued (and this is where the evidence does not seem to justify all the claims) that traditional urban patterns which predate colonialism would disintegrate and be replaced by Western values which would eventually lead to the flight of the élite to the suburbs so that the form of the urban spatial structure would, with time, converge on that of the American city. This indeed is the convergence thesis of McElrath (1968) and Abu-Lughod (1969) based on their studies of Accra, Ghana, and Cairo, Egypt, respectively.

The convergence thesis is not only presumptious, as Friedman and Wulff (1972) argue, but also lacks any deep appreciation of the history of urbanisation in these parts of the world as well as showing a proper grasp of the dependency relationship between many of these cities and their metropoles. Basically these cities have not arisen as a result of the Euro-American industrial revolution and to that extent are 'premature metropolises'. In short, they exist within a value system that respects the preservation of cultural features such as the centrally located Oba's palace of Yoruba cities, the planned downtown shrines of Japanese cities or the funeral quarters in Cairo, whose central location are not based on capitalist land-use monopoly. Furthermore, it is conceivable to expect that present rapid rates of immigration into these cities, which can hardly cope with such problems as housing, employment and other infrastructural provision, are likely not to lead into a convergence into the Western model. Moreover, planning orientation, whether social welfare or capitalist, could be a militating force for or against convergence. Where then lies the utility of these models in urban analysis?

Similar arguments have been raised by David Harvey (1973), on the utility of the micro-economic land-use theories which, he argued, are based on the concept of monopoly rent and exchange value of urban land. Harvey differentiates between what he called use value and exchange value, the former referring to the numerous considerations a house buyer or renter puts forth, such as its utility as a shelter, its spaciousness, accessibility characteristics and its location within a satisfactory neighbourhood; and the latter referring to the value of the house on the housing market. Micro-economic models in general assume that these two values are the same at *the margin*, i.e. the purchaser or renter will in determining exchange value bid exactly that extra quantity of money which represents the value to him of obtaining the extra quantity of use value. This assumption will only be true in a situation of a perfect market, which the urban land or housing market is definitely not. Harvey's observation (even though he advocates a revolutionary Marxist approach to a reformulation of urban land-use theory) is a timely warning about the complexities of the urban land market as well as about the need to relate theories to a society's social and value systems.

Nevertheless, both the classical models and the micro-economic models are not unrealistic, especially when considered *per se* as normative models. In fact it might be argued that the classical models and factorial ecology emphasise the use value characteristics of the urban land while micro-economic approaches focus on the exchange value. A fuller explanation of urban spatial configuration requires a synthesis of these two approaches which, put together, would constitute a fair characterisation of the forces shaping urban land use. It is in this sense that the models are seen as constituting a useful framework for the studies of concepts and techniques in urban analysis.

References

Alonso, W. 1964. *Location and Land Use: Toward a General Theory of Land Rent.* Cambridge, Massachusetts: Harvard University Press

Abu-Lughod, J.L. 1969. Testing the Theory of Social Area Analysis: The Case of Cairo, Egypt. *American Sociological Review, 34*, 198–212

Bell, W. 1955. Economic, Family and Ethnic Status: An Empirical Test. *American Sociological Review, xx*, No. 1, 45–52

Berry, B.J.L. and Horton, F.E. (eds.). 1970. *Geographical Perspectives on Urban Systems: With integrated Readings.* Englewood Cliffs, New Jersey: Prentice-Hall

Burgess, E. 1927. The Growth of the City: An Introduction to a Research Project. In R.E. Park *et al.* (eds.), *The City.* Chicago: Chicago University Press

Davie, R. 1937. The Pattern of Urban Growth. In G.P. Murdock (ed.), *Studies in the Science of Society.* New Haven: Yale University Press, pp. 133–61

Firey, W. 1947. *Land Use in Central Boston.* Cambridge: Harvard University Press.

Firey, W. 1950. Residential Sectors Re-Examined. *The Appraisal Journal, 18*, 451–3

Friedman, J. and Wulff, R. 1972? *The Urban Transition: Comparative Studies of Newly Developing Societies.* University of California, Los Angeles: School of Architecture and Urban Planning

Haig, R. 1926. Toward an understanding of the Metropolis. *Quarterly Journal of Economics, 40*

Harman, H. 1960. *Modern Factor Analysis.* Chicago: University of Chicago Press

Harris, C.D. and Ullman E.L., 1965. The Nature of Cities. *Annals of the American Academy of Political and Social Sciences,* Nov. 1945, 7–11

Harvey, D. 1973. *Social Justice and the City.* Baltimore, Maryland: The Johns Hopkins University Press

Hawley, A. and Duncan, O.D. 1957. Social Area Analysis: A Critical Appraisal. *Land Economics, 33,* 4, 37–45

Herbert, J.D. and Stevens B.H., 1960. A Model for the Distribution of Residential Activity in Urban Areas. *Journal of Regional Science, 9,* 3, 451–7

Hoyt, H. 1939. *The Structure and Growth of Residential Neighborhoods in American Cities.* Washington, D.C. : The United States Federal Housing Administration

Hoyt, H. 1950. Residential Sectors Revisited. *Appraisal Journal, 18,* 415–50

Hoyt, H. 1964. Recent Distortions of the Classical Models of Urban Structure. *Land Economics, 40,* 199–212

Hurd, R. 1924. *Principles of City Land Values,* New York: The Record and Guide

Johnson, J.H. 1972. *Urban Geography: An Introductory Analysis.* Oxford: Pergamon Press

Mabogunje, A.L. 1968. *Urbanization in Nigeria.* London University Press

McElrath, D. 1968. Societal Scale and Social Differentialism, Accra, Ghana. In Scott Greer, *et al., The New Urbanization.* New York: St Martin's Press

McKenzie, D. 1933. *The Metropolitan Community.* New York: McGraw-Hill

Murphy, R. 1966. *The American City: An Urban Geography.* New York: McGraw-Hill

Muth, R. 1969. *Cities and Housing.* Chicago.

Park, R.E., Burgess, E.W. and McKenzie, R.D. (eds.) 1925. *The City.* Chicago: University of Chicago Press

Penderson, P.O. 1967. *Modeller for Befolkningsstruktur og Befolkningsudvikling i Storbyomrader Specielt med Henblik pa Storkobenhavn.* Copenhagen: State Urban Planning Institute

Quinn, J.A. 1940. The Burgess Zonal Hypothesis and its Critics. *American Sociological Review, 5,* 210–80

Rees, P.H. 1970. Concepts of Social Space: Toward an Urban Spatial Geography. In B.J.L. Berry and F.E. Horton (eds.), *Geographical Perspectives on Urban Systems.* Englewood Cliffs, New Jersey: Prentice-Hall

Rodwin, L. 1950. The Theory of Residential Growth and Structure. *The Appraisal Journal, 18,* 451-3

Rummel, R. 1970. *Applied Factor Analysis.* Illinois: Northwestern University Press

Shevky, E. and Bell, W. 1955. *Social Area Analysis: Theory, Illustration, Application and Computation Procedures.* Stanford, California: Stanford University Press

Wingo, L. 1961. *Transportation and Urban Land Use.* Washington D.C.: Resources for the Future, Inc.

2 URBAN POPULATION

1. Introduction

The urban population represents one of the most important aspects of the city. First, it is the nature and composition of the households that make up this population that differentiate it from the countryside, while second, the amount of space utilised by this population as living apartments accounts for a significant proportion of the built-up area of a city. The nature and composition of urban populations are reflected not only in their demographic and socio-economic characteristics but also in the range of economic activities in which the populations are engaged. Consequently, it is not surprising that there are many approaches to the study of urban populations ranging from purely sociological analysis (Weber, 1899) to micro-economic considerations in the location and distribution of urban populations (Alonso, 1964; Wingo, 1961; Muth, 1969) and the spatial distribution of urban population densities (Clark, 1951; Betty *et al.*, 1962).

The purely sociological investigation typified by Weber (1899), examines the demographic, socio-economic and occupational characteristics of urban populations and shows in what ways these differ from those of the rural countryside. Research findings show that urban populations are generally more literate, younger and earn higher incomes than rural populations. Furthermore, they engage mostly in secondary and tertiary activities, thus contrasting drastically with rural populations, whose major preoccupations are in primary production such as farming and mining.

The demographic studies of urban populations, focusing on the sex composition as well as their distribution by age cohorts and origins show that there could be a preponderance of males in the labour force although it is usual to find that the number of women in the labour force could also be very high. Furthermore, the age-sex pyramid shows most of the population to belong to the ages 15—50 year cohort. Thus it is usual for it to have the 'characteristic bulge' in the middle (Berry, 1973, p. 6), implying that there are relatively fewer children and people in the older age classes. This demographic situation is usually explained in terms of the origin of the inhabitants of the city, most of whom are migrants and hence people born outside the city.

Other sociological studies of urban populations focus on social interrelationships and social interactions of the inhabitants. In this respect, the city differs markedly from the village, where the role of family ties and kinship relations could not be underrated. The nature of the interrelationship of urban populations in an industrial society is aptly put by Weber that it

> engenders the essential egotistic self seeking and materialist attitude ... No one can view with equanimity the continual drift of the population to the cities where it will be subject to such demoralizing influences ... The larger the town, the feebler the bonds of moral cohesion (quoted from Berry, 1973, p. 5).

The city therefore is where there is much isolation; where individuals are mainly self-seeking in a complex society. This, according to Berry, creates anomie at 'the societal level, alienation at the perceptual level and resulting individual deviance'. On the other hand, the pattern of social interaction is best summarised by Delos F. Wilcox, who wrote that

> the city is indeed the visible symbol of the annihilation of distance and the multiplication of interests ... Among the business and professional classes, a man's most intimate associates may be scattered over the whole city while he scarcely knows his next door neighbor's name ... The city transforms men as if by magic and newcomers are absorbed and changed into city men (quoted from Berry, 1973, p. 11).

It might be argued that such descriptions as above are not fair on the urban population as they connote that the city is bad. None the less there are many good things in the city and in fact in Weber's balance of the city, it is a place where there is more good than evil. The city indeed is a very complex mechanism, where different organisations strive to achieve various aims and goals. These include the wealth of opportunities it affords for the economic well-being of the inhabitants, the amenities and services it provides to satisfy the masses of people, the benefits it communicates to its surroundings and the market it provides for a country's production. Of course in the thinking of Weber, it represents the highest achievements of political, intellectual and industrial life.

While sociological analysis has dominated studies of urban populations, there is a growing body of literature dealing with its spatial distribution (as described in Chapter 1) and this had led to an examination of the spatial distribution of urban population densities. To this, one might add the methods and techniques that could be utilised in forecasting the growth and composition of urban populations. This chapter will provide a review and an examination of some issues of this spatial dimension.

2. Spatial Aspects of the Socio-economic Characteristics of Urban Populations

Urban populations are made up of households which may be defined as a group of people who live together and eat communally. Such a definition necessarily excludes family members who eat and sleep elsewhere. The household is an important unit in understanding the behavioural characteristics of an urban population. In many urban surveys, it constitutes the sampling unit while many theoretical considerations about urban residential population are framed in terms of units of households.

Generally the characteristics of household that interest us include size, age and sex composition, their educational, marital and social characteristics, their tastes and preferences and their spatial behaviour. Such data as these are not easy to come by even in the most comprehensive population censuses of the developed countries. Researchers therefore may be forced to collect data on variables that interest them or use those that are readily available in censuses or allied publications.

When all or some of these variables are available, it is worth while to examine their spatial variation. Depending on the number and quality of the variables, the technique of examination varies from simple analysis of variance to factorial ecology. Spatial variations may be examined over wards or enumeration areas in a city, planning zones or even areas that represent the historical growth of the city. In such an investigation the set of descriptive statistics of means, standard deviations, etc. (Blalock, 1960) could be used in throwing light on the nature of the spatial variations while factorial ecology will generally describe the dimensions of variation in these socio-economic characteristics. Factorial ecology has been described in the last chapter and it will suffice here to describe and use the technique of the analysis of variance using a specific example.

The example we are using is Jos, a city in Nigeria founded as a mining headquarters about 1915. Jos is presently the headquarters of the Plateau State of Nigeria and its economy is much diversified as it includes not only mining but administration, transportation, education and manufacturing. The choice of Jos is based partly on data availability and the fact that as a result of its historical growth, there is *a priori* evidence to expect spatial variations in the socio-economic characteristics of the population. For instance, at the founding of the city, there was a tripartite division into a European Reservation, a Native town or Birni, where indigenous people lived, and a Sabon Gari or Township, where only migrants lived. In recent years, the city has extended arealy to include a number of suburbs and settlements such as Sabon Gwong and Anglo Jos (see Figure 2.2.1). The source of data for the analysis is the author's research, conducted in 1972, and reported in Ayeni (1974, Chs. 2–4). Some of the variables collected are the age of the head of household, his length of stay in the city, his education measured in terms of years spent in school, the size of his household, the number of workers in the household, the number of rooms a household occupies and the annual rent which was shown to vary significantly with the household income (Ayeni, 1975).

Table 2.2.1: Spatial Variation of Mean Household Characteristics in Jos, 1972

Zone	Age	Length of Stay	Years of School	Size	Workers/ House-hold	Rent	Rooms/ House-hold
Native Town	31.43	9.55	8.18	4.35	1.26	65.38	1.97
Sabon Gwong	30.15	5.64	6.73	4.36	1.22	59.05	1.45
Anglo Jos	35.30	10.48	9.47	4.60	1.28	78.55	2.00
Township	28.74	5.89	9.49	4.15	1.37	84.62	1.71
Reservation	35.69	5.42	12.23	5.37	1.43	165.52	3.09
Jos	31.18	7.78	8.98	4.42	1.30	79.35	1.96

Source: Field-work in Jos, 1972.

From the table, we see that the mean age of the residents is only 31.18, while the short length of residence in the city, only 7.78 years, suggests that most of the inhabitants are migrants. The average number of years spent at school is 9, barely sufficient to cover a secondary school education, while the average size of a family is 4.42; a figure that does not differ much from those obtained by the Federal Office of Statistics, Nigeria, for towns of similar status. Furthermore, in a household of some four or five people, as many as 1.30 are workers. Thus, if the head is a worker, 30 per cent of the wives and other dependents are also workers. Finally, at an average of two rooms per

Figure 2.2.1: Jos, Nigeria, Showing Major Areas of Growth

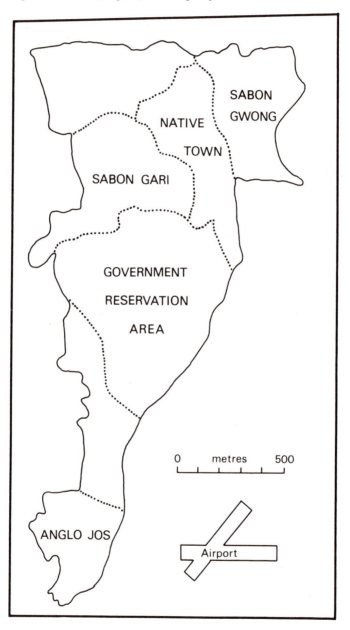

household of 4.2 people, one could conclude that there is some congestion.

The spatial variation of these characteristics is obvious from the table. One might proceed to examine its significance using an analysis of variance technique (Blalock, 1960) and one might even proceed further, if the differences in means are significant, to analyse which areas are markedly different from the others using some of the numerous 'post mortem' tests such as Scheffe's Multiple Comparison of Means, Newman-Keul's Method of Comparison Between Ordered Means or Duncan's Multiple Range Test (see Winer, 1962). These tests are designed to compare the range of the differences between an observed set of means with an expected set of least significant ranges without disturbing the level of significance used in the analysis of variance test. Many of these are not affected even when the assumptions of normality and equal variances are not satisfied.

The significance of the pattern of variation of the socio-economic characteristics over space is tested via a standard one-way analysis of variance. The difference in age, length of residence in the city, years of formal education, annual rent and rooms occupied by households are significant at the 0.01 level, while the number of workers per household is only significant at the 0.05 level. On the other hand, there are no significant variations in the sizes of households.

It is possible to argue that the statistically non-significant observation on the size of household variable reflects a major characteristic of cities in this part of the world. In the American or European city, it is expected that urbanism and urbanisation result in lower fertility levels, and hence smaller family sizes, and it is usual to expect variations in fertility levels within socio-economic groups who again are spatially differentiated. A general argument in support of low fertility levels is that the weight of urban living and the urban milieu is not conducive to maintaining large families. Could this be true of the study area and could we generalise to all cities in Nigeria or the developing countries? While Jos is not the ideal Nigerian city, it has characteristics which are typical of cities in the developing world. None the less, the evidence at hand does not support this general hypothesis, as household sizes are even greatest in areas of higher socio-economic status, although some caution is needed in interpretation. One may note, however, that households in many Nigerian cities sometimes include members of the extended family or even friends and acquaintances. On the other hand, the lower level of significance of the number of workers variable reflects that the incorporation of women into the labour force is still an evolving process, the impact of which is not discernible at present.

The mean age in the Reservation area is the highest in Jos. It is slightly higher than that of Anglo Jos and markedly higher than those of the Native Town, Sabon Gwong and the Township. This may be due to the fact that the Reservation contains people with long years of schooling (12.82 years) who have progressed very high in their employment careers. They are not young school-leavers or fresh rural migrants who tend to seek accommodation in other parts of the city. The relatively older age of Anglo Jos may be due to that place being a heterogeneous zone in terms of household composition. The northern edge of the area contains people of the same calibre as the Reservation while the southern section contains shanty houses and huts of Plateau people, many of whom are miners.

The spatial variation in education shows that the most educated people are in the Reservation area while the least educated are in Sabon Gwong and the Native Town. Both Anglo Jos and the Township do not seem to differ significantly. On the basis of the above, the Township and the Reservation are the areas where the educated migrant to Jos settles.

In terms of the length of stay of households in Jos, the shortest periods were observed for the Reservation area (4.89 years), the Township and Sabon Gwong. Except in the case of Sabon Gwong, it would seem that education, proxied by the number of years of formal education, is negatively correlated with the length of stay so that the more educated, the more migratory one is likely to be. On the other hand, the short length of stay may be due to civil service transfer, especially after the creation of states in 1967.

Household sizes are generally larger in the Reservation than in any other part of the city. This larger size of households in the Reservation may be explained as resulting from the extended family system. It was gathered during the field-work that many occupants of the servants' quarters were indeed not servants but members of the extended family. In many cases such people depend on the head of household in the main house for subsistence. Another reason why sizes of households may be higher in these two areas may be related to their higher education which implies a probable higher income. Furthermore, it may be due to the absence of relatively few single-person households, many of whom are really fresh rural-urban migrants.

It is, however, not surprising that the highest number of workers per household was observed in the Township and the Reservation. These are areas where both husband and wife usually engage in some gainful employment because of their higher level of education, as distinct from the Native Town where many of the women live in purdah.

Our analysis of the pattern of distribution of some socio-economic characteristics of Jos shows that the character of growth is a pertinent issue in the emerging spatial pattern. Thus it is not fortuitous to visualise the city as a coalition or an amalgamation of a number of discrete residential areas or settlements which have become fused in the wake of urban expansion. This indeed is to argue that market forces have hardly been given a free hand in the overhall spatial expansion, at least not to the same extent in the different sub-areas of the city.

Although social segregation was characteristic of the city, as in many cities of the developing world, from its inception, the analysis gives some insight into the identifiable social areas or social segregation tendencies that may eventually evolve. This undoubtedly would be the realm of social area analysis or factorial ecology but then much care might be necessary not only in interpreting emerging dimensions or constructs but also in making comparisons with the constructs of social area analysis in an industrial society.

3. Spatial Distribution of Urban Population Densities

There is a consensus among researchers that the pattern of distribution of population within the city is such that densities decline exponentially from the city centre into the surburbs (Clark, 1951; Berry *et al.*, 1962; Newling, 1966). It is also agreed that a first-order mathematical representation of this phenomenon is

$$d_x = d_0 \ \exp{(-bx)} \tag{1}$$

where d_x is the population density at a distance x from the city centre d_0 is the central density while b is the density gradient. Equation 1 may be expressed in terms of logarithms as

$$\ln d_x = \ln d_0 - bx \tag{2}$$

Most empirical investigations have used equation 2 for this analysis (Rees, 1968; Berry and Horton, 1971).

Nowhere is the spatial distribution of urban population more studied than for the city of Chicago. Rees (1968), for instance, conducted the analysis for the entire metropolitan area (SMSA) as well as for five other sectors, namely the North, the North-west, the West, the South-west and the South of the city. The results of his analysis are shown in

Table 2.3.1 as well as Figure 2.3.1. In all cases very high coefficients of correlation (> 0.90) were recorded and the hypothesis was validated as all the *b* values have negative signs (Table 2.3.1).

Table **2.3.1**: The Decline of Population Density with Distance from the Centre of Chicago, Whole SMSA and Five Sectors, 1960

Parameter*	Whole SMSA	North	North-west	West	South-west	South
			Sector			
r	−0.908	−0.909	−0.930	−0.947	−0.900	−0.957
a	4.51	4.591	4.442	4.574	4.465	4.909
d_0	33.0	39.0	27.7	37.5	29.2	81.1
b	−0.056	−0.037	−0.050	−0.062	−0.063	−0.080

Source: Berry and Horton (1970), p. 277.

* The parameters are:
  r = coefficient of correlation
  a = intercept of line of regression with density measured in $\log_{10}$ units
  d_0 = extrapolated central density (in thousand persons per square mile)
  b = density gradient measured in units of $\log_{10}$ density/miles

It is possible to say that while population densities decrease from the city centre into the suburbs, the rates of decrease need not be the same, as can be seen from Table 2.3.1 and Figure 2.3.1. None the less, the analysis is coarse and we might proceed further by reducing the scatter of points, using small distance rings. In the Chicago study, it emerges that the highest densities do not actually occur at the centre but some short distance away, i.e. the density increases from the centre, reaching a peak some ten miles away before the decline begins. Figure 2.3.2 summarises the situation for the city of Chicago between 1940 and 1966. We see therefore that the hypothesis that the urban population density declines exponentially is only a rough approximation.

Recognising the approximate nature of the exponential equation in fitting urban population densities and related phenomena, Lionel March (1971) argued that it is possible to evolve a generalised distribution function. First he notes that if we ignore constants that may be accounted for by linear co-ordinate transformation and multipliers that weight, scale or normalise the distribution, the following functions

Figure 2.3.1: The Decline of Population Density with Distance from
the Centre of Chicago, Whole SMSA and Five Sectors, 1960

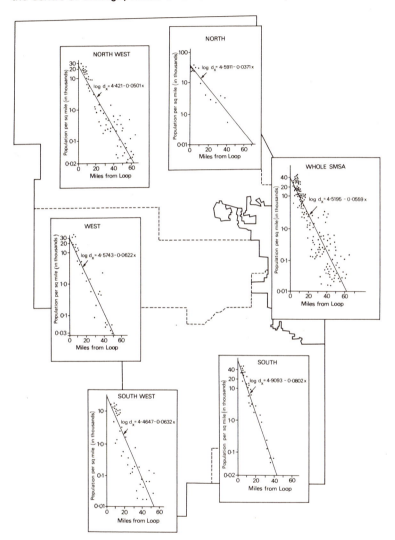

Figure 2.3.2: Density—Distance Graphs: The Chicago SMSA, 1940—66

P   =   Population
      P_t =   Total population
      P_m =   Population of the suburban municipalities
      P_r =   Residual or pseudo-rural population = $P_t - P_m$
A   =   Area
      A_t =   Total area
      A_m =   Area covered by the suburban municipalities
      A_r =   Residual or pseudo rural area = $A_t - A_m$

X   =   Distance
      X_0 =   Centre of the city
      X_1 =   Distance at which population densities reach a peak
      X_2 =   Limit of the continuously built up urban area
      X_3 =   Limit of suburbs built as suburbs
      X_4 =   Limit of commuting to Chicago
      $X_0 - X_1$ =   Range within which population densities rise with distance
      $X_1 - X_2$ =   Range within which total population densities begin to fall with distance
      $X_2 - X_3$ =   Range within which suburban, urban and rural population densities fall exponentially with distance at differing rates, but total population density declines in a curvilinear fashion
      $X_3 - X_4$ =   Range within which only a small proportion of the population commutes to Chicago

Distance—Density—Curves
      I   =   Curve of total density of population (P_t/A_t) within the continuously urbanised area
      J_1 =   Curve of the population density of the suburban municipalities
      J_2 =   Satellite town municipal density curve
      K   =   Curve of total population density (P_t/A_t) beyond X_2
      L   =   Curve of density or urban population (P_m/A_t)
      M   =   Curve of density or rural population ($P_r/A_t - A_m$) curve

Source: Derived from Brian J.L. Berry and Peter Gobeen, *Metropolitan Area Definition: A Re-evaluation of Concept and Statistical Practice* (Washington. DC: US Bureau of the Census Working Paper No. 28, 1968).

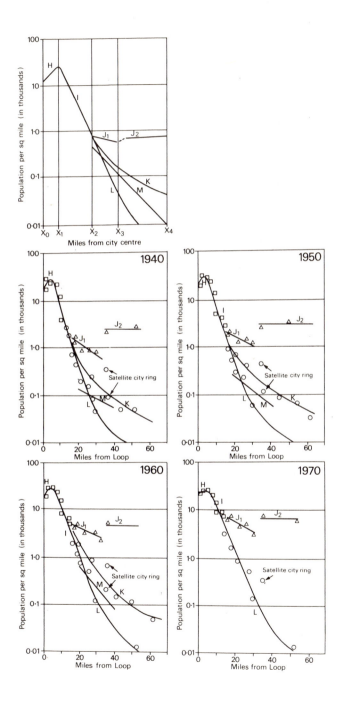

are known to fit the decline of urban population densities and related phenomena:

$$y = x^{-a} \tag{3}$$
$$y = x^{-a} \exp(-x) \tag{4}$$
$$y = x^{-1} \exp(-x) \tag{5}$$
$$y = \exp(-x^{1/2}) \tag{6}$$
$$y = \exp(-x) \tag{7}$$
$$y = \exp(-x^2) \tag{8}$$
$$y = x \exp(-x^2) \tag{9}$$
$$y = x \exp(-x^b) \tag{10}$$
$$y = x^a \exp(-x) \tag{11}$$

The first equation, 3, is the simple logarithmic gravity or Pareto model, while equation 4 is a generalisation of the gravity model. Equation 5, on the other hand, is the physical analogy of the absorption of a flow emanating from a centre while equation 6 is the leptokurtic exponential or the square root exponential. Equation 7 is the simple exponential, equation 8 the Gaussian normal model and equation 9 the circular normal model described by Lowry (1964) as a differentiated product model. Equation 10 is a simple generalisation of equation 9, while equation 11 is a gamma distribution of the kind proposed by Harris (1964).

A simple generalisation of these equations is

$$y = x^a \exp(-x^b) \tag{12}$$

for particular values of a and b. Equation 12 is the same as Dacey's equation (Dacey, 1963) derived in his consideration of the jth nearest neighbour problem. However, it is possible to further generalise these equations in terms of a three-parameter function $m(x: a, b, c)$ given by

$$m(x: a, b, c) = \begin{cases} \dfrac{bc^{a/b} \, x^{a-1} \exp(-cx^b)}{(a/b)} & x > 0 \\ 0 & x \leqslant 0 \end{cases} \tag{13}$$

where $a, b, c > 0$.

March proceeds further to show that the function $m(x)$ is a probability distribution function which for acceptable values of a, b and c is asymptotic to the x axis at infinity. Furthermore the function is at

Figure 2.3.3: Sketch Plots of the Function $m\,(\,|\,x\,|\!:a,b,c)$

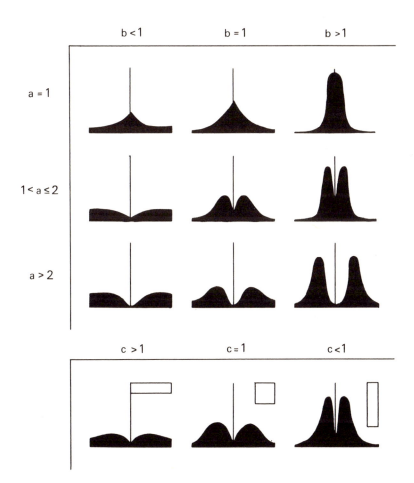

This shows typical cross-sectional portrayals of the distribution for varying shape parameters *a* and *b*, and (bottom) varying scales for different values of *c*.

most unimodal at

$$x = \left\{ \frac{a\text{-}1}{cb} \right\}^{1/b} \qquad a > 1 \tag{14}$$

for positive values of x. The mode occurs before, at or after $x = c^{-1/b}$ according to whether $a-1 < b$; $a-1 = b$ or $a-1 > b$. Furthermore it is possible to calculate the mean m and variance σ^2 of $m(x: a, b, c)$. Figure 2.3.3 is a sketch of the function for various ranges of values of a, b and c.

The interest in these functions should not to be just that of curve fitting to empirical data on urban population densities. Pertinent questions should be asked as to why urban population densities are distributed the way they are and hopefully the answer may lead to the identification of the processes underlying urban population densities. It is then that the differences in the performance of the various functions as descriptive mechanisms of urban population densities could be related not only to the sizes of urban centres but also urban areas in different sociocultural parts of the world. It is strongly suspected that many of these functions might fit, if only poorly, the urban population densities in many parts of the world.

The exponential function and its family of equations should be seen as having a wider application than shown in this chapter. It definitely has some theoretical and empirical applications into human spatial behaviour both in an urban and regional context, mainly as determinants of trip lengths and patterns of interaction. Future researches therefore should concentrate on the causes and characteristics of the variations between each of these functions and their relevance to the spatial structure under examination, as well as providing theoretical justifications in the form of deriving postulates from micro-level behaviour.

4. The Growth of the Urban Population

The growth of population in cities constitutes the most important phenomenon of urbanization in the nineteenth and twentieth centuries. This growth is ascribable to two factors: natural increase and migration. While migration plays a major role in the redistribution of people into the cities, natural increase is still very important, especially in the developing countries where cities possess the best health facilities and where greater attention is paid to the quality of life. None the less any attempt to understand the growth of an urban population must focus on these two categories.

It must be mentioned at the outset that almost all methods of forecasting and analysing national or global populations can (at least in principle) be applicable to urban and metropolitan areas. However, demographers are extremely chary of forecasts for 'small areas' (McLoughlin, 1972) because they are very conscious of the nature of the assumptions of these techniques. In real-life situations, it is easier to meet the assumptions at the regional or national level than at the local area level because of the vagaries that attend small-area data collection. None the less, to the extent that urban analysts might be 'forced' to make small-area projections and analyses, we shall be constrained to describe some of these useful techniques.

There are numerous methods of analysing growth of populations. McLoughlin (1972), for instance, described six mathematical and graphical methods: the employment ratio method, ratio and apportionment methods, the migration and natural increase method, the cohort survival method and matrix methods. These techniques possess different levels of accuracy and mathematical sophistication. We shall describe only two methods which particularly consider the two components of the urban population in addition to the sub-area distribution of this population. These are the cohort-survival method and a method described by Hudson (1970) using a set of differential equations.

(i) The Cohort-survival Method

The age cohort-survival method evaluates the population of a given area by age groups according to the pattern of fertility and mortality that has been observed. It is usual to consider population in age cohorts of five-year intervals. In its most simplified version, the age cohort-survival method assumes that a population is made up of age cohorts $1, 2, \ldots, n$, viz.

$$P_t = (a_1, a_2, \ldots, a_n) \tag{15}$$

where P_t is the population at a specific time t and a_i are the components in the age cohorts. In addition to this, we define a survivor matrix S whose elements are the survival and birth rates for each of the cohorts. The survival rate is '1 -- the death rate' and usually also allows for out-migration. This matrix, usually of n by n dimensions has the form

$$S = \begin{bmatrix} 0 & 0 & & \dots & b_1 & b_2 & \dots & b_v & \dots & 0 & 0 & 0 \\ d_1 & 0 & & \dots & 0 & 0 & \dots & 0 & \dots & 0 & 0 & 0 \\ 0 & d_2 & & & & & \dots & 0 & \dots & 0 & 0 & 0 \\ 0 & 0 & d_3 & \dots & 0 & 0 & \dots & 0 & \dots & 0 & 0 & 0 \\ . & & & & & & & & & & & \\ . & & & & & & & & & & & \\ . & & & & & & & & & & & \\ 0 & 0 & \dots & & & d_{n-1} & & & \dots & 0 & 0 & 0 \end{bmatrix}$$

Basically the matrix S shows that birth rates apply only to a certain section of the age cohorts while the survival rate applies to all except the first age cohort. The vector b_i are the birth rates, while d_j are the survival rates respectively. If P_{t+r} is the column vector of the population of an area by n cohorts at the rth period from t, it may be shown (Keyfitz, 1968) that this vector is given by

$$P_{t+r} = S^r P_t \qquad (16)$$

The process represented by the matrix equation 16 is simply one of ageing a population through successive time periods and simultaneously performing the calculation of births and deaths. This is why the method is so elegant.

Both Rogers and Keyfitz have shown ways by which the technique may be applied to incorporate the effects of migration in an inter-regional framework. Rogers' (1968) method was to introduce the effect of migration by replacing the initial population vector by a matrix in which columns are regions or areas, and rows are age cohorts. To these there will correspond sets of survivorship matrices, one for each region or area. Migration is then introduced through a set of transition matrices (one for each age group) in which the elements represent the probability that an individual in area i will move to area j within the next time period. In projecting with this more complex model, the initial population matrix is multiplied by the survivorship matrix and the result added to net migration.

This method was criticised on account of its basis of inferring migration exchanges among a number of regions from a knowledge of their several populations on several occasions, because empirical data had not borne out the technique. Therefore Keyfitz proposed a similar technique which not only bears out empirical findings but is also more elegant in terms of the use of matrices and more easily manageable in making projections for practical planning purposes.

Keyfitz (1968, pp. 320–2) proceeded as follows. Let there be three regions in a country such that their survivorship matrices are R, S, T, while the initial age cohort vectors are J, K, L respectively. If we assume that there is no migration between the regions, we could express the matrix equation for the simultaneous projection of population as

$$\begin{bmatrix} R & 0 & 0 \\ 0 & S & 0 \\ 0 & 0 & T \end{bmatrix} \cdot \begin{bmatrix} J \\ K \\ L \end{bmatrix} = \begin{bmatrix} RJ \\ SK \\ TL \end{bmatrix} \tag{17}$$

Assume, for the second case, that there is migration from the second region to the first. This implies that the value of SK will be diminished while RJ is increased. Now let there be a second matrix M whose diagonal elements are the fractions moving at each age, then this matrix will appear in the second position of the first and second rows of the operator. Furthermore, if migration is to take place at the end of the interval of projection, the matrix equation is given by

$$\begin{bmatrix} R & MS & 0 \\ 0 & (I-M)S & 0 \\ 0 & 0 & T \end{bmatrix} \cdot \begin{bmatrix} J \\ K \\ L \end{bmatrix} = \begin{bmatrix} RJ + MSK \\ (I-M)SK \\ TL \end{bmatrix} \tag{18}$$

If, however, the migration is to take place at the interval and if the migrants retain during one interval, the mortality and fertility of the group they have, the projection equation is given as

$$\begin{bmatrix} R & SM & 0 \\ 0 & S(I-M) & 0 \\ 0 & 0 & T \end{bmatrix} \cdot \begin{bmatrix} J \\ K \\ L \end{bmatrix} = \begin{bmatrix} RJ + SMK \\ S(I-M)K \\ TL \end{bmatrix} \tag{19}$$

The nature of the migration could still be improved upon in numerous ways. For instance, if we change our assumptions slightly to migration taking place at the beginning of the interval, but the migrants immediately assume the mortality and fertility of the groups to which they go, then the equations are

$$\begin{bmatrix} R & RM & 0 \\ 0 & S(I-M) & 0 \\ 0 & 0 & T \end{bmatrix} \cdot \begin{bmatrix} J \\ K \\ L \end{bmatrix} = \begin{bmatrix} RJ + RMK \\ S(I-M)K \\ TL \end{bmatrix} \tag{20}$$

It is now easy to see how these equations could be generalised into the case of migrations taking place between all regions in an *n* regional set-up. It is simply that the zero elements of the super matrix will be filled by elements that express the nature of these migrations. The reader is encouraged to ponder more on this and fill the empty cells. What is, however, evident from this discussion is the ease with which life tables could be manipulated to provide population projections; since once the data could be cast into the above forms of matrices and vectors, the operations required are simply those of matrix algebra.

These methods have an important appeal in the study of urban population projections as they could easily lead to a complete model of the metropolis. Let the different regions considered here be sub-areas of a city. Let us assume in the meantime that there are no immigrations into the city. Then, interregional migrations are simply those of residential change within the city. Consequently, given the various sub-matrices describing the urban system, one has a useful technique not only for projecting the populations of this system but also of studying the ways these populations are redistributed. Furthermore, if the assumptions of a closed urban system are relaxed, then it is possible to introduce migration into the city through some improvement in the conceptualisation of the super matrix, possibly in terms of birth and death processes in Markov chain analysis (Feller, 1960). Of course, such endeavour makes the population projection more complex and difficult, especially in terms of data collection and analysis, but then we have at hand a useful, if unexplored, method of developing a valuable model of the urban spatial system.

(ii) The Reproductory and Migratory Model

Another method that more explicitly recognises the crowding of the urban environment and the depopulation of rural areas due to both reproductory and migratory processes has been described by Hudson (1970). The most biting criticism of the model is perhaps that it is framed in terms of differential equations and it is in fact a modification of the Lotka-Voltera differential equation model of population inter-action. Theoretically, it is developed as follows.

In a closed environment where population is classified as metropolitan *M* or hinterland *H*, let us assume that a place attracts migrants according to its size; then in a two region case we state that

$$\frac{d_1 H(t)}{dt} = a_1 H(t) + a_{12} M(t) \tag{21}$$

$$\frac{d_1 M(t)}{dt} = a_{21} H(t) + a_2 M(t) \tag{22}$$

where $a_1, a_2 > 0; a_{12}, a_{21} < 0$

These equations describe the rates of change of the hinterland and metropolitan populations respectively. The natural increase component of the rate of change is represented by the balance between births and deaths and is

$$\frac{d_2 H(t)}{dt} = [b_h(t) - d_h(t)] H(t) = a' H(t) \tag{23}$$

$$\frac{d_2 M(t)}{dt} = [b_m(t) - d_m(t)] M(t) = b' M(t) \tag{24}$$

where $b(t)$ and $d(t)$ are the crude birth and death rates respectively at time t.

The complete growth equations for the metropolitan system are

$$\frac{dH(t)}{dt} = \frac{d_1 H(t)}{dt} + \frac{d_2 H(t)}{dt} = a_{11} H(t) + a_{12} M(t) \tag{25}$$

$$\frac{dM(t)}{dt} = \frac{d_1 M(t)}{dt} + \frac{d_2 M(t)}{dt} = a_{21} H(t) + a_{22} M(t) \tag{26}$$

where $a_{11} = a_1 + a'_1; a'_1 = b_h(t) - d_h(t)$
$a_{22} = a_2 + a'_2; a'_2 = b_m(t) - d_m(t)$

A solution of the system of differential equations 25 and 26 will give values for $H(t)$ and $M(t)$ respectively as

$$H(t) = c_{11} \exp(\lambda_1 t) + c_{12} \exp(\lambda_2 t) \tag{27}$$
$$M(t) = c_{21} \exp(\lambda_1 t) + c_{22} \exp(\lambda_2 t) \tag{28}$$

where λ_1 and λ_2 are the two roots of the second-order differential equation formed from equations 25 and 26, and the coefficients c_{ij} represent the initial conditions of population balance in the system. Note that λ_1 and λ_2 could be positive or negative and that they represent some structural characteristics of the birth and death processes in the system.

Equations 27 and 28 may be combined in a matrix form if we allow

$H(t) = Y_1$, $M(t) = Y_2$ and $\exp(\lambda_1 t) = X_1$, $\exp(\lambda_2 t) = X_2$ to give

$$\begin{bmatrix} Y_1 \\ Y_2 \end{bmatrix} = \begin{bmatrix} c_{11} & c_{12} \\ c_{21} & c_{22} \end{bmatrix} \begin{bmatrix} X_1 \\ X_2 \end{bmatrix} \tag{29}$$

None the less, the results of this model would be empirically unacceptable as neither the metropolitan area not its hinterland could have a finite population.

It is obvious that the above model does not possess any characteristic that reflects migration and population growth processes. Consequently, modifications could be made to incorporate these processes. The first is to view migration as based on an information flow network and assume that the amount of migration between two areas at a point in time is some function of the amount of information flowing between them. Consequently the migration component might be expressed as

$$\frac{d_1 H}{dt} = K_{12} H(t) \cdot M(t) \tag{30}$$

$$\frac{d_1 M}{dt} = K_{21} H(t) \cdot M(t) \tag{31}$$

where K_{12}, K_{21} could be of any sign. Furthermore if we assume that growth can be checked, the natural increase component might be expressed by second-degree equations

$$\frac{d_2 H}{dt} = K_1 H(t) - K_{11} H^2(t) \tag{32}$$

$$\frac{d_2 M}{dt} = K_2 M(t) - K_{22} M^2(t) \tag{33}$$

implying that natural growth rate declines proportionately to the square of size.

Combining equations 30 to 33, it is possible to derive the growth equations of the metropolitan and hinterland regions as

$$\frac{dH}{dt} = K_1 H(t) - K_{11} H^2(t) \pm K_{12} H(t) \cdot M(t) \tag{34}$$

$$\frac{dM}{dt} = K_2 M(t) - K_{22} M^2(t) \pm K_{21} H(t) \cdot M(t) \tag{35}$$

Setting the growth rate in equations 34 and 35 equal to zero, the equilibrium situation produces interesting results, which correspond to a complete depopulation of either the hinterland or the metropolis or both. A fourth solution obtained, if we set equations 34 and 35 equal to zero gives

$$0 = K_1 - K_{11} H \pm K_{12} M \tag{36}$$
$$0 = K_2 - K_{22} M \pm K_{21} H \tag{37}$$

and shows how a stable population might be attained if one manipulates and interprets the signs of K_{12} and K_{21}. For instance, there would be a stable population if the hinterland growth kept pace with metropolitan growth, i.e. if

$$K_2 + K_{21}H = K_{22}M \tag{38}$$

It can be shown (Hudson, 1970) that if the mechanisms postulated exist, the long-run result will be a finite population size in both the metropolitan area and its hinterland. In this way, it would be seen that the models offer an approach to more comprehensive analysis of growth and distribution of urban populations to the extent that they indicate which variables are capable of control and which are not by means of the coefficients.

Perhaps the most interesting aspects of this model concern the explicit relationship of the urban population to that of its hinterland. In short, there is an explicit recognition of the role of migration in urban population growth. It therefore stands to reason to expect the possibility of integrating this conceptualisation into the analytical framework of the last section. Such a procedure would be an alternative to the birth and death process of Markov chain analysis in incorporating the immigration component into studies of urban population change.

An important problem that faces these methods of urban population analysis could be in the assemblage of the necessary data for their calibration. However, in recent years researchers are paying more attention to the study of the migratory and reproductive components of urban populations, although most studies have not progressed further than making initial estimates. For instance, in the author's study in Jos, an attempt was made to estimate the growth of the city population in terms of that component due to natural increase and that due to migration between 1931 and 1963 for which data was available (see Table 2.4.1).

Table 2.4.1: The Population of Jos 1931–63, Showing the
Reproductory and Migratory Components

Year	Population	Increase	Reproductory		Migratory	
			Absolute	Per Cent	Absolute	Per Cent
1931	11,854	11,134	4,532	–	3,322	–
1952	38,527	26,673	10,196	38.23	16,477	66.77
1963	110,361	71,834	17,203	23.95	54,004	75.18
Total		109,641	27,399	34.14	70,481	64.34

Note: The totals for reproductory and migratory components do not include 1931 figures.

Source: Ayeni (1974).

The overall rate of growth of population was 5 per cent per annum between 1931 and 1952, while between 1952 and 1963, this rate was 8.5 per cent. On the other hand, the rate of natural increase has been around 3.5 per cent per annum. The facts that emerge from the table are as follows. First, Jos is a rapidly growing city in Nigeria, the majority of whose population is made up of migrants who in 1963 constituted about 65 per cent of the population. The proportion in subsequent years is expected to be higher in view of the fact that the city, as with many other Nigerian urban centres, continues to witness large-scale immigration of people as a result of the changing political scene, notably the creation of states. Furthermore, since only 34 per cent of the increase in population is due to natural increase, one might conclude that the city would be conducive to the spread and assimilation of the processes of modernisation, as migrants in general are known to be important agents of diffusion.

While the above analysis is very gross and useful only for descriptive purposes, it is conceivable to note that a synthesis of the techniques of urban population analysis described in previous pages are the theoretical prerequisite for studying the changing characteristics of urban populations. These indeed are challenges for future research.

5. Conclusion

It is obvious from our discussions so far that there is a wide variety of models of urban populations, some dealing with the age structure, others focusing on migration while still others deal with reproduction. Consequently, our discussions do not pretend to be exhaustive of these models and neither do they pretend to cover all the researches conducted on urban population growth analysis nor on the descriptions of the form of urban populations. To attempt to do this is no doubt a Herculean task, the successful accomplishment of which transcends the aims and objectives of this book. To the extent that many discussions of this very important topic usually neglect or touch marginally on the spatial dimension, we have in the above pages therefore outlined approaches that not only synthesise current ideas on the analysis of urban populations but also open up the gaps in conceptual thinking about population processes.

References

Alonso, W. 1964. *Location and Land Use: Toward a General Theory of Land Rent.* Cambridge, Massachusetts: Harvard University Press

Ayeni, M.A.O. 1974. Predictive Modelling of Urban Spatial Structure: The Example of Jos, Benue-Plateau State, Nigeria. Ph.D. thesis, University of Ibadan, Nigeria

Berry, B.J.L. 1973. *The Human Consequences of Urbanisation.* London: Macmillan

Berry, B.J.L. Simmons, J.W., and Tennant, R.J. 1963. Urban Population Densities: Structure and Change. *Geographical Review, 53,* 2, 389–405

Berry, B.J.L. and Horton, F. 1970. *Geographical Perspective on Urban Systems: with Integrated Readings.* Englewood Cliffs, New Jersey: Prentice-Hall

Blalock, H.M. 1960. *Social Statistics.* New York: McGraw-Hill

Clark, C. 1951. Urban Population Densities. *Journal of the Royal Statistical Society,* Ser. A, *114,* 490–6

Dacey, M.F. 1963. Order Neighbor Statistics for a Class of Random Patterns in Multi-Dimensional Space. *Annals of the Association of American Geographers, 53,* 505–15

Feller, W. 1960. *An Introduction to Probability Theory and its Applications,* Vol. 1. New York: Wiley International

Harris, B. 1964. A Note on the Probability of Interaction at a Distance. *Journal of Regional Science, 5,* 2, 31–5

Hudson, J.C. 1970. Elementary Models for Population Growth and Distribution Analysis. *Demography, 7,* 8, 261–365

Keyfitz, N. 1968. *Introduction to the Mathematics of Population.* Reading, Massachusetts: Addison-Wesley

Lowry, I.S. 1964. *A Model of Metropolis.* Santa Monica, California: Rand Corporation

March, L. 1969. Urban Systems: A Generalized Distribution Function. In A.G. Wilson (ed.), *London Papers in Regional Science,* Vol. 1. London: Pion

McLoughlin. J.B. 1969. *Urban and Regional Planning: A Systems Approach.* London: Faber and Faber

Muth, R. 1969. *Cities and Housing.* Chicago: University of Chicago Press

Newling, B.E. 1966. Urban Growth and Spatial Structure: Mathematical Models and Empirical Evidence. *Geographical Review, 56,* 2, 213–25

Rees, P.H. 1970. Concepts of Social Space: Toward an Urban Social Geography. In B.J.L. Berry and F.E. Horton (eds.), *Geographical Perspective on Urban Systems.* Englewood Cliffs, New Jersey: Prentice-Hall

Rogers, A. 1966. Matrix Methods of Population Analysis. *Journal of the American Institute of Planners,* 32, *1*, 40–4

Weber, A.F. 1899. *The Growth of Cities in the Nineteenth Century.* New York: Macmillan

Winer, B.J. 1962. *Statistical Principles in Experimental Design.* New York: McGraw-Hill

Wingo, L. 1961. *Transportation and Urban Land Use.* Washington, D.C.: Resources for the Future, Inc.

3 URBAN ECONOMIC ACTIVITY

1. Introduction

Cities all over the world are characterised by a set of activities which actually account for the concentrations of people in them. Such activities are distinctively urban and may include those arising from manufacturing, trading and finance, transportation and tertiary activities. All these combine to generate the spatial configuration of the city because their requirements are sometimes functionally differentiated and also spatially segregated. In addition, these activities generate various occupations in which urban dwellers engage.

There are various approaches to the understanding and analysis of urban economic activity. One such approach focuses on the factors of their location, taking particularly into consideration the effect of large-scale agglomerations of people in cities (Pred, 1967; Logan, 1966), while another approach regards the locations of these activities as given and focuses attention on the interrelationships between these activities on the one hand, and between the activities and the areas which the urban centre serves on the other. The first approach is considered marginally of interest here as it has been very well covered in standard textbooks on locational analysis (Losch, 1954; Isard, 1956; Smith, 1955). The second approach, on the other hand, is of particular interest, as it provides very challenging techniques in spatial analysis. A discussion and illustration of some of these techniques is the objective of this chapter.

We shall therefore focus on urban economic activity, especially as this relates to the hinterland, as well as the ways of summarising it using such techniques as the economic base concept and the input-output technique. We shall also examine techniques for studying the spatial and sectoral changes that take place between urban industrial areas and within groups of industries. In this latter context we shall discuss the shift and share or the allocation of growth components technique which is the most widely used method for studying these changes. Furthermore, since our interest sometimes lies in the way these techniques or models predict the future growth of urban centres, we shall also be interested in seeing these techniques within a predictive framework. We shall begin with the economic base concept as it provides a convenient gateway into looking at the other models.

2. The Economic Base Concept

The words *economic base* involve a distinctive way of looking at the relations that exist between an industry and the area which the industry serves. The urban economic base is defined to consist of all activities that export goods and services to points outside a community. Such goods and services are described as basic, as they are supposed to be the income-earners to the community. All other goods and services are said to be non-basic, as they do not bring money from outside the community. In other words, they are population-serving (Tiebout, 1962).

The concept may be traced to ideas expressed by Frederick L. Olmstead and later by Aurousseau (1921). Olmstead, for instance, wrote that

> productive occupations may be roughly divided into those which can be called primary, such as ... manufacturing goods for general use (i.e. not confined to use within the community itself), and those occupations which may be called ancillary, such as devoted directly or indirectly to the service and convenience of the people engaged in the primary occupations (quoted from R. Murphy, 1966, p. 100),

while Aurousseau wrote as follows:

> It is well known that towns have an extraordinary power of growth. This appears to be due to the relationship between the primary occupations of the townsfolk. The primary occupations are those directly concerned with the functions of the town. The secondary occupations are those concerned with the maintenance of the well being of the people engaged in those of primary nature.

The extensive development of the concept was due to Homer Hoyt (1939), while Richard B. Andrews provided the most extensive review and applications of the concept (Andrews, 1953, 1954, 1955). Basically, the use of the concept involves a calculation of total employment (or some other surrogate) in each basic activity and the estimation of the ratio of basic to non-basic employment. In many studies, the technique has been used for the projection and analysis of employment and population, using concepts similar to that of classical economic multiplier.

The urban economic base has been much criticised (Andrews, 1953; Alexander, 1954; Alexanderson, 1956; and Roterus and Calef, 1955). Many of these criticisms deal with the operationalisation of the concept as regards the definition of the area of interest or the unit of measurement (e.g. employment payrolls, community income and expenditure, volume of sales measured in monetary units or even value added by manufacturing). None the less, the economic base concept has a number of uses, many of which had been summarised by Alexander (1945) as follows. First, it is a way of providing the degree of the tie or relationship between a city and the outside world. Second, it has a potentially useful role in the classification of cities and finally it is a method of investigating the role of each business or firm in a city's economic life. In recent years, it has played a notable role in the construction of spatial interaction models of urban and regional structure (Lowry, 1964; Batty, 1970). This aspect of the concept is discussed in Chapter 12 of this book.

(i) Techniques for Determining the Economic Base Ratio

The classical method of determining the basic—non-basic ratio was due to Homer Hoyt (1961), who, using employment or any other data set systematically collected on a national or regional basis, developed a method for comparing the employment pattern of the area under study with that of the nation. This technique usually described as the quotient approach is given by the formula

$$E^B_{ic} = E_{ic} - \frac{P_c}{P_N} \cdot E_{iN} \tag{1}$$

where E^B_{ic} is the basic employment in industrial or activity i in city c, E_{ic} is the total employment in the industrial or activity i in this city while E_{iN} is the total employment in this activity i in the entire nation. P_c, P_N are the city and national populations respectively.

The total basic employment in the city is then calculated from equation 1 by adding all the basic employment in each industry group, viz.

$$E^B_c = \sum_{i=1}^{n} E^B_{ic} \tag{2}$$

Now if E^s_c represents the non-basic component of the employment, then the basic—non-basic ratio is given by

$$E^B_c / E^s_c \tag{3}$$

and the accounting identity

$$E_c^B + E_c^s = E_c \qquad (4)$$

holds.

The calculation of the basic component of urban employment as done above may be criticised on the basis that there is no justification for expecting the amount of basic employment in a city to be a function of the ratio of its population and the national total population. Recognising this criticism, Alexanderson (1956), and subsequently Ullman and Dacey (1960), proposed an alternative approach called the minimum requirement approach.

The minimum requirement approach is based on the notion that there is a minimum percentage of the labour force of an urban area that is required in each sector to maintain its viability, and that any employment beyond this minimum requirement, called 'excess employment' is the basic component while the minimum requirement is the non-basic component.

There are many problems associated with providing an operational definition of a minimum requirement. For instance, Alexanderson (1956), using a 'firm by firm' approach, arrayed 864 cities of the United States with a population greater than 10,000 from the smallest to the largest in terms of their total employment in a cumulative distribution and used the value of the fifth percentile as the minimum requirement. This he called the K-value for the industry. The sum of the K-values for the 36 industry groups used in the analysis yielded the total non-basic employment. Many questions have been raised by the method of Alexanderson. For example, why the lower fifth percentile? And what about the variations that may occur as the size of the city increases? Ullman and Dacey (1960) provided a way of answering some of these questions.

Ullman and Dacey (1960) divided the cities of the United States into six population size classes and picked random samples from each class. For each class and for each industry group the percentage of the total labour force is calculated for each of the cities. For instance, this may be 8 per cent for the textile industry for city A and 2 per cent for city B. If we assume that city A has the highest and city B the lowest, then (8—2) per cent is the amount that is basic for city A while city B has no basic component in this industry. In a similar way, the basic components in the other industries and for the groups of cities are calculated, and hence the basic—non-basic ratio. It was evident that there were variations between the size classes of cities and non-basic employment in a given category was related directly to size (see Figure 3.2.1).

Figure 3.2.1: Minimum Requirements for 14 Industry Types, Based on Regression Lines

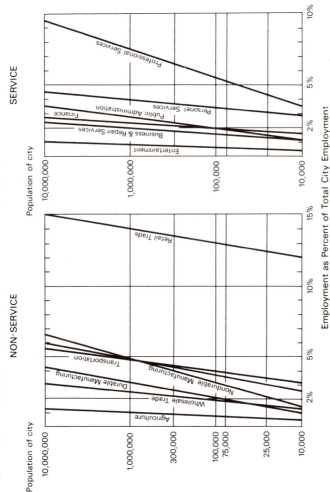

Source: Proceedings of the IGU Symposium in Urban Geography, p. 129.

Besides criticisms of the method of calculation of the urban economic base for a well-defined area, a more fundamental criticism is that not only activities producing for an external market are income-generating (Andrews, 1954). Recognising this criticism, Goldner (1964) has presented within a land-use modelling framework a schematic representation of the urban economy in terms of basic and non-basic components. He provides an extended definition of these terms and says that the basic sector may be defined in terms of their export-import considerations and also in terms of the locational orientation of the industries. According to this scheme (Table 3.2.1), the basic sector is made up of all industries that export goods and services, thereby

Table 3.2.1: Schematic Classification of an Economy into Basic and Service Sectors

Economic Base	Locational Orientation	
Orientation	Basic	Service
	Locate with respect to interregional transportation routes, resources and unique site features; inter-industry linkages, agglomeration economies	Locate with respect to residential population and purchasing power, daytime population concentration
Exports Generate income from sources out- side the city	(1) Agriculture (2) Mining (3) Manufacturing (4) Transportation (5) Regional admini- stration (government) (6) Finance and banking (7) Some educational institutions, e.g. universities and grammar schools. (8) Some services, e.g. tourist hotels etc.	
Local Consumption Generates income from local production	(1) Wholesale trade (2) Building and construction industries (3) Other service activities	(1) Retail trade, including traditional marketing activities (2) Intra-city transporta- tion (3) Services and service industries (4) Local government

Source: Modified after Goldner (1968).

generating income from outside the city; all industries whose locational orientations are deemed as non-local population-oriented, and all other firms which actually generate new income and new employment, even though their products may be consumed locally.

An important criticism of Goldner's approach, perhaps, is the fact that any industry can belong to one and only one class, i.e. either basic or non-basic, but not both. This means that the sort of details and inference in the methods of Hoyt and Ullman and Dacey are lost. Moreover, there is much subjectivity in this method.

In an application of the methodology discussed by Goldner (1968) and shown in Table 3.2.1 for Lagos and Jos in Nigeria, the basic ratio is 0.544 for Lagos and 0.450 for Jos (Table 3.2.2). For Lagos, this means that for one basic employment in the city there are 1.84 service employments while in Jos there would be 2.22 service employments. While it must be accepted that there is not enough evidence for a non-impeachable comparison of the basic–non-basic ratios over city sizes in Nigeria, it might be hypothesised from Table 3.2.2 that this ratio would increase with the size of cities. This contrasts with observations on cities in developed countries because recent urban development has decreased the number of people engaged in agriculture (and hence basic employment) in all cities, and substituted in its stead large numbers of people engaged mostly in the informal urban service sector. Moreover, it is only in some of the larger urban centres that there is any appreciable development of manufacturing and administrative activities which increase the basic component of the urban labour force.

The method of classification proposed by Goldner undoubtedly increases the number of the criticisms of the economic base concept. For instance, it is very subjective, as the researcher has to allocate the employment or other measures of activities on the basis of his knowledge of the area under study. Consequently, two researchers studying

Table 3.2.2: Basic and Non-basic Employment in Lagos (1975) and Jos (1972)

City	Population Estimate	Total Employed	Basic Employment	Non-basic Employment	B/N Ratio
Lagos (1975)	2,496,898	674,160	237,381	436,779	0.54 or 1:1.84
Jos (1972)	98,944	32,951	10,227	22,724	0.45 or 1:2.22

Sources: Ayeni, 1974, p. 256; Ayeni, 1976.

the same city and using this method may arrive at different results. The only benefit of the method is that it is easy to operationalise. A warning is therefore in order, that results based on this approach should be viewed with caution, as with the results that emerge from an economic base study as a whole.

The greatest benefit from using the economic base concept is the simplicity of the technique. Consequently, if the method of determina-, tion of the components of the base concept becomes complex, then one is bound to be discouraged. It is, however, likely that as more and more data become available the economic base concept will not be used for any rigorous research, but rather in an exploratory framework.

(ii) Predicting with the Economic Base Concept

In the absence of a wealth of data that permit the development of more sophisticated techniques of urban economic analysis, it is possible to predict with the economic base concept using the notion that total employment E in an urban region can be related to the population through an equation of the form

$$P = \alpha E \quad \alpha \geqslant 1 \tag{5}$$

where α is the inverse of the activity rate. The activity rate is the proportion of workers per household. Since we know from the assumptions of the economic base concept that service employment E_s is related to total population P, we can define a population-serving ratio β, the ratio of service employment to total population and write and equation of the form

$$E^s = \beta P \quad 0 < \beta < 1 \tag{6}$$

With the accounting identity that

$$E = E^B + E^S \tag{4}$$

we can combine equations 5 and 6 by substituting for P to derive basic employment in terms of total employment. The equation is of the form

$$\begin{aligned} E^B &= E - \alpha\beta E \\ &= (1 - \alpha\beta) E \end{aligned} \tag{7}$$

Using equation 7 we can always calculate the total employment generated from a given basic employment E^B as follows:

$$E = \frac{E^B}{1 - \alpha\beta} = (1 - \mu)^{-1} E^B; \quad \mu = \alpha\beta \tag{8}$$

Once E is known, it is possible to calculate the total population. We shall see that equation 8 is of the form of the input-output model. It suffices here to note that the similarity is merely apparent, as there are structural differences in them.

It is even possible to formulate this set of equations within a quasi-dynamic framework. Such an approach, described by Paelinck (1970), involves the introduction of time lags into equation 7 to give

$$E^B_t = E_{t+1} - \mu E_t \qquad (9)$$

This is a first-order linear difference equation and if we assume E^B_t is a constant, the solution of equation 9 in terms of an initial employment E_0 is given by

$$E_t = \frac{E^B_t}{r} + (E_0 + \frac{E^B_t}{r})(1-r)^t \qquad (10)$$

where $r = 1 - \mu$. Equation 10 will be suitable for tracing the repercussions of a given basic employment throughout an economic system for suitably defined time periods $t = 1, 2 \ldots, n$.

Surprisingly, this approach has formed the point of departure for the development of growth models of the urban economy. Batty (1972) argues that it is possible to expand the multiplier $1/r$ as

$$\frac{1}{(1 - \mu)} = 1 + \mu + \mu^2 + \ldots + \mu^n \qquad (11)$$

and that given an increment of employment ΔE^B_t where the difference operator Δ is defined as

$$\Delta E^B_t = E^B_{t+1} - E^B_t \qquad (12)$$

The total population P generated from this increment is

$$P = \alpha \Delta E^B_t (1 + \mu + \mu^2 + \ldots + \mu^n) \qquad (13)$$

If we assume that μ is a constant parameter and that each increment of activity is generated in successive time periods, then any particular increment of population ΔP_t may be derived from the equation

$$\Delta P_t = \alpha [\Delta E^B_t + \Delta E^B_{t-1}\mu + \Delta E^B_{t-2}\mu^2 + \ldots + \Delta E^B_{t-n}\mu^n] \qquad (14)$$

which could be shown to be equivalent to

$$\Delta P_t = \alpha(1 + \mu) \, [\Delta E^B_t \mu + \Delta E^B_{t-1} \mu^2 + \ldots + \Delta E^B_{t-n} \mu^{2n}] \quad (15)$$

Using a similar argument, it was shown that the distributed lag equations for the employment is equivalent to

$$\Delta E_t = \Delta E^B_t + (1 + \mu) \, [\Delta E^B_t \mu + \Delta E^B_{t-1} \mu^2 + \ldots + \Delta E^B_{t-n} \mu^{2n+1}] \, (16)$$

While Batty developed his model around the disaggregation of the multiplier to generate increases of employment and population in forms similar to geometric lag equations of dynamic models of the classical economic multiplier, it is possible to extend this approach and develop equations that trace the paths of many inputs of basic employment into the space economy (Ayeni, 1975).

We assume that it is possible to define time periods t over which the repercussions of inputs of basic employment may be traced. It may then be reasoned that given some basic employment E^B_1, the total employment at the first time period is the sum of the initial employment E_0 plus the inrease in employment generated from the input basic employment. Thus, if the increase in employment generated from an increase in basic employment is $\delta_t \Delta E_t$, where ΔE_t is as defined in equation 12, then

$$\delta_t \Delta E_t = \frac{\Delta E^B_t}{r} + (\Delta E_0 - \frac{\Delta E^B_t}{r})(1 - r)^t \quad (17)$$

and

$$E_1 = E_0 + \delta_1 = \Delta E^B_0 \quad (18)$$

At the second time period, the total employment will be the sum of the employment E_1 at the previous time period, the increase due to the first change in basic employment $\delta_2 \Delta E^B_0$, and the increase due to the new change in basic employment $\delta_1 \Delta E^B_1$, namely

$$E_2 = E_1 + \delta_2 \Delta E^B_0 + \delta_1 \Delta E^B_1 \quad (19)$$

The case for the third time period may be similarly argued to show that the total employment is

$$E_3 = E_2 + \delta_3 \Delta E^B_0 + \delta_2 \Delta E^B_1 + \delta_1 \Delta E^B_2 \quad (20)$$

Generalising the argument to E_t and substituting backwards for all values of E_t, E_t satisfies the equation

$$E_t = E_0 + \sum_{t=1}^{n} \delta_t \Delta E_0^B + \sum_{t=1}^{n-1} \delta_t \Delta E_1^B + \sum_{t=1}^{n-2} \delta_t \Delta E_2^B + \ldots$$

$$+ \sum_{t=1}^{3} \delta_t \Delta E^B + \sum_{t=1}^{2} \delta_t \Delta E_{t-2}^B + \sum \delta_t \Delta E_{t-1}^B \qquad (21)$$

The total population at each time period may be calculated from the relation specified in equation 5, the increase or changes in total employment may be calculated from equation 12, while increases in population would be given by

$$\Delta P_t = P_{t+1} - P_t \qquad (22)$$

The above are many ways in which the economic base concept could be used within a forecasting framework. As has been often noted, the greatest appeal of the formulations lies in the ease with which the relevant data could be assembled either from published sources or by a field investigation. The fact that economic base analysis is an aggregate technique, as it neglects inter-industry relationships, remains a major criticism.

3. The Urban Input-Output Method

In the forecasts of the urban economic activity of the last section, we have presented an almost total neglect of the role of the individual industries and activities. A better perspective of the picture would be provided by a technique that first projects the levels of output of various activities, since various activities grow at differential rates. This differential growth is necessary to appreciate the role of individual activities. If such a method were available, it is feasible to argue that such output levels for each activity could be related to the needs and requirements of every other activity and the final demand, i.e. the consumer. The traditional method of expressing these relationships is the input-output technique.

The first empirical formulation of an inter-industrial table was by Leontief (1941) in his studies of the structure of the American economy; although the theoretical bases of the technique can be traced to Leon Walras' equilibrium analysis of an economy (see Walras, 1954). The technique has seen wide application in the studies of national economies, (Leontief, 1951; Cao-Pinna, 1956), regional and inter-regional economies (Isard, 1951; Moore, 1955) and is gradually being applied to studies of metropolitan and urban economies (Isard, Kavesh and Kuenne, 1953; Artle, 1955; Morrison, 1973).

The input-output method possesses a number of advantages over the economic base concept. Like the economic base method, it could be a measure of the relationship between an urban centre and its hinterland, but it also shows the links that exist between the elements or sectors of the economic system. As a result of this, it is a better technique for studying the growth of an economy, especially in the impact analysis of possible changes which it accomplishes through the effect of its multiplier.

The input-output method is a sort of inter-industrial accounting whereby the flow of goods measured either in physical or monetary terms is traced from one productive sector to another. It is shown in a two-way table (matrix) representing each sector of the economy twice, once as a producer along the rows; and then as a user of input (consumer) along the columns. A typical input-output table is shown in Table 3.3.1.

The flow of goods between sector i and sector j is indicated by x_{ij}

Table 3.3.1: An Input-output Table

Purchasing Sectors (Outputs)

	Intermediate Use						Final Use	Total Supply
Producing Sectors	Sectors 1 to n							
	1	2	3 $\;\cdot\;\cdot\;\cdot$			n		
1	x_{11}	x_{12}					Y_1	$X_1^{(S)}$
2							Y_2	$X_2^{(S)}$
3							Y_3	
.								
.			x_{ij}					
.								
n	x_{n1}	x_{n2}	x_{n3}				Y_n	$X_n^{(S)}$
Primary Inputs	U_1	U_2	U_3				U_n	
Total Prod.	$X_1^{(P)}$	$X_2^{(P)}$	$X_3^{(P)}$				$X_n^{(P)}$	X

while the following accounting identities can be seen to hold (see Table 3.3.1).

$$X_i^{(S)} = \sum_{j=1}^{n} x_{ij} + Y_i \tag{23}$$

$$X_j^{(P)} = \sum_{i=1}^{n} x_{ij} + U_j \tag{24}$$

and in general

$$X_i^{(S)} = X_j^{(P)} \tag{25}$$

and henceforth below we drop the labels and S and P and assume that equation 25 holds. Where Y_i is the part of the output of industry or activity i that goes into the final demand, e.g. household and government uses and investment; and U_j represents the primary inputs or the value added by that industry or activity. Equation 25 states that the total output of any activity is equivalent to the total consumption of the outputs of that activity. The formulation therefore is that of a 'closed' system.

In input-output analysis, attention is often devoted not only to the construction of the table above but also to the technological coefficients which constitute 'the cooking recipe' of each sector of the economy. These coefficients, determined by the level of technology, are the units of every activity required in the unit production of a given level of output. It is defined as:

$$a_{ij} = \frac{x_{ij}}{x_j} \tag{26}$$

The input-output table can be used as a multiplier in forecasting future states of an urban economic system. It depends on the use of equation 23 which, using the substitution in equation 26, may be written as

$$X_i - \sum_{j=1}^{n} a_{ij} X_j = Y_i \tag{27}$$

where as before Y_i are the bills of final demand. In matrix notation this becomes

$$[\mathbf{I} - \mathbf{a}] \ \mathbf{X} = \mathbf{Y} \tag{28}$$

and $\mathbf{I}$ is an identity matrix. Now, given this bill of final demand one could calculate the outputs of each industry by the equation

$$X = [I - a]^{-1} Y \tag{29}$$

The matrix $(I - a)^{-1}$ is called the Leontief inverse and its elements show how much output must be produced in a given industrial sector in order that a unit of final demand sales can be made. The production so derived includes both the unit of final goods sold directly by the industrial sector and the monetary value of the goods sold indirectly to the final demand sector. The reader might wish to compare equation 23 with equation 8 of the economic base concept.

The input-output model is no doubt a concise way of studying an economy, be it national, regional or metropolitan. The crucial factor in the use of the method is the availability of data, which is a problem even in national economies where short-cut techniques are often used. Such techniques involve the adjustment of a national accounts table to reflect the industrial composition of specific regions. However, there is no reason to be very pessimistic as to its application in metropolitan economic analysis, for with the aid of computerised data banks, the next few years could be eventful in terms of data assemblage. It is therefore useful to explore further developments arising from equation 29.

Since urban centres or metropolitan areas are usually large economic systems that encompass a number of urbanised regions, it is possible to extend the interregional input-output model into the study of metropolitan economies (Isard, 1951). Thus, if there are r regions or subsystems in the metropolitan area, an interregional input-output model of this could be written as

$$_rX_i - \sum_{s=1}^{n} \sum_{j=1}^{m} {}_{rs}X_{ij} = {}_rY_i$$

$$i = 1, 2 \ldots, m$$

where $_rY_i$ represents the final demand for the products of industry i in region r, $_rX_i$ the total output of industry i in region r. The technological coefficients may be defined as

$$_{rs}a_{ij} = \frac{_{rs}x_{ij}}{_rx_i} \tag{31}$$

and the forecasting model can be written as

$$_rX_i = \left[I - {}_{rs}a_{ij} \right]^{-1} {}_rY_i \tag{32}$$

Such a model possesses not only the ability to show the intrametropolitan and interregional industrial relations but could also provide highly valuable insights into the operation of an economic system.

(ii) Towards a Dynamic Input-output Method

One of the most important criticisms of the input-output model in forecasting is the assumption of the stability of the technological coefficients. It is known that in real life these coefficients do vary with time, and this has led to attempts at introducing dynamic considerations into the input-output method. One such consideration is due to Leontief himself, who developed a dynamic theory of input-output systems. The theoretical basis of a dynamic input-output model arises from considerations that the stock $S_{ik(t)}$ of a commodity produced by an industry i and used by an industry k at time period t as well as the rate of change of that stock i.e. $dS_{ik(t)}/dt = \dot{S}_{ik}$, need not be considered as part of final demand. Thus they do not need to be subsumed as part of the technological coefficients a_{ij}, but rather should be accounted for separately. Consequently, the simple input-output equation 23 may be modified as

$$X_i - \sum_{k=1}^{m} x_{ik} - \sum_{k=1}^{m} \dot{S}_{ik} = Y_i \qquad (33)$$

which is interpreted to mean that the bill of final demand for an industry group Y_i is made up not only of the production of the industry group X_i but also the input flows $\sum_{k=1}^{m} x_{ik}$ which serve the various sectors of the economy as well as the changes $\sum_{k=1}^{m} \dot{S}_{ik}$ on the stocks of that particular good used throughout the economy.

It follows from the above reasoning that the set of structural coefficients a_{ik} of the simple input-output model must be supplemented by a corresponding set of structural stock-flow relationships b_{ik} defined as

$$S_{ik} = b_{ik} X_k \qquad (34)$$

where b_{ik} represents the stock or capital coefficients of the system. This is the stock of goods produced by sector i which sector k must hold per unit of its full capacity output, and includes the stock of buildings, machinery as well as inventories of raw materials, spare parts and other supplies used by that industry. By differentiating equation 34 with respect to time we might express b_{ik} in terms of the changes in S_{ik} and X_k as

$$\dot{S}_{ik} = b_{ik}\dot{X}_k \qquad (35)$$

Substituting equations 34 and 35 into equation 33 gives

$$X_i - \sum_{k=1}^{n} a_{ik}X_k = \sum_{k=1}^{n} b_{ik}\dot{X}_k = Y_i \qquad (36)$$

which is a system of differential equations involving structural inter-relationships between inputs and outputs of the various sectors and their rates of change. It is obvious that a solution system to this equation would only be feasible for the n outputs of the various industry classes or sectors, given the components of final demand $Y_i(t)$, the output levels of $X_i(t)$ at an initial time period as well as the time path represented by $\dot{X}_i$.

Mathematically, the differential equation might be solved by first finding the roots of the homogeneous equation represented by

$$X_i - \sum_{k=1}^{n} a_{ik}X_k - \sum_{k=1}^{n} b_{ik}\dot{X}_k = 0 \qquad (37)$$

before finding the solution to the non-homogeneous equation system represented by equation 36. Leontief (1951, pp. 59–62) describes this solution method and the interested reader is referred to this work.

Dynamic input-output method is a complex undertaking not only in terms of data availability but also in terms of defining an appropriate solution system. This is because difference rather than differential equations would have to be used in practice and this has an associated problem of providing a definition for the rates of growth. These techniques require an advanced knowledge of calculus and difference equations not usually within the grasp of the student of urban analysis. Consequently the development of a dynamic input-output analysis has remained for a long time only of theoretical interest.

Finally, it must be pointed out that the simple input-output technique, as well as its dynamic formulation, are basically linear in the extent that they assume that the effect of carrying on several types of production is the sum of the separate parts. This additivity assumption rules out the effect of both external economies and diseconomies in the production process. Consequently a valuable theoretical exploration of the input-output technique could proceed in the direction of incorporating these issues which are outside the scope of this book. None the less, a feasible line of approach for urban analysts is the development of techniques which mathematically and operationally are less complex than the input-output method but which at the same time allow the researcher insights into the mechanism of the urban economy. Such is the approach described in the next section.

(iii) Operational Semi-input-output/Economic Base Method

Recognising the difficulty of data assemblage for the construction of an input-output table, both Czamanski (1965) and Paelinck (1970) developed techniques that can be described as lying between the economic base concept and the input-output analysis. These techniques used the method of distributed lags considered in projections with the economic base concept. It is, however, more comprehensive as it went further than the economic base method in defining categories of urban populations as well as basic and service employments which are related to one another through equations and structural parameters of the economic system. Many of these techniques are not only elegant but are also sophisticated in terms of the levels of disaggregation. The simplest example described by Paelinck is discussed below.

Let P be the total population,
   A be the total active population,
   E^B be the basic urban activities,
   E^S be the service activities.

Relationships between these variables are defined using a number of structural parameters as follows

$$\Delta E^B_{t+1} = E^B_{t+1} - E^B_t$$

$$= \alpha (A_t - E_t) + \alpha^* E^B_t \tag{38}$$

The equation states that basic urban activities are attracted by the available labour pool (active population minus employment) plus an autonomous component. The parameter α scales the total active population to give the urban population while α^* acts like a policy parameter; with a policy that favours attraction increasing the value of α^*. Then,

$$\Delta E^S_{t+1} = E^S_{t+1} - E^S_t$$

$$= \beta (\beta^* P_t - E^S_t) + \beta^{**} E^S_t \quad 0 < \beta \leqslant 1 \tag{39}$$

Equation 39 states that service activities adapt themselves to a desired level $\beta^* P_t$ at a speed β. The autonomous component that serves the city's hinterland is given by $\beta^{**}E_t^s$, while β^{**} is a ratio of population to total employment and β^* is the marginal city serving equilibrium parameter. The next relation is given by;

$$\Delta A_{t+1} = A_{t+1} - A_t$$

$$= \gamma\Delta P_{t+1} + \gamma^*(E_t - A_t) \tag{40}$$

which states that the active population is a function of total population with a component induced by the demand for labour. The constants γ and γ^* are parameters of these relationships. Furthermore,

$$\Delta P_{t+1} = P_{t+1} - P_t$$

$$= \psi E_t + \psi^* P_t \tag{41}$$

This states that total production is attracted from outside by the level of employment plus an autonomous growth rate. ψ, ψ^* are the parameters of the relationships. Finally, the fifth relationship is given by the well-known accounting identity that

$$E = E^B + E^S \tag{42}$$

The formulation of these difference equations of various aspects of urban form shows that urban development is subject to built-in cyclical processes that can be easily triggered off due to the interplay of certain strategic parameters. Paelinck (1970) shows that the general model that presents solutions for all the variables is a problem with systems of difference equations, viz.

$$\begin{bmatrix} P_{t+1} \\ A_{t+1} \\ E_{t+1} \\ E_{t+1}^B \\ E_{t+1}^S \end{bmatrix} = \begin{bmatrix} 1+\gamma^* & -\gamma & \psi & 0 & 0 \\ \gamma\psi^* & 1-\gamma\psi-\gamma & \gamma\psi+\gamma^* & 0 & 0 \\ \beta\beta^* & \alpha & -\alpha & 1+\alpha^* & 1-\beta^{**}-\beta \\ 0 & \alpha & -\alpha & 1+\alpha^* & 0 \\ \beta\beta^* & 0 & 0 & 0 & 1-\beta+\beta^{**} \end{bmatrix} \cdot \begin{bmatrix} P_t \\ A_t \\ E_t \\ E_t^B \\ E_t^S \end{bmatrix}$$

which in matrix form is

$$\mathbf{Y}_{t+1} = \mathbf{A}\mathbf{Y}_t \tag{43}$$

The solution to equation 43, for a given initial state Y_0, of the urban system is

$$Y_t = A^t Y_0 \tag{44}$$

and A^t is the tth power of the matrix A of the parameters of the urban system.

A solution can always easily be obtained to the matrix equation 44 using the Cayley-Hamilton theorem which expressed powers of A in terms of its eigenvalues, which are simply the diagonal elements of this matrix. From an examination of these equations, one readily sees that the crucial information required concerns the parameters of the economic system. The derivation of this is based on empirical relationships that exist between the equations (Paelinck, 1970). The utilisation of the equation system would provide results that lie between the highly aggregative approach of the economic base method and the urban input-output analysis.

4. Shift-share Analysis of the Urban Economy

There are many techniques that could be utilised to analyse either the interregional or sectoral changes in manufacturing activities, but only very few combine both approaches. For instance, the economic base method focuses mainly on the sectors of the economy with an almost total neglect of the spatial dimension. On the other hand, the interregional input-output method discusses in detail the spatial and sectoral components of an economy. However, it suffers from two major shortcomings. Basically, it is not a technique that could be easily used to analyse the nature of the changes in an economy and, second, its data requirements are far from modest. However, the technique of the shift-share analysis is a simple method that adequately copes with both the spatial and sectoral changes that have taken place within an economy. It was first developed by Craamer (1943) but was popularised by Dunn (1965) in his study of the changes in the structure of manufacturing industries in the United States. In recent years, it has been used by Beaud (1960), Stilwell (1969, 1970) and Schatzl (1969) in the analysis of employment data. Furthermore, Paris (1970) has described a methodology for extending the technique into the analysis of population while in the realm of prediction, notable contributions have been made by Brown (1969) and James and Hughes (1973).

The method of shift-share analysis attempts to identify some of the causes that underlie interregional differences in growth, in terms of two major components. The first component recognises the fact that different regions of a national or macro-regional space possess different powers of attraction to industrial development and hence would grow at different rates. On the other hand, the second component recognises that within a particular region or area, industries could be of a type that have great propensities to grow, so that areas where such industries are concentrated would be expected to grow much faster than other areas of the national space.

The mathematical formulation and empirical operationalisation of the technique of the shift-share are based on the notion that the growth of activities or industries in one region or area could be compared with an expected growth in a larger area of which the region is just one of many. Consequently, there are criticisms as to the validity of any analysis based on this notion of expected growth (Houston, 1967). Of course, while these criticisms may be justifiable, they do not in any way reduce the usefulness of the technique as a descriptive tool of historical data because its assumptions do not differ too significantly from those of other techniques, particularly the economic base concept. In fact, if judiciously used, the shift-share technique not only contributes to the theory of interregional resource allocation, but could also provide very useful predictions (Stilwell, 1969, 1970).

To fix ideas about the development of the equations of the methodology, we define a number of terms as follows:

$X_{ij(t)}$ is the output of an activity in sector i and in region or area j at time t. If there are n industry or activity groups and m regions, then $i = 1, 2, \ldots n$; and $j = 1, 2, \ldots m$. Let the change in an activity output between two time periods t and $t + r$ be ΔX_{ij} where r is the number of years between the two periods. For simplicity, let the rate of change be assumed constant; then

$$\Delta X_{ij} = X_{ij(t+r)} - X_{ij(t)} \tag{45}$$

The national or macro-regional output change in each activity group is ΔX_{iN} where

$$\Delta X_{iN} = \sum_{j=1}^{m} \Delta X_{ij} \tag{46}$$

while the national change in all the activities is ΔX_N where

$$\Delta X_N = \sum_{i=1}^{n} \sum_{j=1}^{m} \Delta X_{ij} \tag{47}$$

If we assume that all regions or areas should grow at the national rate, then we can define a total net shift S_{ij} representing both the structural and spatial dimensions of growth in terms of changes in output levels as

$$S_{ij} = \Delta X_{ij} - \left[\frac{\Delta X_N}{X_{N(t)}}\right] X_{ij(t)} \tag{48}$$

S_{ij} is the net shift in industry or activity group i and in region j of the m-region national space.

The first component of the net total shift is called the *differential shift* (Whipple, 1966), *competition shift* (Dunn, 1965), or the *regional effect* (Beaud, 1966) and it is a measure of the locational advantage of the sub-areas. If we define this as D_{ij}, then

$$D_{ij} = \left[\frac{\Delta X_{ij}}{X_{ij(t)}} - \frac{\Delta X_{iN}}{X_{iN(t)}}\right] X_{ij(t)} \tag{49}$$

The reason for calling this the differential shift is obvious if one examines the terms of equation 49 in brackets. It expresses the differential of the rate of growth of each industry group by area and the total rate of growth of all industry groups by areas. It is possible for the value of equation 49 to be either positive or negative. If positive, then the sub-area has a better environment than the nation as a whole and consequently attracts more activities. On the other hand, if negative, then the environment is less conducive to that activity.

The second component of the total net shift has been called the *composition shift* (Dunn, 1966), *proportional shift* (Whipple, 1966) or the *structural effect* (Beaud, 1966). It actually measures the effect of the mix of industries in an area. If we define this as P_{ij}, then

$$P_{ij} = \left[\frac{\Delta X_{iN}}{X_{iN(t)}} - \frac{\Delta X_N}{X_{N(t)}}\right] X_{ij(t)} \tag{50}$$

As in the case of the differential shift, the reason for calling this the composition effect or the industry mix effect can be deduced from the terms in brackets. The bracketed term measures the expected change that is due to differences existing between the national rate of growth of each industry and the total national growth rate for all industries. A positive value for equation 46 implies that the particular industry group in the specified region has a high potential for growth.

Conceptually, the method of shift and share analysis recognises that the total shift in any activity must be accounted for by the locational and structural effects. This is easily verified mathematically by summing the components as given in equations 49 and 50 above, viz.

$$\left[\frac{\Delta X_{ij}}{X_{ij(t)}} - \frac{\Delta X_{iN}}{X_{iN(t)}} \right] X_{ij(t)} + \left[\frac{\Delta X_{iN}}{X_{iN(t)}} - \frac{\Delta X_N}{X_{N(t)}} \right] X_{ij(t)} \qquad (51)$$

$$= \Delta X_{ij} - \left[\frac{\Delta X_N}{X_{N(t)}} \right] X_{ij(t)} = S_{ij}$$

The above is summarised as

$$S_{ij} = P_{ij} + D_{ij} \qquad (51a)$$

In practice, it might be sufficient to calculate any two of the three components, although independent calculations of the three would always validate equation 51a.

Equations 48, 49 and 50 actually define the total shift and its two components spatially and sectorally and thus provide requisite tools for the examination of how industries grow over areas and through industrial groupings. Shifts by areas are generally calculated by summing these equations over industry groupings so that equation 51a, for example, will be written as

$$S_j = P_j + D_j \qquad (52)$$

One major advantage of using the shift-share technique is that it is always possible to compare the roles played by each of the components. For instance, Dunn (1965) proposed a number of ratios that express each component as a proportion of total shift. However, the most useful way for the comparison was proposed by Whipple (1966) and modified by Beaud (1966). Beaud's presentation is discussed by Paris (1970) and adapted below.

Beaud's system consists of two pairs of rectangular axes *OD*, *OP*, inclined at an angle of 45° to the vertical and horizontal rectangular Cartesian axes (*OX* and *OY*). Total regional difference or shift is measured along the *OX* axes while the differential shift is measured along −*DOD* and the proportional shift along −*POP* in such a way that the scale of the *OD*, *OP* axes is √2 times the scale of the *OX*, *OY* axes (see Figure 3.4.1). The advantage of Beaud's graph is that it represents a very effective means of presenting the results as it defines eight sectors that show interesting relationships between the total shift, the proportional shift and the differential shift (see Figure 3.4.2). At the same time, the graph ensures the relationship expressed in equation 52.

(i) An Application of the Shift and Share Technique in Lagos, Nigeria

Lagos metropolitan area is the foremost industrial area in Nigeria, as it accounts for about 40 per cent of all industrial establishments and 60 per cent of the value added by manufacturing activity. This area, which is located in the south-western part of the country, possesses six industrial estates. The industrial centres are Lagos Island, Apapa, Yaba, Ebute Metta, Mushin and Ikeja (see Figure 3.4.3). In recent years there have been significant structural and locational changes among industries and between areas, and the nature of these changes is unravelled through the use of the shift-share techniques. Our variables are the employment and the value-added figures of these industries.

Figure 3.4.1: Standard D–P Graph.

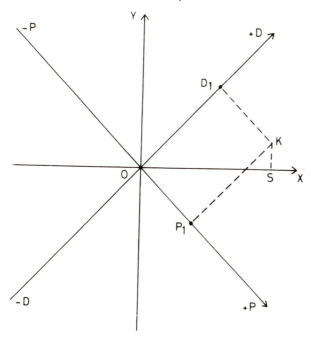

OP_1, OD_1 are the proportional and differential shifts respective for the area K.
OS is the total shift.
The scale of OX, OY is $1/\sqrt{2}$ times scale of OD, OP.
Source: After Stilwell (1970).

Figure 3.4.2: Relationships between D, P and S in the Standard D–P Graph

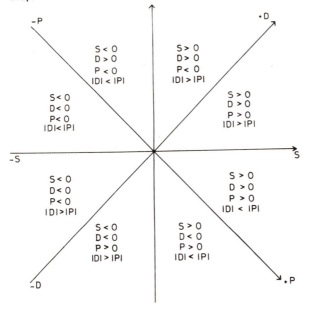

Source: After Stilwell (1970).

The nature of the shifts in manufacturing actvity is shown in Tables 3.4.1 and 3.4.2. From Table 3.4.1, which uses the value-added criterion, it is seen that the greatest negative shifts occurred in Lagos Island and Ebute Metta, while positive shifts occurred in Ikeja, Mushin and Apapa. When related to the components of shift, the high negative total shift of 83.55 per cent on Lagos Island is accounted for by both locational (differential) shift and proportional shift respectively (see Figure 3.4.4). The interpretation is that the negative shifts in manufacturing employment on Lagos Island are a result of both locational disadvantages as well as the structure of the industries. The same statement could be made about Yaba. On the other hand, Ebute Metta and Mushin can be seen to possess good locational advantages but a rather unsatisfactory mix of industries that could generate growth. The industries in Apapa could be seen to possess some satisfactory mix of activities while Apapa itself is becoming locationally disadvantaged. Ikeja is the only industrial area that emerges as having good locational advantages as well as a satisfactory mix of industries.

Figure 3.4.3: Industrial Zones of Lagos, Nigeria

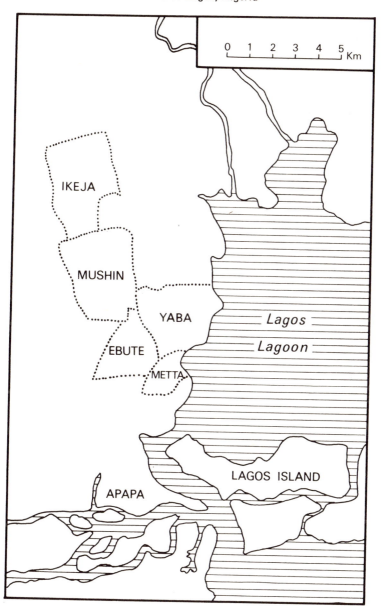

Table 3.4.1: Shift and Share Analysis of Industrial Change in Lagos, 1965–72; Value Added Criterion

Area	Total Shift		Differential Shift		Proportional Shift	
	Million Naira	Per Cent	Million Naira	Per Cent	Million Naira	Per Cent
Lagos Island	−28.613	−83.55	−19.346	−79.67	− 9.268	−39.13
Apapa	5.272	15.39	− 4.759	−19.60	−10.032	42.36
Yaba	− 0.280	− 0.82	− 0.177	− 0.73	−0.103	− 0.43
Ebute Metta	− 5.353	−15.63	0.986	4.06	−6.339	−26.76
Mushin	9.883	28.86	17.857	73.54	−7.974	−33.67
Ikeja	19.091	55.75	5.439	22.40	13.652	57.64

One need not expect that there would be a high degree of correspondence between the growth-generating potential of area measured either by value added or the total employment criterion. This indeed is the case as the components of the shifts even change signs in addition to relative magnitudes when the employment criterion is used. Thus the highest negative shift is now in Apapa while Lagos Island, Ebute Metta and Yaba follow, in that order. An examination of the components of shift (Table 3.4.2) shows that in Apapa much of the change is due to differential shift, while in Lagos Island and Ebute Metta this is due to the lack of strong linkages in the industrial structure. The highest positive shifts occur in Ikeja and Mushin. It is pertinent to note that both components of shift are positive for Ikeja, while only the locational aspect of positive for Mushin (see Figure 3.4.5)

A number of interesting conclusions can be drawn from these analyses about the structure of manufacturing activity in Lagos. First, we see that Ikeja is the most important employment centre and the one that is generating most of the value added by manufacturing activity in Lagos. Second, we are able to identify in terms of locational advantages

Table 3.4.2: Shift and Share Analysis of Industrial Change in Lagos, 1965–72; Employment Criterion

Area	Total Shift		Differential Shift		Proportional Shift	
	No. of employed	Per Cent	No. of employed	Per Cent	No. of employed	Per Cent
Lagos Island	−4,820.31	−23.42	−2,313.52	−15.48	2,506.79	−34.06
Apapa	−10,604.72	−51.53	−9,332.15	−62.39	−1,272.58	−17.29
Yaba	−1,130.74	5.49	−1,637.18	−10.95	506.47	6.88
Ebute Metta	−4,022.52	−19.55	−1,674.88	−11.20	−2,347.64	−31.90
Mushin	7,925.93	−38.52	9,158.80	61.23	−1,232.89	−16.75
Ikeja	−12,652.36	61.48	5,798.93	38.77	6,853.43	93.12

Figure 3.4.4: Shift-share Analysis of the Lagos Economy, Using Value Added by Manufacturing Activities

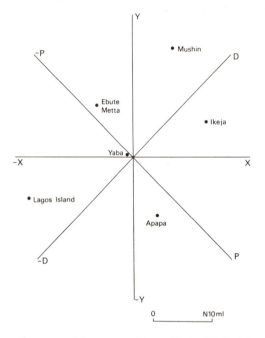

of areas and the composition effect of industries, which of the industrial centres lag behind. To this effect, Lagos Island was seen as an area of both locational disadvantage and lack of proper industrial linkages. Of course, it is known that in recent years, Lagos Island has lost the initial advantage it had to such places as Mushin and Ikeja, and it is today not unusual for firms to move out of Lagos Island to other parts of the metropolitan area. We have also seen that there are centres like Apapa with good linkages but poor locational advantages. The shift and share technique can therefore be seen as a useful technique for identifying the emerging strengths and weaknesses that exist in the structure of manufacturing (or any other) activity.

The identification of the structure of an economic system is fundamental to planning and monitoring of the economy. In the case of Lagos the areas which suffer from locational disadvantage, e.g. Lagos Island and Yaba, need infrastructural improvements, especially as may relate to the increasing traffic congestion, while in areas which lack linkages, as revealed by the negative shifts of the industrial mix component, the injection of propulsive industries might be the only solution.

Figure 3.4.5: Shift-share Analysis of Lagos Economy Using
Employment Figures

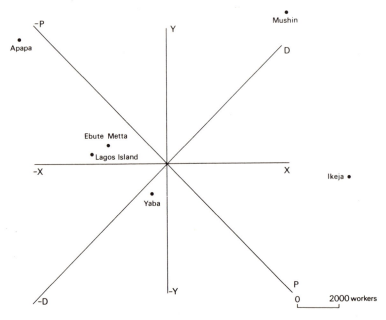

(ii) Predicting with the Shift and Share Technique

There are essentially two approaches towards developing the shift-share
technique into a predictive framework. The first one assumes that a
region's ability to generate growth remains constant (the constant share
method), while the other incorporates a differential growth rate with
the assumption that regional shifts remain constant (constant shift
method). These methods are essentially ratio methods and could be
derived as follows.

Let the growth in a metropolitan area's 'import' demand for industry
i be ΔY_{iN}. If the share of region j in the national production in industry
i is s_{ij}, then the region's growth in export sales is

$$\Delta Z_{ij} = s_{ij} \Delta Y_{iN} \qquad (53)$$

and if we assume constant shares, i.e. we assume that the region's share
of the national market is also s_{ij}, then

$$Z_{ij} = s_{ij} Y_{iN} \qquad (54)$$

If now we divide equation 53 by 54 we obtain

$$\frac{\Delta Z_{ij}}{Z_{ij}} = \frac{\Delta Y_{iN}}{Y_{iN}} \tag{55}$$

and hence

$$\Delta Z_{ij} = \left[\frac{\Delta Y_{iN}}{Y_{iN}} \right] Z_{ij} \tag{56}$$

The crucial point in using equation 56 is the estimation of the ratio in brackets. Once projections have been made of the rates of growth of specific industries, the method comes in handy. However, since such rates are hardly available, it is possible to use other surrogates, such as national commodity-specific output growth rates ($\Delta Q_{iN}/Q_{iN}$) and equation 56 becomes

$$\Delta Z_{ij} = \frac{\Delta Q_{iN}}{Q_{iN}} Z_{ij} \tag{56a}$$

The case of the constant shift technique begins from equation 49 above which expresses D_{ij} in terms of the differential rates of growth. If this equation is divided by $X_{ij(t)}$, we arrive at

$$\frac{D_{ij}}{X_{ij(t)}} = \frac{\Delta X_{ij}}{X_{ij(t)}} - \frac{\Delta X_{iN}}{X_{iN(t)}} \tag{57}$$

the differential growth rate for the industry i and region j. Equation 57 may be written for ΔX_{ij} as

$$\Delta X_{ij} = \left[\frac{\Delta X_{iN}}{X_{iN(t)}} + \frac{D_{ij}}{X_{ij(t)}} \right] X_{ij(t)} \tag{58}$$

Equation 58 is the projection equation under the constant shift assumption. It takes account of the possibility that regional shares may be important by the addition of the differential growth rate to the national industry growth rate. It would seem therefore that the constant shift method is more data-demanding, more comprehensive and hence more accurate. It is difficult to take sides. Reviewing the two most outstanding works using these techniques, Krueckeberg and Silvers (1975) claim that the constant share technique is better than the constant shift method as the latter method gave greater expected error than the former. It has been argued that one reason for this (Brown, 1969) is that the competitive rate component is not stable through time, although in a later study by James and Hughes many of the criticisms of Brown were seen either as resulting from his classification of the industries or from their locational grouping. While any judgements must be passed with caution, one is bound to agree with James and Hughes, who found that in a simple majority of cases the constant shift approach produces far superior results, especially for short-term projections.

The present formulation of the shift and share technique represents two of the easiest approaches in forecasting. Consequently, they are springboards from which further developments and refinements could be made. One such refinement is the method of projected shift described by Krueckeberg and Silvers (1975, p. 442). On the other hand, it is possible to relate the constant shift method to the processes of regional and national growth, as done by James and Hughes (1969, p. 224).

5. Conclusion

Our discussions of the economic base concept, the input-output method and shift and share technique show that even when the same variables are used in analysing the economic structure of an urban system, they differ significantly both in their aims and objectives, as well as in the quality and quantity of information required. Consequently, there are differences in their levels of explanation both as descriptive and predictive tools. Thus, while the economic base method remains a very handy tool for describing the relationship between and industry and the area it serves, the input-output goes further to incorporate inter-industry relations. The shift and share method, on the other hand, evaluates changes that have already taken place in an economy in terms of the locational advantages of areas and overall industrial mix of activities. Unlike the other techniques, it cares very little about inter-industry relationships or the relationship between one industry and the area it serves.

In terms of data requirements, the input-output method needs information that relates to the flow of goods or money between different industries or sectors in an economy. Consequently, it is often criticised on the basis that this information is difficult to obtain in most metropolitan areas. Furthermore, and even when this information is available the computations involved in manipulating the input-output table could be very demanding, especially where there is no access to computer facilities. While these could be reasons why the economic base method could prove a more handy method, it must be realised that the extra effort needed in constructing an input-output table could be justified on the basis of the greater degree of explanation and greater precision in prediction achieved.

None the less, the three techniques of this chapter are indeed complementary and could be judiciously used to provide different insights into the working of an economic system. Consequently, their further development and refinement is bound to be eventful in the literature on urban analysis, as well as providing props for the control and manipulation of the economic system.

References

Alexander, J.W. 1954. The Basic–Nonbasic Concept of Urban Economic Functions. *Economic Geography, 30*, 251–5.

Alexanderson, G. 1956. City Forming and City Serving Production. In H.Mayer and C.F. Kohn (eds.), *Readings in Urban Geography*. Chicago: University of Chicago Press, 1959.

Andrews, R.B. 1953. Mechanics of the Urban Economic Base: Historical Development of the Base Concept. *Land Economics, 29,* 161–7

Andrews, R.B. 1954. Mechanics of the Urban Economic Base. *Land Economics, 30,* 260–9

Andrews, R.B. 1955. Mechanics of the Urban Economic Base: The Concept of Base Ratios. *Land Economics, 31,* 47–53

Artle, R. 1965. *The Structure of the Stockholm Economy*. Ithaca, New York: Cornell University Press

Aurousseau, M. 1921. The Distribution of Population: A Constructive Problem. *Geographical Review, 11,* 563–92

Ayeni, M.A.O. 1974. *Predictive Modelling of Urban Spatial Structure: The Example of Jos, Beneu–Plateau State, Nigeria.* Ph.D. thesis, University of Ibadan, Nigeria

Ayeni, M.A.O. 1975. A Predictive Model of Urban Stock and Activity: 1 Theoretical Considerations. *Environment and Planning A, 7, 8,* 965–79

Ayeni, M.A.O. 1976. A Regional Plan of Lagos State: Planning Lagos Metropolitan Area. *Final Report, Planning Studies Programme,* University of Ibadan, Nigeria

Batty, M. 1970. An Activity Allocation Model for the Nottinghamshire-Derbyshire Subregion. *Regional Studies, 4,* 307–32

Batty, M. 1970. Dynamic Simulation of An Urban System. In A.G. Wilson (ed.), *London Papers in Regional Science,* Vol. 3. London, Pion: pp. 44–82

Beaud, M. 1966. Analyse Regionale–Structurelle et Planification Regionale. *Revue Economique,10,* 2, 254–98

Brown, H.J. 1969. Shift and Share Projection of Regional Economic Growth: An Empirical Test. *Journal of Regional Science, 9,* 1, 1–18

Cao Pinna, V. 1958. Principali Caratteristiche Strutturali di due Economie Mediterranee: Spagna e Italia. *Economia Internazionale, XI,* 2, 3–55

Craamer, D. 1943. *Industrial Location and Natural Resources.* Washington D.C.: Natural Resources Planning Board

Czamanski, S. 1965. A Method of Forecasting Urban Growth by Distributed Lags. *Journal of Regional Science, 5,* 15–20

Dunn, E.S., Jr. 1965. A Statistical and Analytical Technique for Regional Analysis. *Papers Regional Science Association, 6,* 97–112

Fuchs, V. 1962. Statistical Explanations of the Relative Shift of Manufacturing Among Regions of the United States. *Papers Regional Science Association, 8,* 105–26

Goldner, W. 1968. *Projective Land Use Model.* Berkeley California: Bay Area Transportation Study, Technical Report 219

Houston, D. 1967. Shift and Share Analysis: A Critique. *Southern Economic Journal, 32,* 577–81

Hoyt, H. 1961. The Utility of the Economic Base Method in Calculating Urban Growth. *Land Economics, 37,* 51–8

Isard, W. 1951. Interregional and Regional Input-Output Analysis: A Model of a Space Economy. *Review of Economics and Statistics, 33,* 4, 318–28

Isard, W. 1956. *Location and Space Economy.* New York: John Wiley

Isard, W. 1960. *Methods of Regional Analysis.* Cambridge, Massachusetts: M.I.T. Press

Isard, W., Kavesh R., and Kuenne, R.E. 1953. The Economic Base and Structure of Urban Metropolitan Region. *American Sociological Review, 18,* 317–21

James, F., Jr., and Hughes, J. 1973. A Test of Shift and Share Analysis as a predictive Device. *Journal of Regional Science, 13,* 2, 223–32

Krueckeberg, D.A. and Silvers, A.L. 1974. *Urban Planning Analysis: Methods and Models.* New York: John Wiley

Leontief, W., *et al* 1953. *Studies in the structure of the American Economy.* New York: Oxford University Press

Logan, M.I. 1966. The Location Behavior of Manufacturing Firms in Urban Areas. *Annals, Association of American Geographers, 56,* 451–66

Losch, A. 1953. *The Economics of Location.* Yale University, New Haven:

Lowry, I.S. 1964. *A Model of Metropolis.* Santa Monica, California: Rand Corporation

Moore, F.T., and Peterson, J.W. 1955. Regional Analysis: An Interindustry Model for Utah. *Review of Economics and Statistics, 37,* 368–83

Morrison, W.I. 1973. The Development of an Urban Interindustry Model 1. Building the Input-Output Accounts. *Environment and Planning, 5,* 369–83

Murphy, R.E. 1966. *The American City: An Urban Geography.* New York: McGraw-Hill

Paelinck, J. 1970. Dynamic Urban Growth Models. *Papers Regional Science Association, 214,* 25–38

Paris, J.D. 1970. Regional Structural Analysis of Population Changes. *Regional Studies, 4,* 425–43

Pred, A. 1967. *Behavior and Location Part 1.* Lund Series in Geography, Series B No. 27. Lund, Gleerup

Proceedings of the IGU Symposium in Urban Geography, 1960. Lund Series in Geography, Ser. B. No. 24, (1962), p. 129.

Roterus, V., and Calef, W. 1955. Notes on the Basic–Nonbasic Employment Ratio. *Economic Geography, 31,* 17–20

Schatzl, L. 1973. *Industrialization in Nigeria: A Spatial Analysis.* Munich and Ibadan

Smith, W. 1955. The Location of Industry. *Transactions Institute of British Geographers, 21,* 1–18

Stilwell, F.B.J. 1969. Regional Growth and Structural Adaption. *Urban Studies,* 268–82

Stilwell, F.B.J. 1970. Further Thoughts on the Shift and Share Approach. *Regional Studies, 4,* 451–8

Tiebout, C.M. 1962. *The Community Economic Base Study.* Committee for Economic Development, N.Y.: Sup. Paper 16

Ullman, E.L. and Dacey, M. 1960. The Minimum Requirements Approach to Urban Economic Base. Lund Series in Geography, ser. B. No.24, 121–43

Walras, L. 1954. *Elements of Pure Economics.* Homewood, Illinois: Richard D. Irwin

Whipple, R.T.M. 1966. Regional Differentials and Economic Planning. *Australian Planning Institute Journal, 4,* 180–7

4 SPATIAL INTERACTION IN THE URBAN SYSTEM

1. Introduction

Spatial interaction provides the means for the satisfaction of certain needs arising from the locational separation of producers and consumers. It depends on reciprocal relations between different places on the earth's surface and it is based on the principles of complementarity, intervening opportunities and transferability (Ullman, 1956). Complementarity implies areal differentiation and the existence of supply and demand in different areas, while intervening opportunities set up a constraint as to the possibility of interaction taking place. The argument is that even when there is a supply in one area and a demand in another, interaction would only take place if there are no alternative sources of the same material. Transferability, on the other hand, relates to the ease with which such demands could be met and, in fact, it is distance measured in real terms of transfer and time costs. Thus, while complementarity may generate interaction, 'the factor of *intervening opportunity* results in a *substitution of areas* and the factor of *transferability* results in a *substitution* of products' (Ullman, 1956, p. 868).

The urge or desire to satisfy felt needs arising from the separation of activities may be said to constitute a major focus of interest for many studies in geography. These include, for instance, studies on permanent and semi-permanent migrations, trading and marketing activities, transportation and traffic flows and even changes of residence within cities. To these, one would add other studies concerned with the communication of ideas by telephoning, telegraphing and letter-writing.

Spatial interaction in an urban setting could be of at least two types, namely: those that involve physical contacts like the day-to-day movements of people; and those that do not require such contacts, like telephoning. Particularly important in studying the structure of a city are the day-to-day movements which embrace such activities as trip-making to and from places of work, markets and shopping centres and recreational and educational facilities. Although these are just forms of movements in the city, they represent both a function and a process. They are functions as long as they perform the duty of maintaining the *status quo* in the spatial relation of different parts of the city, while they are processes when changes in their volume, intensity and direction come to determine the pattern of growth and organisation of the spatial

structure of the city. Such movements provide vital clues to the understanding of human spatial behaviour in all cities, especially in developing
countries where measures of telephoning, telegraphing and letter-writing
are not likely to prove of much value, given the low level of literacy and
the generally poor economic conditions.

The importance of using trips to characterise the urban system can
therefore not be over-emphasised, as these represent the fundamental
measures of the interdependence of the components of the city (Goddard,
1970). Trips can therefore be made to relate to city structure, as in the
case of the journey to work and residential location (Kain, 1962) or
even to economic and spatial growth through a linking of the factors of
growth to the changes in employment and consequent changes in
interaction (Lowry, 1964). Therefore, an examination of interaction
patterns in a city should follow at least two approaches, namely an
examination of some of the determinants of the propensity to generate
trips at the household, firm or individual level (Ayeni, 1975; Clark,
1965); and the capacity of the various land uses to generate and attract
trips. Such an approach lays emphasis not only on the interrelationships
that exist between land-use categories but also on the relationship
between activities and people. The simultaneous consideration of both
households and land-use zones in the study of trips sees these two
aspects as complementary. The travel behaviour of urban residents is
viewed both as the prerequisite and the consequence of spatial separation
of activities. These are the two major ideas explored in this chapter,
which also puts in perspective notions of efficiency in the spatial
organisation of urban land uses and activities.

2. The Household's Propensity to Interact in an Urban System

The household frequency of making trips per specified time period was
defined by Marble as transport inputs at the household level (Marble,
1957). In this often-quoted work which was carried out in Cedar
Rapids, Iowa, USA, Marble employed a linear regression model to relate
trip frequency, *inter alia,* to household location with respect to the
other elements of the spatial system; for instance, levels of retail
hierarchy. It emerged from the study that there was no significant
relationship between trip frequency and distance to trip termini as well
as between trip frequency and the type of road, 'although the places
visited could definitely be a function of distance'.

On the basis of the above, it would seem that different sets of
hypotheses concerning trip frequency need be postulated. In particular,
such hypotheses must identify the relationship between trip frequency

and the socio-economic characteristics of trip-makers, using such variables as age, income, length of stay in the city, size of household, number of workers per household, annual house rent and marital status. Each of these variables would be assumed as likely to contribute significantly to the propensity of households to generate trips. For example, one would expect that middle-aged households would generate more trips than either very young households or the very old ones. So also one would expect trip generation to increase with income, size of household, and length of stay in the city.

We might proceed to test some of these hypotheses using various statistical techniques, ranging from simple tests of differences between two means using the 't' test, to an analysis of variance technique or even a multiple regression analysis, depending on the levels of measurement of the data and the specific research objective. For instance, if data is available in a classificatory scale, e.g. male and female or even income groups, then the 't' test or the analysis of variance technique might be sufficient. On the other hand, if our measurement meets at least the criteria of the interval or ratio scale, multivariate regression analysis would be appropriate. However, it might seem worth while to attempt a multiple regression analysis of data on a mixed scale of measurement provided the researcher is aware of the problems and limits of interpretation of the results. In the examples that follow, the three different techniques are used partly to illustrate relevance in urban analysis.

For purposes of illustration, let us assume that income classes have been given as low, middle and upper, corresponding to annual incomes of under 600.00 Naira, 600.00 to 1,600.00 Naira, and above 1,600.00 Naira respectively.

In Jos, Nigeria, the mean frequency of trips per household for a specified period is shown in Table 4.2.1. The low-income group can

Table 4.2.1: Household Trip Frequency by Wage Classes, Jos, 1972

Income Group	No. of Observations	Mean Frequency of Trips	Standard Deviation
Low Income 600.00 Naira p.a.	114	16.59	8.96
Middle Income 600.00 – 1,600.00 Naira	114	22.96	15.35
Upper Income Above 1,600.00 Naira	56	23.50	12.62

Table 4.2.2: The Standard Analysis of Variance Table between Trip Frequency and Income Groups in Jos

Source of Variation	Sum of Squares	Mean Sum of Squares	Degrees of Freedom	F
Between Groups	2,936.8	1,468.28	2	9.28**
Error	44,436.4	159.21	281	
Total	47,373.2	1,626.49	283	

** Significant at $\alpha = 0.01$

be seen to generate only 17 trips per week, the middle-income group generates 23, while the upper-income group generates 24. If the methods of the one-way analysis of variance described in Chapter 2 were applied to the data, the standard table is as shown in Table 4.2.2. The F value of 9.28 is highly significant at the 0.01 level.

We might proceed further to examine where the difference in means actually lies, using one or more of the tests after means also discussed in Chapter 2. Using the Newman-Keul's test it emerges that the low and the upper income on the one hand, and the low income and the middle income on the other, differ. There is no significant difference between the volume of trips of the middle-income or upper-income groups at the 0.01 level of significance. Hence it can be stated that above an income of 600 Naira, differences in trip frequency of households are not very significant. The conclusion, then, is that the higher-income groups generate more trips than the low-income group.

The 't' test is, in general, used to test whether there are differences between two means. In this sense, the analysis of variance is an extension of this technique where there are more than two means. If all heads of households have been grouped either as single or married, then this is a suitable technique. In Jos, the trip-generating capabilities of these categories of households are shown in Table 4.2.3, where it is seen that there are differences in their trip-generating capabilities. For instance, households headed by spinsters or bachelors generate only 16 trips per week while those headed by married people generate as many as 36 trips per week. The highly significant nature of the difference between these two volumes was confirmed by the 't' test (Table 4.2.3). In addition to the fact that households headed by married people are generally larger in size, one may also suggest that even though the extended family system may result in certain households headed by unmarried people being large, the preponderance of one-person households resulting from the migratory nature of the population of this

Table 4.2.3: Trip-generating Frequencies of Households Headed by Single and Married Heads

Group	Mean Frequency of Trips	Standard Deviation	Degrees of Freedom	*t* value
1 Single Man as Head	16.43	8.35	124	5.36**
2 Married Man as Head	35.52	19.92		

**Significant at $\alpha = 0.01$

particular city might have contributed to the lower trip frequency of this category of households. Furthermore, both types of households are known to contain members of the extended family system, although, they may be more in households headed by single men or women.

When variables are satisfactorily measured, say on a ratio or interval scale, a multiple regression model would be preferred. A multiple regression model has an equation of the form

$$Y = a_0 + \sum_{i=1}^{n} b_i X_i + e \tag{1}$$

where Y is the criterion or dependent variable, a_0 is the intercept of the regression plane or hyperplane, X_i are the predictor or explanatory variables and e is the error term of prediction. The b_i are the partial regression coefficients. For purposes of explanation, it is usual to transform the partial regression coefficients into standard forms by dividing each coefficient by its standard error to yield Beta coefficients (β_i). The beta coefficients have the advantage that they represent the weights of the contribution of each variable into the predictive or explanatory model (see Anderson, 1958, or Cooley and Lohnes, 1971, for explicit statements on this model). There is a version of the multiple regression model, the Stepwise Regression method which has the distinguishing ability to perform the regression analysis by identifying the relative importance of the predictor variables which are entered accordingly. This version is used in our illustration below.

Six predictor variables have been selected. These are the age of the head of household, his length of stay in the city, his level of education measured by the number of years spent in school, his total annual rent (which was known to correlate highly with his income) and the number of workers in the household. The criterion or dependent variable is

Table 4.2.4: Order of Importance of the Predictor Variables of Trip Generation at the Household Level

Step**	Variable Name	Prop. of Variance	R
1	Total annual rent	0.344	0.587
2	No. of workers per household	0.101	0.667
3	Size of household	0.008	0.674
4	Age of head	0.004	0.676
5	Length of stay in city	0.001	0.677
6	Education	0.000	0.677
Total		0.458	0.677

** Step is the order of importance in the model.
 Number of households used in the model = 176.

the volume of trips generated by each of 176 households within the period of a week. In this type of analysis, at least two types of interpretation may be carried out. The first concerns the order of importance and proportion of the variance explained by each of the predictor variables, while the second concerns the overall interpretation of the regression model. On the first score, Table 4.2.4 shows the variables in their order of importance and their relative contributions to the variance. It is significant to note that total annual rent of the household is the most significant predictor or independent variable of trip generation. It would seem that the higher the rent, the greater is the trip volume ($R = 0.59$, Table 4.2.4). Since it has been observed elsewhere (Ayeni, 1974) that the higher the annual rent, the higher is the socio-economic class of the household, it may be argued that this analysis further substantiates the observation of the importance of the income factor. The number of workers in the household is second, thus confirming the intuitive notion that in household trip generation the number of workers plays an important role.

The size of household, age of the head and his length of stay follow in that order. The level of education is last and does not contribute much to the volume of trips generated at the household level since it can be assumed that its effect is already subsumed under income.

The above results are somehow unexpected, especially for the following variables: the size of the household, the education and the length of stay in town. One would intuitively expect these variables to be more important than they are presently. Of course, their relative unimportance may be due to multicollinearity among the variables. Multicollinearity occurs when the correlation between two or more independent variables is high. Under such a situation the sampling error of the partial slopes and partial correlation coefficients would be large and then there would be a number of different combinations of regression coefficients which would give almost equally good fittings to the empirical data (Blalock, 1963). Although multicollinearity does not constitute a threat when the regression model is being used for prediction, it does when one is merely interested in explanations, as in the present study. It is therefore pertinent to explore this further.

Table 4.2.5 is the matrix of zero-order correlation coefficients between the predictor or independent variables. Generally these correlation coefficients are not high, the highest being 0.48 between years of school and size of household.

There are not many tests that deal with multicollinearity. The rule of thumb has been to examine the zero-order correlation coefficients and note whether they are high or low. How high has always been the subjective decision of the researcher. However, Tintner (1945, 1965) has developed a set of test functions for multicollinearity. These are defined by

$$\Lambda_r = (N-1) \sum_{i=1}^{r} \lambda_i \qquad (2)$$

where N is the number of observations in each type of the independent variables and λ_r is the rth eigenvalue of the matrix of coefficients of the normal equations of the multiple regression model. In the test, the smallest eigenvalue is λ_1. Λ_r is approximately distributed like chi-square with $(N - 1 - p + r) r$ degrees of freedom, where p is the number of independent variables (Tintner, 1965, p. 127). For large samples, it

Table 4.2.5: Zero-order Correlation Coefficients between the Dependent and Independent Variables

Variable	1	2	3	4	5	6	7
1 Age	1.00						
2 Length of Stay	0.35	1.00					
3 Years of Schooling	− 0.23	−0.18	1.00				
4 Size of Household	0.10	−0.19	0.48	1.00			
5 Annual Rent	0.45	0.19	− 0.04	0.17	1.00		
6 No. of Workers	0.12	0.06	0.03	0.23	0.36	1.00	
7 Vol. of Trips/Week	0.31	0.08	0.03	0.24	0.59	0.51	1.0

has been shown that the quantity

$$\frac{\Lambda_r - Nr}{\sqrt{(2Nr)}} \tag{3}$$

is normally distributed with zero mean and unit variance (Tintner, 1965, p. 128; Anderson, 1948). It is this latter function that is employed in this study.

The use of the test functions is basically to estimate the number of independent linear relationships in a data set. It proceeds as follows. First, we form the test functions $\Lambda_1, \Lambda_2, \ldots, \Lambda_r$ and sequentially test at a predetermined significance level until we encounter any Λ_{r+1} that is not significant while Λ_r is significant. The conclusion is then drawn that only r linear independent relations may be established. The values of λ and Λ for the correlation matrix of Table 4.2.5 are tabulated in Table 4.2.6, in addition to their test values on the normal distribution curve (since $N = 176$). The null hypothesis is that the said independent variables are linearly dependent.

It emerges from Table 4.2.6 that the null hypothesis has to be rejected and we have to accept that from all evidence at hand, the independent variables are *truly* independent. This means that the degree of multicollinearity in the data set is not so important as to adversely affect our interpretations.

The above observation is important for the second interpretation of the regression analysis as an explanatory model. This second interpretation should concentrate on the examination of not only the overall coefficient of determination (R^2), but also the significance of the individual partial regression coefficients. This regression equation is

Table 4.2.6: Testing for Multicollinearity

r	Eigenvalues λ_r	Test Functions Λ_r	Test Values Z
1	0.35	61.93	6.08*
2	0.37	125.97	8.52*
3	0.56	219.87	9.48*
4	0.73	348.21	9.48*
5	0.92	508.99	8.84*
6	1.71	807.76	5.40*
7	2.36	1225.00	0.14

* Significant at 0.01 level.

$$Y = 2.13 + 1.11X_1 + 5.56X_2 + 0.01X_3 + 0.08X_4$$
$$(6.24\dagger) \quad (5.3\dagger) \quad (1.10*) \quad (1.21*)$$

$$-0.03X_5 + 0.03X_6 \tag{4}$$
$$(0.49) \quad (0.21)$$

$$R = 0.677 \text{ and } F = 23.84$$

where Y is the volume of trips generated per week by a household. X_i ($i = 1, 2 \ldots 6$) are the socio-economic variables discussed above.

The correlation coefficient of 0.677 is found to be highly significant at the 0.001 level, implying that the correlation between the criterion and predictor variables is not a chance occurrence. The analysis of variance value of $F = 23.84$ also confirms the significance of the regression equation as an explanatory model of some determinants of the propensity to interact. However, when the statistical usefulness of the model for forecasting is taken into consideration a slightly different story emerges. This is so because the partial regression coefficients are not all significant, even at the 0.05 level. The only significant ones are the total annual rent, the number of workers per household, the sizes of households and the age of the head of the household. The former two are significant at the 0.01 level while the latter two are significant only at the 0.25 level. This therefore means that as far as Jos is concerned, the income surrogate (total annual rent) and the number of workers per household determine to a large extent the trip-generating capacity of the household. The length of stay in Jos and the level of education have not proved important as trip-generating variables.

Although the regression model produced a multiple correlation coefficient of 0.677, it should be noted that the coefficient of determination (R-squared) is only 0.46, implying that the socio-economic variables used in the analysis could explain only 46 per cent of the total variation. Even though income and the number of workers in a household have been shown to be highly significant, it would seem that some other relevant variables, for instance the type of occupation of the members of the household and the spatial juxtaposition of household residences and activities in the city should be included. We hope a

---

† Significant at the 0.01 level.
* Significant at the 0.25 level.
The 't' values for the regression coefficient are shown in brackets.

combination of these socio-economic and spatial variables is desirable and should constitute some basis for future research on household trip generation in cities.

3. Aggregate Patterns of Spatial Interaction

In studying aggregate patterns of interaction within an urban system, emphasis should be placed on at least two aspects, namely the distribution of trip end and the trip generation and attraction of the different land uses (Elliot-Hurst, 1968). In the study of the distribution of trip ends, one might characterise trip lengths into distance bands of say less than one kilometre, one to two kilometres, etc. One might then proceed to examine this distribution and express it graphically. To illustrate, let us look at Table 4.3.1, which shows the situation in Jos in 1972 for two categories of trip types.

For the journey to work, quite a high proportion of people (38.50 per cent) travel less than 1 kilometre, while this proportion gradually declines with increasing distance from home. The nature of this decrease is shown in Figure 4.3.1 and it would seem the exponential decay curve might be a good fit to the observation. The line of best fit is given by

$$Y = 401.5 \exp(-0.4596x) \qquad (5)$$

Table 4.3.1: Aggregate Distribution of Trip Ends in Jos

Distance Bands in Kilometres	Journey to Work		Journey to Services*	
	No. of Trips	Per Cent of Total	No. of Trips	Per Cent of Total
0 to 1	446	38.50	954	26.08
1 to 2	247	21.30	1,330	36.36
2 to 3	248	21.40	783	21.40
3 to 4	110	9.50	297	8.12
4 to 5	34	2.90	41	1.12
5 to 6	9	0.80	7	0.19
6 to 7	15	1.30	188	5.14
7 to 8	2	0.20	19	0.52
8 to 9	17	1.50	30	0.82
9 to 10	27	2.30	8	0.22
10 to 11	3	0.30	1	0.03
Total Trips	1,158	100.00	3,658	100.00

* Service trips in this context include the journeys to service centres, schools and recreation.

Figure 4.3.1: Distribution of Trip Ends by Distance Bands for the Journey to Work, Jos, 1972

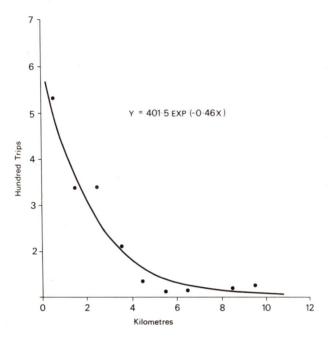

The distribution of trip lengths for the journey to services is more complex, perhaps as a result of the lumping together of many trip types. For instance, the class includes not only the trips to service centres and market-places but also trips to recreational and educational facilities. Consequently, Table 4.3.7 shows that many of the trips (37 per cent) for these services are longer than one kilometre. One can therefore say that the proportion of trips between distance bands rises from the zero to one kilometre class reaching a peak at between one and two kilometres before declining with increasing distance. A more complex decay function, possibly one of the generalisations of Chapter 2, could be applied. Experience would suggest a curve of the form

$$Y = Ax^{\alpha} \exp(-bx) \tag{6}$$

The best-fit curve for this distribution is

$$Y = 1960.6x^{0.148} \exp(-0.661x) \tag{7}$$

and it is shown in Figure 4.3.2.

Figure 4.3.2: Distribution of Trip Ends by Distance Bands for the Journey to Service Centres, Jos, 1972

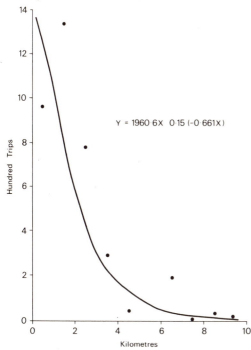

An important observation is the fact that many of the curves being fitted to intra-urban population densities could be found applicable to the case of the distribution of trip lengths. This is a sign of the isomorphic relationship that may exist between these aspects of the urban form. Consequently, one might argue that the city system is characterised by a number of interacting forces, the end product of which gives rise to some regularity of the urban phenomenon.

The second approach to the study of patterns of interaction in an urban system might focus on the trip-generating and attracting capacity of various land-use types or zones of an urban system. Such an endeavour could relate the form and function of an urban system especially when land-use types coincide with zonal delimitation. In either case, it is worth while to be able to differentiate between intra-zonal and inter-zonal trips, as the inter-zonal trips are not only the measure of the functional link between zones, but also a measure of the spatial differentiation of activities. Thus, if intra-zonal trips are large compared with inter-zonal ones, one might conclude that either the zones are too large or the zones are heterogeneous so that zones are origins as well as destinations for trips.

The study of patterns of interaction between zones of an urban system represents the first steps in the analysis of the urban system, for it is possible to represent such interactions by maps and diagrams (Ayeni, 1974, Ch. 5) or in matrices which could later on be factor analysed to yield the dimension of the functional association of land uses. While this latter reasoning is discussed in a wider framework in Chapter 6, let us in this chapter review the patterns of interaction using maps and diagrams.

In the study conducted in Jos, the aggregate patterns of trip generation shows that a rather high percentage of all trips (33.04) per cent) are intra-zonal, possibly as a result of the rather high mix of urban activities. Now if we focus on the inter-zonal trips alone, the pattern of interaction that results is as shown in Figure 4.3.3. It is obvious from the figure that there are probably as many origins as there are destinations and this would suggest that a better perspective of the situation might be produced if trips are broken down by types into say, work trips, trips to service centres, trips to schools, trips to recreational facilities, etc. The resulting diagrams would no doubt be less complex, but the pattern of interaction would yet remain a function of the spatial organisation of the city.

The spatial organisation of a city is definitely a function of the level of economic development of its hinterland, as well as the origin of the city. Cities in developed economies exhibit a highly differentiated spatial organisation, whereas a high mix of land uses and activities characterises cities of the developing economies. It is in this context that the concept of spatial efficiency could produce some useful insights into the organisation of space in the city.

4. Spatial Efficiency

Any attempt to formulate a concept of spatial efficiency must relate it to the ease of movement within the urban system. The ease of movement is a very broad term as it may relate not only to the movement of people but also to those of goods and services. To facilitate the discussion, therefore, it is necessary to define efficiency. *Webster's New International Dictionary* defines efficiency as 'the capacity to produce *desired results* with a minimum expenditure of *energy,* time or money, or material' (emphasis mine). The pertinent words in the definition are the 'desired results' and 'energy'; this is why it is difficult to apply the definition directly to the spatial case. Even though people are known to perceive time or money differently and to differ on what are desired results and the appropriate measures of energy, an efficient spatial system may nevertheless be described as one that minimises the *efforts of movement* subject to the *constraints* that obtain in the system. Constraints in an urban system may be the provision of enough housing opportunities or employment facilities for the city's able-bodied who in turn are required to travel to work daily. On the other hand, efforts of movement may be measured as transportation costs.

The above interpretation lays no claim to absolute originality as it does no more than express ideas similar to those in the optimisation techniques of linear programming, especially in the transportation problem (Hitchcock, 1964). The transportation problem essentially sets out to *minimise* the effort of movement (cost), subject to the constraint that all goods must be moved from their source to their destination, and in such a way that the holding capacities of the destinations are not violated. In the graphical representation of the solution of the transportation problem, cross-hauls are generally minimised. Consequently cross-hauls in intra-city movement of people, as shown in Figure 4.3.3, may be interpreted as representing some degree of spatial inefficiency in a system. In this way, the concept of spatial efficiency may be highly useful in establishing performance criteria for city systems, especially when this is defined in terms of the patterns of spatial interaction.

Of course, the spatial organisation of urban systems is a more complex phenomenon than the transportation problem of linear programming. This is because an urban system is made up of many sub-systems, e.g. journey to work or journey to service centres, etc., that require different assumptions about their spatial organisation and hence different measures of efficiency. Furthermore, it is possible for an urban system to manifest different degrees of efficiency with respect to each of these different sub-systems. It would seem therefore that an approach to understanding the degree of the spatial efficiency of the urban system should proceed cautiously, even when recognising the presence of the various sub-systems.

Furthermore, and perhaps more importantly, is the fact that linear programming *per se* merely solves a distribution problem and assumes that both origin and destination constraints are given. A more consistent approach should not hold these two sets of variables constant or given but rather generate at least one of them, since efficiency in an urban system should relate not only to the ease of movement but also the aggregation of land-use activities. It is in this context that methods of

Figure 4.3.3: Patterns of Interaction in Jos, 1972

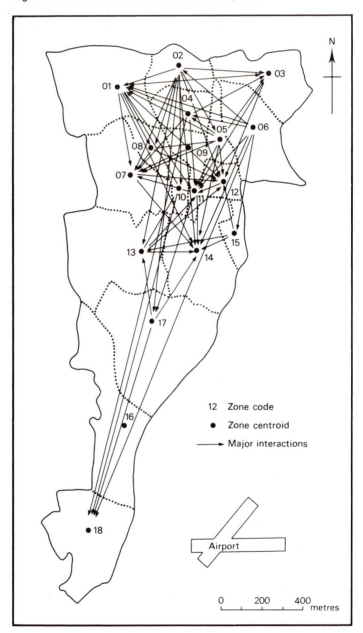

location-allocation could prove useful in investigating the notion of spatial efficiency. Both the location-allocation method and the transportation problem of linear programming are discussed in Chapter 9.

5. Conclusion

The urge and desire to satisfy human felt needs are the requisites of urban spatial interaction, which in turn is determined to a large extent by a city's spatial configuration. Thus, how long a man travels to obtain services is determined by where these facilities are located as well as the need to purchase the services. The frequency of interaction or trip-making, on the other hand, is determined not only by a household's socio-economic characteristics, but also by the convenience and comfort of trip-making, represented by the means and costs of transportation, characteristics of the network as well as the general ease of movement. Consequently, the notion of complementarity, intervening opportunities and transferability are crucial to understanding household's spatial behaviour.

On the other hand, the determinants of the trip-generating capabilities of urban land uses are made up of the type and quality of functions therein. For instance, a work centre would generate and attract more trips than a residential zone of the same size, in the same way that a labour-intensive enterprise on the work site would generate and attract more trips in proportion to their populations. None the less, one should expect a different result if trips are broken down by types. The of trips generated by households for journey to work purposes may remain equal, but differences would occur for such trips as service and recreational. It is in this category that socio-economic considerations are particularly crucial to understanding household's spatial behaviour.

Equally important in the analysis of trips is their temporal distribution. Thus expressed over time, this distribution is expected to show some regularities that coincide with the peak hours of the journey to and from work. Such a regularity over time and space may not be observed for the journey to services as well as recreational trips. The journey to work, which incidentally is the most important component of spatial interaction, is highly regular and predictable. This is probably a reason why optimality in the journey-to-work system may be counter-intuitive to the other components of the urban system.

While the analysis of both aggregate land use and households provide some understanding of intra-city spatial interaction, there is need for a synthesis of these thoughts for a full appreciation of their role in the structuring of the urban space. One might start probing into this through an investigation into the reasons why, for the individual household trips, ends decrease exponentially. Is it a result of people's perception of unit distance? Or is it just another of the regularities in the urban system? And to what extent are transportation costs relevant in such structuring of the urban space? These are major research questions, some of which are answered in subsequent chapters of this book.

References

Anderson, T.W. 1948. The Symptotic Distribution of the Roots of Certain Determinantal Equations. *Journal of the Royal Statistical Society*, Supl. 10, 190

Anderson, T.W. 1958. *An Introduction to Multivariate Statistical Analysis*. New York: John Wiley

Ayeni, M.A.O. 1974. Predictive Modelling of Urban Spatial Structure: The Example of Jos, Benue-Plateau State, Nigeria. Ph.D. thesis, University of Ibadan, Nigeria

Ayeni, M.A.O. 1975. Some Determinants of the Propensity of Interact in an Urban System: A Case Study in Jos, Nigeria. *Nigerian Geographical Journal*, 18, 2, 111–20

Blalock, H.M., Jr. 1963. Correlated Independent Variables: The Problem of Multicollinearity. *Social Forces*, 42, 2, 233–7

Clark, W.A.V. 1968. Consumer Travel Patterns and the Concept of Range. *Annals, Association of American Geographers*, 59, 2

Cooley, W.W. and Lohnes, P.R. 1972. *Multivariate Data Analysis*. New York: John Wiley

Goddard, J.R. 1970. Functional Regions within the City Centre. *Transactions, Institute of British Geographers*, 40, 161–82

Hitchcock, F.L. 1941. The Distribution of a Product from Several Sources to Numerous Locations. *Journal of Mathematics and Physics*, 20, 224–30

Elliot-Hurst, M.E. 1964. Traffic Generation and Land Use in Urban Areas. *Scottish Geographical Magazine*, 80

Kain, J.F. 1961. The Journey to Work as a Determinant of Residential Location. *Papers Regional Science Association*, 9, 137–60

Lowry, I.S. 1964. *A Model of Metropolis*. Santa Monica, California: Rand Corporation

Marble D.F. 1959. Transport Inputs at Urban Residential Sites. *Papers Regional Science Association*, 5, 233–66

Tintner, G. 1945. A Note on Rank, Multicollinearity and Multiple Regressions. *Annals of Mathematical Statistics*, 16, 304

Tintner, G. 1965. *Econometrics*. New York: John Wiley

Ullman, E.L. 1959. The Role of Transportation as the Basis for Interaction. In W.L. Thomas (ed.), *Man's Role in Changing the Face of the Earth*. Chicago: University of Chicago Press, pp. 862–80

5 THE LOCATION AND UTILISATION OF URBAN SERVICES

1. Introduction

One of the most pressing problems faced by cities all over the world, and in developing countries especially, is that of serviceability. In a different context, Mabogunje (1973) has argued that the issue of serviceability involves not only the inability of cities to stimulate rural production by creating a constantly expanding market for agricultural products, but also their inability to adequately provide amenities and essential services for the teeming populations both within cities and in their tributary areas. To city-dwellers, essential services and amenities include the provision of housing, health facilities, sewage disposal systems, convenient means of transportation, water and electricity, and educational and recreational facilities. The inability of cities to adequately cope with the provision of these services is due, on one hand to the rather phenomenal way cities increase their populations through rural-urban migration, and on the other to the fact that urban management in many of these countries lacks the administrative and technical machinery to plan and maintain the cities.

The provision of these different amenities requires fundamentally different considerations. For instance, the nature of the demand for water and electricity may not require any intra-city locational considerations, while facilities like education and outdoor recreational centres are point-specific in the sense that they must be located in particular areas of the city. Consequently, an important aspect of the provision of some of these facilities is the degree of accessibility and the burden of travel time and travel cost which their provision puts on the citizens who demand them.

Educational, and to some extent recreational, facilities are urban goods consumed mainly by young people. The question is, how accessible and how adequate are these for urban youth? To such people, these facilities are of the utmost importance, as they represent avenues for the development of sound minds and sound bodies. Their location and utilisation can therefore be seen as crucial to the socio-psychological well-being of the consumers.

The intra-city location and consequent utilisation of educational and outdoor recreational facilities have not been given much prominence in the research efforts of developing countries; perhaps because hitherto their towns and urban centres are small in population and areal expansion. However, in recent years, many of these urban centres have witnessed not only population growth but attendant vertical and horizontal expansion. The result has been a gradual removal from the cities of most natural phenomena and the creation of a highly artificial environment and, possibily, society. Both of these factors emphasise the point that accessibility could be as crucial in the provision of these facilities within a city or metropolitan area as between a city and its hinterland.

Consequently, the aim of this chapter is to identify the particular problems of the location and utilisation of two urban services enjoyed mainly by youths. Therefore the analysis will begin by examining the structure of cities with respect to the provision of these facilities. To this end, our attention will be focused on the fundamental principles of supply and demand of these two facilities and on an examination of their patterns of consumption by youths. It is hoped that from these, a number of pertinent issues that affect the spatial behaviour of people more generally are raised and discussed.

The rest of this chapter is therefore as follows. The next section examines the theoretical issues concerning the location of urban facilities, in particular welfare services such as educational and recreational centres. In the third section, we present some empirical evidence as to the location and consumption of these facilities in Nigeria, while in the fourth section attention is focused on the identification of the associated problems and their possible solutions. In the last section we conclude on the notion that increasing suburbanisation of our cities calls for more concerted efforts in researching into the range of these facilities and the need to make them accessible to consumers.

2. Theoretical Issues on the Location of Urban Facilities

The most crucial discussions concerning the location of urban facilities can be seen in Walter Christaller's (1933) central place theory. As a theory for the location of cities, it sees central places (cities) as existing to provide goods and services for the consumption of people both within and without the city boundaries. To this end, it is argued that goods and services are of different orders and that each good or service possesses a trade area or range from which people travel to the central place to purchase it. It is further argued (Berry, 1968) that this trade area has two limits, the upper and the lower. The lower limit is the threshold as it encompasses the area that assures the viability of the good or service. The upper limit, on the other hand, defines the maximum reach above which nobody travels to the central place to purchase the good or service. Consequently, goods of a higher order would have longer ranges than goods of a lower order.

Although central place theory deals with the location of cities, it has come to be applied to the location of services within the city. When applied to the intra-urban case, the theory also has implications for functional specialisation, as the efficient production of goods and services requires both high capital investment and areal differentiation within the city. For instance, in terms of retailing activities, it is possible to identify retail centres of different orders as well as of functions within the orders of centres. However, an assumption of central place theory is that all goods and services are economic, so that land-use differentiation and functional specialisation arise from the operation of purely economic forces. Of course, not all urban goods and services are purely economic. The cases of schooling and recreation are important in this respect, as their operation in Nigeria, as well as in most developing countries, is basically social welfare in orientation. None the less, to the extent that the establishment of any recreational or educational facility requires considerations as to range and threshold, central place theory is still a convenient basis for discussion.

Consequently, it is crucial to examine the applicability of the central place theory by looking at both the structure of the supply and demand functions of these facilities. The supply function of either the educational or recreational facility no doubt depends on some sort of threshold. For instance, the location of a primary school in a section of a city implies the existence of a sufficient number of children of primary school age in the neighbourhood. Where this is not properly considered, as happened in the old Western Region of Nigeria between 1955 and 1960, the result is usually one whereby schools would have to be closed down. In the same way, location of a playground, a golf course or an amusement centre requires some amount of threshold. In the city, population sizes or income levels could serve as appropriate measures of the thresholds required. The demand, on the other hand, may vary according to age and sex. For instance, primary schools are consumed by youths between the ages of six and eleven while secondary schools are utilised by youths between the ages of eleven and eighteen. In the same way the recreational schools, just as those of males could differ from those of females.

To the extent that the urban zonal populations could serve as thresholds for the location of urban facilities, their supply and demand functions emphasise the structure of accessibility which has been described as the essential link between the supply and demand of these facilities at the level of the individual (Mabogunje, 1974). Accessibility *per se* is one of the most frequently used and yet little defined terms in urban studies. A definition by Ingram (1971) gives it as 'the inherent characteristic or advantage of a place with respect to overcoming some form of friction'. Ingram notes further that there are two related notions; that of relative accessibility, which measures the degree to which two places or things are connected and that of integral accessibility, which measures the degree of interconnections of points or things in the system. In the location and utilisation of urban facilities, what is interesting to us is relative accessibility between the consumers of these facilities on the one hand and their locations on the other.

The measurement of accessibility could be either in terms of physical distance, time costs, monetary and inconvenience costs or combinations of these. The crucial thing about accessibility as far as it relates to the location of intra-urban facilities is that it necessitates considerations of issues of centrality where facilities can easily serve the largest possible number of people. Thus, unlike most other economic activities, such as the production of goods, the educational and recreational facilities should be located more closely to the areas of dense population. If this is accepted, it would be expected that these facilities would have low centrality indices and hence a high covariation with the intra-city distribution of population. The argument may be put the other way round that, to the extent that both the supply of and demand for these facilities are concentrated in the city, the distribution of population is a crucial factor in their location.

Accessibility, mobility and efficiency of a spatial system are no doubt fundamental not only to the physical and mental development of youths, but also of other city inhabitants. These three concepts are really more involved than as described above, but since they are not the major issues of this chapter, they are not discussed further. However, we hope the empirical works discussed below go a long way to reveal the possible structure of these concepts and the way they reveal the problems encountered by youths.

3. Location of Schools and Recreational Centres and the Spatial Behaviour of Youths in Nigerian Cities

The spatial behaviour of youths with respect to the location of educational and outdoor recreational facilities are the patterns of interaction that result from the needs of youths to study and enjoy recreation. This spatial component is important to the extent that it identifies some aspects of traffic generation in the city and hence could be related to the spatial structure. However, this same component is a means of verifying the relevance of the concept of accessibility as it affects these facilities in cities in general.

The data used in this section come from two major sources. The first was the study conducted in Jos by the author in 1972 (Ayeni, 1974) while the second source is a similar study conducted in Lagos in 1974 (Ayeni, 1976). Although the two studies were designed to unravel spatial interaction in cities as a means of urban model-building for planning purposes, the nature of the journey to schools and recreational centres was given sufficient attention for present purposes. Thus in the former study, a total of 873 pupils were interviewed for the journey-to-school behavioural pattern, while 1,376 were interviewed on their patterns of interaction for the journey to recreation facilities. In the latter study, 1,041 youths were interviewed on the journey to school and 1,316 on petterns of recreation. The administration of the question-naires require that zones be delimited for each of the cities (see Figures 5.3.1 and 5.3.2).

The relevant sections of the research that are used in this section deal with two categories of youths. The first class consists of people between the ages of six and eighteen. These are mostly primary school pupils or students of secondary institutions. The information on these sets of people was sieved to ensure that only data relating to upper primary school pupils and day students in secondary institutions were used in subsequent analysis. The second group of people is made up of young men, most of whom had passed the age of schooling and were engaged in productive economic activity in the cities. It is felt that this design gives a cross-sectional view of the nature of the problems youths encounter during intra-city movement processes to consume certain urban facilities.

The decision to use the cities of Jos and Lagos for illustrative purposes is rather one of convenience.* However, it could be argued that these two cities could be compared to illustrate the problem of scale in facilities in Nigeria. In the first place, they are fast growing in size and population; between 1952 and 1963 they had growth rates of 8.1 per cent and 11.5 per cent per annum respectively. In the second place, the two cities could be compared to illustrate the problem of scale in urban studies. Thus, while it may be thought that the size of an urban centre could be vital in the patterns of interaction generated, it is quite conceivable that the locational and consumption characteristics are not size-dependent. The area of Lagos covered in the research is the area

---

* Most of the empirical results used in this and subsequent chapters are based on these two cities and their study zones shown in Figures 5.3.1 and 5.3.2.

Figure 5.3.1: The Study Areas in Jos, 1972

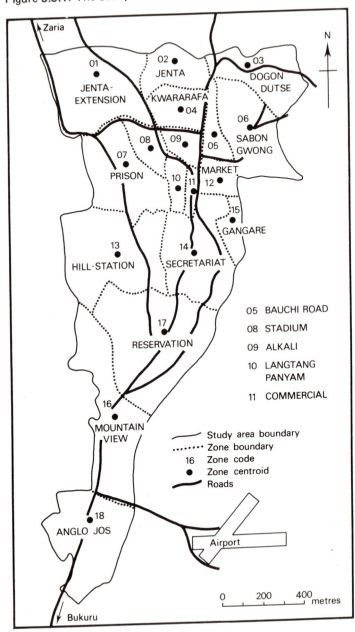

Figure 5.3.2: The Study Areas in Lagos, 1975

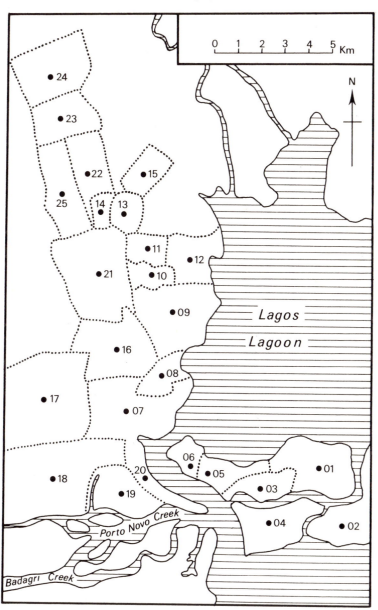

generally referred to as the Greater Lagos area which has a population estimate of some two and a half million people in 1975 and covers the suburbs of Mushin, Ikeja, Oshodi and Agege. Jos, on the other hand, covers the built-up area of Jos city and the suburbs and villages of Kabong, Tudan Wada and Anglo Jos.

In 1972, there were 40 schools, made up of 8 secondary schools and 32 primary schools in Jos. The intra-city location of these primary schools *vis-à-vis* the estimated population of the zones of the city where they were located is shown in Table 5.3.1. An examination of the table shows a rather high concentration of primary schools in three major areas of the city. These are Jenta Extension (1) which has 8 out of the 32, Sabon Gwong (6) which has 6 and the Prison Area (7) which has 5. These zones are peripheral to the city (see Figure 5.3.3). It is also obvious from comparing columns five and six of the table that the distribution of schools in the city is not population-orientated. Furthermore, using the Spearman's Rank correlation coefficient which measures the association between population and number of schools, we see that this is only 0.021, a figure that is statistically insignificant. It may therefore be concluded that there is a rather high centrality index in the location of primary institutions in the city of Jos.

The pattern of consumption of the educational facilities is shown in Figure 5.3.3, which has been constructed from an interaction matrix of the journey to school. It again emphasises the concentrated nature of the schools. An interesting aspect of the figure is in the volume of trip-makers to schools. Again Jenta Extension (1) and the Prison Area (7) stand out as receiving the biggest volume, which invariably originates in the zones of high populations. The nature of the interaction pattern is better revealed by zonal summaries of trip lengths and other characteristics shown in Table 5.3.2. The average trip length to school in Jos is 2.2 kilometres. This in itself is believed to be long, considering the fact that such distances involve rather young people, most of whom travel on foot.

There are considerable variations between the zonal mean trip lengths, as these range between as low as 0.52 kilometres in Jenta Extension (1) to 4.46 kilometres in Anglo Jos (18). If we examine the last column of Table 5.3.2, we can identify which zones make a journey of over 3 kilometres on average to school. Here Gangare (15), Anglo Jos (18) and Hill Station (13) have more than 45 per cent of all trips to school longer than 3 kilometres. This is to say that these represent some of the areas where more educational facilities should be provided in the city. Other zones like Jenta (2) and the Reservation have about 10 per

Table 5.3.1: Population and Distribution of Primary Schools in Jos, 1972

Zones	Description	Population 1972	No. of Schools	Zone Proportion of Schools	Zone Proportion of Population
1	Jenta Extension	6,332	8	0.25	0.06
2	Jenta	9,101	1	0.03	0.09
3	Dogon Dutse	1,101	2	0.06	0.01
4	Kwararafa	10,002	1	0.03	0.10
5	Bauchi Road	7,828			0.08
6	Sabon Gwong	19,571	6	0.19	0.20
7	Prison Area	3,286	5	0.16	0.03
8	Stadium Area	7,923	3	0.09	0.08
9	Alkali Street Area	10,586			0.11
10	Lengtang-Panyam Area	3,552	1	0.03	0.04
11	CBD	409			0.004
12	Market Area	10,108			0.10
13	Hill Station	1,314			0.01
14	Secretariat	1,269			0.01
15	Gangare	3,681			0.04
16	Mountain View	40	2	0.06	0.00
17	Reservation	1,340	1	0.03	0.01
18	Anglo Jos	1,503	2	0.06	0.02
	Total	98,946	32	0.99	0.994

Source: Author's field-work in Jos, 1972. Population figures were estimated from a sample survey of households in Jos.

Figure 5.3.3: Patterns of Interaction of the Journey to Schools, Jos, 1972

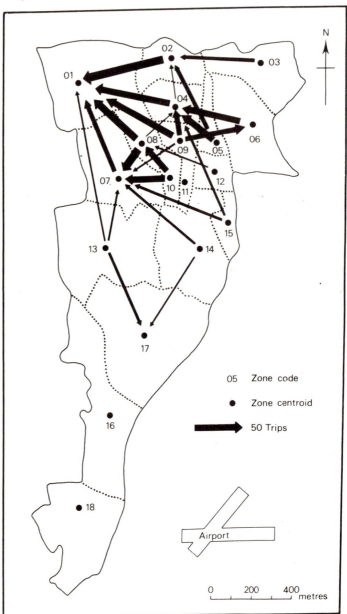

Table 5.3.2: The Spatial Behaviour of Students Over Selected Areas of Jos, 1972

Zone Code	Name	Mean Distance km	Cumulative Percentage of Total Trips in Distance Groups			
			0 – 1 km	1 – 2 km	2 – 3 km	3 – 4 km
1	Jenta Extension	0.52	66.67	100.0	—	—
2	Jenta	2.22	0.0	75.00	81.82	81.82
3	Dogon Dutse	2.94	0.0	8.11	86.49	97.30
4	Kwararafa	0.85	38.27	100.0	—	—
5	Bauchi Road	2.34	40.04	50.62	90.62	100.0
6	Sabon Gwong	1.07	74.79	96.77	100.0	—
7	Prison Area	1.28	19.92	59.92	73.07	100.0
8	Stadium Area	2.64	0.0	0.0	70.37	100.0
9	Alkali Street	1.57	11.97	72.65	100.0	—
10	Langtang	0.81	30.95	97.01	97.01	100.0
12	Market	1.38	42.42	100.0	—	—
13	Hill Station	2.34	11.76	56.86	56.86	90.20
14	Secretariat	1.90	2.70	56.76	56.76	100.0
15	Gangare	2.43	0.0	35.71	35.71	100.0
17	Reservation	2.64	0.0	20.00	20.00	92.00
18	Anglo Jos	4.46	0.0	0.0	0.0	54.54

Average trip length is 2.2 km.

Source: Calculated from author's field-work.

cent of their children making trips longer than 4 kilometres.

The situation in Lagos is similar to that of Jos. Here again, there are four centres where these schools are located. In particular, they are Surulere (16), Yaba (9), Lagos Island (5 and 6), Mushin (21) and Oshodi (25). These zones, except Lagos Island, are also peripheral to the overall configuration of the city. The pattern of interaction shown in Figure 5.3.4 also emphasises the concentrated nature of the schools.

As in the case of Jos, meaningful summaries of the spatial behaviour are provided by Table 5.3.3, which indicates that the average trip length to school is 3.24 kilometres, a figure only slightly greater than that of Jos. There are considerable variations in the zonal mean trip lengths ranging from 4.68 kilometres in Itire Lawanson (17) to 2.22 kilometres in Yaba (9) and 2.72 kilometres in Agege (24).

Of great importance, however, is the third column, which shows that a very small percentage, and only in Igbobi (10) and Yaba (9), make trips of less than 1 kilometre to school. Furthermore, if we examine the

Figure 5.3.4: Patterns of Interaction of the Journey to Schools, Lagos, 1975

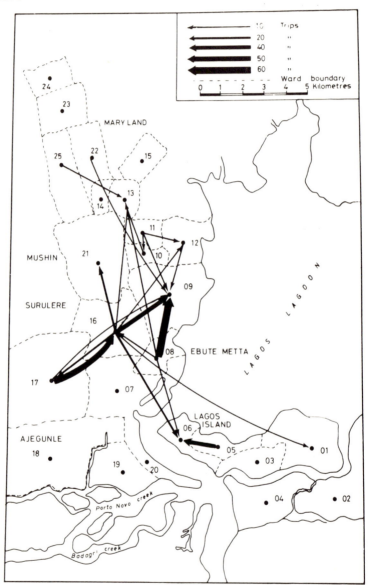

Table 5.3.3: The Spatial Behaviour of Students over Selected Areas of Lagos, 1975

Zone Code	Description	Mean Distance km	Cumulative Percentage of Trips over Distance Groups					
			0 − 1	1 − 2	2 − 3	3 − 4	4 − 5	5 − 6
5	Lagos							
6	Island	3.40	0.0	85.57	85.57	85.57	85.57	85.57
	Ebute							
8	Metta	3.28	0.0	56.95	56.95	60.98	88.78	92.37
9	Yaba	2.22	1.92	90.38	90.38	90.38	90.15	96.15
	Igbobi-							
10	Fadeyi	3.52	15.78	42.10	42.10	84.21	84.21	89.47
11	Shomolu	2.91	0.0	56.75	72.97	75.67	86.47	91.89
12	Bariga	3.25	0.0	51.35	62.16	62.16	83.78	83.78
13	Palm-							
	Grove	3.36	0.0	55.00	57.40	65.00	74.00	75.00
16	Surulere	3.10	0.0	60.37	66.29	68.14	90.37	90.37
17	Itire-							
	Lawanson	4.68	0.0	0.0	22.98	22.98	80.45	80.45
19	Apapa	3.17	0.0	81.08	81.08	81.08	81.08	81.08
21	Mushin	3.12	0.0	0.0	77.96	79.66	91.52	93.22
22	Ikeja	3.39	0.0	54.54	65.45	65.45	65.45	70.90
24	Agege	2.72	0.0	5.37	91.39	91.39	91.39	94.62

Average trip length in Lagos is 3.24 km.
Source: Author's field-work.

last column, we find that average trip lengths to school could be considerably greater than six kilometres. Considering the traffic problems in Lagos, this is rather unfortunate.

Recreational facilities appealing to youths involve such facilities as playing fields, cinemas, amusement centres, theatres, parks and sporting clubs. These facilities require some sort of threshold before a site can be chosen, and population is a crucial element for consideration. In Jos there are many outdoor recreational facilities, notably parks and playing fields, near major road intersections. There are also a few centres where other facilities are located, and they include Kwararafa (4), Stadium (8), Commercial Zone (11) Hill Station (13) and the Reservation (17). Kwararafa (4) is probably the largest centre as it has two of the four cinemas and many hotels and bars. The Stadium (8) area contains the Jos Stadium in addition to a number of hotels. The Hill Station is the site of two international hotels in addition to a museum and a zoological

Figure 5.3.5: Patterns of Interaction of the Journey to
Recreational Centres in Jos, 1972

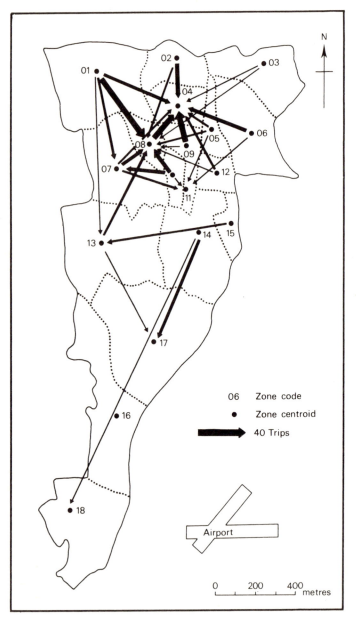

Table 5.3.4: The Spatial Behaviour of Youths on Recreational Trips in Selected Areas of Jos, 1972

Zone	Description	Mean Distance (km)	0 — 1 km	1 — 2 km	2 — 3 km	3 — 4 km
1	Jenta Extension	1.17	17.65	94.12	100.00	—
2	Jenta	4.72	0.0	27.43	33.33	33.33
3	Dogon Dutse	3.89	0.0	0.0	39.13	65.22
4	Kwararafa	0.68	66.67	91.11	97.78	97.78
5	Bauchi Road	3.82	0.0	0.0	0.0	2.63
6	Sabon Gwong	1.21	65.00	88.33	96.67	100.00
7	Prison Area	3.64	2.94	2.94	17.65	67.65
8	Stadium Area	2.30	0.0	8.77	98.25	100.00
9	Alkali Street	1.66	8.11	35.14	100.00	—
10	Langtang	0.88	33.82	94.12	100.00	—
12	Market	1.20	12.50	100.00	—	—
13	Hill Station	3.05	6.25	6.25	56.25	—
14	Secretariat	2.21	13.64	68.19	68.19	100.00
15	Nangare	1.52	42.86	50.00	78.57	100.00
17	Reservation	2.91	0.0	0.0	87.50	87.50
18	Anglo Jos	1.73	0.0	64.29	100.00	100.00

Average trip length is 2.43 km.
Source: author's field-work.

garden. The zoological garden attracts more than two hundred thousand visitors annually.

The consumption pattern of recreational facilities is shown in Figure 5.3.5, which further confirms the observation that outdoor recreational facilities are rather more concentrated than dispersed. It is also important to observe that the arrows from the origins to the destinations are not proportional to the populations at the origins, implying that the generation of such trips may be constrained by the socio-economic and other characteristics of the inhabitants. Consequently, one can note that there are certain long trips, made by youths usually of the higher socio-economic status, notably from the Secretariat area (14) to Anglo Jos (18) and other parts of the city.

The spatial behaviour of the youths may also be summarised through their average trip lengths. For the whole city, the mean length of recreational trips is 2.43 kilometres, although it could be as low as 0.68 kilometres in Kwararafa (4) and as high as 3.82 in Bauchi Road (5). Furthermore, only six zones have means that are greater than average. If, however, we examine the last column of Table 5.3.4, we find that a considerable number of people make recreational trips of more than

4 kilometres. Jenta (2), Bauchi Road (5) and Prison Area (7), which belong to this category, represent some of the areas which are either inadequately catered for or not at all.

The situation in Lagos is more critical, as there is a general absence of parks except in the very high-class areas of Ikoyi, Apapa, etc., where in any case few youths reside. However there are a number of cinemas, hotels and a few sporting clubs. These facilities are so few that there is almost nothing added by showing them on a map. It is obvious that such recreational centres as hotels and beer parlours are widely dispersed, while recreational facilities which develop the psychophysiological characteristics of youths are few and concentrated in yet fewer locations (see Figure 5.3.6), notably Victoria Island (4) where there is the Bar Beach, Surulere (16) where there is the National Stadium Complex; the Central Business District of Lagos (6), Ebute Meta (8), Shomolu (11), Palm Grove (13) and Ikeja (22). These are zones where cinemas are concentrated, or where there are parks and playing fields. Although it may not be very obvious that there is a lack of recreational facilities in Lagos, an examination of the average trip length, which is a staggering 10.04 kilometres, dispels all doubts. In general, average trip lengths range between 3.38 kilometres in Palm Grove (13) and 18.88 in Ikeja (22). These rather large figures may be due to the fact that the beach on Victoria Island (4) is probably the most important recreational centre in Lagos (see Figure 5.3.6).

From Table 5.3.5, it is seen that very few people make short recreational trips. These few are found in Palm Grove (13), Ashodi (25), Ogbobi-Fadeyi (10) and Surulere (16). On the other hand, quite a large proportion of the people make rather long trips. This is true of people in such areas as Bariga (12), Itire-Lawanson (17), Apapa (19), Mushin (21), Ikeja (22) and Agege (24). Considering the poor traffic situation in Lagos, any recreational trip longer than six kilometres may be said to be highly undesirable.

It emerges so far that the location of schools and recreational facilities in Lagos and Jos, and possibly in other Nigerian towns, is peripheral to the overall growth of the cities and hence is not population-orientated. While this could be adduced as a reason for the rather long trips, it is also conceivable, especially in the case of education facilities, that long trips may also be due to either religious or socio-economic considerations. For the former, it is known that people of certain religious sects would always prefer their children to attend schools of their sect, their locations notwithstanding. This may be adduced as a reason why as many school trips were made from Sabon Gwong (6)

Figure 5.3.6: Pattern of Interaction of the Journey to Recreational Centres in Lagos, 1975

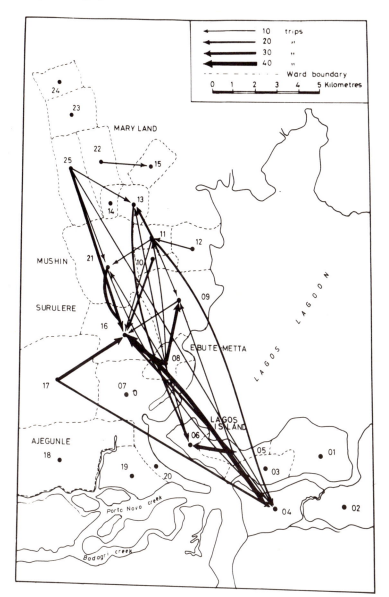

Table 5.3.5: The Spatial Behaviour of Youths on Recreational Trips over Selected Areas of Lagos, 1975

Zone	Description	Mean Distance (km)	Cumulative Percentage of Total Trips in Distance Groups					
			0 – 1 km	1 – 2 km	2 – 3 km	3 – 4 km	4 – 5 km	5 – 6 km
8	Ebute Meta	4.57	0.0	30.0	30.0	30.0	30.0	100.0
9	Yaba	6.97	0.0	11.39	11.39	11.39	32.91	32.91
10	Igbobi Fadeyi	5.71	0.0	0.0	0.0	0.0	0.0	100.0
11	Shomolu	6.02	0.0	.67	7.5	7.5	7.5	90.83
12	Bariga	7.02	0.0	2.81	7.75	18.31	40.14	45.07
13	Palm Grove	3.38	0.0	29.63	55.56	81.48	81.48	85.19
16	Surulere	5.29	9.09	0.09	9.09	9.09	72.73	74.03
17	Itire-Lawanson	10.77	0.0	0.0	0.0	0.0	0.0	0.0
19	Apapa	11.14	0.0	0.0	0.0	2.90	2.90	2.90
21	Mushin	11.52	0.0	0.0	0.0	0.0	15.38	15.38
22	Ikeja	18.88	0.0	0.0	0.0	0.0	0.0	0.0
24	Agege	11.32	0.0	1.33	1.33	1.33	1.33	16.00
25	Oshodi	3.66	0.0	63.64	81.82	81.82	81.82	90.91

Average trip length is 10.04 km.

Source: Calculated from author's field-work.

into Jos as those made from Jos to Sabon Gwong. The influence of socio-economic considerations is to ensure that people of the higher socio-economic status educate their children in the best schools (which incidently may be fee-paying) which may be long distances from their homes. In Lagos, this is true of such long school trips from Surulere (16) to Ikoyi and in Jos for trips from the Secretariat (14) and Hill Station (13) to the Reservation where the Hill Crest School is.

Recreational trip-making, on the other hand, is not so easy to explain in terms of religion and perhaps socio-economic characteristic only. Thus, to the extent that the recreational trip-makers are generally older than the school trip-makers, the best explanation is that the presence or location of these centres, their powers of attraction in terms of the ranges of conveniences and facilities provided, and their degree of accessibility to the people are vital to the consumption process. To these one may possibly add that socio-economic considerations, such as the level of education, the nature of occupation and even stages in a man's life cycle are critical elements in studying the volume of recreational trips generated by youths. This is an aspect in which much research is needed if we are ever going to identify the needs and problems young people face in adapting to the effects of urbanisation and the growing affluence that is becoming characteristic of urban centres.

4. The Spatial Dimensions of the Problems of Youths in the Consumption of Urban Facilities

The harmonious utilisation of urban facilities by youths is confronted by a number of problems both spatial and aspatial, but we shall concentrate on those with a spatial orientation. Perhaps the greatest problems are those associated with the rather long trips either to school or to recreational facilities. These problems have two important dimensions. The first one concerns the strain suffered by youths as a result of long distances they trek to school. Although the author has not conducted researches into the nature and consequences of such strains, it is believed that this could be one of the causes of drowsiness shown at odd times by pupils during lessons. The situation becomes even worse if certain inadequacies of the facilities are taken into consideration. In the case of the primary schools, these inadequacies relate to the lack of infrastructure, especially buildings, desks and tables, with the result that many urban centres run two school sessions daily, the morning from 7.30 a.m. to 12.30 p.m., and the evening from 2.00 p.m. to 6.30 p.m. in order to maximise the use of available resources. In such circumstances, one would expect the strain of long trips to be greater on the set of pupils that attend schools in the afternoon or evening sessions. A possible hypothesis arising from this consideration is that pupils in the morning sessions perform better in their class lessons than those of the afternoon.

The situation is worse in the case of secondary schools. Considering the fact that secondary schools possess a longer range than primary schools, one could expect many secondary-school day students to make very long journeys to and from schools. These long journeys are occasioned by the fact that these secondary schools are really very few in number and are known to be grossly inadequate both in number and facilities. One way by which secondary schools minimise these strains is through the provision of afternoon meals to all students and their encouragement to stay behind in the afternoon for preparatory classes. None the less, the strains remain.

The second dimension of the long trip length actually identifies the rather inaccessible nature of these educational facilities. This is to argue that even when long trips are made in cars or buses, the cost of purchasing education has been unwittingly increased. To a very poor man, this may be a major determinant as to whether a child attends a school or not. In addition to cost constraints, the child may also become disillusioned. For recreational trips, on the other hand, long distances between points of supply and demand represent great disutilities which may reduce the frequency of recreation. This is already becoming obvious from our field investigations. For instance, in Lagos, where traffic problems are considerable, the mean frequency of trip-making for recreational purposes was only 2.56 per week, while on Jos it was 4.86. Trip frequency may therefore be said to be very elastic to increases in travel costs and sizes of urban centres. This may be because the individual trip-maker has fixed disposable time and monetary resources which he can expend in the search for leisure. Consequently, personal mobility and the nature of the transportation network could be important variables that explain the number of trips made.

A major problem that arises from the consumption of both educational and recreational facilities within the city is that of the flow of traffic. Pupils usually go to school in the morning at about 7.00 a.m., when workers are setting out for work. The meeting of these two groups of people at bus stops leads to scrambling for the few places available on the buses. The provision of school buses may alleviate the problem, but will surely not solve it, as it is likely to lead to traffic hold-ups as a result of overcrowding on the roads.

There is a set of problems that underlies the worsening situation of the dimensions of the spatial problems. In the case of education, it finds expression in the over-utilisation of existing facilities and infra-structure as a result of the two-session system. Consequently, it is not unusual to find that half the chairs, tables and desks are broken or in unusuable condition, while the state of disrepair of classrooms, toilet facilities and playing apparatus show that stocks are gravely over-used. In the case of recreational facilities, this finds expression in the non-provision of the wide range of facilities required by the youths and general lack of repair and proper upkeep of parks and fields. The result is always a tendency to over-use the few available ones that meet the minimum specifications.

Most of these problems could be summarised under one or two headings. First, it would seem that as a result of many reasons, notably the fact that both formal educational and outdoor recreational facilities are innovations (in the sense that they are different from pre-European educational and recreational needs) whose corresponding land uses are being grafted to an existing, often pre-industrial land-use pattern, it has been very difficult to locate these facilities as near to the people as possible. This difficulty has been heightened by the unfortunate fact that the realisation that modern urban planning requires consideration of goals and objectives that relate to different classes of people, especially youths, eludes current planning machinery. For example, a more comprehensive planning would have noted the relevance of a sound data base concerning the social functions of recreation and the expectations of the users of recreational facilities, in addition to their efficient management. In the same way, planners for educational facilities would consider both the socio-economic and the geographical consequences of their location within the city.

Secondly, and perhaps more fundamentally, there is a general lack of awareness on the scope and dimensions of the educational and recreational needs of youths, as well as other residents. For instance, it is unfortunate to think that the educational needs of urban residents stop with the provision of the facilities for the formal educational system. It is a truism to state that much of the urban labour force in Third World cities acquires its skills and practices from systems outside the formal educational system. If there is appreciation of this fact, then there is the need on the part of the government or of city managements to make facilities accessible to this section of the population. Furthermore, there is an urgent need by employers to recognise their system of instruction. This same lack of awareness of scope and dimensions is probably most manifest in the case of recreational facilities where nobody actually thinks of the range of recreational facilities that could be provided for the different age and sex groups of the residents. The promotion of sporting activities in Nigeria by the Ministry of Social Development, Youths and Sports goes only a short way to solving the problem, as the emphasis is in competitive sporting rather than sporting for leisure. It is to this end that private clubs and associations have proved useful, but these only cater for a very small proportion of urban residents. There is therefore a need for a city department whose aims are to research into, provide and maintain the recreational needs of people of all categories.

Conclusion

The more urban centres increase their population and spatial extent, the more the cities grow vertically and the more complex the functional interrelationships become, the more there will be a demand for the satisfaction of basic human needs. To the Nigerian urban youth, the demands include the provision of adequate employment facilities, the provision of water, electricity and health facilities. However, the two that are essential to psychophysiological, social, sanitary and economic well-being are the educational and recreational facilities. The provision of leisure-time activities in addition to educational centres are needed to compensate for the strains and stresses that attend migration to the cities and the use of top-storey buildings as homes and offices. While a well-organised school system develops the minds of the youths, the urban parks which act as 'the lungs and breathing spaces of the city' aid physical development.

Consequently, we have shown how locational patterns of these urban activities influence the spatial behaviour of youths and what consequences such behaviour may have on their sociopsychological development. We have also emphasised the fact that for educational and recreational centres, in particular to attract people, they must possess qualities which make them different from the rest of the city. Furthermore, they must provide a variety of activities for the various age/sex groupings of our youths. Of course the provision of these in the most accessible way is seen as very crucial to their efficient utilisation.

Finally, it must be said that while urban centres all over the world probably enjoy more organised forms of educational and recreational facilities than rural areas, it must be accepted that as a result of a lack of comprehensive planning that particularly considers various groups of people, especially young people, these facilities could be inaccessible to the majority of consumers. There is therefore a need to emphasise more in our researches and planning efforts the factors of location, inventory and classification of these facilities and their roles in the adjustment of people to the highly artificial milieu which has become our urban centres.

References

Ayeni, M.A.O. 1974. Predictive modelling of Urban Spatial Structure: The Example of Jos, Benue-Plateau State Nigeria. Ph.D. thesis, University of Ibadan, Nigeria

Ayeni, M.A.O. 1976. *Lagos State Project, A Regional Plan of Lagos State: Planning Lagos Metropolitan Area Final Reports*. Submitted to the Planning Studies Programme, Faculty of the Social Sciences, University of Ibadan, Ibadan

Berry, B.J.L. 1968. *Geography of Market Centres and Retail Distribution*. Englewood Cliffs, New Jersey: Prentice-Hall

Christaller, W. 1933. *Die Zentralen Orte in Siiddentshland* Jeno. Translated by W. Baskin, 1966. *Central Places in Southern Germany*. Englewood Cliffs, New Jersey: Prentice-Hall

Ingram, R. 1971. The Concept of Accessibility: A Search for an Operational Form. *Regional Studies, 5,* 101–7

Mabogunje, A.L. 1973. Towards an Urban Policy in Nigeria. An address presented at the 17th Annual Conference of the Nigerian Geographical Association, Lagos, Dec. 1973

Mabogunje, A.L. 1974. Cities and Social Order. Inaugural lecture, University of Ibadan, April 1974

6 FORMAL AND FUNCTIONAL SPATIAL ORGANISATION OF THE CITY

1. Introduction

The formal spatial organisation of an urban system has been shown to involve at least two dimensions. These are the geometrical framework within which distinctive cultural groups live and interact and characteristics of social areas as perceived by the residents (Bourne and Murdie, 1972). Functional organisation, on the other hand, refers to the ways in which land uses and social areas interact, and emphasises the delimitation of areas of economic and social domination by some nodes of the urban system (Symanski *et al.*, 1973). Consequently, both formal and functional organisation of an urban system could be seen as integral components of its spatial structure.

An analysis of the formal and functional organisation of a city should essentially be concerned with the grouping or classification of its sub-area units, either on the basis of a single very important criterion or through the use of more than one distinguishing characteristic. In the former case, single-feature regions or classes result while the latter gives rise to multi-feature regions. Each of these has its advantages and disadvantages (Grigg, 1967, pp. 492–3). However, since there is always a high spatial covariance of two or more properties being classified in a regional system, the multi-feature classification should possess some appeal.

Classification may be based upon either the similarity between objects classed, or on the basis of the relationship between the objects (Grigg, 1967; Simpson, 1961, p. 3). Classification based on a single most or very important criterion or sets of distinguishing characteristics produce uniform or formal regions while those based on interrelationships between objects produce functional or nodal regions. While formal or uniform regions are easy to construct and hence more widely used for study and analysis, functional or nodal regions could be more suitable for planning purposes (Fair, 1957, p. 32). None the less the two are not necessarily mutually exclusive and there could be strong relationships between them. This indeed is the argument of this chapter which sets out, using some important characteristics of an urban spatial form, first to show that it is possible to establish (inductively) the dimensions of the formal or unform structure of Jos, Nigeria; as well as those of its nodal or functional organisation. Second, the chapter analyses the characteristics of the interrelationships between formal and functional organisation of this urban system.

2. The Concept of the Field and Canonical Correlation

The formal organisation and functional association of any stem of interest are known to possess interdependent patterns in space (see Webber, 1964; Philbrick, 1957). An integrating concept of this interrelationship is found in field theory. Field theory originated in physics but was first used in the social sciences by Kurt Lewin as a framework for studying the complex interplay among forms of social interaction and social conditions which engender or might potentially engender interaction (Lewin, 1951). Berry (1966) provides a rationale for its usage in spatial analysis when he states that:

> spatial processes must involve simultaneous congruent changes in spatial structure and behavior and neither structure nor behavior can be asserted to be the sole source through which external influences freed the process and compel change . . . Behavioral changes may call forth structural changes as well as the converse.

The emphasis of this quotation lies in the symbiotic relationship that exists between form and function. In spatial analysis, one could view the elements of spatial form as being arranged in a matrix **A**, an attribute matrix, whose rows are made up of places but whose columns consist of the attributes of these places. Similarly, the spatial process or function could be seen as another matrix **B**, a behavioural matrix, whose rows and columns represent the same set of places in matrix **A** but whose elements represent some form of interaction between these places. Field theory may then be seen as an integrating concept that emphasises the relationships between these two matrices. However, there is a need to develop an operational technique which could identify the nature and significance of any interrelationships that might exist between the attribute and behavioural matrices. Canonical correlation analysis offers a suitable methodology.

Canonical correlation analysis is a general method for dealing with two sets of data, one of which may be or may not be dependent on the other. In this way it is a suitable technique for operationalising the ideas embedded in the field concept. It may be characterised as a sort of 'double-barrelled principal components analysis' (Tatsuoka, 1971, p. 183) as it identifies the components of one set of variables that are most highly linearly related to the components of the other set of variables. Thus if there are s variables $X_1, X_2 \ldots, X_s$ of the first set and p variables $Y_1, Y_2 \ldots, Y_p$ of the second, canonical analysis obtains a pair of linear functions or canonical variates U and V of these two sets of variables in such a way that they have maximum (canonical) correlation. The canonical variates U and V have the form:

$$U = a_1x_1 + a_2x_2 + \ldots + a_sx_s$$

$$V = b_1y_1 + b_2y_2 + \ldots + b_py_p$$

where a_i, $i = 1, 2, \ldots, s$ and b_j, $j = 1, 2, \ldots, p$ are the canonical coefficients. If p is less than s, there will, in general, always be p pairs of these variates which are interpreted like component loadings in factor analysis.

Since Berry produced a formal and functional regionalisation of India (Berry, 1966), numerous studies have employed the technique of canonical correlation. Among these were the studies by Ray on the interrelationship between economic and cultural differences in Canada (Ray, 1972) and the studies by Clark on the formal and structural components of Wales (Clark, 1973). None the less, besides the studies by Bourne and Murdie on the dimensions of the social and physical space of Toronto (Bourne and Murdie, 1972), few studies have utilised this technique at the level of the urban or metropolitan area, even though urban centres constitute valuable areas not only for testing ideas about human spatial behaviour, but also of exploring the symbiotic relationship embedded in the concept of the field.

Canonical correlation analysis is based on an assumption that all the variables within a variable set are independent and normally distributed. Therefore, in the analysis of social investigation, where data seldom meet these assumptions, it is always necessary either to standardise (normalise) or 'clean' the variables. The latter approach uses methods of principal components or factor analysis. Principal component analysis is a multivariate technique for expressing a matrix of m groups of attributes (or variables) measured over n areas in terms of r orthogonal dimensions ($r \leqslant m$), in such a way that these dimensions preserve most of the original variance of the m variables. Besides the parsimony involved in this technique, the independent dimensions that result are interpretable and completely describe through component scores the performance of each of the n areas of the system of interest (see Harman, 1960; Anderson, 1958; and Cooley and Lohnes, 1971, for descriptions of these techniques).

Our research strategy is as follows: from two sets of data, one explaining the functional space and the other explaining the formal space, attempts are made through the use of the technique of principal components analysis to define both the functional and formal spatial organisation of Jos. Component scores by sub-areas of the city on each of the two sets of components then constitute the data base for the analysis of the symbiotic relationship between the two sets of data. The rationale for this approach is provided by Cattel (1952, p. 17) who writes that: 'Factor Analytic Investigation has its function predominantly in basic research to provide the measurement foundations for later special problems in pure and applied research' (quoted from Rummell, 1970, p. 3). Furthermore the approach also provides an intermediate investigation of the nature of the formal and functional spatial organisation of a city.

The data sets used in the present chapter are derived from studies conducted by the author and partly described in Chapter 5.

The information in the attribute matrix of Jos was collected over eighteen zones, the delimitation of which reflected land-use considerations as well as administrative convenience. For each zone, information on land-use characteristics as well as the socio-economic characteristics of the residents were obtained. The former includes the distribution of land, houses and floor space, the distribution of manufacturing and service employment, and population as surrogates for industrial, service and residential land uses respectively. The second category includes the average zonal age of the head of household, his length of residence in the city, his years of formal schooling, the size of his household, the number of working people in the household, the average number of rooms a household occupies and the average total annual rent. Total annual rent which varies by wage classes (Ayeni, 1975) was used as as surrogate for the income variable which could not be measured on a ratio scale.

The second set of data describes the movement characteristics of the same set of households in the attribute matrix. These movements were made as comprehensive as possible to include total day-to-day movements such as journeys to places of work, markets and shopping centres and journeys to recreational facilities and schools as reflected over a one-month period. The choice of households was based on a 7.5 per cent sample of all houses in the city by 1972. This gave a total of 374 houses and 1,703 households. The execution of the sampling procedure was systematically random, involving a systematic choice of streets, followed by a random selection of houses. All households within a housing unit were interviewed.

Table 6.3.1: Dimensions of Formal Spatial Organisation

Dimensions	I	II	III
Eigenvalues	6.812	2.217	1.366
Per cent variance	52.40	17.05	10.51
Cumulative per cent variance	52.40	69.45	79.96

3. The Formal Spatial Organisation of Jos.

Following the findings of Bourne and Murdie (1972) that the spatial organisation of a city involves both the city's geometrical framework and its social areas, the groups of variables of the attribute matrix (13 in all) described in the last section were subjected to a principal components analysis from which emerged three dimensions. The three dimensions explain a total of 80 per cent of the variance contained in the original variables. The first dimension, which dominates the urban system of Jos, accounts for 52.4 per cent of this explained variance while the other two components explain 17.05 and 10.51 per cent respectively (see Table 6.3.1).

The first component is characterised by low positive loadings on the socioeconomic variables and rather low positive loadings on population, employment and floor space variables (see Table 6.3.2). An interpretation of this factor is facilitated by the pattern of scores shown in Table 6.3.3 and Figure 6.3.1. These clearly demonstrate that this dimension is a socio-economic one as it tries to divide the city into three historically important groups; the north, the west and the south. The north is made

Table 6.3.2: Rotated Factor Loadings on the Formal Spatial Structure

Dimensions	I	II	III
1 Population	0.338	−0.922	0.015
2 Employment	0.134	0.131	−0.103
3 Area	−0.617	0.243	0.258
4 Number of houses	0.123	−0.948	−0.102
5 Total floor space	0.102	−0.914	−0.125
6 Service floor space	−0.070	0.205	0.223
7 Age of head	−0.943	0.110	−0.089
8 Length of residence in city	0.268	−0.124	−0.858
9 Years of schooling	−0.831	0.297	0.336
10 Household size	−0.540	0.141	0.202
11 Workers per household	−0.274	0.207	0.170
12 Rooms per household	−0.936	0.172	0.124
13 Annual rent	−0.821	0.181	0.303

Figure 6.3.1: The Social Space of Jos

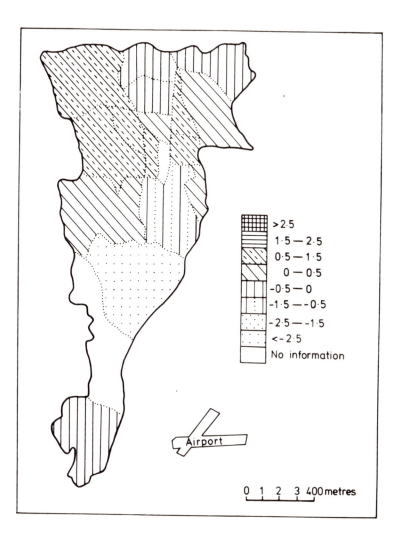

up of Jenta (2), Dogon Dutse (3) and Kwararafa (4). To these may be added Sabon Gwong (6) and Alkali (9). These zones have factor scores ranging between -0.5 and $+0.5$ (see Figure 6.3.1). The west, on the other hand, is made up of zones with scores between 0.5 and 1.5 and includes Jenta Extension (1), Prison Area (7), Stadium (8) and Langtang-Panyam (10) while the south is made up of the Secretariat (14) and the Reservation (18). These latter zones have negative high scores (< -1.5). The divisions correspond roughly with the tripartite delimitation (from colonial days) of cities in these parts of Nigeria into the Birnin (the old city), Sabon Gari (the new city) and the European Reservation. The Birnin was where the indigenous people lived, while Sabon Gari was inhabited by other Nigerian ethnic groups.

The second component loads in an exactly opposite way to the first, as high negative loadings occur on such variables as population, number of houses and floor space while the socio-economic variables possess rather low positive loadings. The pattern of scores (see Figure 6.3.2) shows that the zones which are large in terms of population and area have high scores. Consequently, it may be said that this dimension is measuring the 'size' of zones. The component divides the city into two size-spaces made up roughly of Jenta Extension (1), Prison Area (7), Stadium (8), Langtang-Panyam (10), Hill Station (13), Secretariat (14), Reservation (17) and Anglo Jos (18) on the one hand, and Jenta (2), Kwararafa (4), Alkali (9), Bauchi Road (5) and Market Area (12) on the other. Zones in the first set occupy large areas of land while those of the second, though occupying smaller areas, have larger populations. Furthermore, factor scores of the first set of zones are positive while they are negative in the second set. In view of these observations, this component is a 'size-space' dimension.

While the first two components identify both the socio-economic and the size structure of the city, the third dimension identifies an important characteristic of Jos. This component, accounting for only 10.51 per cent of the variance, loads highly (-0.858) on the length of stay variable which it weakly contrasts with the years of formal education and rent. The pattern of scores (Figure 6.3.3) shows that areas such as Jenta (2), Kwararafa (4), Alkali (9), Gangare (15) and Anglo Jos (18), where most of the people indigenous to the plateau live, have the highest scores (see Table 6.3.3). On the other hand are Jenta Extension (1), Prison (7), Stadium (8), Langtang-Panyam (10), Secretariat (14) and the Reservation (18) where most migrants live. This dimension therefore may be described as the 'migrancy' component of urban social space of Jos. It could be compared with the migrant component

Figure 6.3.2: The Physical Size Space of Jos

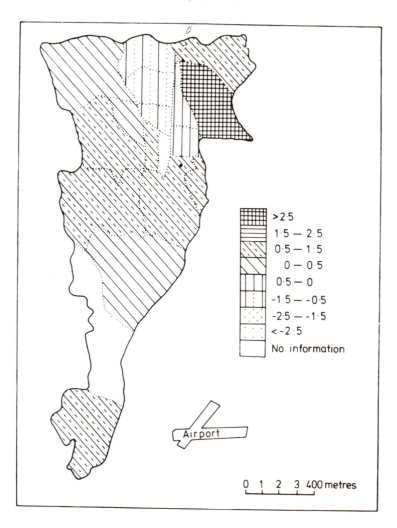

	>2·5
	1·5 — 2·5
	0·5 — 1·5
	0 — 0·5
	0·5 — 0
	-1·5 — -0·5
	-2·5 — -1·5
	<-2·5
	No information

Airport

0 1 2 3 400 metres

Table 6.3.3: Zonal Factor Scores on the Dimensions of Formal Spatial Association

Zone	Descriptions	I	II	III
1	Jenta Extension	0.835	0.412	0.450
2	Jenta	−0.479	−0.995	−1.155
3	Dogon Dutse	−0.107	1.092	0.109
4	Kwararafa	−0.300	−0.918	−2.080
5	Bauchi Road	0.555	−0.166	0.065
6	Sabon Gwong	0.475	−2.768	1.341
7	Prison Area	0.531	0.580	0.401
8	Stadium	0.755	0.211	1.562
9	Alkali	0.183	−0.824	−0.603
10	Langtang-Panyam	0.975	0.813	0.751
11	CBD*			
12	Market	0.578	−0.334	−0.443
13	Hill Station	0.106	0.578	−0.243
14	Secretariat	−1.013	0.539	0.839
15	Gangare	0.216	0.684	−0.852
16	Mountain View*			
17	Reservation	−3.190	0.006	0.954
18	Anglo Jos	−0.119	1.092	−1.095

*   Sample sizes in zones 11 and 16 were too small (because of its non-residential nature) for meaningful estimates of socio-economic characteristics to be made. They were therefore omitted in the analysis reported in this study.

of social area — factorial ecology analysis of cities in Third World countries (see Rees, 1970).

The analysis of the formal spatial organisation of Jos could be described in terms of three major dimensions of socio-economic or social space, the 'size space' and 'migrancy space' of variation. While they do not show any discernible spatial variation in terms of being either concentric, sectoral or found in nucleations, they undoubtedly outline the historic development of the city. It is of course not surprising that these dimensions neither correspond in name nor spatial variation to findings from social area analysis or factorial ecology. First, social area analysis is based on a number of postulates concerning an industrial society. While Jos could be described as an industrialising city, the Nigerian society which feeds it with people is not yet an industrial society, so that many of the postulates of social area analysis would not be applicable. Furthermore, the selection of variables for this analysis is not guided by a desire to replicate in Jos findings of social area analysis, but rather by a desire to find the dimensions of the spatial structure.

Figure 6.3.3: The 'Migrancy' Component of Social Space

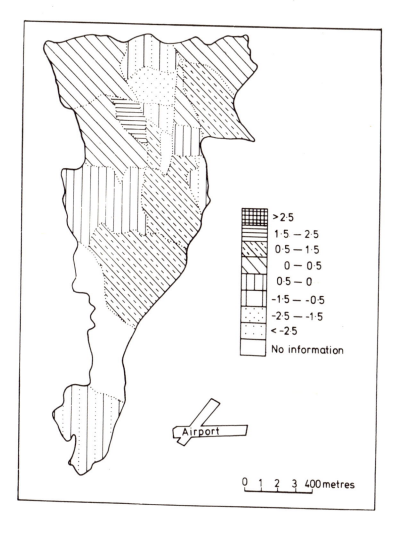

4. The Functional Association of Activities

The functional association of activities in Jos is sought through a conventional principal components analysis of the product-moment correlation coefficient matrix derived from the aggregate matrix of the $(n^2 - n)$ volumes of interaction. The correlation coefficient matrix itself shows the degree of interrelationships that exist between one zone and every other zone of the urban system in terms of trip generation and attraction characteristics. The use of principal components analysis on interaction data is to produce groupings of both destinations and origins in terms of the similarities of their linkage patterns (Humphreys, 1965). This is usually achieved through a simultaneous interpretation of both component loadings and component scores. Thus, while component loadings produce a regionalisation of the flow system in terms of the destination patterns, the factor scores identify the set of origins that interact significantly with these destinations. This approach gives a more precise indication of the functional nature and zonal composition of the factors, as factor scores represent the relative importance of flows from particular origins (Wiseman, 1976).

The analysis of the interaction matrix produced seven dimensions or components which describe various aspects of the functional association of activities in the city. In all, the seven components account for 84 per cent of total variance (Table 6.4.1). The first two components accounting for 25 and 19 per cent of total variance respectively could be said to dominate the spatial system. The other five components together explain only 42.30 per cent of explained variance. In so far as principal components analysis produces dimensions in order of magnitude, the analysis may be seen as identifying seven hierarchies of functional association of activities. It is possible to justify such a hierarchical interpretation by the argument that household trips could be ordered since most household travels are purposeful (Marble, 1959).

The most dominant pattern of interaction in Jos centres on the Prison Area (7), Stadium (8), the Central Business District (11) and the Secretariat (14) as destination zones (Table 6.4.2). The set of important origins as revealed by the factor score matrix (Table 6.4.3) are made of Jenta Extension (1), Sabon Gwong (6), the Stadium Area (8) and Langtang-Panyam (10). The set of destination zones contain most of the labour force in the State Administration. Consequently, it might be argued that this pattern describes the behaviour of white collar workers in Jos (see also Figure 6.4.1).

The second dominant pattern of interaction embraces Dogon Dutse (3) and Bauchi Road (5) as prominent destinations while the areas of

Figure 6.4.1: Functional Associaton of the Interaction Pattern of White-collar Workers in Jos

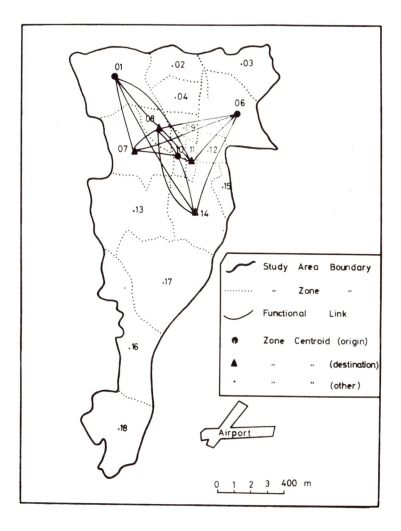

Table 6.4.1: Dimensions of Functional Association

Dimensions							
Eigenvalues	4.496	3.438	2.232	1.590	1.445	1.295	1.043
Per Cent Variance	24.98	19.10	11.39	8.83	8.09	6.17	5.80
Cum. Per Cent	24.98	44.08	55.47	64.30	72.39	78.56	84.36

Secretariat (14) and Anglo Jos (18) were of secondary importance (Table 6.4.2). Associated origins, on the other hand were Dogon Dutse (3), Sabon Gwong (6), Prison (7) and Secretariat (14). The set of destinations are principally industrial zones, especially Anglo Jos (18) (Makeri Industrial Estate) and parts of the Secretariat (14) where most of the manufacturing firms which employ more than ten people locate. The Bauchi Road area (5) is also a major industrial centre, particularly along Delimi Street, which was the location of motor vehicle repair yards, bakeries and service industries which employ fewer than ten people. It would seem therefore that this dimension represents the location of manufacturing activities and the spatial behaviour of blue-collar workers in Jos. This pattern of functional organisation is revealed in Figure 6.4.2.

The third dimension accounts for 11.39 per cent of total variance and centres on three major zones, namely the Hill Station (13), Mountain View (16) and Gangare (15). These zones are linked mostly to one

Table 6.4.2: Rotated Factor Matrix of Functional Organisation

Zone Description	I	II	III	IV	V	VI	VII
1 Jenta Extension	0.206	−0.002	−0.124	0.170	−0.143	0.913	0.057
2 Jenta	−0.002	0.223	0.156	−0.021	0.052	0.046	−0.029
3 Dogon Dutse	0.211	0.685	0.011	−0.002	0.322	−0.165	−0.191
4 Kwararafa	0.111	−0.063	−0.103	−0.373	0.414	0.529	0.352
5 Bauchi Road	0.014	0.894	0.159	−0.031	−0.111	0.056	0.190
6 Sabon Gwong	−0.058	−0.014	−0.152	0.073	−0.959	0.090	−0.053
7 Prison Area	0.963	−0.033	−0.039	−0.004	−0.065	−0.029	0.051
8 Stadium	0.435	−0.119	−0.052	0.003	−0.158	0.031	0.180
9 Alkali	0.152	0.137	−0.046	0.385	0.090	0.095	−0.084
10 Langtang-Panyam	−0.001	−0.030	−0.095	0.951	−0.084	0.124	0.024
11 CBD	0.808	0.053	−0.111	−0.060	−0.022	0.330	0.144
12 Market	0.289	0.209	−0.121	0.028	−0.128	0.252	0.169
13 Hill Station	−0.075	−0.078	0.938	0.074	0.048	−0.150	−0.042
14 Secretariat	0.706	0.395	−0.131	0.122	0.129	0.305	0.121
15 Gangare	−0.194	0.195	0.766	−0.100	0.013	0.160	0.297
16 Mountain View	0.018	0.212	0.774	−0.273	0.227	0.126	−0.244
17 Reservation	−0.173	−0.095	0.016	−0.021	−0.059	−0.096	−0.948
18 Anglo Jos	−0.060	0.354	−0.137	−0.030	0.086	−0.149	0.121

Figure 6.4.2: Functional Association of the Interaction Pattern of Blue-Collar Workers in Jos

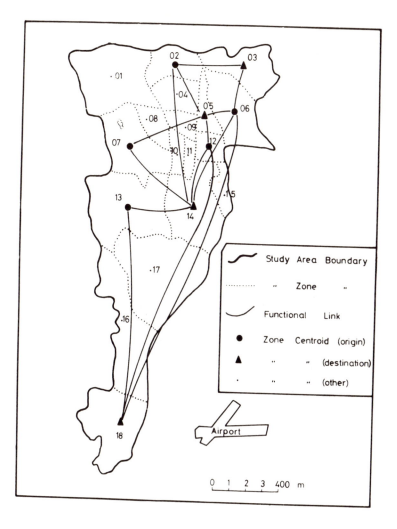

another (see Table 6.4.2) and then weekly to Jenta Extension (1), Langtang-Panyam (10) and Sabon Gwong (6). This component of functional association (see Figure 6.4.3) seems to describe certain aspects of the recreational behaviour, as the destination zones of Mountain View (16), the Hill Station (13), Sabon Gwong (6) and Jenta (2) contain a couple of recreational facilities.

The fourth dimension accounts for only 8.83 per cent of total variance and centres mainly on the Langtang-Panyam area (10). Other less important destinations are Jenta Extension (1), Sabon Gwong (6), Stadium (8), Alkali Street (9), the Market (12), the Hill Station (13) and the Secretariat (14). Many of these areas are also origins. To the extent that most of the origin zones of Jenta Extension (1), Stadium (8), Hill Station (13), Secretariat (14) and Anglo Jos (18) belong to the township of Jos, it may be said that this functional association describes certain aspects of the behaviour of people in the Sabon Gari (Figure 6.4.4). People in the Sabon Gari were generally more educated, younger and possibly wage-earners. Hence this unique pattern of interaction.

The fifth component of functional organisation identifies Kwararafa (4) as the most important destination, although other less important ones are Jenta (2), Dogon Dutse (3), Mountain View (16) and Secretariat (14). The most associated origins are Jenta Extension (1), Sabon Gwong (6) and Alkali Street (9). In the main, this is a north of the city component (Figure 6.4.5) as it links the northernmost parts of the city, an area occupied mostly by the lower-income group, and an extension of the Native Town. The sixth pattern of functional association, on the other hand, identifies destinations that are scattered over the city, e.g. Jenta Extension (1), Jenta (2) in the north, Kwararafa (4) and Stadium (8) in the centre and the Secretariat (14) and Mountain View (16) in the south. Most of the primary and secondary schools and colleges are located here. This dimension clearly describes the educational component of spatial interaction (see Figure 6.4.6).

The last component is less easy to interpret as it is characterised by rather low positive loadings. However, if the patterns of loading (i.e. negative or positive) are considered, then the destinations are made up of Jenta Extension (1), Kwararafa (4), Bauchi Road (5), Prison (7), Stadium (8), CBD (11), Market (12), Secretariat (14), Gangare (15) and Anglo Jos (18). The origins (Table 6.4.3) are equally as many as the destinations (Figure 6.4.7). The common activities of these destination zones are trading and retailing. Retailing land-use activities in Nigerian cities lack the area differentiation associated with them in American

Figure 6.4.3: Aspects of the Functional Organisation of Recreational Behaviour

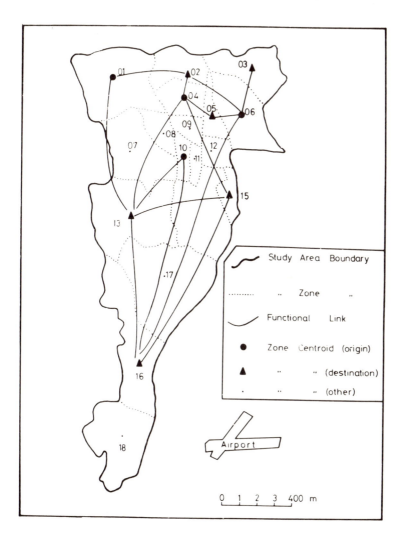

Figure 6.4.4: Functional Regionalisation of Behaviour of Dwellers in Sabon Gari

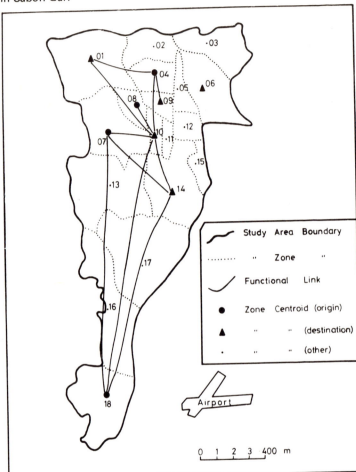

Figure 6.4.5: The 'North of the City' Functional Association

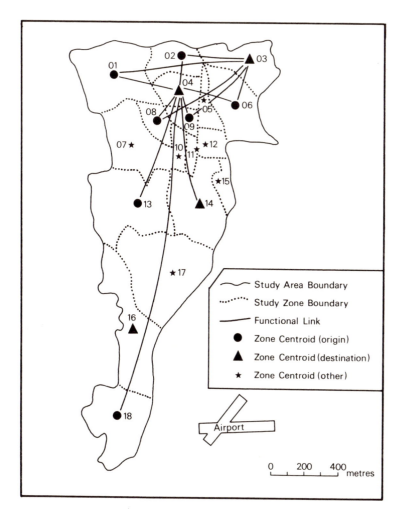

Study Area Boundary	
Study Zone Boundary	
Functional Link	
●	Zone Centroid (origin)
▲	Zone Centroid (destination)
★	Zone Centroid (other)

Airport

0   200   400
metres

Figure 6.4.6: The Educational Dimension of Functional Association

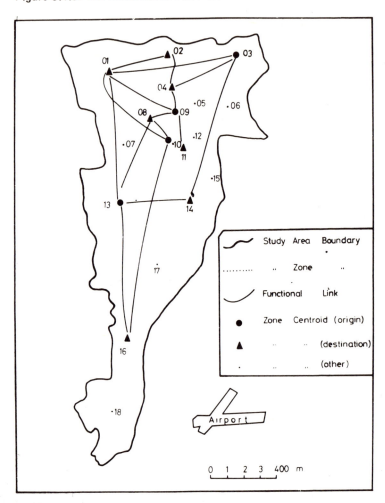

Table 6.4.3: Factor Scores on the Dimensions of Functional Organisation

Zone Description	I	II	III	IV	V	VI	VII
1 Jenta Extension	0.645	−0.335	0.122	0.754	1.110	−1.719	0.293
2 Jenta	−0.111	0.108	−0.094	−1.004	0.547	1.454	0.435
3 Dogon Dutse	−0.834	1.094	−0.160	−0.553	−0.678	0.625	0.688
4 Kwararafa	−0.260	−0.215	0.065	2.608	−0.813	1.517	−0.776
5 Bauchi Road	−0.080	−1.746	−0.181	−1.004	0.263	−0.402	1.164
6 Sabon Gwong	0.582	2.858	0.345	−0.261	0.939	−0.330	0.029
7 Prison Area	−0.722	0.406	−4.469	1.105	−1.699	−0.760	0.732
8 Stadium	2.029	−0.449	−0.328	1.190	0.692	−0.407	0.492
9 Alkali	−0.119	−0.567	−0.617	−0.197	1.349	2.061	0.271
10 Langtang-Panyam	2.389	−0.178	0.154	−1.181	−2.097	0.503	−0.020
11 CBD							
12 Market	−1.159	0.149	0.253	−0.640	−0.730	−0.396	−0.339
13 Hill Station	−0.153	−0.459	1.514	−0.044	0.819	0.174	−2.007
14 Secretariat	−0.158	0.799	−1.257	0.008	0.602	−0.408	−0.221
15 Gangare	−0.714	−0.243	2.922	−0.052	−0.177	−0.374	0.924
16 Mountain View							
17 Reservation	0.266	−0.506	−0.738	−0.861	−0.386	−0.925	−2.416
18 Anglo Jos	−1.068	−0.715	−1.024	0.133	0.260	−0.615	0.751

cities, although some concentrations, such as at market centres and European-created central business districts, do exists. Therefore shopping trips are characterised by much intra-zonal travelling. This probably accounts for the low proportion of variance (6.19 per cent) contributed by this dimension.

The analysis of the functional association of land uses and activities in Jos reveals not a predominance of few centres but a rather mixed and complicated pattern resulting from the relative lack of areal differentiation of activities. None the less the emergence of interpretable dimensions such as those describing the link between the places of work of white-collar and blue-collar workers *vis-à-vis* their places of residence not only identifies the fundamental differences in the trip-generating ability of the two groups but also suggests the nature of the traffic associated with them. Planning to meet the exigencies of traffic flow in Jos must take into consideration these different demands. These comments are true to some extent of the dimensions that describe school utilisation and service centres.

The emergence of dimensions describing the spatial interaction of people in particular areas of the city, especially Sabon Gari (new town) and north of the city (an extension of the Birnin), would suggest a continuation or an extrapolation of colonial patterns of urban growth in

Figure 6.4.7: The Service Component of Functional Organisation

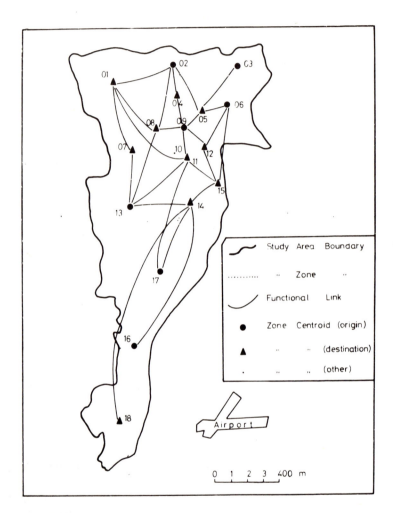

Nigeria into a post-colonial phase. An aim of Lord Lugard's indirect rule policy was to effect minimum intervention in the growth of the cultural values of various ethnic groups in Nigeria. Just as this policy possessed locational implications in the growth of cities in the country, one is tempted to suggest that it probably also had impressions on the movement behaviour of people. This situation is definitely not a desirable one, as locational and spatial behaviour militates against the cosmopolitanisation of urban centres. In the past, segregation based on ethnic origin is known to have been conducive to rioting and ethnic animosity (Plotnicov, 1967).

When the results of the analyses in the last two sections are combined, one sees principal components analysis as a useful technique for deciphering the nature of the form and function of an urban system. Explanations of the evolving dimensions suggest that there is some degree of structural overlap, as such explanations utilised extensively the author's knowledge and familiarisation with the city. The next section provides a more objective analysis of the nature of structure overlaps and interrelationships.

5. Formal and Functional Spatial Organisation

The principal hypothesis of the 'field' theoretic framework and what makes it of utmost significance for the present study is the assertion that patterns of interaction may be explained in terms of social forms or conditions which engender or might potentially engender interaction. In Jos, the formal spatial organisation as revealed through a principal components analysis of socio-economic and other characteristics represents such social forms or conditions, while the functional regions that resulted from an analysis of interaction represent the patterns of interaction. We are thus interested in the extent and amount of interrelationships that exist between these two sets of components, three of the formal and seven of the functional structure. Since the dimensions within each set are orthogonal the only relationships between the two sets are between each of the three components of formal and each of the seven components of functional association. This relationship is expressed in a correlation sub-matrix R_{12} and shown in Table 6.5.1. A canonical analysis of this sub-matrix produced three canonical variates with correlation coefficients of 0.903, 0.766 and 0.651. Although the canonical correlations are high, they are only significant at the 0.049, 0.231 and 0.326 levels respectively (Table 6.5.2). Consequently, much care is needed in subsequent interpretations and generalisations.

The first pair of canonical variates of the formal and functional

Table 6.5.1: Correlation Sub-matrix between the Dimensions of the Formal and Functional Organisation

		I	II	III
Function	I	0.316	−0.086	0.555
	II	0.032	−0.456	0.327
	III	0.276	0.029	−0.209
	IV	0.156	−0.027	−0.233
	V	−0.026	−0.345	0.060
	VI	0.018	−0.309	−0.527
	VII	0.618	0.096	−0.076

Table 6.5.2: Canonical Correlations

Canonical Variate	Corresponding Eigenvalues	Canonical Correlation	Wilk's Lambda	Chi-Square	Degrees of Freedom	Significance
I	0.815	0.903	0.044	32.781	21	0.049
II	0.587	0.766	0.234	15.674	12	0.231
III	0.424	0.651	0.576	5.800	5	0.326

Table 6.5.3: Coefficients for Canonical Variables

		I	II	III
Functional	1	0.662	0.310	0.068
	2	0.437	−0.122	0.598
	3	−0.193	0.385	0.092
	4	−0.226	0.220	0.148
	5	0.120	−0.133	0.489
	6	−0.517	0.006	0.605
	7	0.012	0.821	0.055
Formal	1	0.127	0.974	0.186
	2	−0.154	0.205	−0.967
	3	0.980	−0.094	−0.176

organisation share a total variance of 81.5 per cent between them and loads positively highly on the linkage patterns of the white-collar and blue-collar workers' dimensions of spatial interaction, and the 'migrancy space' of the formal organisation (see Table 6.5.3). This variate therefore indicates a strong relationship between patterns of interaction of wage-earners, many of whom are migrants, and their socio-economic characteristics. Since the pattern of canonical scores (Table 6.5.4 and Figure 6.5.1) shows that Jenta Extension (1), Sabon Gwong (6),

Table 6.5.4: Canonical Variate Scores

Code	Zones	Variate I		Variate II		Variate III	
		1st set	2nd set	1st set	2nd set	1st set	2nd set
1	Jenta Extension	1.106	0.483	0.538	0.855	−0.516	−0.322
2	Jenta	−0.473	−1.040	−0.011	−0.561	1.071	0.075
3	Dogon Dutse	−0.331	−0.075	0.083	0.109	0.586	−1.094
4	Kwararafa	−1.742	−1.935	0.022	−0.284	0.723	1.198
5	Bauchi Road	−0.328	0.160	0.817	0.500	−1.265	0.253
6	Sabon Gwong	1.911	1.800	−0.195	−0.232	2.002	2.528
7	Prison Area	−0.280	0.371	0.611	0.598	−0.935	0.532
8	Stadium	1.230	1.595	1.130	0.631	0.134	−0.339
9	Alkali	−1.070	−0.441	−0.193	0.067	1.488	0.937
10	Langtang-Panyam	1.228	0.735	0.828	1.045	−0.826	−0.736
11	CBD						
12	Market	−0.388	−0.309	−0.800	0.537	−0.723	0.509
13	Hill Station	−0.551	−0.314	−1.175	0.245	0.243	−0.496
14	Secretariat	0.771	0.610	−0.892	−0.956	0.387	−0.857
15	Gangare	−0.968	−0.912	1.702	0.431	−0.194	−0.471
16	Mountain View						
17	Reservation	0.400	0.527	−2.432	−3.196	−1.397	−0.769
18	Anglo Jos	−0.512	−0.256	−0.030	0.211	−0.778	−0.884

Stadium (8), Langtang-Panyam (10), Secretariat (14) and the Reservation (17) (zones already identified as containing mainly migrants) have positive scores, it might be concluded that this variate validates previous interpretation of the dimensions of form and function.

The second pair of canonical variates explains only 58.7 per cent of the variance between themselves, and the correlation coefficient of 0.77 is only significant at the 0.23 level. However this pair of variables loads strongly on the socio-economic space of formal organisation (Table 6.5.3) and the functional association of service activities. It has been observed elsewhere (Ayeni, 1974) that there is some sort of association between economic status of a resident in Jos and the particular centres he visits for service activities. It was noted, for instance, that while people of high economic status patronise the central business district (11), people of lower economic status patronise the Market (12). It seems, therefore, that this canonical variate has identified the nature and amount of this relationship. The patterns of scores (Table 6.5.4 and Figure 6.5.2) which contrast the Secretariat (14) and the Reservation (17) with the rest of the city also confirm such interpretations. It is noted that these two zones are occupied by people in the upper rung of the socio-economic structures.

The last pair of canonical variates explain between them only 42.4

Figure 6.5.1: Patterns of Scores on the First Canonical Variate

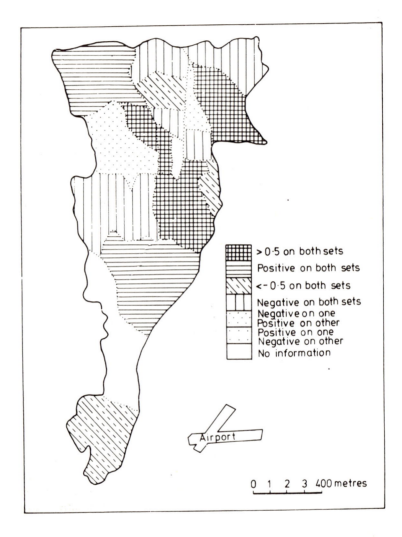

per cent of total variance. It has a high negative loading on the size dimension of formal spatial organisation, and high positive loadings on blue-collar workers, the north of the city and the educational components of functional organisation. It thus shows the sensitivity of spatial behaviour to the 'size' of zones of the urban system. The pattern of variate scores (Table 6.5.4 and Figure 6.5.3) shows that zones which are large in size are negatively associated with this pair of variates. For instance, the Prison Area (7), Jenta Extension (1), the Reservation (17) and Anglo Jos (18), which are physically large zones, have high negative scores. On the other hand, Jenta (2), Kwararafa (4), Sabon Gwong (6) and Alkali (9), though fairly small in size, have large populations, large numbers of people in the labour force and many children who go to school, and hence positive scores on the pair of variates (Table 6.5.4 and Figure 6.5.3). Furthermore, the positive loading of the socio-economic space dimension on this variate (0.186) could be seen as validating the influence of social and economic characteristics of households in generating interaction within an urban system.

The interpretation of the canonical variates confirms some of the interpretations of the previous two sections although at a higher level of abstraction and a higher degree of specificity. This indeed is the main contribution of the study. It was thus shown that wage-earners (the white-collar and blue-collar workers), most of whom are migrants, generate the most important patterns of interaction within the urban system. As in other parts of the world, the location of the places of work represents a critical aspect of the spatial and functional association of land uses. Similarly, it was shown that linkage patterns that result from the spatial behaviour of urban residents on the utilisation of urban service facilities reflect to a very significant degree the influence of the social status of the residents. This bias is probably a consequence of changing values and value systems of people undergoing processes of urbanisation. The continued coexistence of market places with modern central business districts represents some of the functions maintaining traditional, sometimes pre-industrial, values in the city. Finally, it is seen that while linkage associations would generally correlate positively with the socio-economic variables, the converse is true with the physical size variables of an urban form. It may therefore be argued that the analysis has revealed the interdependence among the formal and linkage dimensions of spatial organisation within the urban system of Jos. Consequently, it has produced an identification of those components of the city hitherto unknown or unrevealed. Inasmuch as these components represent general descriptions of the urban form and the processes

Figure 6.5.2: Patterns of Scores on the Second Canonical Variate

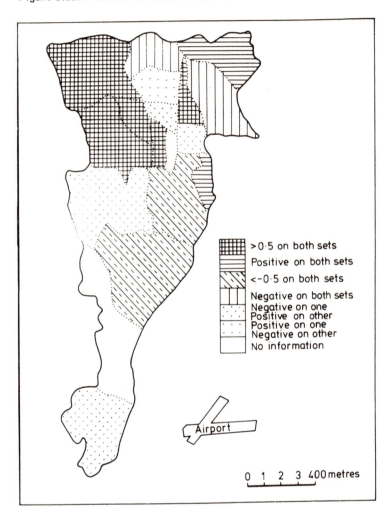

Figure 6.5.3: Patterns of Scores on the Third Canonical Variate

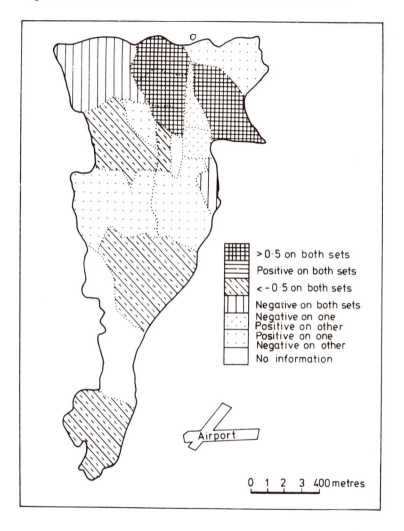

> 0·5 on both sets
Positive on both sets
< − 0·5 on both sets
Negative on both sets
Negative on one
Positive on other
Positive on one
Negative on other
No information

Airport

0 1 2 3 400 metres

therein, they can be made to bear on policy decisions that relate to arranging or rearranging the city.

6. Conclusion

The study of form and function is a fundamental research undertaking in geography. This is because it is possible to regard the functions of a system of interest as the processes that maintain the *status quo* of the phenomenon. Consequently, a study of form and function is indirectly a study of the interplay between patterns and processes. Therefore the flow of people and goods in an urban system is as much a process that generates urban spatial structure as a component of this structure. The present study has attempted to analyse some of the relationships between these two aspects of a city structure. It is possible that a synthesis of such relationships could provide alternative avenues for the development of models that recognise symbiotic relationships between patterns and processes of the urban spatial and social structure.

Field theory offers a powerful framework for the study of symbiosis that may exist between form and function, and the multivariate technique of canonical correlation offers a practical way of operationalising the field concept. When applied to an urban system, these analyses not only deepen our understanding of man's behaviour within the urban environment but also give a broader ecological perspective of spatial behaviour. Such understanding is necessary for making useful suggestions as to how man's innumerable problems in the city might be solved.

References

Anderson, T.W. 1958. *An Introduction to Multivariate Statistical Analysis.* New York: John Wiley

Ayeni, M.A.O. 1974. Predictive Modelling of Urban Spatial Structure: The Example of Jos, Benue-Plateau State of Nigeria. Ph.D. thesis, University of Ibadan, Nigeria

Ayeni, M.A.O. 1975. Some determinants of the propensity to interact in an urban system: A case study of Jos, Nigeria. *Nigerian Geographical Journal, 18*, 2, 111–19

Berry, B.J.L. 1966. Interdependency of flows and spatial structure: A general field theory formulation. In *Essays on Commodity Flows and the Spatial Structure of the Indian Economy.* Chicago: University of Chicago, Department of Geography, Research Paper No. 111

Bourne, L.S., and Murdie, R.A. 1972. Interrelationship of Social and Physical Space in the City: A Multivariate Analysis of Metropolitan Toronto. *The Canadian Geographer, 26*, 3 211–29

Cattel, R.B. 1952. *Factor Analysis: An Introduction and Manual for Psychologists and Social Scientists.* New York: Harper and Row

Clark, D. 1972. The Formal and Functional Structure of Wales. *The Annals of the Association of American Geographers, 63*, 1, 71–84

Cooley, W.W., and Lohnes P.R., 1971. *Multivariate Data Analysis.* New York: John Wiley

Fair, T.J.D. 1957. Regions for Planning in South Africa. *South Africa Geographical Journal, 39*, 26–50

Grigg, D. 1967. Regions, Models and Classes. In R.J. Chorley and P. Haggett, *Models in Geography.* London: Methuen, Chapter 12, pp. 461–510

Harman, H. 1960. *Factor Analysis.* Chicago: University of Chicago Press

Humphreys, G. 1965. The Journey to Work in Industrial South Wales. *Transactions, Institute of British Geographers,* No. 36

Lewin, K. 1951. *Field Theory in Social Science.* New York: Harper Torchbooks

Marble, D.F. 1959. Transport Inputs at Urban Residential Sites. *Papers and Proceedings, Regional Science Association, 5,* 253–66

Philbrick, A.K. 1959. Principles of Areal Functional Organization in Regional Human Geography. *Economic Geography, 33,* 299–336

Plotnicov, L. 1969. *Strangers to the City: The Urban Man in Jos.* Pittsburgh: Pittsburgh University Press

Ray, D.M. 1971. From Factorial to Canonical Ecology: The Spatial Interrelationships of Economic and Cultural Differences in Canada. *Economic Geography, 47,* 344–55

Rees, P.H. 1970. Concepts of Social Space: Toward an Urban Social Geography. In B.J.L. Berry and F.E. Horton (eds.), *Geographical Perspectives on Urban Systems.* Englewood Cliffs, New Jersey: Prentice-Hall

Rummell, R. 1970. *Applied Factors Analysis.* Evanston, Illinois: Northwestern University Press

Simpson, G.G. 1961. *Principles of Animal Taxonomy.* New York: Columbia University Press.

Symanski, R., and Newman, J.L. 1973. Formal, Functional and Nodal Regions: Three Fallacies. *The Professional Geographer, 25,* 4

Tatsuoka, M.M. 1971. *Multivariate Analysis Techniques for Educational and Psychological Research.* New York: John Wiley

Webber, M.M. 1964. The Urban Place and the Non-place Urban Realm. In M.M. Webber *et al.* (eds.), *Explorations into Urban Structure.* Philadelphia: University of Philadelphia Press

Wisemann, R. 1976. Interpretation of Factored Flow Data, A Comparison of two Traffic Systems. *The Professional Geographer, 28,* 2, 172–7

Part Two

SIMULATION TECHNIQUES IN URBAN ANALYSIS

7 SIMULATION MODELLING AND THE URBAN SYSTEM

1. Introduction

One of the outcomes of the methodological shift in geography resulting from the quantitative revolution was the need to unravel the web of interrelationships that exist between spatial patterns and processes. This goal found expression in quantitative analysis of point patterns (Rogers, 1969; Harvey, 1966; Dacey, 1964), line patterns (Kansky, 1963; Haggett and Chorley, 1969) and areal pattern (Bunge, 1966). Then came the realisation that pattern analysis does not usually give a one-to-one relationship between patterns and processes. Consequently geographers have been urged to analyse spatial processes (Harvey, 1969; Ackerman, 1963) in order to deduce the spatial patterns. The two approaches that evolved in this endeavour are the behavioural approach which focuses on decision-making at the individual level (Rushton, 1969; Pred, 1967, 1968) and process-pattern studies through mathematical formulation of the problem under investigation.

The impacts of these developments were felt most in human geography in general and urban geography in particular. To this end, geographers have had to quantitatively appraise and evaluate current theories and models in economics and other social sciences and much reliance has come to be placed on the allied fields of mathematics, engineering, operations research and systems analysis. This approach to a large extent is hypothetico-deductive as it involves, first, the definition of the problem and the variables of interest, their mathematical formulation in terms of hypotheses, which are then tested and compared with reality. Thus geography has fully embraced the methods of the experimental sciences through the use of models in the investigation of the systems of interest.

Modelling in urban analysis as well as in other sciences has traditionally followed two approaches generally described as analytical and simulation. Analytical approaches require the development of models whose solutions could be deduced by recourse to the analytical methods of mathematics. Consequently they require the necessary identification of the components of the system of interest as well as an unambiguous specification of relationships and equations. The models of Alonso and Wingo discussed earlier in this book are examples. Inasmuch as urban analysts face the insurmountable problem of identifying the complexity of relationships between the objects of the urban system, this approach, apart from its theoretical importance, is of limited use. On the other hand, simulation modelling recognises the inability of analysts to know and specify all the relationships and hence develop a series of approximating techniques towards finding solutions. Consequently, simulation modelling has been a field of intensive research in recent years. In this chapter, we shall dwell on issues regarding the definition of simulation modelling, its relevance to urban analysis and its link with the conceptualisation of the city as a system. In this way, we hope to bring into proper perspective the techniques and concepts described and operationalised in the rest of the book.

2. What is Simulation?

It was Kibel (1972) of the Association of American Geographers who defined a simulation as 'a cross between a portrait and a caricature of reality', It is, according to him, an attempt to present reality in a convincing manner for purposes of explanation, manipulation and analysis. According to him, every work of interaction, both fiction and non-fiction, is a form of simulation in the sense that it systematically selects certain aspects of life to illuminate and manipulate and that it collapses time so that the reader can experience hours, days, years and centuries in minutes.

A more technical definition of simulation is provided by Batty (1972) who argued that a simulation is a process of modelling in which solution to complex situations are reached without recourse to mathe-mathematics. Social systems are characterised by many variables which act or interact simultanously. Besides the fact that researchers find it difficult to specify unambiguously all these variables and identify their interactions, simulation methods produce good results as deductive solutions might be impossible. Even in cases where deductive solutions are theoretically possible, one is often faced with practical problems of data collection and synthesis so that the method of simulation is often considered the only feasible approach (Orcutt *et al.*, 1961).

The central feature of simulation modelling is that it signifies the scientific approach to the understanding of the system of interest. For instance, by continuously changing the variables in the investigation, it is possible not only to identify the more important ones but also to generate new knowledge about how the system works. In this way, simulation modelling provides an understanding framework as well as a way of monitoring and changing the system of interest. It is therefore

logical to argue that in a field as urban geography where there are complex variables, the actions of some of which can be counter-intuitive,
simulation modelling provides one technique of researching the
dynamics of systems.

A simulation model is a set of procedures which is governed by some
predetermined and consistent rules for handling and manipulating events
and information as they are introduced into the simulation. In the social
sciences, where the phenomenon of interest is made of very complex
entities and where social scientists are trained to use computers, it is
usual to associate simulation with computer modelling. However, not all
simulation models need be handled by the computer, although computer models have the added advantage of logicality of rules and clearly
stated theory (Kibel, 1972). Thus it is possible to classify simulation
models as computer simulation and gaming simulation.

Computer simulation models include the broad category of
computer-based models that in some way attempt to represent, re-
create or simulate the systems of interest through the use of mathematical equations or sets of equations. On the other hand, gaming
simulations are models which may or may not be computer-based,
but are driven in part or totally by human actions and decisions. Thus,
unlike computer models, human beings participate directly in the
process of simulation. Most of the simulation models discussed later on
in this book are computer-based because of the added advantage mentioned above.

A way of classifying simulation models is through their structural
complexity, expressed in the number of variables, their interrelationships and their levels of unpredictability. If we use the dichotomy that
a model may be simple or complex, predictable or unpredictable, four
classes of models are produced (see Table 7.2.1). Thus a model can be
simple and understood as in the case of an urban street pattern or simple
and unpredictable as in the voting behaviour of city-dwellers. On the
other hand, an understood system may be complex, e.g. the totality of
the urban spatial system (Kibel, 1972).

While a classification as above may provide insights into the nature
of sub-systems of an urban system and perhaps modelling problems, it
does not provide us with the numerous approaches which could be
utilised in modelling urban systems. One such approach is to focus
attention on whether the equations of our model are to be probabilistic
or deterministic and in what ways time is to be treated, whether in a
one-shot comparative static type, or whether it is dynamic. For instance,
if time is to be included explicitly in the model, then it is dynamic and

Table 7.2.1: A Classification of Simulation Models Based on Complexity and Predictability

		Structural Complexity	
		Simple	Complex
	Understood	A city street pattern	The journey to ¡work
Levels of Unpredictability			
	Unpredictable	Urban voting behaviour	The urban spatial system

Source: Kibel, 1972.

we may have to specify its treatment, whether as a continuous or discrete variable. When these sets of considerations are combined it is possible to provide six types of models. These are the deterministic comparative static model, the probabilistic comparative static model; dynamic, discrete time deterministic model; dynamic discrete time probabilistic; dynamic continuous deterministic and dynamic continuous time probabilistic models. Table 7.2.2 summarises these approaches. The major difference between a static and dynamic model is that the former explicitly incorporates time in its equations while any incorporation of time in the latter is at best implicit. If a model is dynamic and time is treated as discrete, difference equations are employed, while if time is treated as continuous, differential equations are used. If, however, the model's conceptualisation is probabilistic, stochastic difference and differential equations are used respectively.

The classification presented in Table 7.2.2 is a very ambitious one, as operational models so far developed in urban analysis are of the com-

Table 7.2.2: The Range of Urban Models

| | Static | Dynamic | |
		Discrete Time	Continuous Time
Deterministic	Comparative static, e.g. linear programming formulation of location models	Dynamic with difference equations	Dynamic with differential equations
Probabilistic	Monte Carlo simulation technique, e.g. Hagerstrand's model, Markov chain models	Dynamic with stochastic difference equations	Dynamic with stochastic differential equations

parative static type because the development of dynamic models is faced with problems of defining time in terms of leads and lags and finding the associated parameters. Furthermore, dynamic modelling requires the accumulation of a statistical set of data collected over a long period of time. As of now, the runs of statistics on which the society is based are too short for an unimpeachable analysis. None the less, researchers are approaching the development of dynamic models from two major perspectives. The first involves the introduction of change and change-producing forces into the formulation of comparative static models. For instance, the consideration of a potential mover class in residential location modelling is of this type (Wilson, 1970; Ayeni, 1975). The second approach introduces lags into comparative static models (Paelinck, 1970; Batty, 1972).

Most practical approaches to urban simulation modelling begin by recognising the complexities of the urban system, and then proceed to develop models of certain aspects of the city such as residential location or location of industrial activities. Models that deal with single aspects of the urban system shall be called partial models in this book while those that deal with two or more aspects shall be described as general models. While the above terminology will be for purposes of convenience, it also recognises the view that an urban area would be conceived as a system of interacting parts.

3. Systems Modelling in Urban Geography

Modern systems theory provides a means of conceptualising and understanding the objects of study. Such an understanding has proceeded through the use of terms and concepts such as feedback, homeostasis and control, entropy and methods of operations research. It has also been characteristic of various branches of knowledge to view the object of study as a system of interrelated components. In urban studies, Berry (1964) has shown how cities and groups of cities may be regarded as systems, while Brown (1969) has sought an understanding of urban land use in terms of cybernetics. At a more abstract level, Medvedkov (1967) has shown how the concept of entropy from systems analysis may be employed in the study of random and clustered aspects of settlement patterns, while Wilson (1970) demonstrates the use of these concepts in the development of models of urban and regional structure.

Although many of these developments have contributed immensely to the advancement of our understanding of the objects of study, they are not without problems. Sometimes the problem arises from over-generalisation of analogies without adequate attention to the fundamentals of the origin and use of concepts, as in the use of entropy by Medvedkov (op. cit.) or Brown's (op. cit.) verbal description (or prescription?) of the use of cybernetics in studying land use in cities. At other times we have relied on broad similarities in describing entities as systems rather than defining from first principles (Berry, 1964). The greatest shortcoming of these developments lies in the inability of many students and researchers to relate the conceptualisation of their object of study as a system to the use of the systems method of analysis and to the articulation of the nature of their 'system'.

The present section attempts to correct some of these failures, using the city as an example. First we try to show from first principles, how a city constitutes a well-defined system whose components are more successfully modelled within a system framework such that their inter-actions become the variables of investigation. Second, we try to show that systems analysis provides requisite tools in the concept of entropy, for the study of urban systems 'in terms of organizing concept and the opportunity to develop a unique group of underlying principles' (Barrows, 1923, pp. 3 and 9).

The most well-known definition of a system is that given by Hall and Fagen (1956). According to them, a system is 'a set of objects, together with relationships between the objects and between their attributes'. None the less, Rapoport's recent description of a system seems not only to have extended the original definition but also to have brought it into a new conceptual framework for analytical and predictive purposes. According to him, a system is 'a *portion of the real world* which at a given time can be characterized by a given *state* together with a set of *rules and laws* that permit the *deduction* of future states from partial information' (Rapoport, 1970; my emphasis).

Hall and Fagen's definition emphasises objects, attributes and relationships. The objects are the components of the system; the attri-butes are their properties whilst the relationships represent the mecha-nisms that link the various components and the attributes. In Rapoport's terminology, this system can be *a portion of the real world* such as the city which is the focus of the present study. The functional and spatial characteristics of this city at a point in time, represent the state of the system, while the various hypotheses posited to facilitate an under-standing of its operations may be interpreted as the rules and laws that will enable deductions to be made about the future states of the system.

Conceptualising the city or a group of cities as a system therefore requires that we apply the whole battery of systems analytical tools to our investigation. Such conceptualisation is, however, not new in the literature. Berry (1964), for example, examining the city structure, through the spatial organisation of retailing and urban population density patterns, asserts that a city is a 'system within a system of cities'. This conceptualisation has further been extended by Brown (1969), who sees cybernetics, the science of control in animals and machines, as highly applicable to urban land use, which according to him is a product of a negative feedback that is always tending to bring the system into equilibrium.

Our approach in this book is therefore to characterise the city as a system in the terms defined above, and to go further to identify what constitutes objects, attributes, relationships, the state, rules and laws of this system. The point is that if a city must be viewed as a system, there is a need for precise and explicit definitions of pertinent concepts. Once this is achieved, it is possible to introduce such ideas as 'energy', 'temperature', 'forces' and 'external and internal co-ordinates' into our conceptualisation. In this way, we shall be at the threshold of utilising a well-developed body of ideas and techniques in analysing and understanding social systems in general and urban systems in particular (Wilson, 1970, p. 121).

In order to employ some of these ideas and techniques, one needs to identify what the major components of the city system are. One way of doing this is to use Wilson's categorisation of these components into 'objects, activities, physical infrastructure, land and policy' (Wilson, 1969). The 'objects' comprise the population, the goods and the vehicles in the city; activities include those of residing, production of goods and services and trip-making for the consumption of these goods and services. Infrastructure, on the other hand, comprises not only buildings (houses, schools, stores, factories and shops) but also roads, parking spaces, pipes, electric and telecommunication lines. Land refers to areas under different land uses while policy refers to the various decision-making agencies (public or private), which affect the volume of these other aspects of the city system (see Table 7.3.1).

The entities defined above in Table 7.3.1 form the first steps in the building of sub-systems of interest within the city. Our approach is to consider these entities and amalgamate them into sub-systems that lead most to a fuller understanding of urban functional organisation and spatial structure. Such sub-systems should include the residential, which comprises population as its object, buildings as its infrastructure and residing as its activity; the workplace, which comprises the production of goods and services as its activity, factories, schools and offices as its infrastructure. To these we may add an economic sub-system which

Table 7.3.1: The Components of a Metropolitan System

Objects	Activities	Physical Infrastructure	Land	Policy
Population Goods	Residing Production of goods and services	Buildings Houses Schools Factories Offices	Land in different uses	Decisions
Services	Services			Goals
Vehicles	Jobs Making trips Shopping Education	Shops Transport facilities Roads, Railway lines Airports Ports, etc.		Plans

Source: Wilson (1969).

comprises shops and markets as infrastructure and the distribution and consumption of goods as the activity; and a transportation sub-system. Figure 7.3.1 shows these major sub-systems and underscores the point that the transport and infrastructural sub-systems provide the frame over which the other sub-systems rest.

The city as a system also involves the definition of what are the interactions, as these are responsible for its social, economic and spatial structure. The interactions that determine the economic structure, are the monetary and other financial transactions while the social structure may be seen as determined by flows of information and ideas. The spatial structure, on the other hand, is dependent on spatial interaction which has its expression in the form of all aspects of human spatial behaviour as the journeys to work, services, schools and recreational centres. The volume and direction of these physical trips represent the relationships between the objects of the city system.

Conceptualising the city as a system possesses two major advantages. First, since we are forced to look at an interacting whole as distinct from individual parts, we are constrained to define explicitly our objects and interactions, and produce classifications of these where necessary, into sub-systems that may be further studied in depth. Such an approach provides new insights into old problems and leads to greater precision of findings (Mabogunje, 1969).

Second, the systems approach provides us with tools for the analysis

Figure 7.3.1: A View of the City as a System

Environment (national city system)

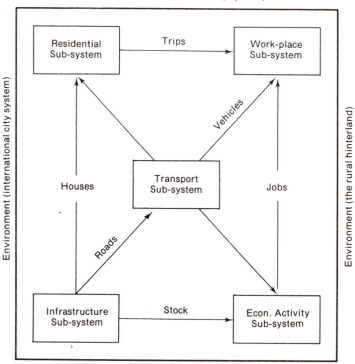

Environment (regional city system)

of urban systems, which is particularly concerned with events in both spatial and temporal dimensions. Provided our definitions are precise, the resolution of these dimensions is facilitated by the use of systems analytic techniques which provide a conceptualisation of change in a way that involves a continuous evaluation of the significance of the entities that constitute the processes of change. The concept of entropy is particularly useful in this respect. First, it could be used to derive process-oriented planning models of urban spatial structure by viewing spatial interaction as processes that generate spatial patterns as done by Kain (1962) for residential location using the interaction mechanism of the journey to work. This is in contrast to many classical models (the concentric, the sector and the multiple-nuclei models) which were derived from considerations of patterns without due appreciation of the symbiotic relationship between processes and patterns. Furthermore, dynamic modelling of urban spatial structure may be tied to this concept as related to the changes that take place in the transactions of energy between various parts of a system (Wilson, 1970, pp. 112–24). In such a case, the functional relationship between 'internal' and 'external' co-ordinates of the social system will have to be identified in terms of its entropy.

4. Urban Problems and Simulation Modelling

The twentieth century has produced urban centres whose important characteristics involve change. Such changes include both growth of population and the areal extent of the cities. The salient characteristics of these changes are the phenomenal rate at which they occur. Consequently, all over the world, city planners are faced with the problem of maintaining a rational balance between man, his agents and the urban environment. Broadly defined, the major problem of the city may be said to be that of liveability, which includes not only the problems created by environmental stress and deterioration, but also those created by the movement of people and the circulation of goods on the transportation networks.

The problem of environmental deterioration arises because the optimal range of environmental conditions which embraces the web of interrelationships between man and the natural surrounding has long been reached and surpassed. Consequently, the problem of environmental deterioration comes in two forms. The first results from the many man-made elements which are directly poisonous or harmful. This class includes the pollution of an area as a result of industrial production, scientific investigation and transportation, which fill the air with such gases as carbon monoxide, sulphur oxides, hydrocarbons, nitrogen oxides, etc. The second results from the rapid changes that take place between the man-made and the natural ecosystem. These changes are characterised by the rapid rate of water usage and water disposal, the impact of man in rapidly clearing a once wooded land to provide habitation for the ever-increasing population of the cities. To this list, one would add the problem of solid waste or garbage disposal from residential houses as well as commercial, institutional and industrial sources. The need for an efficient method of removal of this waste need not be emphasised as their accumulation creates not only filthy but also unhealthy environments.

The problem created with the rapid conversion of wooded land into areas for habitation arises when little thought is placed on man's need in terms of the creation of open spaces, green belts and the use of urban

PERCEPTION (margin annotation)

fringe areas for settlements. The problem is compounded by the growth of ghettos and squatter settlements where basic urban facilities such as water, electricity and even roads might be inadequate or absent. Even when basic urban facilities are available, the rather high rate of population increase leads to over-utilisation of existing facilities, overcrowding and environmental deterioration.

Circulation within the city is as important as that between the city and its tributary area. Circulation involves both the day-to-day movements of people on work or service trips as well as pleasure trips. The intra-city movement of goods and services contributes another important component of circulation. The crucial issue is the ease with which people, goods and services interact. This is a critical element of the liveability of a city as the more difficult interaction is, the more inefficient is the urban spatial system and the greater the diseconomies of city size. Of course, the problem of easy circulation cannot be divorced from that of the spatial organisation of land uses, as urban land uses are as much a generator as an attractor of urban trips. It is therefore necessary for those concerned with the issue of liveability to realise this critical relationship.

While the issue of liveability is crucial to the twentieth-century urban centre, there are other problems which need to be tackled, as they relate closely to liveability. Such include the problem of the inability of some cities to adequately cater for its inhabitants through the provision of essential services, and the problem of urban management. Many urban centres have been faced with problems of financing both the city administration and the provision of essential services because of a declining tax base arising in part from suburbanisation of both urban activities and urban labour force. The city in any part of the world is therefore forced to cater for more people than maintain it. In very many situations, it is the environment which bears the brunt of the actions of city governments and the inhabitants.

It must be emphasised that the interrelationships between the above components of the contemporary problems of our urban centres are complex and little understood. Attempts to study or solve particular problems may fail because of the lack of consideration of the sets of interactions between that problem and many related ones. It is really in this way that the characterisation of a city as a system with interacting set of sub-systems could be beneficial. Thus one might, as a first step, focus on the understanding of particular sub-systems which might subsequently be combined to produce a true picture of the urban spatial structure. The point being made is that the study of sub-systems *per se* is a barren exercise, as the whole is more than the sum of the parts.

There are now numerous models of the various sub-systems of the urban spatial structure, just as there are models dealing with the total spatial structure. These models in general have achieved a number of successes. First they have been used in the need to understand the mechanisms which govern the structure and behaviour of urban systems within a hypothetico-deductive framework, as mentioned above. The emerging result is a synthesis of major variables to be used in the subsequent development of theory. Second, and more important, is the increasing use of models in predicting outcomes of policies and decisions. Such a development is based on the notion that any meaningful planning must be based on an evaluation of possible alternative paths of growth. Consequently, these models are playing significant roles in the decision-making aspects of structure planning, whereby emphasis is on the distribution of activities such as population, patterns of land use and the interactions between them, as well as the network of communications and the system of utility services.

Understanding of systems of interest constitutes an important stage in the monitoring and planning process. Simulation models offer a valuable tool in all these fields as they generally present a wider range of solutions which constitute valuable alternatives to the planning decision-making process. They could also contribute avenues for exploring new concepts of the future of mankind.

Urban modelling no doubt has been of immense use in the planning field and in fact has effected changes in the planning framework of many countries, in particular Britain and America. None the less it must be appreciated that a model of an urban system, or any system whatsoever, is a direct reflection of its underlying theory so that any model of society, to be useful, must be based on an appropriate theory of the society. Consequently, while the construction of urban models might be tailored to meet the needs of the society in solving urban problems, at the same time such endeavours must appreciate the need to incorporate theory. The extent to which current models satisfy these ambitions is difficult to define, but it is safe to say that much has to be done in integrating theory and practice. The models discussed in subsequent chapters strive to achieve such balance.

5. Conclusion

The aim of urban analysis is not to produce a set of tools which is at best technocratic and at worst barren and devoid of any meaningful applications. Simulation models become technocratic when they are not based on acceptable theories and concepts in the literature but rather become heuristic devices for achieving some type of aims. On the other hand, simulation modelling becomes a barren exercise or an exercise in applied mathematics and computation when its utility cannot be easily demonstrated. The utility of urban models can be justified as follows: first, there is a pedagogic role as a model is a useful teaching device, especially of the mechanisms of the urban spatial structure. Second, as a technique of understanding the urban system, its role is probably unsurpassed as it uses the experimental approaches of the natural and many social sciences. Third, as an evaluative device for policies and decisions on the growth and development of urban centres, simulation modelling is an invaluable tool for discovering and analysing the characteristics of the 'city of the future'.

Urban simulation modelling is necessarily tied to the notion of a city as a system in order to achieve these aims. Such a realisation enables us to focus our research interests on the city as a whole as well as on the interacting parts of this city. Provided that our terms and concepts are unambiguously defined, the methods of systems analysis constitute a 'useful arsenal' for probing into the mechanisms of the urban spatial structure. In subsequent chapters, a number of different approaches to urban modelling will be discussed in addition to their relative merits. It is obvious that even when models cannot solve all the problems, they can provide valuable answers to some of them.

References

Ackerman, E.A. 1963. Where is a Research Frontier? *Annals, Association of American Geographers, 53*, 429–40

Ayeni, M.A.O. 1975. A Predictive Model of Urban Stock and Activity: 1: Theoretical Considerations, *Environment and Planning A, 7*, 8, 965–79

Barrows, H.H. 1923. Geography as Human Ecology. *Annals, Association of American Geographers, 13*, 1–14

Batty, M. 1972. Dynamic Simulation of Urban System. In A.G. Wilson (ed.), *London Papers in Regional Science*, Vol. 3. London: Pion, pp. 44–82

Berry, B.J.L. 1964. Cities as Systems within Systems of Cities. *Papers Regional Science Association, 13*, 147–63

Brown, R.K. 1969. City Cybernetics. *Land Economics, 45*, 406–16

Bunge, W. 1966. *Theoretical Geography.* Lund Series in Geography, Series C, No. 1, Gleerup

Dacey, M.F. 1964. Two Dimensional Random Point Patterns: A Review and an Interpretation. *Papers Regional Science Association, 13*, 41–55

Haggett, P., and Chorley, R.J., 1969. *Network Analysis in Geography.* London: Arnold

Hall, A.D., and Fagen, R.E. 1956. Definition of a System. *General Systems Yearbook, 1,* 18–27

Harvey, D. 1966. Geographical Processes and Point Patterns: Testing Models of Diffusion by Quadrat Sampling. *Transactions, Institute of British Geographers, 40,* 81–95

Harvey, D. 1969. *Explanation in Geography.* London: Arnold

Kain, J.F. 1962. The Journey to Work as a Determinant of Residential Location. *Papers Regional Science Association, 9,* 137–60

Kansky, L.J. 1964. *Structure of Transportation Networks.* Chicago: University of Chicago, Department of Geography Research Paper, No. 84

Kibel, B.M. 1972. *Simulation of the Urban Environment.* Commission on College Geography, Technical Paper No. 5. Washington D.C.: Association of American Geographers

Mabogunje, A.L. 1969. Systems Approach to a Theory of Rural Urban Migration. *Geographical Analysis, 1,* 1–18

Medvedkov, Y.V. 1966. The Concept of Entropy in Settlement Pattern Analysis. *Papers Regional Science Association, 18,* 165–88

Orcutt, G.H., Greenberger, M., Korbel, J., and Revlin, A.M., 1961. *Micro-analysis of Socioeconomic Systems: A Simulation Study.* New York: Harper and Row

Paelinck, J. 1970. Dynamic Urban Growth Models. *Papers Regional Science Association, 24,* 25–37

Pred, A. 1967. *Behaviour and Location.* Part 1, Lund Series in Geography, Series B, No. 27. Lund, Gleerup

Pred, A. 1969. *Behaviour and Location.* Part 2, Lund Series in Geography, Series B, No. 29. Lund, Gleerup

Rapoport, A. 1970. Modern Systems Theory–An Outlook for Coping with Change. *General Systems Yearbook,* 15–25

Rogers, A. 1969. Quadrat Analysis and Urban Dispersion. 1. Theoretical Techniques. *Environment and Planning, 1,* 47–80

Rushton, G. 1969. Analysis of Spatial Behaviour by Revealed Space Preference. *Annals Association of American Geographers, 59,* 393

Wilson, A.G. 1969. Forecasting Planning. *Urban Studies, 6,* 348–69

Wilson, A.G. 1970. *Entropy in Urban and Regional Modelling.* London: Pion

8 PROBABILITY MODELS OF URBAN ANALYSIS

1. Introduction

Stochastic models incorporate some probabilistic notions in their formulation. In the social sciences in general and geography in particular, one is often faced with the philosophical implications of the role of chance in human decision and behaviour. Consequently, the researcher is wary of the probabilistic approach because it suggests that one might be 'regarding the earth's surface as governed by the mechanisms of a roulette wheel and its development as a permanent floating crap game' (Curry, 1966). None the less, most researchers withdraw from this philosophic position but subscribe to the view that observable results of location decision and action appear to the observer as though they are governed by probabilistic laws (Dacey, 1975).

The element of chance enters our studies therefore principally as a surrogate for the aspects of behaviour that we cannot yet incorporate into our models or as a means by which we discriminate the effects of alternative decisions. In this way, stochastic models can effectively be used as a process model to understand reality. Consequently, when we conceptualise the urban system in terms of a Monte Carlo procedure, we accept our inadequate knowledge of the processes at hand and seek to unravel these in a series of experimentation. Thus the development of stochastic models, whatever the philosophical bases, has definite pedagogic uses; and it is these that recommend their study and analysis. In this chapter, we shall look at two simple stochastic models, the Monte Carlo and Markov chain models, that serve a wide range of uses in urban analysis. To this end, we shall focus not only on the techniques involved but also on the contributions thay make to understanding.

2. The Monte Carlo Approach to Simulation Modelling

The Monte Carlo approach to simulation had been described by Hägerstrand (1965) as

> a game of the dice in which the gaming table represents a part of the earth's surface, the pieces represent individuals living in the area, and the rules of the game constitute the particular factors which we want to study in operation.

The technique can therefore be seen as one that possesses not only

179

pedagogical uses but also one that creates increased understanding of the phenomena of investigation as the emphasis of this definition is on the study of the particular factors that give rise to our systems of interest. The complexity and the amount of intercorrelation and inter-relatedness of these factors constitute crucial variables of the processes of the game. In this context, Morrill's definition that the technique is 'a stochastic model of an experimental procedure for the mathematical evaluation where no unique mathematical solution is possible' (Morrill, 1965) provides the *raison d'être* for their study.

The important characteristic of the Monte Carlo method is the decision process which fundamentally is stochastic, i.e. based on the throw of dice or a set of random numbers from random number tables or generated by the computer. Consequently, new situations or states of the phenomenon of interest are outcomes of a selection process that is probabilistic in operation.

Monte Carlo simulation, according to Ackoff (1962) has four main uses. It can be used to determine the values of control variables and to test the effects of changes in probability values and parameters. Third, a simulation model can be made to trace the trajectory of dynamic systems while parameters could be easily estimated and sensitivity analysis carried out. Finally, and probably more importantly, it can be used to experiment with different inputs and parameters in addition to the examination of the effects of certain constraints. In these ways, Monte Carlo models will not only provide the understanding but may also provide means of studying the 'city of the future'.

The Monte Carlo technique has very wide applications in the physical sciences and engineering, but its usage was imported into geography through the pioneering studies of Hägerstrand on diffusion processes (Hägerstrand, 1965). The earliest intrusion into urban modelling were due to the large-scale urban models developed by Chapin and his colleagues at the University of North Carolina whereby the decision to build on vacant land was conceived in probabilistic terms (Donelly *et al.*, 1964). Morrill utilised the technique in a study of Seattle and focused on the development of black ghettos (Morrill, 1965). In another study, he applied a refinement of these ideas to the growth and spread of settlements in Sweden (Morrill, 1965a); while Colenutt (1970) describes an application of the technique to the development of roadside land uses, particularly the diffusion of bill-boards in urban centres.

Several criticisms might be levelled against Monte Carlo methods. First, it is difficult to derive independently the probability surface for the allocation process, as theoretically this derivation should be based on some empirical surfaces. In practice, authors have used the actual pattern to derive these probabilities, which are subsequently used in replicating observed patterns. In addition, there is a more difficult problem of conceptualising the probability surfaces in a dynamic framework. This is because with successive iterations of the model, these probability surfaces should change. Authors have either neglected the problem or introduced subjective rules which no doubt help in unravelling some of the hidden structures of the processes. Although one cannot but agree with Colenutt (1970) that Monte Carlo models are not truly time-orientated, as they merely simulate spatial patterns that result from processes implicitly assumed to operate over time, the Monte Carlo technique does possess intrinsic qualities that make them require examination.

(i) Procedures in the Monte Carlo Technique

The steps involved in the use of the Monte Carlo technique may be carried out manually or by the computer. The computer has the added advantage of speed, absence of human error and the fact that it can produce many runs of the same problem, and thus provide the opportunity to compute means and standard deviations. This latter aspect becomes an advantage when we bear in mind that since we assume a stochastic process through the use of dice or a random number table, any one run of the simulation is just one of many possible outcomes if the processes are repeated over and over again.

The steps involved in using a Monte Carlo technique consist of:

(i) the formulation of a set of possible hypotheses on the factors governing the system of interest;
(ii) the construction of a matrix of probabilities from theoretical considerations about the system of interest;
(iii) the allocation procedure using both the probability matrix and a random number table.

The formulation of hypotheses about the systems of interest is perhaps the most important single aspect of the simulation process. This is so because the set of hypotheses we generate must emanate from some theoretical considerations concerning the nature of our system. For instance, if we want to simulate residential location within the city we might begin by examining the postulates of micro-economic residential location theory which generally emphasises the cost of the journey to work *vis-à-vis* the cost of housing and the cost of other composite goods.

The construction of a probability surface should be derived directly from the same set of theoretical considerations, although surrogates are often used. For instance, Hägerstrand argued that the network of social interaction, measured by telephone traffic (or other measures of spatial interaction) is a useful surrogate for defining the processes of innovation diffusion. In the case of intra-city residential location, it might be argued that this could be based on the benefits derivable from locating on particular sites within the city, or on accessibility to jobs and other urban amenities.

It is also important in using the Monte Carlo technique to partition the city into sub-areas. This could be done in a number of ways, e.g. by using wards, enumeration areas or other administrative divisions and by using equal areal divisions. The use of political divisions suffers from the disadvantages introduced by varying shapes and sizes, while equal areal divisions are purely arbitrary and difficult to transfer from map into reality. To the extent that many methods for testing the goodness of fit of Monte Carlo simulation models depend on the use of quadrats, squares or hexagons are generally used. In theory, the hexagon is preferred, although the square is more convenient to handle.

Let us illustrate the the principles and procedures involved by a hypothetical example simulating population growth in a city divided into fifteen square cells. We know the distribution of population densities in most urban systems follows the exponential law given by Clark (1951) as

$$d_x = d_0 \exp(-bx) \tag{1}$$

where d_x is the population density at distance x from the city centre, d_0 is the city centre population density, and b is the density gradient. This equation is basically an empirical formula whose theoretical explanation has been difficult to give. However, let us assume it arises from the rent gradient in the city and for our hypothetical case let this gradient be given as in Table 8.2.1.

The construction of a probability matrix using the hypothetical rent gradient is a two-stage process which involves, first, the allocation of

Table 8.2.1: A Hypothetical Rent Gradient

Distance from Centre in km	0	1	2	3	4
Rent in Naira	200	74	27	10	4

scores to each cell of the urban system on the basis of the rent gradient and, secondly, the conversion of the scores into a probability matrix. The method of awarding scores to cells could be the point score method which involves using the hypothesis(es) posited to explain growth. In our hypothetical city and using Table 8.2.1 above, the highest value of 200 is awarded to the central zone while the adjacent sets of zones receive 74, etc. Table 8.2.2 summarises the procedure.

Table 8.2.2: Point Score Matrix

	1	2	3	4	5
A	10	27	74	27	10
B	27	74	200	74	27
C	10	27	74	27	10

If we now add all the elements of the points score matrix and then divide each element by the total, we shall have constructed a growth probability matrix. Now let each element of Table 8.2.2 be S_{ij}, then

$$S = \sum_{i=1}^{n} \sum_{j=1}^{m} S_{ij} \tag{2}$$

and

$$P_{ij} = \frac{S_{ij}}{S} \quad i = 1, \ldots, n; \; j = 1, \ldots, m. \tag{3}$$

We note that

$$\sum_{i=1}^{n} \sum_{j=1}^{m} P_{ij} = 1.0 \tag{4}$$

where n and m are the dimensions of the growth matrix. These results are given in Table 8.2.3.

Table 8.2.3: A Growth Probability Matrix

	1	2	3	4	5
A	0.0143	0.0387	0.1060	0.0387	0.0143
B	0.0387	0.1060	0.2865	0.1060	0.0387
C	0.0143	0.0387	0.1060	0.0387	0.0143

Such a probability matrix described above has all the characteristics of a mean information field (MIF) as described by Hägerstrand (1965). This is not surprising since conceptually we are operating on the same plane. In the operation of our simulation, if differs from the mean information field of Hägerstrand in the sense that it is fixed on the urban landscape, while Hägerstrand's MIF is moved from one origin of the diffusion process to another. Of course, it is possible to see the probability matrix being used as an MIF when the focus is on the diffusion of ideas, innovations etc., within the city.

The idea of using the probability matrix like the MIF of Hägerstrand in urban analysis could be worthwhile, as studies have shown that urban areas are not necessarily monocentric but rather polycentric, as shown by Harris and Ullman (1945) for the American city or by Mabogunje for cities in developing countries (Mabogunje, 1968). In the latter case there are at least two centres, one a traditional centre which served as the preindustrial core of the city and the other a modern centre that emerged during the colonial period.

It is usual to convert the probability surface above into random number fields for the allocation process. This is done again in a two-stage process that involves neglecting the decimal signs and then making successive cumulations for rows beginning with the first row and moving from left to right. Let the cell elements of our probability matrix after we have neglected the decimal points be denoted by r_{ij}, then each element of the random number matrix q_{ij} is given by

$$q_{ij} = \sum_{i=1}^{n} \sum_{j=1}^{m} r_{ij} \tag{5}$$

Thus for the first cell of the first row $q_{11} = r_{11}$ while for the fifth cell of the second row it is

$$q_{25} = \sum_{j=1}^{5} r_{1j} + \sum_{j=1}^{5} r_{2j} \tag{6}$$

The resulting table is given in 8.2.4. Note that the grand summation, represented by the fifth element of the third row is 9,999. This is as expected, since our table is simply a two-dimensional cummulative table. The figures in each cell therefore are upward limiting numbers for the conversion of the table into a random number field.

Table 8.2.4: Upward Limiting Numbers of a Random Number Field

	1	2	3	4	5
A	143	530	1,590	1,977	2,120
B	2,507	3,567	6,432	7,492	7,879
C	8,022	8,409	9,469	9,856	9,999

It is now an easy matter to convert Table 8.2.4 into a random number field that specifies the range of values of the numbers to be used in allocating factors of growth. This is done by specifying the lowest and highest values in each cell. For instance, the first cell would have the values 0000–0143 while the second has 0144–0530 and so on. Table 8.2.5 summarises this procedure.

Table 8.2.5: The Random Number Field

	1	2	3	4	5
A	0000–0143	0144–0530	0531–1590	1591–1977	1978–2120
B	2121–2507	2508–3567	3568–6432	6433–7492	7493–7879
C	7880–8022	8023–8409	8410–9469	9470–9856	9857–9999

At this stage we are in a position to perform our simulation using the Monte Carlo approach. Basically this involves three things. First, we must know how many items we want to allocate. This could be an exogenous input into our model. Second, we must know how to use a standard random number table and, third, how to use this in conjunction with our random number matrix. Let us assume that for our city, there are 1,500 people made up of 150 households. It would be reasonable to use households as the basis of our allocation and we would have to allocate only 150 households instead of 1,500 people. This takes considerable time besides the fact that it is logical to expect that people live in households rather than as single individuals in a city.

Our experiment is simple enough to be carried out manually. The procedure for allocating houses is simply one of comparing our random number field with that generated by a computer or made available in a statistical table. Let us illustrate by using the random number table in Lindley and Miller (1968, p. 12). Using the first four columns as our four-digit number system, the allocation procedure is to tally for each

Table 8.2.6: Allocation of the First Fifty Households

	2	5	4	2
1	3	18	4	2
1		4	4	

Table 8.2.7: Allocation of the First One Hundred Households

2	3	11	5	2
2	7	36	6	6
1		9	8	2

Table 8.2.8: Final Outcome of the Experiment

3	9	13	6	3
5	12	46	13	10
1	1	16	10	2

cell the number of times any number between the upper and lower limits of each of the cells comes up. At every tallying, it is deemed that that cell has received a household. In this way, the first fifty households are as allocated in Table 8.2.6, while Table 8.2.7 shows the allocation of the first one hundred households; and Table 8.2.8 the final outcome of the simulation.

The sequential description of the steps involved illustrate a number of points, some of which are often taken as assumptions. First we are able to see that if the experiment has been performed by many students using different cross-sections of the random number table, different answers would emerge, but they would not be statistically significantly different. The same conclusion will be true if the experiment has been done by one man using different cross-sections of the table. It might be worth while for students to try this out and compare results.

Second, the procedure is flexible as it gives an opportunity of introducing density constraints on any of the zones. These constraints may arise as a result of the factors of physical features, e.g. the presence of a lake or a mountain or it may be a result of zoning regulations. Whatever these are, they are barriers in the spread or growth of the city. It is even possible to characterise them by types such as permanent or temporary; reflecting or absorbing. Thus while a lake may be a permanent and absorbing barrier, it is conceivable to see an area liable to flooding as a temporary barrier (Abler, Adams, and Gould, 1972).

As a final step, it is desirable to test the results of our simulation experiment to ensure whether the hypothesis posited are sufficient or whether more have to be added if the posited hypothesis fail to replicate reality. This is the experimental use of a simulation technique. Tests that could be used are of various forms. In particular the chi-square test or the more powerful Kolmogorov-Smirnov two-sample test can be used on the cell by cell populations. So also are correlation and regression methods, which not only tell the degree of correspondence between observed and predicted populations but also could be made to identify possible growth hypotheses through an examination of residuals from the analysis. The chi-square test, on the other hand, merely compares the cell frequencies with observed ones. It could be less effective where some frequencies are too few. In such cases, the Kolmogorov-Smirnov test should be preferred, as it is not only more powerful but also preserves the property of relative location of individual cell values (i.e. the appropriate distance decay characteristic), as well as ensuring that the hierachy of the two sets of observations is maintained (Morrill, 1965).

3. A Monte Carlo Simulation of Urban Development

The example described below was carried out by the author in 1969 (Ayeni, 1970). The aim of the experiment was to be led through the Monte Carlo technique to discover which factors had in recent years affected the pattern of town expansion; and which might help to adumbrate the future patterns of growth. The area of study was Ikere-Ekiti, a town with a population of 107,000 in 1963. It lies some 30 kilometres north of Akure, the capital of Ondo State, Nigeria. By all standards the town is rather a small one and its choice at that time for study was due partly to this small size and the ease with which relevant information for the simulation experiment could be assembled.

Ikere-Ekiti belongs to that characterisation of many Nigerian towns as agro-towns, in the sense that most or a large percentage of the inhabitants are engaged in agricultural activities while secondary and tertiary jobs are few. Consequently, the land use is simple as residential activity covers about 80 per cent of all built-up land while institutional and commercial land uses are next important. The land-use characteristics in 1969 are as given in Figure 8.3.1.

The study is made possible by the availability of town plans and aerial photographs for 1959. The town plan on scale 1:4800 is detailed enough to show all houses, roads and other infrastructure at that time. Consequently it was possible to divide the areas occupied by the town

Figure 8.3.1: Land-use Activities in Ikere-Ekiti, 1969

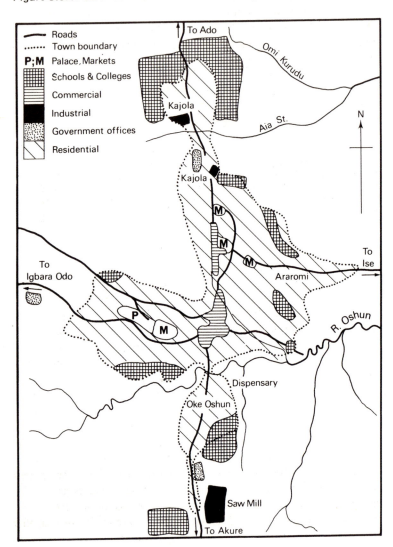

into 15 by 11 squares of 0.16 square kilometres each. From this, the number of houses were counted and this constituted the data base for the simulation experiment. To these we added the information on the number of houses built and their location between 1959 and 1969 to derive the state of the system for 1969.

Table 8.3.1: Some Factors Affecting the Location of Houses in Ikere-Ekiti, 1969

	Factors	Number	Percentage
1	Location of family land	80	61.07
2	Exhaustion of building plots on family land	20	15.27
3	Nearness to raods plus economic rent	12	9.16
4	Nearness to urban facilities, e.g. schools	5	3.82
5	Nearness to workplace	0	0.00
6	Good land and desirable site	4	3.05
7	Others, amenities, etc.	10	7.63
Total		131	100.00

Source: Ayeni (1970).

Our aim is to study the processes of urban development through the spatial distribution and growth of houses in the town. Consequently, in an earlier part of the research we tried to find what the people considered as the determinants of the location of their houses. The response is as shown in Table 8.3.1 below. It emerges from this table that the important factors of residential area selection are socio-cultural rather than economic. For instance, about 61 per cent of landlords claimed that the location of family land is the major determinant while another 15 per cent who were not living on family land did so because there were no available plots for them. In the Nigerian context in general and the Yoruba cities (of which this is one), much urban development in recent years has been by what has been described as growth by fission (Mabogunje, 1968, p. 226). Growth by fission involves a continuous breakdown of traditional family compounds into smaller individual housing units. Indeed, this is a major determinant of high population densities in Nigerian cities. Table 8.3.1 also shows the rather insignificant rates of such factors as accessibility to work, urban facilities and amenities. Accessibility to work was unimportant since most households engaged in agricultural activities, while considerations as to income from real estate represented by nearness to major roads and urban arteries are of very recent emergence in the house location decision process. This latter consideration is spatially manifested in the recent fanning out of the city along the major north-south and east-west routes, representing a form of suburbanisation.

Nevertheless, the central area is till the most valued part of towns in traditional cities. Consequently people do not wish to be too far away as it was imperative that homage be paid to the Oba or King whose residence is at the centre of the town. To this extent and the extent that modern urban development involves suburbanisation it might be argued that the rent gradient would apply with the proviso that rent is measured in terms of the people's value system rather than in monetary terms. These considerations led to the following hypotheses:

(i) that the people's valuation of the town is highest for the central area but decreases as one moves towards the outskirts;

(ii) that house-seekers would as much as possible want to build houses near the major tarred roads (since such houses now command higher rents);

(iii) that site characteristics would be important in the selection process.

The first hypothesis no doubt is the most important and in our point score method it was rated as such. The central area was awarded 50 points while the points decrease to 22 at 400 metres away, 10 at 800 metres and zero at about 2 kilometres away. In the same way the most accessible parts were awarded 5 points which decrease gradually to zero at 2 kilometres. Site suitability was less objectively considered. Areas of level and well-drained soils were considered as best and were awarded 4 points while areas of steep gradient had 3 and areas of bare rocks and inselbergs scored zero. In this way probability surfaces were derived for the town for both 1959 and 1969 (see Tables 8.3.2 and 8.3.4). Tables 8.3.3 and 8.3.5 represent the random number fields. In 1959, there was a total of 4,070 houses in the town and since the simulation was manually done, it was arbitrarily decided (to save time) that each tally from the simultaneous use of the random number field and a table of random numbers meant that the cell concerned received four houses. This meant an allocation of 1,018 houses. The correlation coefficient between the observed and simulated housing densities for 1959 was 0.98, a value that is statistically highly significant ($\alpha = 0.001$). The regression equation was

$$Y = 0.272 + 0.926X \qquad (7)$$

Table 8.3.2: Probability Surface for 1959 Simulation Pattern

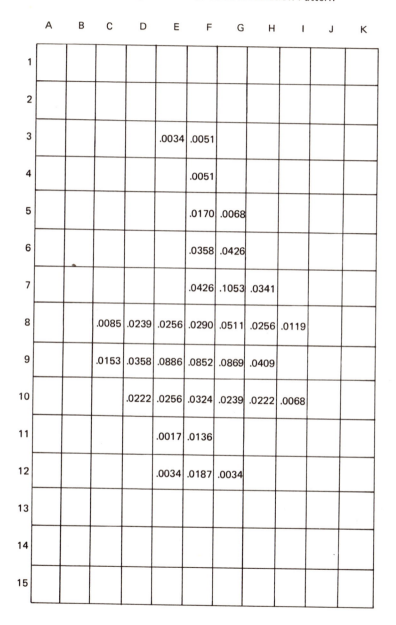

	A	B	C	D	E	F	G	H	I	J	K
1											
2											
3					.0034	.0051					
4						.0051					
5						.0170	.0068				
6						.0358	.0426				
7						.0426	.1053	.0341			
8			.0085	.0239	.0256	.0290	.0511	.0256	.0119		
9			.0153	.0358	.0886	.0852	.0869	.0409			
10				.0222	.0256	.0324	.0239	.0222	.0068		
11					.0017	.0136					
12					.0034	.0187	.0034				
13											
14											
15											

Table 8.3.3: Random Number Field for 1959 Simulation Pattern

	A	B	C	D	E	F	G	H	I	J	K
1											
2					0001 0034	0035 0085					
3						0086 0136					
4						0137 0306	0307 0374				
5						0375 0732	0733 1158				
6						1159 1584	1585 2637	2638 2978			
7			2979 3063	3064 3302	3303 3558	3559 3848	3849 4359	4360 4615	4616 4734		
8			4735 4887	4888 5245	5246 6131	6132 6983	6984 7852	7853 8261			
9				8262 8483	8484 8739	8740 9063	9064 9302	9303 9524	9525 9592		
10					9593 9609	9610 9745					
11					9746 9779	9780 9966	9967 1.0000				
12											
13											
14											
15											

Table 8.3.4: Probability Matrix for 1969 Simulated Pattern

	A	B	C	D	E	F	G	H	I	J	K
1											
2											
3					.0169	.0339					
4					.0085	.0085					
5					.0085	.0425	.0339	.0169			
6					.0085	.0592	.0592	.0254	.0085		
7						.0169		.0425	.0339	.0085	
8			.0254	.0169	.0169	.0169	.0169	.0254	.0509	.0254	
9			.0524					.0254	.0165		
10			.0085	.0339	.0169	.0085	.0085	.0085	.0254		
11						.0169	.0425				
12					.0169	.0339	.0425				
13						.0254					

Table 8.3.5: Random Number Field for 1969 Simulated Pattern

	A	B	C	D	E	F	G	H	I	J	K
1											
2											
3					0001 0169	0170 0508					
4					0509 0593	0594 0578					
5					0679 0763	0764 1188	1189 1527	1528 1696			
6					1697 1781	1782 2373	2374 2965	2966 3219	3220 3304		
7						3305 3473		3474 3898	3899 4237	4238 4322	
8			4323 4576	4577 4745	4746 4914	4915 5083	5084 5252	5253 5506	5507 6015	6016 6269	
9			6270 6694					6695 6948	6949 7117		
10			7118 7202	7203 7541	7542 7710	7711 7795	7796 7880	7881 7965	7966 8219		
11						8220 8388	8389 8813				
12					8814 8982	8983 9321	8322 9746				
13						9747 0000					
14											
15											

where Y represents the expected housing density and X the observed density. A residual map of this equation identified over-predictions of housing density in the central zones and some under-predictions in the southern parts. The over-prediction of the central zones resulted from the blanket assumption of the exponential decrease of population. Further reflections show this decrease could not be as smooth in a comparable Western urban centre. The gradient curve should be one whereby the central zones, if defined to mean the oldest parts of the town, would have a more or less equal housing density which would subsequently decrease outwards in those areas that represent the surburbs. Thus a density decay function that would adequately describe our phenomenon of interest would be the right-hand side of a platy-kurtic normal distribution curve.

On the other hand, over-prediction in the northern zones and some under-predictions in the southern zones could result from our assumption that the town is monocentric. The town, in fact, though mostly residential, is made of three or more quasi-independent settlements whose common bond was the need for defence. Although by the time of this study, the sub-areas had merged into each other, it was not impossible that by 1959 these areas were still spatially differentiated.

While the simulation would in general be described as successful, there was a need to examine the extent to which it reproduced the size classes in the distribution of housing density. Table 8.3.6 represents a summary for the 1959 situation and shows that in general minor differences do exist for the size class distribution. A Kolmogorov-Smirnov Test (Siegel, 1958) for the comparison of the two distributions focusing on the maximum observed difference D_0 and predicted D_e of the accumulated density proportions (Table 8.3.7) show that the differences that existed were not statistically significant.

Table 8.3.6: Size Classes of Housing Density

	Number of Cells	
Size Classes of Density	Observed	Simulated
Less than 1	12	11
1 — 2.5	8	9
2.6 — 4.0	5	6
4.1 — 5.5	2	3
5.6 — 7.0	3	1
Greater than 7	4	4

Table 8.3.7: Size Classes and Accumulated Proportions

| Size Classes | | Accumulated Proportions | |
	Observed	Simulated	Difference
Less than 1	0.353	0.324	0.030
1 − 2.5	0.588	0.588	0.000
2.6 − 4.0	· 0.735	0.765	0.030
4.1 − 5.5	0.794	0.852	0.058
5.6 − 7.0	0.882	0.882	0.000
Greater than 7	1.000	1.000	0.000

Maximum $D_0 = 0.058$; Maximum $D_e = 0.324$ $\alpha = 0.01$

Monte Carlo simulation techniques could provide useful insights into the mechanisms of an urban system. First, it is a simple technique that could be manually done or computer-based after the specification of a set of hypotheses derived from a sound theory. Consequently, it is permissive and possesses high pedagogic value. In the experiment described above, it emerges that improvements could be made either in the operationalisation of the probability surface by making it moveable, i.e. using it as a mean information field. Furthermore, it could be made more useful by increasing its robustness through the incorporation of variables that are specific to that particular urban system. In this way, crucial variables that pertain to the operation of the housing market could be introduced and the model run again.

Perhaps a major contribution of the technique is its identification of the mechanisms of the urban system. Our study shows that a blanket transfer of the concepts of rent and population density decay function of the Western city may be dangerous as it obscures real causes of urban growth in the developing countries. While general 'laws' and rules may exist for describing urban growth, it is probably still true that each case should be treated on its own merits within these laws and rules. This is an important contribution of the simulation technique.

4. Markov Chain Models in Urban Analysis

Markov chain models are the simplest of the dynamic and quasi-dynamic models currently in use in urban analysis. It is a very simple type of variation over time in which the development at any time is controlled entirely by the present states of the system and not by the history which led up to the present state. It includes concepts such as those of absorbing and reflecting states. Consequently there are as many types of

Markov chains and because of their simplicity there are many applications in the social sciences. There were at least two trends in the use of Markov models in geography. The first represents an attempt to develop stochastic process models as represented in the geographical literature by the works of Brown (1970), Drewett (1969) and Harris (1968) on urban land-use succession; Blumen *et al.* (1955), Adelman (1958) and Collins (1970) on industrial migration. The second approach accepts the possibility of interpreting processes within a Markov chain framework but sought to improve on its predictions of spatial behaviour. In this class were the contributions of Lee (1955) and Madansky (1959) who proposed least square optimisation procedures for estimating the transitional probabilities and Scott (1965) who outlined a linear programming approach. Other authors, notably Ginsberg (1971), Goodman (1961) and McGinnis (1968) sought the use of semi-Markov chains while Ginsberg (1973) and Spilerman (1972) proposed approaches for relaxing the inherent homogeneous assumption about the elements of the states of the Markov system.

A sequence of trials with possible outcomes $E = (E_1, E_2, \ldots, E_n)$ is called a Markov chain if the probabilities of sample sequences are defined in terms of a probability distribution (e_k) for E_k at the initial trial and fixed conditional probabilities p_{jk} of E_k given that E_j has occurred at the preceeding trial (Feller, 1968, pp. 312–74). The possible outcomes $E = (E_1, E_2, \ldots, E_n)$ are referred to as the possible states of the system, while p_{jk} is the probability of transition from E_j to E_k. The set of probabilities (p_{jk}) is sometimes arranged in a square transition matrix P as

$$
P = \begin{bmatrix}
p_{11} & p_{12} & \cdots & \cdots & p_{1n} \\
p_{21} & p_{22} & & & p_{2n} \\
\cdot & & & & \cdot \\
\cdot & & & & \cdot \ \cdot \\
\cdot & & & & \cdot \ \cdot \\
p_{n1} & p_{n2} & \cdots & \cdots & p_{nn}
\end{bmatrix}
$$

where $p_{jk} \geqslant 0$

$$
\sum_{k=1}^{n} p_{jk} = 1.0 \tag{8}
$$

The matrix P of transition probabilities represents the fundamental characteristic of the processes involved in the system of interest and in fact it may be used to produce a classification of the type of chain as well as to predict subsequent states of the system. Thus if all elements of P are greater than zero, the chain is said to be regular, while a p_{jk} that is equal to 1.0 defines an absorbing state for the system. All other states will be transient or reflecting. The above no doubt suggests that the Markov chain model would be useful in the study of diffusion processes. This indeed has been the case (Brown, 1963).

The behaviour of a Markov process in time period r is known to depend on p_{jk} as follows. Let $p_{jk}^{(r+1)}$ be the probability of transition from E_j to E_k in exactly $r + 1$ steps, then

$$P_{jk}^{(r+1)} = \sum_v p_{jv} \; P_{vk}^{(r)} \tag{9}$$

which expressed in matrix form is

$$\mathbf{P}^{r+1} = \mathbf{P} \cdot \mathbf{P}^r \tag{10}$$

i.e. the probability of a transition from E_j to E_k in exactly $r + 1$ steps is only dependent on the probability at the rth step and not on how that step was reached. Thus if $E^{(0)}$ is the initial state of our system, the state of the system after $r + 1$ steps, $E^{(r+1)}$ is given by

$$E^{(r+1)} = E^0 P^r \tag{11}$$

Let us illustrate by a possible geographical situation of a hypothetical step migration processes between three cities of a country in which the first city is primate. This means that in the long run we might expect all migrants to end up in this city. Markov chain terminology, such a city would constitute an absorbing state. Let the transition probability matrix be

$$\mathbf{P} = \begin{bmatrix} 1 & 0 & 0 \\ \frac{1}{3} & 0 & \frac{2}{3} \\ 0 & \frac{1}{2} & \frac{1}{2} \end{bmatrix}$$

If the initial probability vector of population distribution between the cities is $E^{(0)} = (\frac{1}{2}, \frac{1}{4}, \frac{1}{4})$, i.e. half the population are in the primate city while the rest are shared equally by the other two cities, the state of the system after one time period is $(\frac{14}{24}, \frac{3}{24}, \frac{7}{24})$. Note that this proportion, calculated by the equation

$$E^{(1)} = E^{(0)} P \tag{12}$$

shows that the proportion in state (1) keeps increasing. We can similarly calculate the situation at our second time period by

$$E^{(2)} = E^{(1)} P = E^{(0)} P^2 \tag{13}$$

which is $(^{30}\!/_{48}, {}^{7}\!/_{48}, {}^{11}\!/_{48})$.

We can also use some properties of the matrix **P** to derive the migration history of people in our system. For instance, we may be interested in how long it takes a typical migrant before he is absorbed into the primate city and how many times he takes part in the step migration process. Procedures for doing this are discussed in Kenemy and Snell (1960).

(i) Criticisms of Markov Chain Models in Social Research

While Markov chains provide a way of examining the dynamic process of social systems, it is often argued that its assumptions are sometimes too simplistic to reflect reality. None the less, it is these same assumptions that allow the derivation and readily interpretable dimensions of social systems. The principal assumption is the Markov property that history is irrelevant in the analysis, i.e. that the future states of a system are determined not by the history of the system but by its current state. Although very few social systems fall into this category, this assumption generally works well where the time periods are short enough to obliterate the effects of history. On the other hand, it is possible to modify the Markov chain by formulating the problem in terms of higher-order Markov chains (Feller, 1968) at the expense of increasing computations and data availability.

Furthermore, it is often argued that our conceptualisation of time in discrete units does not reflect reality. Social systems, like any other system, do not behave so discretely although observations on social systems must be collected on a discrete basis. For instance, it is a truism that migration occurs at different times rather than at the end of a specified time period. A semi-Markov chain whereby the time between one period and the next is a result of a separate stochastic process could be formulated to obviate this problem. For instance, it could be argued that the transition between two periods is a function of both current and future states. Such a formulation will make the length of residency of the Markov process in any state a random variable. Associated with this problem is that of defining the states of the system. It is usual in

Markov chain analysis to assume that there is a finite number of states which are discrete, mutally exclusive and collectively exhaustive.

In urban studies where we use data collected on the basis of well-defined area units, these assumptions would necessarily hold. However, when we deal with continuous variables such as city sizes or *per capita* income, the characterisation of the system states may introduce some artificialities. Again, at the expense of computational simplicity and data availability, we can obviate this problem by using a more general stochastic difference equation of the form

$$x(t) = f[x(t-1), z(t)] \tag{14}$$

where f is a single valued function, $x(t)$ is the system's state of the process at time t and $z(t)$ is a stochastic variable with known time-dependent probability distribution.

Simple Markov chains often assume that the transition probabilities are constant over time. This is the stationarity assumption. The effect of technological changes is to cause sometimes rapid and serious changes to occur in social systems. While this assumption is not peculiar to Markov chains, as it is basic to most forecasting techniques, the stationarity assumptions can at least in theory be relaxed so that one uses instead non-stationary Markov models where the probability matrix **P** is time-dependent.

A rather strong criticism of Markov chain models concerns the homogeneity assumption, which considers all the elements of the Markov state as homogeneous. For instance, if one considers intra-urban residential change as a Markov process, the homogeneity assumption presumes that all households in an area of the city are homogeneous. This could be very far from the truth. There are really two approaches to a solution. First, if these are good reasons to believe that a Markovian state is not homogeneous, one could always disaggregate the state populations into classes and then proceed to estimate different trans-action probabilities for the different states of the system. An equally good and probably better approach is that introduced by Ginsberg (1973) and Spilerman (1972), who sought to introduce independent variables into the estimation of the transition probabilities. Such an approach would then, through some regression analysis, make predictions for the heterogeneous populations in the states.

Markov chains do have great potentialities in the investigation of social processes, in particular as a first approximation technique whereby it is used to identify either problems associated with social behaviour or in the initial formulation of the stochastic processes involved. Like any other mathematical technique, there is need to use common sense and judgement in evaluating its applicability and interpreting the results. One very illustrative application is described by Bourne in his studies of land-use change in Toronto.

5. Bourne's Urban Land-use Allocation Conversion Model

One of the most recent, realistic and well-documented Markov chain models of urban spatial structure is that developed and used by Bourne in his studies on the redevelopment of the central city of Toronto (Bourne, 1967, 1969). Conceptually, the model integrates the dynamics of land-use conversion into land-use allocation through the use of probability matrices which relate the units of growth assigned to each sub-area of the urban system by an allocation model to changes in existing land-use structure. Operationally, there was a deep awareness of some of the criticisms of Markov models, especially that of stationarity. Bourne mitigated this criticism by using a weighted average of transition probability matrices in addition to using short time periods.

The model consists of two components, a set of spatial allocation multiple regression equation designed to account for the distribution of new construction in each area of the city, and a set of Markov chain probability matrices, one for each sub-area of the city and measuring the structure of land-use succession resulting from new construction. In developing the multiple regression equations, estimates of the volume of new construction were related to such variables as sizes and areas of residential lots, distance from peak land-use intersections, total employment in an area, total population, proximity to major thoroughfares, residential density, socio-economic status, age of residential property and concentration of apartments. In all, there were different multiple regression models for five dependent variables, the total residential construction, commercial office, parking, apartment and single family. Multiple correlation coefficients of between 0.60 for apartments and 0.80 for parking were recorded.

The multiple regression models produce outputs that become inputs into the land-use conversion model which is a Markov chain model. Thus the outputs multiplied by the transition matrices yield the new land-use structure in an area. Used iteratively, it is possible to use the technique for forecasting. The land-use succession model is developed as follows;

LU_i^t is a column vector of the initial land-use distribution at time f for ith land-use type in the jth area;

$P_{ik}^{t,\ t+1}$ is a matrix of row probabilities for each of j areas representing the probability of conversion of existing land-use type i to new construction type k in time period t and $t + 1$;

$R_{ik}^{t,\ t+1}$ is a matrix of column probabilities, the same order as P, measuring the probability of conversion be each new construction type k;

$C_k^{t,\ t+1}$ is a row vector for each of j areas representing the volume of new construction;

$TC_j^{t,t+1}$ is a column vector of total land-use conversion in each of i types for j areas;

LU_j^{t+1} is the final output vector containing the land-use distribution at time $t + 1$ for each of j areas;

LC_{ik}^{t+1} an intermediate output matrix containing the amount of land area converted;

$NC_k^{t,\ t+1}$ an intermediate output vector representing the total land converted to use k in each of j areas, i.e.

$$NC_k^{t,t+1} = \sum_i LC_{ik}^{t,t+1} \tag{15}$$

The land-use conversion model is then made up of the following equations. First there is an intra-urban land-use distribution model given by

$$TC_i^{t,t+1} \cdot P_{ik}^{t,t+1} = LC_{i,k}^{t+1} \tag{16}$$

This model provides the aggregate conversion of land uses through new construction. The second matrix R_{ik} is derived from intermediate tables and it represents the probability of new construction locating in each of i initial land-use types.

First iteration

$$C_k^t \cdot R_{ik}^{t,t+1} = LC_{ik}^{t,t+1} \tag{17}$$

$$\sum_{k=1}^{i} LC_{ik}^{t,t+1} = LC_i^{t,t+1} \tag{18}$$

(total land conversion by land-use type i)

$$\sum_{i=1}^{k} LC_{ik}^{t,t+1} = NC_k^{t,t+1} \tag{19}$$

(total land conversion by new construction type k)

After the first iteration, a new land-use structure is generated from the equation:

$$LU_i^t - LC_i^{t,t+1} + NC_k^{t,t+1} = LU_i^{t+1} \tag{20}$$

The model then proceeds to the second iteration which repeats equations 17 to 19 above, but each time using a new probability matrix. Thus for the second iteration

$$C_k^{t+1} \cdot R_{ik}^{t+1,t+2} = LC_{ik}^{t+1,t+2} \tag{21}$$

All along, it must be ensured that the following constraints hold

$$\sum_{k=1}^{i} R_{ik} = 1.0 \text{ for each of } j \text{ areas} \tag{22}$$

and

$$P_{ik} \geqslant 0.0 \text{ in matrix product } LC_{ik}$$

i denoting land-use types and j the number of sub-areas in the system

Bourne's model is an operational one but its beauty lies in the way both land-use allocation and land-use conversion mechanisms have been integrated. In the past, most urban models have concentrated on either but not both approaches with the consequence that these approaches have been rather simplistic. Structural changes in urban development is represented by the conversion of one land use to another and it is in this respect that Bourne's contribution becomes of significance to model-builders. Any criticism of Bourne's model will not be in its conceptualisation but rather in its applicability as it requires a type of data that hardly exists: accurate measures of land-use succession. None the less, it represents an important step in understanding urban land-use conversion process.

6. Conclusion

While the surface of the earth is not a 'floating crap game' and the activities of men not necessarily governed by the mechanism of a roulette wheel, the probabilistic approach to urban modelling would seem to be a valuable area of research in urban studies. It is obvious that urban development is a complex process, the variables of which we may never totally comprehend. Consequently the Monte Carlo technique could be suitable as a way of discerning these variables of the urban development process. On the other hand, our conceptualisation of land conversion as a stochastic process is an acceptance of our inability to identify the pertinent processes rather than a philosophical acceptance of the role of chance.

Granted, then, that geographical processes in the city are either not very well known or not easily identifiable, the probability approach should be an inspiring framework towards furthering our understanding. In that case, one might proceed from such aggregate considerations represented in Markov chains or Monte Carlo techniques to producing stochastic models of individual locational and spatial behaviour. It would seem that using this probabilistic approach with stochastic difference or stochastic differential equations (depending on whether our treatment of time is as a discrete or continuous variable) should be our goal, as there is an urgent need to move from the comparative static approach of Markov chains or Monte Carlo techniques into a dynamic framework. This no doubt should constitute a research frontier for the serious-minded urban modeller.

The probabilistic approach is one of at least two approaches to urban model-building. The other approach, the deterministic, in the sense that all the equations of the system of interest must be known and interaction identified, constitute another major thrust. Some of the approaches to the development of deterministic urban models are discussed in the next chapter.

References

Abler, R., Adams, J.S., and Gould, P.R. 1972. *Spatial Organization: The Geographer's View of the World.* Englewood Cliffs, New Jersey: Prentice-Hall

Ackoff, R.L. 1962. *Scientific Method: Optimising Applied Research Decision.* New York: John Wiley

Adelman, I.G. 1958. A Stochastic Analysis of the Size Distribution of Firms. *Journal of the American Statistical Association, 53,* 893–904

Ayeni, M.B. 1970. The Built-Up Area of Ikere-Ekiti; Past, Present and the Future: A Simulation Study. B.Sc. dissertation, Department of Geography, University of Ibadan, Nigeria

Blumen, I. *et al.* 1955. *The Industrial Mobility of Labour as a Probability Process.* Ithaca, New York: Cornell University Press

Bourne, L.S. 1967. *Private Redevelopment of the Central City: Spatial Processes of Structural Change in the City of Toronto.* Department of Geography, Research Series No. 112, University of Chicago

Bourne, L.S. 1969. A Spatial Allocation-Land Use Conversion Model or Urban Growth. *Journal of Regional Science, 9,* 2, 261–71

Brown, L.S. 1963. The Diffusion of Innovations: A Markov Chain Type Approach. Northwestern University, Department of Geography, Discussion Paper No. 3

Brown, L.S. 1970. On the use of Markov Chains in Movement Research. *Economic Geography, 46,* 393–403

Clark, C. 1951. Urban Population Densities. *Journal of the Royal Statistical Society,* Ser. A, *114,* 490–6

Colenutt, R.J. 1970. Building Models of Urban Growth and Spatial Structure. In C. Board *et al.* (eds.), *Progress in Geography,* Vol. 2. London: Arnold, pp. 109–52

Collins, L. 1970. Markov Chains and Industrial Migration: Forecasting Aspects of Industrial Activity in Ontario. Unpublished Ph.D. thesis, Department of Geography, University of Toronto

Curry, L. 1966. Chance and Landscape. In J.W. House (ed.), *Northern Geographical Essays in Honor of G.H.S. Daysh.* Newcastle

Dacey, M.F. 1975. Comments on Papers by Isard and Smith. *Papers Regional Science Association, 35,* 51–6

Donelly, T.G., Chapin, F.S. Jr., and Weiss, S.F. 1964. *A Probabilistic Model for Residential Growth: An Urban Studies Research Monograph.* Chapel Hill, University of North Carolina: University of North Carolina Press

Drewett, J.R. 1969. A Stochastic Model of the Land Conversion Process: An Interim Report. *Regional Studies, 3,* 3, 269–80

Feller, W. 1968. *An Introduction to Probability Theory and Its Applications,* Vol. 1. New York: Wiley International, third edition

Ginsberg, R.B. 1971. Semi-Markov Processes and Mobility. *Journal of Mathematical Sociology, 1,* 233–62

Ginsberg, R.B. 1973. Stochastic Models of Residential and Geographic Mobility for Heterogeneous Populations. *Environment and Planning, 5,* 113–24

Goodman, L.A. 1961. Statistic Methods for the Mover-Stayer Model. *Journal of the American Statistical Association, 56*

Hägerstrand, T. 1953. *Innovationsfoploppet ur Korologisk Synpunkt.* Lund, Gleerup, Sweden. Tr. A. Pred, 1967, *Innovation Diffusion as a Spatial Process.* Chicago: University of Chicago Press

Hägerstrand, T. 1967. On Monte Carlo Simulation of Diffusion. In W.L. Garrison (ed.), *Quantitative Geography.* Evanston, Illinois: Northwestern Studies in Geography

Hägerstrand, T. 1965. A Monte Carlo Approach to Diffusion. *European Journal of Sociology, 6,* 43–67

Harris, C.C. 1968. A Stochastic Process Model of Residential Development. *Journal of Regional Science, 8,* 29–39

Harris, C.D., and Ullman, E.L. 1945. The Nature of Cities. *Annals of the American Academy of Political and Social Sciences,* Nov., 7–11

Kenemy, J.G., and Snell, J.L. 1960. *Finite Markov Chains.* Princeton, New Jersey: D. Van Nostrand

Lee, T.C. *et al.* 1955. On Estimating the Transitional Probabilities of a Markov Process. *Journal of Farm Economics, 47,* 742–62

Lindley, D.V. and Miller, J.C.P. 1968. *Cambridge Elementary Statistical Tables.* Cambridge: Cambridge University Press

Mabogunje, A.L. 1968. *Urbanization in Nigeria.* London: University of London Press

Madansky, A. 1959. Least Squares Estimation in Finite Markov Processes. *Psychometrika, 24,* 2

Marble, D.F. 1964. A Simple Markovian Model of Trip Structures in a Metropolitan Region. *Papers, Regional Science Association,* Western Section, *1,* 150–6

McGinnis, R. 1968. A Stochastic Model of Social Mobility. *American Sociological Review, 33,* 712–22

Morrill, R.L. 1965. The American Ghetto: Problems and Alternatives. *The Geographical Review, 50,* 339–61

Morrill, R.L. 1965a. *Migration and the Spread and Growth of Urban Settlement* Lund, Gleerup, Sweden

Scott, A.J. 1965. A Procedure for the Estimation of Markov Transition Probabilities. *Regional Science Research Institute Discussion Paper,* No. 8

Siegal, S. 1958. *Non-parametric Statistics for the Behavioural Sciences.* New York: McGraw-Hill

Spilerman, S. 1972. The Analysis of Mobility Process by the Introduction of Independent Variables into a Markov Chain. *American Sociological Review, 37,* 227–94

9 OPTIMISATION MODELS

1. Introduction

Optimisation models consist of a set of methods for the evaluation of a system in terms of what 'ought to have been' rather than what is. These techniques, which include as simplest examples methods of linear programming, game theory and many other techniques under the cover name of operation research, are used to find the optimum relationship between a number of independent variables. They were extensively developed during World War Two but since the end of the war, like most other inventions and discoveries, the techniques have been applied most widely in management and industry, especially in analysing the best methods of product allocation, distribution and shipping, blending and production planning. In economics, Dorfman, Samuelson and Solov pioneered the use of linear programming (Dorfman *et al*, 1958) while extensive application of game theory to economic behaviour was made by von Neuman and Morgenstern (1953).

The use of linear programming in spatial analysis and regional science is due to the Wharton School of the University of Pennsylvania who, under Walter Isard (1958, 1966), not only extended the simple linear programming framework into interregional formulations but also monitored its usage in metropolitan planning (Stevens and Coughlin, 1958). Initially, the use of linear programming in spatial analysis derived from attempts to generalise the limited models of von Thunen, Weber and later spatial theorists. Thus the location of firms and industries was a primary focus of interest by Beckman and Marschak (1955) on the one hand, and Koopmans and Beckman (1957) on the other. The latter authors even considered the associated problem of handling indivisibilities in a linear programming framework. Furthermore, attempts at understanding the spatial distribution of goods from a set of origins to a set of destinations led to the now famous transportation model of linear programming (Koopmans, 1947; Hitchcock, 1941). In recent years, partial or general models of the urban or metropolitan spatial structure have been presented within the linear programming framework (Herbert and Stevens, 1960; Ochs, 1969) and efforts have been made to view development planning in terms of the maximisation of some objective function. All these no doubt provide a rationale for the study of linear programming.

Game theory, on the other hand, is less widely used in spatial analysis despite the fact that the two techniques are similar, as many game theory problems can be framed in terms of a linear programming model (Vajda, 1956). Basically, they are underlain by the same mathematics and one cannot but agree with Peter Gould that ' . . . a key made from a little modern algebra may often open many doors' (Gould, 1963). None the less game theory is a method used extensively in engineering, business, statistics, economics, sociology and anthropology. The useful insights provided by Gould in his analysis of the agricultural practice of the Jantialla farmer in Ghana or the cattle traders of Ghana and Upper Volta through the use of the game theoretic framework are pointers to the potential of game theory in understanding human spatial organisation.

It would be preposterous to attempt a catch-all presentation of the use of these optimisation techniques. Instead, we feel we should emphasise the essential and show how they have been and can be made to relate to the urban spatial structure. While ardently pursuing this goal, it is proper to warn the reader that linearity which is a vital assumption of these models is an approximation to reality. Thus these two optimisation techniques are first-order approximations to dynamic or non-linear programming, the discussion of which is beyond the aims and scope of this book. Thus much caution and discretion are necessary in the use of the models.

2. Linear Programming: An Introduction

Linear programming is both a decision-making aid as well as an analytical mechanism. As a technique that produces an optimum configuration given an objective function and a set of restraints, it enables policy-makers to choose the best solution while its analytical ability enables the academician to possess greater weights into the problem at hand. Let us illustrate this by a simple example.

Consider an urban area where two types of residential buildings are to be constructed. Let these be single-family and multi-family units respectively. Let us assume that only three inputs, namely site rent, labour and capital are required and let us assume that these vary for the two types of housing units. Furthermore, let us assume that we have 600 units of land, 360 units of labour and 240 units of capital. In order to build a single unit of these two house types, the following combination of the inputs are required:

Required Units	Type I	Type II
Land/site Rent	0.6	0.5
Labour	0.3	0.4
Capital	0.16	0.3

Our problem is to find out how many houses of each type that must be built using the units of land, labour and capital available in such a way that income from real estate would be maximised. Let x_1, x_2 be the units of Types I and II houses that must be built and let the income from each house type be c_1, c_2, the total income Z is

$$Z = c_1 x_1 + c_2 x_2 \tag{1}$$

Since all the inputs must be used and since we can not use more than the quantities that we have, we may express the restraints on our action as

(i) $0.6x_1 + 0.5x_2 \leqslant 600$
(ii) $0.3x_1 + 0.4x_2 \leqslant 360$
(iii) $0.16x_1 + 0.3x_2 \leqslant 240$

Of course we can generalise the above as:

(i) $a_{11}x_1 + a_{12}x_2 \leqslant r_1$
(ii) $a_{21}x_1 + a_{22}x_2 \leqslant r_2$
(iii) $a_{31}x_1 + a_{32}x_2 \leqslant r_3$

The linear programming problem may now be stated as

maximise $z = c_1 x_1 + c_2 x_2 \tag{1a}$

subject to

$$\left.\begin{array}{l} \text{(i) } a_{11}x_1 + a_{12}x_2 \leqslant r_1 \\ \text{(ii) } a_{21}x_1 + a_{22}x_2 \leqslant r_2 \\ \text{(iii) } a_{31}x_1 + a_{32}x_2 \leqslant r_3 \\ x_i \geqslant 0 \text{ for all } i \end{array}\right\} \tag{2}$$

and the above is the general form in which linear programming problems are stated.

Linear programming problems may be solved by the simplex method for which general algorithms have been developed; or graphically if the number of types of activities is not more than two. Let us illustrate the latter by solving our problem graphically. We shall proceed by representing on a graph the locus of points for which the equalities hold. Let us start by drawing the lines

$$0.6x_1 + 9.5x_2 = 600$$
$$0.3x_1 + 0.4x_2 = 360$$
$$0.16x_1 + 0.3x_2 = 240$$

Thus line *ED* represents the restraint on land. The area under that line satisfies the restraint that land must be used in the specified proportion. Similarly, *FG* and *AH* represent the restraints on labour and capital respectively (see Figure 9.2.1).

From the above, it is obvious that the area that satisfies the three

Figure 9.2.1: Graphical Solution of a Linear Programming Problem

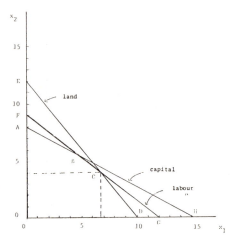

Scale : 1 unit = 100 houses.

Solution : x_1 = 670 , x_2 = 400.

constraints is made up of all points on and under the curve *ABCD* and within the figure OABCD. The point where income is maximised is *C*, where 670 units of House Type 1 and 400 units of House Type II are to be located in the city.

The total income will be

$$c_1(670) \quad + \quad c_2(400) \quad = \quad 1,070$$

since by assumption above $c_1 = c_2 = 1$. The reader is advised to test as many points in and on the figure OABCD to verify that income is truly maximised at point *C*.

It should be noted that not all linear programming problems can be solved by the method of graphs. Indeed graphs can only be used where no more than two types of activities are being considered as graphical representation becomes difficult when these are more than two dimensions. The general method for solving linear programming problems is the simplex method and to the extent that is is also used in solving some game theory problems, we shall discuss it briefly.

(i) The Simplex Method

The simplex method, due to G.B. Dantzig, is an iterative method for the solution of linear programming problems. At each stage of the iteration it indicates whether a solution obtained is optimal and where it could be bettered if it is not optimal. The rationale is based on the general method of solving linear equations by a means of a simplex tableau. The method consists simply of finding an initial feasible basis (one is always obvious), and then changing this basis by substituting, one at a time, an activity not in the basis for one formerly in it. Each activity entering the basis is chosen so that the new basis will remain feasible. The exposition below is framed in terms of matrix algebra and is very precise and convenient. It is modified from Almon's book, *Matrix Methods in Economics* (Almon, 1967, pp. 58–73).

Let us begin by writing the linear programming problem in matrix algebra. Let *C* be the vector of costs, *X*, the vector of inputs, then the inequalities are

$$a_{11}x_1 + a_{12}x_2 + \ldots + a_{1n}x_n \leqslant r_1$$
$$a_{21}x_1 + a_{22}x_2 + \ldots + a_{2n}x_n \leqslant r_2$$
$$\cdot$$
$$\cdot$$
$$\cdot$$
$$a_{m1}x_1 + a_{m2}x_2 + \ldots + a_{mn}x_n \leqslant r_m$$

The first step is to reduce the inequalities to equations by introducing slack variables. A slack variable is any positive number that causes equality to exist and may be interpreted economically as idle inputs. We thus have

$$a_{11}x_1 + a_{12}x_2 + \ldots + a_{1n}x_n + x_{n+1} + 0x_{n+2} + \ldots = r_1$$
$$a_{21}x_1 + a_{22}x_2 + \ldots + a_{2n}x_n + 0x_{n+1} + x_{n+2} + \ldots = r_2$$
$$\vdots$$
$$a_{m1}x_1 + a_{m2}x_2 + \ldots + a_{mn}x_n + 0x_{n+1} + 0x_{n+2} + \ldots + x_{n+k} = r_m$$

$$
\begin{bmatrix}
a_{11} & a_{12} & \cdots & a_{1n} & 1 & 0 & \cdots & 0 \\
a_{21} & a_{22} & \cdots & a_{2n} & 0 & 1 & \cdots & 0 \\
\vdots & & & & & & & \vdots \\
a_{m1} & a_{m1} & \cdots & a_{mn} & 0 & 0 & \cdots & 1
\end{bmatrix}
\begin{bmatrix}
x_1 \\ x_2 \\ \vdots \\ x_n \\ x_{n+1} \\ \vdots \\ x_{n+k}
\end{bmatrix}
=
\begin{bmatrix}
r_1 \\ r_2 \\ \vdots \\ r_m
\end{bmatrix}
$$

Our discussions of the economic base concept, the input-output method Let the matrix of coefficients in the above equation be **A**, then the linear programming problem may be stated in matrix algebra as

Maximise $\mathbf{Z} = \mathbf{CX}$ (3)

Subject to

$$\mathbf{AX} = \mathbf{R} \quad (4)$$

$$\mathbf{X} \geqslant 0 \text{ for all } \mathbf{X} \quad (5)$$

A solution of the equation $\mathbf{AX} = \mathbf{R}$ which uses only linearly independent activities is called a basic solution (and the m-dimensional geometric figure having the basic solutions as vertices is called simplex — hence the name of the method). The square matrix formed of the columns of **A** which it uses is called the corresponding basis and we shall denote this by **B**.

Let us define a use-level vector, U^B which is the solution of the equation $BU = R$. If this use-level vector is non-negative, then the basis **B** is said to be feasible, for the corresponding solution * of $AX = R$. Let C^B be the row vector of elements of **C** correspnding to the columns of **B****, and let $Z^B = C^B U^B$ be the value of the objective function for the basic feasible solution corresponding to the basis **B**. Let us define vector Π^B, called the vector of simplex multiplier corresponding to the basis **B** by the equation

$$\Pi^B = C^B B^{-1} \tag{6}$$

and V^B, the vector of simplex criteria by

$$V^B = C - \Pi^B A \tag{7}$$

We may now give a procedure for the computation. It is as follows.

(1) Find an initial **B**.
(2) Find B^{-1} and $U^B = B^{-1} R$.
(3) Calculate $\Pi^B = C^B B^{-1}$, the simplex multiplier.
(4) Calculate $V^B = C - \Pi^B A$, the simplex criteria. This is the opportunity cost of using each activity.
(5) If $V^B \leqslant 0$, the optimal solution has been reached. If some element, V^B_k is positive, any one of the positive elements may be chosen but usually use as A_k, the activity that has the largest simplex criterion.
(6) Calculate $P = B^{-1} A_k$. These are the rates of substitution between A_k and the activities in **B**.
(7) Find the value of r such that

$$\frac{U^B_r}{P_r} = \min_{[i \,|\, P_i > 0]} \left(\frac{U^B_i}{P_i} \right) \tag{8}$$

(8) Return to step 2 with the basis $(B_1, B_2, \ldots B_{r-1}, A_k, B_{r+1}, \ldots, B_n)$.

---

* If A_i the ith column of **A** is not in B then $X_i = 0$; if A_i is B_j then $X_i = U^B_j$.
** If A_i is B_j, then $C^B_j = C_i$.

The above steps of the solution of the linear programming problem by the simplex method may be illustrated by the example of the last section. Thus if we express the inequalities in terms of equations we have

$$6x_1 + 5x_2 + x_3 + 0 \cdot x_4 + 0 \cdot x_5 = 6{,}000$$
$$3x_1 + 4x_2 + 0 \cdot x_3 + x_4 + 0 \cdot x_5 = 3{,}600$$
$$1.6x_1 + 3x_2 + 0 \cdot x_3 + 0 \cdot x_4 + x_5 = 2{,}400$$

In order to make computations easy, let us divide the **R** vector by 100, so that $\mathbf{R}' = (60, 36, 24)$. We begin by selecting a basis – usually x_3, x_5 is a good combination. Proceeding as outlined above, the first tableau is

	Basis	C^B	P	U		B^{-1}			A_k	b			A		
Tableau	$-\Pi$			0	0	0	0			60	6	5	1	0	0
I	x_3	0	5	60	1	0	0	5		36	2	4	0	1	0
	x_4	0	4	36	0	1	1	4		24	$\frac{8}{5}$	3	0	0	1
	x_5	0	3	24	0	0	1	3		V^0	1	(1)	0	0	0

We have the option of introducing A_1 or A_2 into the new basis. Let us choose A_2, then our new basis is x_3, x_4, x_2, since we must pivot on x_5. Repeating the processes above, Tableau II is as shown below.

	Basis	C^B	P	U		B^{-1}		A_k	b			A		
Tableau	$-\Pi$			8	0	0	$-\frac{1}{3}$		60	6	5	1	0	0
II	x_3	0	$\frac{10}{3}$	20	1	0	$-\frac{5}{3}$	6	36	3	4	0	1	0
	x_4	0	$\frac{13}{15}$	4	0	1	$-\frac{4}{3}$	3	24	$\frac{8}{5}$	3	0	0	1
	x_2	1	$\frac{8}{15}$	8	0	0	$\frac{1}{3}$	$\frac{8}{5}$	V^1	$\frac{7}{15}$	0	0	0	$\frac{1}{3}$

A check on columns headed P and U shows that we must pivot for the third tableau on x_4 using x_1 since A_1 has the highest score on V^1. Continuing the processes, Tableaux III and IV here

	Basis	C^B	P	U		B^{-1}		A_k	b			A		
Tableau	$-\Pi$			$\frac{12}{13}$	0	$\frac{23}{13}$	$-\frac{35}{13}$		60	6	5	1	0	0
III	x_3	0	0	$\frac{60}{13}$	1	$-\frac{50}{13}$	$\frac{45}{13}$	6	36	3	4	0	1	0
	x_1	-1	1	$-\frac{60}{13}$	0	$-\frac{45}{13}$	$\frac{60}{39}$	3	24	$\frac{8}{5}$	3	0	0	1
	x_2	1	0	$\frac{72}{13}$	0	$-\frac{8}{13}$	$\frac{15}{13}$	$\frac{8}{5}$	V^2	(2)	0	0	$\frac{23}{13}$	$-\frac{35}{13}$

	Basis	C^B	P	U	B^{-1}		A_k	b	A				
Tableau IV	$-$ II			$-\frac{32}{3}$	$-\frac{1}{9}$	$-\frac{1}{9}$		60	6	5	1	0	0
	x_1	1		$\frac{20}{3}$	$\frac{4}{9}$	$-\frac{5}{9}$		36	3	4	0	1	0
	x_2	1		4	$-\frac{1}{3}$	$\frac{2}{3}$		24	$\frac{8}{5}$	3	0	0	1
								V^3	0	0	$-\frac{1}{9}$	$\frac{1}{9}$	0

have been constructed. It will be seen that after the fourth tableau none of the values of V is greater than zero. Consequently we know we have arrived at an optimum solution which is found under the U column. Thus the optimum values of x_1 and x_2 are

$$x_1 = 6.67$$
$$x_2 = 4.00$$

i.e. 667 units of House Type I and 400 units of House Type II would give the highest income. This is the value of II.

It must be agreed that the above description of the method of solution is probably of historic significance only since there are standard computer programmes for the algorithms involved. However, a careful examination of the process may afford further insights into the interpretation of the maximisation procedure. This is left as an exercise to the reader. We shall in the next section proceed further with the development of the linear programming framework by looking at the dual problem.

(ii) The Dual of a Linear Programming Problem

For every linear programming problem there is always as associated problem called the dual. Mathematically, the dual provides a check on the original formulation of the problem, the primal; by ensuring that the maximum value of the primal is the minimum value of the dual. Consequently it provides further insights into the structure of the processes at work. Furthermore, it may give an easier or quicker way of arriving at the solution of the primal problem (Churchman *et al.*, 1962).

The dual therefore is usually formulated as the reverse of the primal. Thus, if the primal is a maximisation problem, the dual will minimise. For instance, as in the last example, if the primal maximises income, the dual will minimise costs. Consequently, the costs in the objective function of the primal become the limiting constraints in the dual, implying that there will be as many constraints in the dual as there are choice variables in the primal. Furthermore, the resource variables which are the limiting constraints on the primal become the choice variables of the objective function. In general, the coefficients of the constraints of the primal are transposed in the dual and the sense of the inequalities in the primal are reversed in the dual.

Let us illustrate by a simple example of the location of House Types I and II, involving the constraints of land and capital only. Let the objective function of the primal problem be

maximise

$$Z = x_1 + x_2$$

subject to

$$6x_1 + 5x_2 \leqslant 60$$
$$1.6x_1 + 3x_2 \leqslant 24$$
$$x_1, x_2 \geqslant 0$$

the dual of the above problem is

minimise

$$Y = 60p_1 \ 24p_2$$

subject to

$$6p_1 + 1.6p_2 \geqslant 1$$
$$5p_1 + 3p_2 \geqslant 1$$
$$p_1 p_2 \geqslant 0$$

where p_1 and p_2 are the costs of performing each of the activities. In general $Y = Z$.

Let us illustrate the above relationships by a graphical solution of the primal and dual problems. Figure 9.2.2, showing the solution of the primal problem, gives the values of $x_1 = 6$ and $x_2 = 4.8$ and a

$$Z = 6 + 4.8 = 10.8$$

On the other hand, Figure 9.2.3, which shows the dual solution, gives values of p_1 and p_2 as 0.15 and 0.075 dollars respectively and a

$$Y = 0.15\,(60) + 0.075(24) = 10.8$$

so that the equation that Y should be equal to Z holds.

In the pages above, we have gone to great lengths to show what linear

Figure 9.2.2: Graphical Solution of the Primal Problem

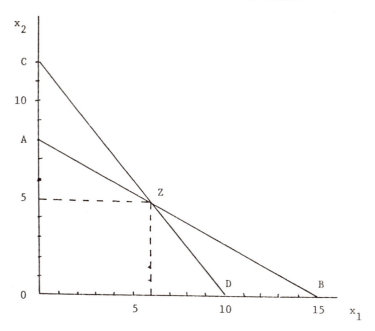

programming is as well as how to use the simplex method to derive a solution. This is because it is often a misunderstood technique even though it is one of the few which could be evaluative of the optimal behaviour of human beings. In fact, in economic analysis, it has been a convenient technique for operationalising the concept of the rational economic man. However, urban systems are more complex as they include not only sub-optimal behaviour but also non-monetary costs where quantitative expression could be difficult. None the less, we shall devote the next two sections to various attempts at modelling residential location as well as the total urban form through the technique of linear programming.

3. A Linear Programming Model of Residential Location: The Herbert-Stevens' Model

One of the classics in the realm of intra-city linear programming formulation is the Herbert-Stevens' model for the distribution of residential activities in urban areas (Herbert and Stevens, 1960). The importance of the model arises from a number of considerations. First, it was

Figure 9.2.3: Graphical Solution of the Dual Problem

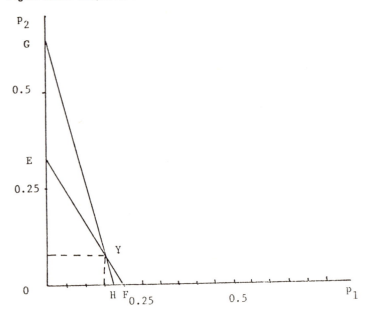

operational, as it was one of the many models used in the Penn-Jersey Transportation Study. The Penn-Jersey Transportation Study involved comprehensive analysis of land uses and other activities, their rates of growth and their projection from the 1960 data base to 1975 and subsequently to 1985 (Penn-Jersey Transportation Study, 1964). Consequently, it made considerable compromise between theoretical elegance and practical applicability. Second, the residential location modelling was based on the important and significant contribution of William Alonso to the theory of residential location (Alonso, 1964) discussed in Chapter 1. Indeed many writers have rightly called it an operational formulation of the Alonso Model (Batty, 1970).

The modelling framework assumes that the amount of land that would be available for residential use as well as the number of households to be located would be exogenously given. Furthermore, given discretely defined time periods (which may be made short enough to avoid errors arising from the linear assumptions of the model, linear programming would produce an optimal configuration of new households on the available land.

The operationalisation of the Alonso framework is as follows. Households would be expected to locate their residences according to their total budget, the items which constitute a market basket and the costs of obtaining these items. A market basket is defined as a unique combination of residential bundle and a bundle of all other commodities consumed annually by the household. The argument proceeds as follows (see Chapter 1, section 3).

(i) There is a set of market baskets among which each household in a household group is indifferent.

(ii) The set of market baskets include, but are not necessarily limited to, the market baskets currently consumed by households of that type.

(iii) Households will optimise not by selecting a market basket from all the conceivable sets from which they could obtain satisfaction by selecting from the posited set the market basket which maximises the household's savings.

The assumptions that households have a fixed total budget, and that the prices of 'other commodities' bundle in a market basket are given, imply that the residential budget varies from market basket to market basket and therefore gives rise to savings. Households would therefore be optimally allocated to houses in such a way no household can increase its savings without reducing the savings of some other households, and hence the aggregate saving.

Let us fix ideas by looking at the mathematical presentation. Let us define the following variables (notations differ slightly from the original):

n number of areas in the urban system subscripted by $i = 1, 2, \ldots, n$

w number of household groups denoted by $l = 1, 2, \ldots, w$

m number of residential bundles, $h = 1, 2, \ldots, m$

b^{lh} is the residential budget allocated by a household group l to the purchase of residential bundle h

c_i^{lh} is the annual cost to a household of group l of the residential bundle h in area i, exclusive of the site cost

s^{lh} is the number of acres in a site used by a household of group l using residential bundle h

L_i is the number of acres (hectares) of land available at area i

p^l is the number of households of group l in the region

X_i^{lh} is the number of households of group l using residential bundle h located by the model in area i.

The function to be maximised is the aggregate savings of all households in the system subject to the constraints that the total land consumption at each zone must not be greater than the total available land and that all the projected (exogenously given) number of household groups must be allocated. The primal problem then is:

maximise $\quad Z = \sum_{i=1}^{n} \sum_{l=1}^{w} \sum_{h=1}^{m} X_{i}^{lh}(b^{lh} - c_{i}^{lh})$ $\qquad$ (9)

subject to

(i) $\qquad \sum_{l=1}^{n} \sum_{h=1}^{m} S^{lh} X_{i}^{lh} \leqslant L_{i} \qquad$ for all i $\qquad$ (10)

(ii) $\qquad \sum_{i=1}^{n} \sum_{h=1}^{m} X_{i}^{lh} = P^{l} \qquad$ for all l $\qquad$ (11)

and

(iii) $\qquad X_{i}^{lh} \geqslant 0 \qquad$ for all i, l, h $\qquad$ (12)

Equation 10, representing the first set of constraints, is n in number while there are w for the second set. The equality sign of constraint set two (equation 11) is to ensure that the model neither fails to allocate all exogenously given population as $\leqslant$ would imply; nor goes on indefinitely with the allocation process as $\geqslant$ would imply.

The above formulation could be improved in a number of ways. First, we may disaggregate the regional household group p^{l} as well as the zonal available land L_{i} to L_{i}^{w}, recognising that zones may be structured in such a way that house types are known. The effect of this on the data base could be immense but it is an approach which entropy maximisation methodology has found useful. Second, it is possible to break down households or household groups into workers and dependants. We could then see the workers as the generators of the journey to work movement system. The problem then would be to link movement behaviour and transport cost into the model. Senior and Wilson (1973) have discussed these approaches within a different conceptual framework, but also show the relationship between that formulation and the linear programming model. Ways of achieving this within the linear programming methodology have been described by Coughlin and Stevens (1959) and by Ochs (1969) in developing general models of the urban spatial structure.

Let us examine the dual of the linear programming problem. Since households maximise aggregate savings, we might expect that this implies the minimisation of rents paid for houses by household groups.

This indeed is the case. Let us define

r_i as the annual rent per unit of land in area i and
v^l the annual subsidy per household for all households of group l.

The dual problem is

$$\text{minimise} \quad \gamma_. = \sum_{i=1}^{n} r_i L_i + \sum_{l=1}^{w} v^l(-p^l) \tag{13}$$

subject to

(i) $s^{lh} r_i - v^l \geqslant b^{lh} - c_i^{lh}$ for all i, l, h (14)

(ii) $r_i \geqslant 0$ for all i (15)

(iii) $v^l \gtrless 0$ for all l (16)

Since linear programming requires that for each constraint in the primal problem, there must be a variable in the dual and vice versa, the land constraints are associated with the rent variables r_i of equation 13 and the requirement that all households must be located makes the subsidy variables v^l a necessary part of the model (Herbert and Stevens, 1960, p. 30, footnote 22). This relationship between v^l and the constraint set (ii) of the primal explains why its signs are unrestricted in the dual.

An interpretation of the dual no doubt throws much light on the operation of the urban land market. For instance, the dual minimises the aggregate net total rent (which is total rent minus subsidies) and hence minimises returns to the *rentier* class. On the other hand, the fact that the subsidies could be positive or negative imply that they add to or subtract from the rent-paying ability of households and hence to the rental income of landowners. Thus the location of a household's residence within the city is controlled by the intersection of his rent-paying ability and the monetary demand of landlords.

Although this model was operational for the Penn-Jersey Study (1964), and to the extent that it was one of many models utilised, it is not possible directly to evaluate its success from the Penn-Jersey report. None the less, one might presume that a suitable degree of confidence was achieved because of the scale of investigation and analysis given in these reports.

4. Metropolitan Area Linear Programming Models

The earliest metropolitan area linear programming model was the one developed by Coughlin and Stevens (1959). Its objective was to plan for industrial land use and commodity transportation in an optimal form, thus recognising the closely related nature of the two variables. As usual, it assumes that the metropolitan area can be broken into n sub-units, for which the planner knows the present land use and for which he could make projections as to consumer demands. Furthermore, the models assume that although the flow of transport between the metropolitan area and the rest of the world is outside the frame of reference, it is expected that the planner knows the level of imports to and exports from the metropolitan area.

In order to plan optimally for the metropolitan area, this model defines its solution in terms of two variables, X the levels of outputs of industries in each area, and S the levels of shipments between areas. Three constraints on the maximisation process were given in terms of land, consumption and commodity flow. The first constraint on land states that the amount of industrial land used up by an industrial plant should not exceed the amount available for that purpose; while the constraint on consumption argues that the amount of commodity produced in an area plus the net imports of the commodity into the area less the industrial requirements for the commodity should be at least equal to the projected consumer demand for the commodity in the area. The third constraint ensures that total imports from and exports to other regions from the metropolitan areas must meet the quota set for such trade while the outputs of each commodity in each area must not be less than present outputs or some other specified minimum.

Let us define the following variables:

S_{ij}^l is the number of units of commodity l shipped from i to j

T_{ij}^l is the ton-miles of transportation required to ship a unit of commodity l from i to j

a_h^k is the number of units of land type h needed per unit output of commodity k

R_j^w is the given number of units of industrial land w available in area j

X_j^k is the number of units of outputs of industry k in area j

I_j^k is the net import of commodity k to area j

D_j^k is the projected consumer demand for commodity k in area j

c_m^k is the fixed number of units of commodity m needed per unit output of commodity k

S_{jr}^l is the number of units of commodity l shipped to the outside region, r

Q_r^l is the projected export of commodity l from our metropolitan area to outside regions.

The objective function minimises the utilisation of transportation in the inter-areal shipment of the conditions, viz.

minimise $\quad Y = \sum\limits_{\substack{i \\ i \ne j}} \sum\limits_{j} \sum\limits_{l} S^l_{ij} \, T^l_{ij}$ $\qquad\qquad$ (17)

subject to

(i) $\qquad \sum\limits_{k} a^{hk} X^k_j \leqslant R^h_j$ $\qquad\qquad$ (18)

(ii) $\qquad X^k_j + I^k_j - \sum\limits_{m} c^k_m X^k_j \geqslant D^k_j$ $\qquad\qquad$ (19)

(iii) $\qquad \sum\limits_{j} S^l_{ij} - \sum\limits_{\substack{v \\ v \notin n}} S^l_{jv} = I^l_j$ $\qquad\qquad$ (20)

and

(iv) $\qquad \sum\limits_{j} S^l_{jr} = Q^l_r$ $\qquad\qquad$ (21)

The dual of this model was not given by the authors. One could, however, speculate that it would be a maximisation function of probably aggregate savings by the industries or plants on their consumption of land and other inputs into their production process. An explicit statement of this dual would have probably indicated the comprehensiveness of this never-tested model of the metropolitan region. Consequently, this model was indeed very speculative and in fact represented one of the earliest ambitions to utilise the linear programming formulation as a general approach for modelling urban and other economic activities.

A similar but more explicit model was the one developed by Ochs (1969). Ochs' model arises from the criticism of a planning procedure which neglects the symbiotic relationship that exists between land uses and the transportation system. For instance, the planning procedure then was one which superimposes over a residential land-use system some exogenous transportation network or vice versa. Ochs saw a recognition of the symbiotic relationship in the design of an optimal land-use transportation system combination instead of an optimal land-use or transportation system.

In effect, the model was a two-stage process. The first part finds a minimum cost combination of housing types, housing locations and flows of traffic from residences to work given a capacitated network and a set of plant outputs. The second part, on the other hand, changes the capacity of the network in a manner which reduces the total cost of housing and transportation. The first part of the problem is solved through a linear programming formulation, the dual solution vector of which constitutes inputs to the second part of the planning problem. Thus, while the primal problem minimises the sum of housing and travel time costs, the dual maximises the marginal cost prices for the use of the transportation system.

Let us define the following variables for the primal problem (again notation differs slightly from the original):

m is the number of plant locations in the metropolitan area. This is subscripted by $j = 1, 2, \ldots, m$

n is the number of residential tracts $i = 1, 2, \ldots, n$

w is the number of different possible types of housing structures, $k = 1, 2, \ldots, w$

$I_{(i,j)}$ is the number of routes connecting destinations j to origin i. This is indexed by $(i,j)r = 1, 2, \ldots I(i,j)$

$T^k_{(i,j)r}$ is the number of people living in housing structures of type k at location i who take route $(i,j)r$ to plant location j

p^k is the unit housing cost of housing structure type k

$C_{(i,j)r}$ is twice the unit cost of traversing route (i,j) r

$C^k_{(i,j)r}$ is the sum of p^k and $C_{(i,j)r}$

D is the number of links in the network; $d = 1, 2, \ldots, D$

$a^k_{d(i,j)r}$ is the unit flow over link d by persons living in housing structure type k at location i traversing route $(i,j)r$

$\bar{s}(d)$ is the velocity per unit of flow over link d

$A^{\bar{s}(d)}$ is the flow capacity of link d at speed $\bar{s}$

L_i the total land available for residential use in tract i

$l^k_{i(i,j)r}$ land required for housing by an individual living in a housing structure of type k in tract i who uses route (i,j) r

E_j is the total work force required at plant site j

$e^k_{(i,j)r}$ is a person who works at plant location j, lives in a structure of type k in tract i and travels along route (i,j) r

The objective function minimising the aggregate housing, and travel time, costs is

$$\text{minimise} \quad Z = \sum_i \sum_j \sum_k \sum_r C_{(i,j)r} T^k_{(i,j,)r} \tag{22}$$

subject to

(i) $$\sum_i \sum_j \sum_k \sum_r - a^k_{i(i,j)r} T^k_{(i,j)r} \geqslant -A^{\bar{s}(d)}_d \qquad (23)$$

(ii) $$\sum_j \sum_k \sum_r - l^k_{i(i,j)r} T^k_{(i,j)r} \geqslant L_i \qquad (24)$$

(iii) $$\sum_i \sum_k \sum_r e^k_{j(i,j)r} T^k_{(i,j)r} = E_j \qquad (25)$$

and

(iv) $$T^k_{(i,j)r} \geqslant 0 \qquad (26)$$

The first set of conditions ensures that the flow of traffic from all sources over a given link does not exceed the flow capacity of that link, while the second ensures that not more than the available residential land is used for residential purposes. The third conditions ensure that the employment requirements of each plant location be met. Since the unit cost of traversing route (i,j) r of the system, i.e. $C_{(i,j)r}$, is definitely a function of the velocity per unit of flow over all links in the particular route, i.e. $\bar{s}(d)$ for all d in the route, it will be realised that the solution vectors of both the dual and the primal will vary with the speeds $\bar{s}(d)$ used to define flow capacity. This is a crucial aspect of the model.

In order to formulate the dual of the primal problem, the following variables are defined:

U_d is the marginal rental value of capacity on link d, i.e. the reduction in aggregate travel and housing costs which could be obtained by a unit increase in the flow capacity of link d

U_i is the marginal rental value of land in tract i and

U_j is the marginal cost of housing and congestion created by employment at plant site j.

The dual then is

maximise $$Y = \sum_j U_j E_j - \sum_d U_d A_d^{\bar{s}(d)} - \sum_i U_i L_i \qquad (27)$$

subject to

(i) $$\sum_d a^k_{d(i,j)r} U_d + \sum_i - l_{i(i,j)r} U_i + \sum_j e^k_{j(i,j)r} U_j \leqslant C^k_{(i,j)r} \qquad (28)$$

for all i, j, k, r

and

(ii) $U_d \geqslant O$; $U_i \geqslant O$ and $U_j \geqslant O$ for all i, j, d (29)

Once the dual problem is solved, one tries alternative possibilities of altering the transportation network, usually by decreasing or increasing the capacity of any link which gives decreases or increases in the total cost of providing capacity on that link greater or less than the increase or reduction in the housing and travel time costs. Since the incremental costs of capacity on a link equals the current rental value of the capital required plus the rental value of the land to provide the increment of capacity, the minimum cost solution to the urban problem is achieved when the dual values for the links specified in the first-stage problem equal the cost of providing increments to those links. Thus this minimum cost solution is reiteratively achieved through a process whereby new capacities determined by the second-stage problem are specified as new constraints for the first-stage linear program.

The same set of criticisms against the Coughlin and Stevens model may be made against this model. In particular is the criticism that it was never operationalised, so that we have no basis of analysing its performance both against models that use the same framework and models that utilise alternative frameworks. However, the explicit statement of urban land uses as well as the flow of transportation is a major contribution of this model. What we however do not know is the extent to which its assumptions reflect reality.

5. Game Theory

Game theory is a widely used technique in both engineering and the social sciences. Its utility in analysing economic behaviour has been demonstrated by von Neumann and Morgenstern (1953) while some applications are emerging in anthropology (Davenport, 1960) and geography (Gould, 1963). Basically, game theory deals with the question of rational decision-making in the face of uncertain conditions by choosing certain strategies to outwit an opponent, or at least to maintain a position superior to others (Gould, 1963). We may see this in terms of intra-city location, whereby an entrepreneur or locater has to visualise the location of his activity *vis-à-vis* the location of others of similar characteristics.

A zero-sum two-person game, so described because the gain of a strategist is the loss of the opponent, is probably the least complicated of the game theoretic approaches. It is in fact a special case of linear programming although it is slightly more complicated. For instance while in linear programming the solution of the dual is not necessarily a required part of the objective, in game theory the solution of both primal and dual problems at the same time is the objective. This is why the solution to a game theoretic problem is always defined in terms of a minimax solution.

In zero-sum two-person game theory it is usual to assume that both players are malevolent, i.e. each is concerned with maximising his own gains or minimising his own losses; and that both are aware of, and intelligent enough to evaluate accurately, the pay-offs associated with both players' alternative strategies. Let us consider two players, A and B, each having two strategies $_sA_1$, $_sA_2$; $_sB_1$, $_sB_2$ respectively. Let the pay-offs (a_{ij}) associated with these strategies be represented in columns for A and rows for B. Then the pay-off matrix is

	$_sA_1$	$_sA_2$	B's prob.
$_sB_1$	a_{11}	a_{12}	y_1
$_sB_2$	a_{13}	a_{14}	y_2
A's prob.	x_1	x_2	

Let the probability associated with A's strategies be x_1 and x_2 and B's strategies be y_1 and y_2, thus

$$\sum_i x_i = \sum_i y_i = 1 \tag{30}$$

$$i = 1, 2, \ldots, n$$

Such a game as above is said to possess a mixed strategy since it is not immediately obvious which of the two strategies either A or B will choose. For A the expected pay-off is given by

$$\sum_i a_{ij} x_i = v \tag{31}$$

meaning that A will not gain less than

$$\min_j \text{ of } \sum_i a_{ij} x_i = v \tag{32}$$

Equations 32 and 30 may be cast around and written as

$$a_{1j} x_1 + \ldots + a_{mj} x_m \geqslant v \quad \text{for all } j = 1, \ldots, n \tag{33}$$

$$x_1 + x_2 + \ldots + x_m = 1.0 \tag{34}$$

$$x_i \geqslant 0 \quad \text{for all } i = 1, \ldots, m \tag{35}$$

Dividing equations 33 and 34 by v gives

$$a_{ij} \frac{x_1}{v} + \ldots + a_{mj} \frac{x_m}{v} \geqslant 1.0 \qquad (33a)$$

$$\frac{x_1 + x_2 + \ldots + x_m}{v} = \frac{1}{v} \qquad (34a)$$

If we define x_i/v as x_i', A's expected behaviour may be described as

minimise $\quad \sum_i x_i' = 1.0 \qquad (36)$

such that

$$\sum_i a_{ij} x_i' \geqslant 1.0 \qquad (37)$$

and using similar arguments and transformations, B's behaviour might be described as

maximise $\quad \sum y_i' = 1.0 \qquad (38)$

such that

$$\sum_j a_{ij} y_i' \leqslant 1.0 \qquad (39)$$

It should be intuitively obvious to the reader that these equations could possibly be solved by the simplex algorithm, since they have the same forms as linear programming problems. This indeed is the case but we cannot go into the details here. The interested reader should consult von Neumann and Morgenstern (1953) or standard texts on game theory (Vajda, 1956; Bennion, 1960, pp. 102-25).

Peter Gould has analysed the behaviour of Jantile farmers of Ghana as well as the market choice of cattle-herders, also in Ghana, in terms of game theory (Gould, 1963). In both cases, the game was two-person, zero-sum between the farmers and the herders on the one hand, and the environment on the other. According to him, valuable insights were provided into spatial behaviour and decision-making. It remains, however, to be seen and shown how urban analysis could be framed in terms of game theory, and in such a way that meaningful models of the urban spatial structure are derived.

6. Location-allocation Modelling

Location-allocation systems constitute a class of combinatorial problems in spatial analysis (Scott, 1971). Since spatially structured combinatorial problems could be identified with mathematical systems whose component elements represent the most basic of spatial entities such as points, lines, regions and areas, it would be seen that these problems could be of immense use in urban analysis as well as planning. Combinatorial problems fall into two general classes, viz. those dealing with network or graph theoretic problems and those dealing with grouping and partitioning problems. The first includes such considerations as the setting up of a one-way system, the establishment and servicing of a network of public transportation facilities or the development of an electricity distribution system. The second deals with such problems as the location of a group of central facilities such as schools, hospitals and warehouses, the establishment of electoral districts or the optimal determination of a set of administrative regions. The commonality between these two sets of problems arises from consideration of efficiency and optimality in the structuring of space.

The quest for accessibility of services and facilities to consumers is as crucial within the city as it is in any geographical investigation. Location-allocation methods provide an approach for analysing the optimality in locational decision as well as efficiency in human spatial behaviour. The general structure of location-allocation methods is as follows: given the distribution in space of a set of n points, their weights (or population), a set of p indivisible centroids or facilities without predetermined locations; and given transportation or shipping costs, the problem is to find location for the p facilities, the allocation of each point to these facilities and the quantities to be transferred in such a way as to optimise an objective function such as the total costs of operation. It is easy to see how location-allocation methods generalise into questions of taxonomic description, regionalisation and optimal spatial clustering (Scott, 1971, p. 118).

Let us reflect on the general location-allocation model described above. If the locations of all central facilities are known in advance, while the assignment of flows is not known, the problem reduces to the ordinary transportation problem of linear programming. On the other hand, if the assignment of flows is known but the geographical disposition of the central facilities is unknown, the problem reduces to a pure locational Weberian problem. The Weberian location problem is to find the location for a single central facility such that the cost of flows between this facility and the n points is a minimum. On the other hand if we want to locate p centres to serve the given distribution of population, our location-allocation problem becomes the well known p

median problem (Cooper, 1967). The transportation problem is easily solved by a variation of the simplex method called the north-west corner algorithm (Hitchcock, 1941) but the solution of the Weberian problem or the p-median problem requires the use of calculus techniques.

The extended Weberian problem may be stated mathematically as follows. Given a set of fixed destinations which may be the distribution of populations we wish to find the locations (x_i, y_i) $i = 1, 2 \ldots p$ in Euclidean space, of a set of p sources (which could be interpreted as schools, for instance) that serve these destinations in some way and to find simultaneously the allocation of populations to schools so as to minimise the sum of distances from the sources to the destinations. This is given by

$$Q = \sum_{i=1}^{p} \sum_{j=1}^{n} \alpha_{ij} \left[(x_{Dj} - x_i)^2 + (y_{Dj} - y_i)^2 \right]^{\frac{1}{2}} \qquad (40)$$

(i) $\qquad \sum_{i=1}^{P} \alpha_{ij} = 1 \qquad (j = 1, \ldots, n) \qquad (41)$

and

(ii) $\qquad \alpha_{ij} = 0,1 \qquad$ for all i,j $\qquad (42)$

where the variable α_{ij} determines whether or not the jth point is assigned to the ith facility. The condition expressed in equation 41 ensures that each point is assigned to one and only one central facility (or partition). It is known (Cooper, 1969; Scott, 1971) that a solution exists for equation 40 if and only if

$$\frac{\delta Q}{\delta x_i} = \frac{\alpha_{ij} (x_{Dj} - x_i)}{\left[(x_{Dj} - x_i)^2 + (y_{Dj} - y_i)^2 \right]^{\frac{1}{2}}} = 0 \qquad (43)$$

and

$$\frac{\delta Q}{\delta y_i} = \frac{\alpha_{ij} (y_{Dj} - y_i)}{\left[(x_{Dj} - x_i)^2 + (y_{Dj} - y_i)^2 \right]^{\frac{1}{2}}} = 0 \qquad (44)$$

While equations 43 and 44 constitute necessary and sufficient conditions for (x_i, y_i) to be a solution of equation 40, various algorithms have to be developed for their solution (Cooper, 1969; Nordbeck and Rystedt, 1971). Many of these algorithms are iterative and proceed as follows. If we set

$$V_j = \left[(x_{Dj} - x_i)^2 + (y_{Dj} - y_i)^2 \right]^{1/2} \qquad (45)$$

the solution can be approximated to any degree of accuracy by the iteration of equations 46 and 47

$$x_{r+1} = \sum_{j=1}^{n} \sum_{i=1}^{P} \frac{\alpha_{ij} x_j}{V_{jr}} \Bigg/ \sum_{j=1}^{n} \sum_{i=1}^{P} \frac{\alpha_{ij}}{V_{jr}} \qquad (46)$$

$$y_{r+1} = \sum_{j=1}^{n} \sum_{i=1}^{P} \frac{\alpha_{ij} y_i}{V_{jr}} \Bigg/ \sum_{j=1}^{n} \sum_{i=1}^{P} \frac{\alpha_{ij}}{V_{jr}} \qquad (47)$$

where r is an iteration parameter. The crucial problem is then in the selection of initial values of (x_i, y_i), since most algorithms developed either for an exact or heuristic solution are known to be very sensitive to these values (Goodchild and Massam, 1969; Rushton et al. 1973). For the one-centre Weber problem, the co-ordinates of the centre of gravity of the set of n points have been found to yield a good starting-point that leads to rapid convergence. For the p-median case, intelligent guesses could always be made, while if one wants to evaluate real locations against an optimum configuration, one could always use real values as initial starting values.

There is an increasing use of location-allocation methods in geographical analysis. Goodchild and Massam (1969) used these techniques in evaluating the siting of regional centres and the determination of administrative areas while a collection of some algorithms for exact and heuristic solutions of location allocation methods is given in Rushton et al. (1973). It is definitely a suitable technique for analysing the spatial efficiency of the intra-city location of such facilities as schools, hospitals and recreational areas. The methods possess one major advantage over the linear programming formulation of earlier sections of this chapter. This advantage stems from the fact that location-allocation methods find the optimal distribution of activities as well as an efficient system of flows or interaction between supply and demand points. To this extent, it constitutes a powerful technique for the evaluation or operationalisation of the concept of spatial efficiency described in Chapter 4 of this book. Its major criticism is the almost total absence of behavioural assumptions about haman spatial interaction. Consequently, location-allocation methods cannot be described as models of the society but rather as models that are prescriptive or evaluative of the degree of optimality in societal spatial and locational behaviour.

There is an increasing use of location-allocation methods in geographical analysis. For instance, Goodchild and Massam (1969) used these techniques in evaluating the siting of regional centres and the determination of administrative areas in Ontario, Canada. This utilisation of the technique which was based on an earlier conceptualisation by Revelle (1968) and Teitz (1967) could be of very great value in studies of regionalisation and spatial clustering of regional systems. In urban centres, it would find ready application in studies of electoral districting and even in efficient partitioning of urban space for planning purposes. Let us explain this by the case of a city whereby one has to located say p polling booths ($p \geqslant 2$) while there are n points of population distribution to be served by these booths. Let us assume further that we want to solve this problem simultaneously such that we produce a partitioning of this population distribution in an optimal way so that the set of points served by a central facility is uniquely served by this facility. The location-allocation problem is simply that of finding an optimal p-fold partitioning of the original point set (see Scott, 1971. p. 122).

As defined above, the problem could involve considerations of partitioning a point set in continuous or discrete space. For the optimal partitioning in a continuous space, the problem is

$$\text{minimise} \quad Z = \sum_{i=1}^{n} \sum_{j=1}^{P} \alpha_{ij} r_j \left[(x_{Dj} - x_i)^2 + (y_{Dj} - y_i)^2 \right]^{\frac{1}{2}} \quad (48)$$

subject to
$$\sum_{i=1}^{P} \alpha_{ij} = 1 \qquad j = 1, 2, \ldots, n \quad (49)$$

and
$$\alpha_{ij} = 0, 1 \qquad \text{for all } i \text{ and } j \quad (50)$$

where the variable α_{ij} determines whether or not the point is assigned to the ith facility. Equation 49 ensures that each point is assigned to one and only one central facility or partition. Scott (1971) notes that the solution of equations 48 to 50 could not only be difficult but could also be computationally expensive. However, if the problem is reduced to a discrete space, it becomes more easily tractable, though at the expense of exactness in the final solution.

The formulation of the location-allocation model for optimal partitioning in a discrete space is due to Revelle (1968). Let us assume as before that there are n discrete regions and that the distance between any two regions i and j is d_{ij}. In addition, let r_j be the specified level of demand upon a central facility which is closest to it and let us assume that any region may be adopted as the location for a central facility (see Scott, 1971, pp. 124–5). The problem is then

$$\text{minimise} \quad Z = \sum_{n=1}^{n} \sum_{j=1}^{n} \alpha_{ij} r_j d_{ij} \tag{51}$$

subject to

$$\sum_{i=1}^{n} \alpha_{ij} = 1 \qquad (j = 1, 2, \ldots, n) \tag{52}$$

$$\sum_{i=1}^{n} \alpha_{ii} = P \qquad (i = 1, 2, \ldots, n) \tag{53}$$

$$\alpha_{ii} - \alpha_{ij} \geqslant 0 \quad \begin{cases} (i = 1, 2, \ldots, n) \\ (j = 1, 2, \ldots, n) \\ (i \neq j) \end{cases} \tag{54}$$

$$\alpha_{ij} \geqslant 0 \qquad \text{for all } i \text{ and } j \tag{55}$$

Whenever $\alpha_{ij} = 1$, region j is assigned to a central facility in i; whereas the condition expressed in equation 53 ensures that exactly p central facilities are located. It is assumed that if a central facility is located in region i, then at optimality, region i will be assigned to that facility. Furthermore, equation 54 ensures that if $a_{ii} = 0$, then no central facility exists at i and no region j may be assigned to i.

Location-allocation models constitute very suitable techniques for analysing the spatial efficiency of the intra-city location of such facilities as schools, health centres and recreational areas. They could also be very useful in delimiting urban areas into efficient zones for planning purposes. The methods of location-allocation systems possess one major advantage over the linear programming formulations of earlier sections of this chapter. This advantage stems from the fact that location-allocation methods find the optimal distribution of activities as well as an efficient system of flows or interactions between supply and demand points. To this extent, the methods constitute a powerful technique for the evaluation or operationalisation of the concept of spatial efficiency described in Chapter 4 of this book. Its major criticism is the almost total absence of behavioural assumptions about human spatial interaction. Consequently, location-allocation methods cannot be described as models of the society but rather as models that are prescriptive or evaluative of the degree of optimality in societal spatial and locational behaviour.

7. Conclusion

All the models described in this chapter have one general characteristic. They are based on the maximisation or minimisation of some objective function. For instance, in the case of the residential location model, this objective function was the minimisation of house rents and transportation costs while deriving a maximum utility from the facilities provided by the housing market. Thus, the models act under the strong but hardly sustained assumption that man the actor is perfectly knowledgeable and rational in his decision-making. Pertinent questions therefore can be asked as to the extent to which man can be regarded as rational and omniscient. Many criticisms of optimising models are based on these questions. A summary of these criticisms were provided by Pred (1967).

Pred argues that there are three fundamental criticisms of this approach in studying human behaviour. First, human behaviour is not optimal because competition in real life is not perfect. Furthermore, it is not accurate to see the urban resident as a rational economic man whose aim is to maximise his utility function since man does not possess the mental acumen of the economic man, which is nothing less than 'preposterously omniscient rationality'. As an alternative, he offered a scheme for explaining the spatial behaviour of people. The scheme involves the acceptance of Simon's concepts of bounded rationality which implies that any decision-maker does not possess the mental acumen to know all the repercussions of his possible actions; and that of satisficing behaviour. Satisficing behaviour implies that people or actors look not necessarily for optimum profits but rather for profits that are considered satisfactory. We consider there criticisms as valid as optimising models tell us what people should do rather than what they do. It is crucial to remember that there is much sub-optimality in human behaviour.

Furthermore, optimality models are deterministic and hence too rigid for modelling human behaviour, which is not only flexible but little understood. The rigidity in these models assume that we can unambigously describe human action in terms of a system of equations. This is often not the case. Nevertheless, optimisation models, as normative models, play the very important role of acting as evaluative criteria of human action. It is in this sense that they can be meaningfully used.

References

Almon. C. Jr. 1967. *Matrix Methods in Economics.* Reading, Massachusetts: Wesley

Alonso, W. 1964. *Location and Land Use: Toward a General Theory of Land Rent.* Cambridge, Massachusetts: Harvard University Press

Batty, M. 1970. Recent Developments in Land Use Modelling. *Urban Systems Research Unit.* Department of Geography, University of Reading

Beckman, M. and Marschak, T., 1955. An Activity Analysis Approach to Location Theory. *Kyklos*, Fasc. 2

Bennion, E.G. 1960. *Elementary Mathematics of Linear Programming and Game Theory.* East Lansing, Michigan: Michigan University Press

Churchman, C.W., Ackoff, R.L., Arnoff, L., *et al.* 1957. *Introduction to Operations Research.* New York: John Wiley

Cooper, L. 1967. Solutions of Generalized Locational Equilibrium Models. *Journal of Regional Science*, 7, 1, 1–8

Davenport, W. 1960. Jamaican Fishing: a Game Theoretic Analysis. *Yale University Publications in Anthropology*, No. 59

Dorfman, R., Samuelson, P.A., and Solow, R.M., 1958. *Linear Programming and Economic Analysis*, New York: McGraw-Hill

Goodchild, M.F., and Massam, B.H. 1969. Some Least Cost Models of Spatial Administrative Systems in Southern Ontario. *Geografiske Annaller*, 52B, 86–94

Gould, P.R. 1963. Man Against his Environment: A Game Theoretic Framework. *Annals, Association of American Geographers*, 53, 290–7

Herbert, J.D., and Stevens, B.H. 1960. A Model for the Distribution of Residential Activity in Urban Areas. *Journal of Regional Science*, 2, 2, 21–36

Hitchcock, F.L. 1941. The Distribution of a Product from Several Sources to Numerous Locations. *Journal of Mathematics and Physics*, 20, 224–30

Isard, W. 1958. Interrogational Linear Programming: An Elementary Presentation and A General Model. *Journal of Regional Science*, 1, 1, 1–59

Isard, W. 1960. *Methods of Regional Analysis.* Cambridge, Massachusetts: M.I.T. Press

Koopmans, T.C. 1951. *Activity Analysis of Production and Allocation.* New York: John Wiley

Koopmans, T.C., and Beckman, M. 1957. Assignment Problems and the Location of Economic Activities. *Econometrica*, 25, 53–76

Von Neumann, J., and Morgenstern, O. 1953. *Theory of Games and Economic Behaviour.* Princeton, New Jersey: Princeton University Press

Nordbeck, S., and Rystedt, B., 1970. Computer Cartography: A Multiple Location Problem. In G. Tornquist *et al.* (eds.), *Multiple Location Analysis.* Lund Series in Geography Series C, No. 12. Gleerup, Lund

Ochs, J. 1969. An Application of Linear Programming to Urban Spatial Organisation. *Journal of Regional Science*, 9, 3, 451–7

Pennsylvania Department of Highways. 1964. *Pennsylvania-Jersey Transportation Study.* PB. 173.327. Springfield, Virginia: Federal Scientific and Technical Information

Pred, A. 1967. *Behavior and Location Part I.* Lund Series in Geography Series B, No. 27. Gleerup, Lund

Revelle, C.S. 1968. *Central Facilities Location.* Center for Environmental Quality Management. Cornell University Report No. 1002

Rushton, G., Goodchild, M.F., and Ostresh, L.M. Jr. 1973. *Computer Programs for Location-Allocation Problems.* Monograph No. 6. Department of University of Iowa

Scott, A.J. 1971. *Combinatorial Programming, Spatial Analysis and Planning.* London: Methuen

Senior, M.L., and Wilson, A.G. 1973. Disaggregated Residential Location Models: Some Tests and Further Theoretical Development. In E.L. Cripps (ed.),

Space-time Concepts in Regional Science, London: Pion

Stevens, B.H., and Coughlin, R.E. 1959. A Note on Inter-Area Linear Programming for a Metropolitan Area. *Journal of Regional Science, 1,* 2, 75-80

Teitz, M. 1967. *Toward a Theory of Urban Public Facility Location.* CPDR Working Paper No. 67. Berkeley, California: Berkeley Center for Planning and Development Research, University of California

Vajda, S. 1960. *An Introduction to Linear Programming.* London: Methuen

10 ENTROPY MODELLING

1. Introduction

The concept of entropy has at least two origins, namely physics and information theory. This duality of origin has generated some contradiction in its usage (Marchand, 1972). The term was first used in the nineteenth century in thermo-dynamics, to represent a certain modality of energy of a system and its interpretation was based on two principles of thermodynamics, known as the principles of the conservation and degradation of energy. The first states that macroscopic systems have definite and precise energies subject to a definite conservation principle while the second, often called Carnot's principle, postulates that energy may change from a superior level (mechanical or electrical) to an intermediate level (chemical) and to an inferior level (heat). It is this second principle that defines entropy as the measure of the differences in the nature and repartition of energy. Thus for a system whose temperature is T and which experiences some change Q in heat, the change in entropy is

$$dS = dQ\left(\frac{1}{T}\right) \tag{1}$$

Entropy is therefore a derived or second-order concept that can indicate the loss or gain in the capacity to do work due to energetic transactions in parts of a system.

The statistical formulation of entropy in thermodynamics is due to Boltzmann. According to him, if matter were made up of populations of molecules and atoms (described as complexions by Planck), whose number for a given mass could be closely estimated; and if there are n energy states such that f_i is the number of particles in a state i, then the entropy is given by

$$S = k \sum_{i=1}^{n} f_i \log f_i \tag{2}$$

where k, the Boltzmann constant, equals approximately 10^{-6} degrees Kelvin in the c-g-s-system.

The second origin of the concept may be traced to modern developments in communications engineering. An offshoot of this is information theory which defines information as 'a measure of one's freedom of choice when one selects a message' (Shannon and Weaver, 1949, p. 100).

237

This theory does not consider the subjective value of a piece of information in terms of its importance to the person who receives it. It deals with the 'statistical rarity' or the 'surprise value' of messages. Consequently, it looks at information in terms of probabilities. For instance, given that messages $E_1, E_2 \ldots, E_n$ have probabilities $p_1, p_2 \ldots, p_n$ of occurrence, *the entropy of the information or the information content H* is defined as

$$H = -\sum_{i=1}^{n} p_i \log P_i \qquad (3)$$

and

$$\sum_{i=1}^{n} P_i = 1 \qquad (4)$$

Equations 2 and 3, which define thermodynamic entropy and information theory entropy respectively, are very similar, and it is this similarity that generated the contradiction in its usage. It must be noted, however, that these formulae cannot be equated for, without a temperature constant, entropy in information theory defines a property of an equation and not the inevitable state of a closed thermodynamic system (Chapman, 1970). Brillouin, who discussed this contradiction extensively, has suggested that the physical entropy S be retained while the information theory entropy H be interpreted as the information content or the negentropy of the system (Brillouin, 1956, p. 288). The two are, however, related through the negentropy principle of information. But it may be argued that while the physical entropy S measures the energetic state of a system, the information theory H measures the structural state. This argument is supported by the observation that entropy in thermodynamics is measured in energy units, viz. degrees Kelvin in the c-g-s system, whereas in information theory the unit of measurement is the base of the logarithm. In this latter case, nits, (natural units) are used when the logarithm is to base e, dits (decimal units) when it is to base 10 while bits (binary units) when the base of the logarithm is 2. Binary units are the most popular since these are easily related to decision processes embedded in information theory (Cherry, 1965). The two entropies can, however, be used complementarily, as any structural state is a function of the disposition and the amount of energy in a system.

2. Entropy and the City System

The concept of entropy provides a number of useful techniques that have been found invaluable in many branches of knowledge ranging from statistics (Kullback, 1958) to psychology (Attneave, 1959), econometrics (Lisman, 1949), economics (Theil, 1967) and geography (Medvedkov, 1970). It is therefore one that offers great potentialities for studies of urban structure. In economics, it has been used to provide greater insights into many economic models while in geography it has been utilised in the study of settlement patterns (Chapman, 1970; Medvekov, 1970), network analysis (Medvedkov, 1967) and in the generation of models of urban and regional systems (Wilson, 1970) and in the development of a theory of settlement location (Curry, 1964). In urban studies, this concept can be used in at least two ways, namely, the analysis of the functional association and spatial structure and also in the generation of *process-pattern* models of urban structure. These models possess two important uses. First, through their derivation within a hypothetico-deductive system, they enable theory development, while second, as process-pattern models, they could be used for planning and monitoring an urban system. These uses employ the two interpretations of entropy discussed above.

The use of the entropy concept to generate models of spatial interaction and spatial structure has been discussed by Wilson (1967) and Curry (1964). It involves the notion of uncertainty in a system (of 'molecules') subject to random motion. The most probable state of the elements of the system is achieved when its entropy is maximised subject to the constraints on the micro-state of the system. The method, developed in statistical physics, is based on the theory of ensembles and is called the entropy maximising methodology (Wilson, 1970). However, an analogy has been found in urban and regional studies in the movement behaviour of people. We may illustrate this by the journey to work-residential location sub-system within a city where there are n residential zones and n places of work. If T_{ij} is the interaction of trips variable between the ith residence and the jth work place, we can define as constraints the following equations.

$$\sum_{i=1}^{n} T_{ij} = E_j \tag{5}$$

which implies that the number of people who go to work is balanced by the number of employment opportunities; and

$$\alpha \sum_{j=1}^{n} T_{ij} = \psi_i \tag{6}$$

where

$$\frac{1}{a} = \alpha, \ 0 < a \leqslant 1 \tag{7}$$

The variable ψ_i is the population at residential zone i and a is the ratio of workers in a household to total number of people in the household. The constant α is the inverse of a. Equation 6 merely states that in a household, there is at least one worker so that the population who lives in a residential zone is easily derivable from the interaction variable scaled by the constant α. We can now introduce a hypothesis about residential location in terms of the cost of the journey to work. If we then define c_{ij} as the generalised cost of movement between residence i and place of work j and C as the total cost of movement for the journey to work-residential location system, then

$$\sum_{i=1}^{n} \sum_{j=1}^{n} T_{ij} c_{ij} = C \tag{8}$$

It has been shown (Wilson, 1970) that if we define P_{ij} as

$$P_{ij} = \frac{T_{ij}}{T} \tag{9}$$

where

$$T = \sum_{i=1}^{n} \sum_{i=1}^{n} T_{ij} \tag{10}$$

in the equations above, the entropy of the journey to work—residential location sub-system is given by

$$S = (\log T! - T\log T + T) - T \sum_{i=1}^{n} \sum_{j=1}^{n} P_{ij} \log P_{ij} \tag{11}$$

which but for the constant in brackets is of the same form as equation 3 above. The most probable state of a system is the equilibrium state which is achieved when the entropy of the system is maximised subject to the system constraints. For the journey to work sub-system, this state occurs when the entropy of equation 11 is maximised subject to equations 5 and 8 as system constraints. The pattern of the journey to work is then described by the interaction model

$$T_{ij} = B_j E_j \exp\left(-\beta c_{ij}\right) \tag{12}$$

and

$$B_j = \left[\sum_{i=1}^{n} \exp\left(-\beta c_{ij}\right)\right]^{-1} \tag{13}$$

The parameter β is the Lagrangian multiplier associated with the cost constraint equation 8 and it governs the worker's propensity to interact on the transport system. The variable B_j is a balancing term which measures the overall attractiveness of the individual zones.

It is interesting to note the similarity between this model represented by equations 12 and 13 and the gravity model (Carrothers, 1956; Isard, 1960). Conceptually, however, the model differs from the gravity model. Equations 12 and 13 have constituted points of departure for the development of models of urban structure (Batty, 1970; Cripps and Foot, 1971). For instance, the residential location component is provided by summing equation 12 over j and scaling by the constant α above. This approach will be utilised to develop not only descriptive models of urban structure but also those that possess some predictive capabilities.

The immediate benefits of the model described above lie in the explicit statement of terms and definition of parameters. For instance, there is an explicit statement of the impedance function, the aspect that describes the function of distance, as exponential. In criticisms of the gravity model it is the uncertainty of the form of this equation that has featured most prominently. Furthermore, there is the ease of interpretation of the parameters of the model and finally the system of equations is very consistent and thus we are able to justify the introduction of the B_j constraints where necessary.

The greatest advantage of the entropy maximisation model does not lie only in its being stochastic. It also concerns the fact that it offers a unique opportunity for studying system dynamics and for developing dynamic or quasi-dynamic models of urban spatial structure. The study of system dynamics may be approached from the interpretation from thermodynamics, that the change in entropy of a system equals the change in system energy plus the work done externally on the system namely

$$dS = \mu dE + \mu \sum_k X_k dx_k$$

where dS is the change in entropy, dE is the change in system energy and X_k is the external force corresponding to external co-ordinate x_k (Wilson, 1970, p. 12). On the other hand dynamic or quasi-dynamic models may be built firstly by recognising that change is represented in the birth, death and migration rates which are best studied at the micro-level, that is, the household or firm level. This in itself involves two types of problems, namely the aggregation of micro-level behaviour into planning models and the incorporation of the processes of change.

The study of system dynamics is beyond the scope of this chapter as it requires major definitional problems of the concepts of social energy and work and measurements of their rates of change. The case of the introduction of dynamic and quasi-dynamic principles falls within the ambit of the book. Some of the approaches are discussed in subsequent chapters. Before we turn to the exploration of these ideas, let us examine the other use of the concept of entropy in urban analysis.

This other use of the concept of entropy is based on the notion that the entropy of a probability distribution as given in equation 3 above is properly defined with both maximum and minimum values thus:

$$0 \leqslant H \leqslant \log n \tag{14}$$

where $\log n$, the maximum value of H occurs when all the probability values are each equal to $1/n$; and zero, the minimum value of H occurs when all but one p is not equal to zero. When all but one p is not equal to zero, there is no uncertainty and there is maximum degree of order. But when all ps are equal, uncertainty is greatest and the amount of order is least.

Attempts have been made in geography to equate the minimum and maximum values with patterns of spatial distribution. The approach has been to interpret organisation in terms relating to the reduction in information from the case of maximum entropy. For example, Medvedkov (1967) compares the case of uniform distribution with maximum information which by the interpretation above means maximum entropy! This does not seem reasonable and it may be well to heed Chapman's (1970) warning that this index has no ability to consider the relative location of points. It therefore seems logical to use the index only in the sense that maximum entropy or minimum information means complete disorder, and therefore greater uncertainty, whereas maximum information implies less uncertainty. It would seem that the major source or error lies in the confusion of the technical meaning of information with its everyday meaning.

Just as interaction can be modelled using the concept of entropy, the information theory entropy provides indices that could be used to describe the structure of flows. To do this, bivariate forms of equation 3 are defined. Following Theil (1967), these are

$$H(P_{ij}) = - \sum_i^n \sum_j^n P_{ij} \log P_{ij} \quad \text{(Joint Information)} \tag{15}$$

$$H(P_{i*}) = -\overset{n}{\underset{i}{\Sigma}} P_{i*} \log P_{i*} \quad \text{(Row Information)} \qquad (16)$$

$$H(P_{*j}) = -\overset{n}{\underset{j}{\Sigma}} P_{*j} \log P_{*j} \quad \text{(Column Information)} \qquad (17)$$

where

$$P_{ij} = \frac{T_{ij}}{\overset{n}{\underset{i}{\Sigma}} \overset{n}{\underset{j}{\Sigma}} ij} \qquad \text{as defined above}$$

Other measures include the expected joint information which may or may not be equal to the joint entropy measured by equation 15. This index, encountered when all origins and destinations are independent, is defined as

$$H(P_{ij}) = \overset{n}{\underset{i}{\Sigma}} \overset{n}{\underset{j}{\Sigma}} P_{ij} \log (P_{i*}/P_{i*}P_{*j}) \qquad (18)$$

$$= H(P_{i*}) + H(P_{*j}) - H(P_{ij}) \qquad (19)$$

and is the first moment of P_{ij}.

Another measure that may be defined occurs when there are both *a priori* probabilities P_{ij} and *a posteriori* probabilities Q_{ij}. This is defined as information gain I and it is

$$(20) \qquad I(Q{:}P) = \overset{n}{\underset{i}{\Sigma}} \overset{n}{\underset{j}{\Sigma}} Q_{ij} \log (Q_{ij}/P_{ij}) \qquad (20)$$

The interpretation of the above indices is facilitated if it is remembered that for any flow pattern, a complete dispersion of inputs and outputs and hence linkages means maximum uncertainty in tracing the course of each flow. Furthermore, whre there is maximum concentration of inputs and outputs, there is little uncertainty in finding a place in the system for a randomly selected flow. The joint information is therefore a measure of statistical linkage between origins and destinations. The information gain index, on the other hand, is a means of comparing the accuracy of one set of forecasts over another. It may therefore be used to compare the structure of two flows. Its minimum value of zero occurs when the *a priori* and the *a posteriori* probabilities are equal. Its maximum value, when the *a posteriori* probabilities are maximised may be shown to be given by

$$I(Q{:}P)_{\max} = H(Q_{ij})_{\max} - 1 \tag{21}$$

where

$$H(Q_{ij})_{\max} = \log n^2$$

It has been shown so far that the concept of entropy from systems analysis produces an 'organising concept' in our ability to utilise the framework to develop models of spatial interaction and spatial structure. It has also been shown that this same concept provides a number of useful techniques for the description and analysis of the structure of spatial interaction. Consequently, the concept of entropy may be seen as a needed integrating concept in urban studies.

3. Empirical Investigation of the Uses of the Entropy Concept in Urban Analysis

In this section we shall illustrate the two uses of entropy described in the previous section. We shall also attempt a synthesis of these uses. The data for the analysis is the pattern of spatial interaction of the journey to work over 18 zones into which Jos was divided for analysis. This pattern of interaction can be related to the residential location by summing the matrix over columns and scaling by the activity rate. Table 10.3.1, which contains the details of the interactional pattern, shows that many of the zones are important work centres. Furthermore, the row totals also show that these same zones are important residential areas, thus highlighting the heterogeneous nature of land use in the city. In order to illustrate the use of entropy in simulating this pattern, the constraint equation 8 is slightly modified to reflect more behavioural assumptions of residential location by the introduction of W_i defined as the benefits that could be derived by locating one's residence in zone i.

It therefore has the form

$$\sum_{i=1}^{n} T_{ij}(c_{ij} - W_i) = C' \tag{8a}$$

which may be interpreted as saying that the actual cost of transport is the differential between the true cost and the benefit (measured in monetary terms) that could be derived from different residential zones. As a result of this modification, the interaction equation becomes

$$T_{ij} = B_j E_j \exp\left[-\beta(c_{ij} - W_i)\right] \tag{12a}$$

Table 10.3.1: Journey to Work Interaction Matrix, Jos, 1972 (samples)

	1	2	3	4	5	6	7	8	9	10	11	12	13	14	15	16	17	18	Total
1	31		6		1		20	7	4	4	5	6	6	17			2	3	112
2	6	21	5				8		2	2	6	26	4	19			3	2	104
3	2		18	1		2	1		1	2		5	1	12				1	46
4	6		2	66	4		10	2	12	2	2	44	4	24			14	12	204
5	6		2	2	46	2	8			3	14	42	2	10	12				130
6	4	9	27	3	15	111	21	6		2	6	45	3	81			1	42	390
7	3		2		5		16	1	1	1	1	4	6	16		2	2	2	61
8	5		5		3	1	8	6	3		6	7	3	40		4	1	7	97
9	5		2		3	1	4	2	31	1	4	18	1	31		3	3	2	109
10		2	2		5		15	8	2	21	14	23	1	30				8	142
11																			
12	6		3		6	3	3				3	132	9	9		3	3	6	174
13	1						4				3	1	1	8		1	1	5	34
14	1						2			1				20			1		27
15			3		6					3		3	6	24	24		3	6	78
16																			
17	1				1		4					1		8			9	1	24
18	1													1			1	30	34
Total	78	32	77	72	95	120	124	32	56	43	64	357	47	350	36	13	43	127	1,766

or

$$T_{ij} = B_j E_j V_i \exp\left[-\beta c_{ij}\right] \tag{12b}$$

where

$$B_j = \sum_{i=1}^{n} V_i \exp\left[-\beta c_{ij}\right]^{-1} \tag{13a}$$

and

$$V_i = \exp\left(\beta W_i\right) \; ; \; V_i > 0 \tag{22}$$

Because of the difficulty of operationally measuring terms like utility or benefits, it was hypothesised that these benefits of locating in a zone, represented by equation 22, covary with the quality and quantity of houses in the zone (Batty, 1970).

The technique of simulation required the use of the computer to calibrate the model, i.e. to derive its crucial parameters. The coefficient of association R, between the observed and simulated zonal populations, and the mean trip length were used as calibration statistics. The coefficient of association R is defined as

$$R = \frac{N\sum_{i=1}^{n} \psi_i \psi_i' - \left(\sum_{i=1}^{n} \psi_i\right)\left(\sum_{i=1}^{n} \psi_i'\right)}{\left[\left\{N\sum_{i=1}^{n} \psi_i^2 - \left(\sum_{i=1}^{n} \psi_i\right)^2\right\}\left\{N\sum_{i=1}^{n} \psi_i'^2 - \left(\sum_{i=1}^{n} \psi_i'\right)^2\right\}\right]^{1/2}} \tag{23}$$

where ψ_i, ψ_i' are the observed and simulated zonal populations respectively and N is the number of zones in the city. The mean trip length $\bar{C}$ is defined as

$$\bar{C} = \frac{\sum_{i=1}^{n}\sum_{j=1}^{n}\left[T_{ij} c_{ij}\right]}{\sum_{i=1}^{n}\sum_{j=1}^{n} T_{ij}} \tag{24}$$

The method of calibration is well documented by Batty (1970) and Evans (1971) and involves a search procedure for the parameter β through many runs of the model on a computer such that the difference between the observed and simulated mean trip lengths is minimised, while the degree of association between observed and simulated zonal populations is maximised. The value of β which satisfies the above criteria is said to give a good fit to the model. Table 10.3.3 shows some of the details of the calibration process. The observed mean trip length of 1.78 was almost correctly predicted by a value of β equal to 0.47. The statistical '*t*' test confirms that the differences between the observed and simulated trip lengths is not significant at the 0.001 level while a correlation coefficient of 0.97 was recorded.

The pattern of interaction resulting from the use of equations 12b and 13a above is shown in Table 10.3.3. An examination of the row and column totals probably confirms the observations made with respect to the observed interaction matrix of Table 10.3.1. The question that remains is, what is the nature of the internal structure of the flows in the two systems? The indices of information theory entropy provide useful avenues for answering this question.

Tables 10.3.2 and 10.3.3 have been constructed to provide certain measures of the information theory entropy of the simulated and observed patterns of interaction. Table 10.3.4 is the value of these indices measured in binary units (bits). Table 10.3.5 is what may be described as a standardisation of Table 10.3.4. It involves defining a scale for all the indices to lie between zero and one, and involves dividing each index by its maximum value thus

Table 10.3.2: Calibration Procedure of the Journey to Work — Residential Location Model

A

Parameter Values	Mean Trip Length (observed)	Mean Trip Length (simulated)	Correlation Coefficient $= r$	Coefficient of determination $= r^2$
0.24	1.78	2.14	0.99	0.98
0.43	1.78	1.85	0.97	0.95
0.45	1.78	1.82	0.97	0.94
0.47	1.78	1.76	0.97	0.93
0.49	1.78	1.74	0.96	0.93
0.50	1.78	1.74	0.96	0.92

Test of Significance on Mean Trip Length

B

Parameter Value β	Mean Trip Length (o)	Mean Trip Length (s)	Degrees of Freedom	t value
0.47	1.78	1.76	322	1.18*

* Not significant at 0.001 level.

Table 10.3.3. Simulated Journey to Work Interaction Matrix

	1	2	3	4	5	6	7	8	9	10	11	12	13	14	15	16	17	18	Total
1	119	49	99	96	78	18	262	43	105	53	45	403	39	186	55	3	13	93	1,759
2	101	121	192	14	127	27	249	41	174	76	69	599	29	278	99	2	13	69	2,280
3	5	4	63	9	10	5	16	2	11	5	5	47	2	20	6	0	0	8	218
4	103	7	192	279	188	39	387	59	20	111	100	876	48	409	121	4	18	124	3,085
5	61	49	157	139	231	66	282	40	185	84	87	945	34	345	148	4	14	111	2,982
6	90	65	496	180	411	234	572	77	288	175	177	2,083	63	700	343	8	29	232	6,223
7	25	11	31	35	55	11	330	22	57	45	43	289	34	211	48	4	16	112	1,379
8	92	43	104	118	110	33	484	87	180	97	83	698	49	333	99	3	23	95	2,731
9	99	80	208	18	221	55	534	79	355	158	140	1,186	64	570	171	6	29	161	4,134
10	27	19	50	53	54	18	239	23	86	73	63	469	30	261	70	2	13	63	1,613
11	2	2	6	5	6	2	26	2	8	7	8	55	3	33	9		1	9	184
12	69	50	162		205	73	508	56	215	157	157	1,799	60	628	254	7	28	196	4,624
13	8	3	8	8	9	2	74	4	14	12	11	74	24	108	20	3	11	81	474
14	4	3	10	10	11	6	57	4	16	13	15	98	13	179	27	2	6	52	526
15	15	13	37	32	52	19	139	13	51	38	43	419	27	292	142	3	12	96	1,443
16													1					8	10
17	3	1	4	4	4	1	41	2	7	6	6	40	13	60	11	5	21	178	407
18			1	1	1	0	7		1		1	7	2	13	2	4	3	973	1,016
Total	823	520	1,820	1,001	1,773	609	4,028	554	1,773	1,110	1,053	10,087	535	4,626	1,625	60	250	2,661	35,088

$$H' = \frac{H}{H_{max}} \qquad (25)$$

This corresponds to what some people describe as the relative entropy (Chapman 1970). This standardisation provides a uniform scale for the comparison of the indices for the different situations.

The interpretation that results from Tables 10.3.4 and 10.3.5 is that the two systems, the observed and the simulated patterns of the journey to work, are rather close. For example, joint entropies are 6.38 and 6.82 bits for the observed and simulated respectively, the row information entropies are 3.73 and 3.48 bits while the column entropies are 3.62 and 3.59 bits.

A cell to cell comparison of the elements of the two matrices is produced by the information gain index of only 0.55 which may be compared with its maximum value of 7.35 in Table 10.3.4.

The results of these comparisons may be improved by further statistical analysis and calculations of variances and subsequent tests of significance. Such an approach would proceed by recognising that the relative frequencies used in calculating the cell to cell probabilities p_{ij} are obtained from random samples of sizes m_{ij}. If for instance, we then assume that the frequencies are subject to a binomial or any other distribution functions, it would be possible to derive the variances of each of the frequencies and hence those of the information entropy indices. Such an investigation, interesting as it may be, is outside the scope of this section.

The rather high values of the indices in Table 10.3.5 imply that there is very little concentration of origins and destinations, that is home places are as dispersed as workplaces. This, in any case is a conclusion that has been reached by a direct examination of the interaction matrices in Tables 10.3.1 and 10.3.2. However, that they are close to their maximum values (See Table 10.3.4) suggests that the amount of

Table 10.3.4: Structural Complexity of the Journey to Work System

	Joint Information (bits)	Row Information (bits)	Column Information (bits)	Informative Gain
Observed	6.38	3.73	3.62	
Simulated				0.55
(modelled)	6.82	3.48	3.59	
Maximum	8.35	4.17	4.17	7.35

Table 10.3.5: Standardised Measures of the Structural Complexity of the Journey to Work System

	Joint Information	Row Information	Column Information	Informative Gain
Observed	0.76	0.89	0.87	
Simulated (modelled)	0.82	0.83	0.86	0.075
Maximum	1	1	1	1

'energy' being expended on the journey to work system is high, in many cases greater than 80 per cent of the maximum. Translated into costs, one could argue that a situation where the transportation cost is some 80 per cent of a maximum that could be spent would imply some unnecessary costs. Furthermore, if it is noted that the most efficient way is represented by the situation when the cost of movement is minimal, a situation as the above is possible but not desirable. This, therefore, is one of the indications which the information theory entropy gives which many other indices cannot show.

A further understanding of a system arises if the above indices of information theory can be related more directly to the energy states of a physical system. Such understanding utilises Brillouin's interpretation of the relationship between information and entropy. According to him, in a scheme where the possible cases of P may be interpreted as 'complexions' of a physical system, entropy is decreased when information is obtained, thus reducing the number of complexions. This inform information must however be furnished by some external agent whose entropy will increase (so that the law of the conservation of energy holds). Information therefore brings a decrease in entropy and an increase in negentropy so that if at any two periods, the entropies are S_1 and S_0, and the information is I_1, this information is the change in the two entropies namely

$$I = S_0 - S_1 \qquad (26a)$$

or

$$S_1 = S_0 - I \qquad (26b)$$

The above is the 'negentropy principle of information' (Brillouin, 1956, p. 153).

The negentropy principle of information defines the relationship between entropy and information or negentropy, and in a sense supports the interpretation of information as a measure of the structural state. The smallest possible amount of negentropy required in any observation is of the order of k (Boltzmann's constant) and it is approximately equal to $k \log 2$. In the c-g-s system, this equals 10^{-16} degrees Kelvin, while in binary units it is 1 bit. Thus a small value of the energy state corresponds to a big value in the binary unit, implying that a small change in entropy corresponds to a higher change in the information or negentropy. Consequently, large structural changes in a system may result from small energetic changes.

Although no attempts have been made in this section to explore the nature of the empirical relationships between entropy changes and information in Jos, as a result of the difficulty of obtaining relevant data temporally disaggregated, it is hoped that future studies would not neglect this very important contribution of the concept of entropy in urban analysis.

It must be agreed that there is a limit beyond which this analogy may not be pursued for social systems. For physical systems, the concepts of work and energy are well defined but this is not true for social systems. Consequently, while the physical scientist compared the physical entropy measured in the c-g-s system with the information measured in bits, the social scientists at best must regard these measures as indications only, until the pertinent concepts are unambigously defined. Nevertheless the entropy concept furnishes him with a valuable research tool.

4. Conclusion

The entropy formalism continues to undergo valuable criticisms that are forcing its proponents to assess critically the philosophical basis of the formalism as well as its applicability in modelling human systems. For instance, Beckmann and Golob regard entropy maximisation 'as a metaphysical method' and feel that 'presumably entropy is a measure of diversity, but its operational meaning in connection with travel decisions, is obscure. The derivation usually given is a non-critical adaptation of an argument from Kinetic Gas Theory to an economic situation' (Beckmann and Golob, 1971, p. 3; quoted from Webber, 1973). Beckmann (1973, p. 2) goes further, to say that 'its proponents have become skilled in subjecting every problem to this approach and inventing *ad hoc* constraints to make entropy fit the case'. The truth is that criticisms of this nature provide the *raison d'être* for a clarification and synthesis of the two important views of entropy as discussed in this chapter.

Further misconceptions about the entropy formalism may be resolved through a realisation that equation 11 usually used in deriving entropy models is indeed an approximation to equation 3 which describes the information content of a message. In fact this approximation based on Stirling's equation that

$$\log x \,! \,\doteq\, x \log x - x \tag{27}$$

is valid for large n only. Furthermore, it is possible to argue that while the analogy with statistical mechanics provides a model of a physical system via an objective probability approach, the use of equation 3 as derived from information theory represents a subjective probability approach which need not be based on the notion of an infinite set of trials. The justification for maximising equation 3 then lies on the notion that the procedure represents the maximally non-commital procedure for deriving a statistical model of a society. This indeed is what the entropy maximising methodology is about. Consequently, it is possible to argue following Jaynes (1957) and Webber (1975) that statistical mechanics may be a particular example of the use of the formulation, and agree that there exists the 'possibility that we have now reached a state where statistical mechanics is no longer dependent on physical hypotheses, but may become merely an example of statistical inference' (Jaynes, 1957, p. 621). Thus, the entropy maximisation approach provides a genuine method for deriving statistical models of society given some characteristics or restraints on the behaviour of this society. It is the duty of the model-builder to ensure that *ad hoc* restraints are not conjured but rather that they are based on theoretically sound premises.

'What we have a right to ask of a conceptual model,' write Dorfman, Samuelson and Solow (1958), 'is that it seizes on the strategic relationships that control the phenomenon and that it thereby permits us to manipulate, i.e. think about, the situation.' The use of the entropy maximising framework lays bare the interrelationships and interactions in a city and it is therefore appropriate for studying human spatial interaction. It must be agreed that it could be a very powerful paradigm in urban and regional analysis as well as in the development of operational planning models. Future researches may therefore be expected to explore its applicability into all fields that involve human spatial interaction.

References

Attneave, F. 1959. *Applications of Informations Theory to Pyschology*. New York: Henry Holt

Ayeni M.A.O. 1974. Predictive Modelling of Urban Spatial Structure, the example of Jos, Benue−Plateau State Nigeria, Ph.D. thesis, University of Ibadan, Nigeria

Batty, M. 1970. An Activity Allocation Model for the Nottinghamshire−Derbyshire Subregion. *Regional Studies, 4,* 307−32

Beckmann, M.J. 1973. Entropy, Gravity, Utility and All That. Unpublished manuscript

Beckmann, M.J. and Golob, T.F. 1971. On the metaphysical foundations of Traffic Theory: Entropy revisited. Paper presented at the Fifth International Symposium on the Theory of Traffic and Transportation. Berkeley, California

Berry, B.J.L. and Schwind, P. 1969. Information and Entropy in Migrant Flows. *Geographical Analysis, 1,* 5−14

Brillouin, I. 1956. *Science and Information Theory.* New York: Academic Press

Carrothers, G.A.P. 1956. An historical review of the gravity and potential concepts of human interaction. *Journal Am. Inst. Plann.,* 94−102

Chapman, C.P. 1970. The Application of Information Theory to the Analysis of Population Distribution in Space. *Economic Geography, 46,* 2, Supplement, 317−31

Cherry, C. 1965. *On Human Communication.* Cambridge, Massachusetts: M.I.T. Press

Cripps, E.L., and Foot, D. 1971. A Land Use Model for Subregional Planning. *Regional Studies, 3,* 243−68

Curry, L. 1964. The Random Spatial Economy; An Exploration in Settlement Theory. *Annals of the Association of American Geographers, 54,* 138−46

Dorfman, R., Samuelson, P.A. and Solow, R.M. 1958. *Linear Programming and Economic Analysis.* New York: McGraw-Hill

Evans, A.W. 1971. The calibration of trip distribution models with potential or similar functions. *Transportation Research, 5,* 15−38

Hall, A.D., and Fagen, R.E. 1956. Definition of a System. *General Systems Year Book, 1,* 18−27

Isard, W. 1960. *Methods of Regional Analysis*: Cambridge, Massachusetts: M.I.T. Press

Jaynes, E.T. 1957. Information Theory and Statistical Methanics I. *Physical Review, 106,* 620−30

Kullback, S. 1959. *Information Theory and Statistics.* New York: John Wiley

Lisman, J.H.C. 1949. Econometrics and Themodynamics: a Remark on Davis' Theory of Budgets, *Econometrica, 17,* 59−62

Marchand, B. 1972. Information Theory and Geography. *Geographical Analysis, 4,* 234−57

Medvedkov, Y.V. 1966. The concept of entropy in settlement pattern analysis. *Papers Regional Science Association, 18,* 165−88

Medvedkov, Y.V. 1967. Topology in Central Place Analysis. *Papers Regional Science Association, 20,* 77−84

Medvedkov, Y.V. 1970. Entropy, an assessment of potentialities in Geography. *Economic Geography, 46,* 306−16

Shannon, C.E., and Weaver, W. 1949. *The mathematical theory of communication.* Urbana, Illinois: University of Illinois Press

Theil, H. 1967. *Economics and Information Theory.* Amsterdam: North Holland Publishing Company

Webber, M.J. 1975. The Meaning of Entropy Maximizing Models. In G.J. Papageorgiou, *Mathematical Land Use Theory.* Massachussetts: Lexington Books, 1975

Wilson, A.G. 1967. A statistical Theory of Spatial Distribution Models. *Transportation Research, 1,* 253−69

Wilson, A.G. 1969. Forecasting Planning. *Urban Studies, 6,* 348−69

Wilson, A.G. 1970. *Entropy in Urban and Regional Modelling.* London: Pion

11 AN ENTROPY-MAXIMISING APPROACH TO RESIDENTIAL LOCATION MODELLING

1. Introduction

Residential use is by far the largest consumer of land in the city. Consequently it is a focus of intense research, as has been shown in this book and as reflected in the works of Park (1915), Park *et al.* (1925) of the Chicago School of urban sociology and in the micro-economic theories of Wingo (1961) and Alonso (1964) — see Chapter 1. Furthermore, residential use *per se* possesses a number of assumptions about human spatial behaviour. Consequently, alongside these researches there is the realisation that the urban spatial structure and human spatial behaviour possess a symbiotic relationship such that one is a cause as well as a consequence of the other (Foley, 1964). The entropy-maximising framework discussed in the last chapter offers a method for developing models that recognise this relationship.

Consequently in this chapter we shall discuss how the framework may be embellished to generate a spatial interaction-cum-location model of urban residents using the well-known relationship between the journey to work and residential location. Thus we shall discuss the theoretical basis of a disaggregated residential location as well as the need for disaggregation, using some of the principles described by Wingo and Alonso. We shall also discuss some of the empirical problems of disaggregation in addition to using the disaggregated residential location model to understand human spatial behaviour in Jos, Plateau State of Nigeria.

2. A Disaggregated Residential Location Model

As statistical averages, spatial interaction models can be very useful at the macro-scale level of investigation in describing static distribution and associated travel patterns. Unfortunately, this highly aggregative nature of the models constitutes their greatest weakness. The model views the city as a homogenous universe of houses, peoples' travel patterns and mode. This is rather unrealistic as a city is in reality a very heterogenous entity. In consequence, it is often argued that micro-economic models of residential location can provide a better basis for designing predictive models of urban structure as such models are based on the decisions of individuals or households. However, if such models are to be used for planning there must be some aggregation of house-holds. The problem then centres around the level of aggregation. There are at least two approaches to the solution of this problem. The first is to generate planning models from micro-economic assumptions using, for instance, the concept of the utility tree developed by Strotz (1957, 1959). This concept involves the notion that if commodities are func-tionally seperable, they can be aggregated to form a hierarchical structure and the individual's or households's utility functions can be broken up into a hierarchy of functions corresponding to these com-modity groups. Using this concept but paying particular attention to the aggregation of households as opposed to sectoral aggregation, it has been shown that where it is theoretically possible to construct aggre-gate models which are functions of parameters of the individual's utility functions, the problem is usually not analytically tractable (Wilson, 1971). The same conclusion applies even when it is possible to define probability density functions in terms of the variables of the utility functions.

Another approach is to proceed from the highly aggregative model of the elementary location model of the last chapter, and to disaggre-gate it to an appropriate level, dictated in the main by sources and relia-bility of the data set. The disaggregation of spatial interaction models will then proceed through a reformulation of the assumptions that resi-dential location is determined by the distribution of workplaces and workers' accessibility to those places as well as through incorporating the location behaviour of the various categories of the city population that constitute important sub-markets. For example, it is obvious that quite a significant proportion of the total set of households in a city may have nobody in the labour force, most especially where the house-holds comprise old and retired men. Furthermore, house ownership or rentage may be an important factor in determining spatial and loca-tional behaviour so that disaggregation may be pursued using the assumptions of micro-economic theory as to the relationship between income, house costs and 'other goods'. Urban structure as identified by factorial ecological studies may also be useful in identifying means and levels of disaggregation.

Consequently, a residential location model should include some or all of the following considerations (Wilson, 1970, pp. 69–80):

(i) different income groups by location;
(ii) the distribution of employment opportunities by wage levels and by location;

(iii) the location and distribution of houses as well as their types and quality; and

(iv) the variations in house prices and house rents for the different zones or areas of an urban system.

In order to fix ideas, let us define the variables of the journey to work—residential location as follows:

T_{ij}^{kw} is the number of workers of income group w who work in zone j, live in residential zone i in a house of type k. This is the interaction variable

H_i^k is the number of houses of type k in residential zone i

E_j^w is the number of jobs in work-zone j offering wage w

P_i^k is the price or rent of a type k house in residential zone i

q^w is the average percentage of income, after transportation costs have been deducted, which a member of income group w spends on housing

c_{ij} is the generalised cost of travel from residence i to work place j

c_{ij}' is that component of the generalised travel cost which is actually paid out. This is the 'out-of-pocket' transportation cost

C^w is the total expenditure on transportation by each income group w.

The constraints on the journey to work system, and hence on residential location, may be defined as follows:

$$\sum_i \sum_k T_{ij}^{kw} = E_j^w \tag{1}$$

$$\sum_i \sum_j \sum_k T_{ij}^{kw} \, [c_{ij} - W_i] = C^w \tag{2}$$

$$\sum_i \sum_j \sum_k T_{ij}^{kw} \, [P_i^k - q^w \, (w - c_{ij}')]^2 = \sigma^2_w \tag{3}$$

σ^2_w is the variance of the distribution of housing expenditure for the income class w. Note that these equations are similar to those of the elementary location model.

The entropy of the disaggregated journey to work system may be defined as

$$\ln T_{ij}^{kw} = \ln \left\{ \frac{T^{kw} !}{\prod_i \prod_j T_{ij}^{kw} !} \right\} \tag{4}$$

If this is maximised subject to the constraints of the three equations above, the resulting spatial interaction model is a hybrid of Wilson's (1970) disaggregated model and its equations are

$$T_{ij}^{kw} = B_j^w E_j^w H_i^k \exp(-\beta_i^w c_{ij}) \exp\{-\mu_i^w [p_i^k - q^w (w - c_{ij})]^2\}$$ (5)

where

$$B_j^w = [\sum_i \sum_k H_i^k \exp(-\beta_i^w c_{ij}) \exp\{-\mu_i^w [p_i^k - q^w (w - c_{ij})]\}]^{-1}$$ (6)

H_i^k, house type by location has been used instead of $\exp(W_i)$ as a measure of the attraction of or the benefits derivable from locating in area i.

The allocation equation described above is purposely singly constrained at the destination end by the non-use of a constraint equation of the form

$$\sum_j \sum_w T_{ij}^{kw} = \psi H_i^k$$ (7)

where ψ is a scale factor on the number of work trip-makers that are in a household. The constraint equation has been dropped for two reasons. First, residential location models should be singly constrained as the function of a spatial interaction and location model changes with the introduction of this constraint. Second, it enables a prediction of houses by types demanded at residential zones as an outcome of the process of allocating workers of wage level w (Cripps and Cater, 1972).

An important aspect of residential location decision processes not considered by the above model is the assumption that there is only one worker in a household. The assumption may be relaxed in at least two ways. First, it may be assumed that it is the income of the head of household that is relevant to locational decision-making. One can then proceed to develop different allocation models for the dependent workers (workers who are not heads of households). On the other hand one can assume that all income of the household is relevant to residential decision-making (Cripps and Cater, 1972; Senior and Wilson, 1973, pp. 6–8). The latter approach is preferred because of the exigencies of reliable data.

It has been mentioned that there are always some people with no member in the labour force. Such peoples' principle of residential location may not include considerations of location of workplaces. Wilson (1970, p. 81) and Senior and Wilson (1973, pp. 6–8) outlined ways of taking care of this sub-population. A further consideration of this group in the present attempt is not deemed feasible, because it was not possible to collect sufficient data to deal with this problem even though it is realised that this may be highly important both for policy and planning purposes.

The significant contribution of the residential location model of equations 6 and 5 lie in the introduction of equation 3 as a constraint and the incorporation of the last exponential term in the allocation function. It is really these two that represent the intersection of supply and demand mechanisms in the urban residential choice decision processes. This view is facilitated by the interpretation of the terms and equations. The constraint expressed by equation 3 above measures the distribution of spread of housing expenditure for each income group. The right-hand side of the equation is an assumption that the spread of this distribution is normal (in the Gaussian sense). The terms in square brackets in equation 5 merely express the complementarity of rent or house price and transportation costs as prominently noted in micro-economic theories of residential location. As noted by Wilson (1970, p. 79) it is really the last exponential term of the allocation equation 5 that makes the disaggregation worth while.

The interpretations and function of μ and β are as follows. The parameters μ_i^w are Lagrangian multipliers associated with the constraint equation 3. Just as β_i^w denotes the type w worker's propensity to travel to work over a network, μ_i^w denotes the worker's propensity to match housing prices or rents by accounting for the differential above or below the worker's money allocation. The values of β_i^w and μ_i^w are determined at calibration by minimising the differences between the observed and prediced mean trip costs and mean household expenditure patterns respectively (see section 3 below).

(i) Empirical Problems of Disaggregation

The empirical development of disaggregated location models is generally faced by a number of measurement problems and the availability of relevant data. The situation is even more serious in developing countries. Consequently, in many cases the researcher may be forced to use regional or national figures in the measurement of certain variables. From the considerations of previous sections, the type of data required include information on the number of houses by types and by location, their prices or rents; as well as the distribution of employment opportunities by wage level and location. In addition to these, one needs a detailed knowledge of household patterns of expenditure for the different socio-economic classes. The difficulties of assembling these data are discussed using Jos as our example.

The stock of houses in a city may be classified using such characteristics as an age-size index, quality and ownership (Cripps and Cater, 1972, p. 120). Although houses in Jos could be classified using quality defined in terms of the availability of utilities such as water, electricity, kitchen, bathroom plus the amount of congestion in these houses, it was difficult to produce a single index. It is, however, possible to classify houses by tenure into owner-occupied and rented houses, using results of the field-work and information from the Town Planning Division of the Ministry of Works and Survey, Jos (1972). This classification of houses by ownerships is shown in Table 11.2.1. From the table, it can be seen that there is a zonal variation in the hoses by types and that most residents live in rented quarters, as owner-occupied houses form only 21 per cent of all dwellings in the city.

There is a problem with measurement of house prices for the

Table 11.2.1: Classification of the Housing Stock in Jos

Zone	Name	No. of Houses	Owner-occupied	Public and Private Rented	Per Cent Owner-occupied
1	Jenta New	178	25	153	14.0
2	Jenta	598	194	395	32.4
3	Dogon Dutse	76	25	51	32.9
4	Kwararafa	529	143	386	27.0
5	Bauchi Road	306	65	241	21.2
6	Sabon Gwong	1,073	144	929	13.4
7	Prison Area	142	16	126	11.3
8	Stadium Area	228	6	222	2.7
9	Alkali Street	593	144	449	24.3
10	Langtang	167	14	123	11.4
11	Commercial	40	3	37	7.5
12	Market	384	92	292	24.0
13	Hill Station	50	14	36	28.0
14	Secretariat	117	21	96	17.9
15	Gangare	356	74	282	20.8
16	Mountain View	20	12	8	60.0
17	Reservation	180	48	132	26.7
18	Anglo Jos	130	58	72	44.6
	Jos	5,167	1,098	4,030	21.3

Sources: Ministry of Works and Survey (Town Planning Division, Jos); see Ayeni, also, 1974.

dwellings listed above since data on their current market values are not available. Nevertheless, the problem is less serious in the rented (public or private) sector where total rents paid by households could be used as such rents are expected to have been progressively adjusted with the continuous rise in the cost of living. The only snag about rent is that some households, especially those in the higher-income group, pay rents that are highly subsidised by their employers. While such rents are not economic rents, they are still the highest paid for any dwelling in the city. Consequently, total rents paid for all spaces consumed may be taken as a composite measure that determines residential selection. The case of the owner-occupied sector is slightly more complex as this falls into two classes. The first class consists of relatively low-quality houses built many years ago and where no mortgages are presently being paid while the second consists of high-quality dwellings occupied by their owners or upper-income employees, who live rent-free. In view of these two constrasting situations, the only assumption that could be made is that the locational decision of households who own their dwellings or live in rent-free quarters is influenced by the current costs of house-building and maintenance in different parts of the city. This approach would substitute for house rent certain monetary values which are not actually paid by these households but which are monthly or yearly equivalents of mortgage repayments for households wishing to locate in such zones. Table 11.2.2. shows the zonal variation of average house prices and rents in Jos. The average rent per month per household is 10.30 Naira ($ 16.40) while the monthly equivalent of mortgage repayments for the owner-occupied dwellings is 26.65 Naira ($ 42.30) per household.

The classification of employment by wage levels and by location (Table 11.2.3) is more straightforward than the determination of house prices. Wages have been regarded as low if they are less than 600.00 Naira ($ 1,000.00), medium if between 600 and 1,600 Naira ($ 2,600) and high if above 1,600 Naira ($ 2,000) per annum.* The survey from which much of the data used in this section came provided pertinent information on the spatial distribution of employment by wages though the disaggregated interaction variable T_{ij}^w. This was used to calculate the total zonal distribution of employment through equation 8, viz.

$$E_j^w = (\sum_i T_{ij}^w / \sum_i \sum_w T_{ij}^w) E_j \qquad (8)$$

---

* Since this research was conducted, wages in Nigeria have doubled in many cases. The minimum wage in the public sector is now 720.00 Naira ($1,142.86) per annum. It could be less in the private sector.

Table 11.2.2: House 'Prices' by Zones of Residence in Jos

Zone	Name	Owner-occupied Naira per month	Public or Private Rented Naira per Month
1	Jenta New	13.15	6.09
2	Jenta	16.79	5.62
3	Dogon Dutse	23.00	8.24
4	Kwararafa	13.00	4.91
5	Bauchi Road	18.92	4.98
6	Sabon Gwong	11.08	4.92
7	Prison Area	25.75	10.63
8	Stadium Area	31.00	5.85
9	Alkali St	13.25	6.19
10	Langtang Area	20.75	6.33
11	Commercial	40.00	10.14
12	Market Area	20.50	4.18
13	Hill Station	40.00	15.14
14	Secretariat	53.35	10.28
15	Gangare	7.33	4.25
16	Mountain View	50.00	30.08
17	Reservation	75.25	36.06
18	Anglo Jos	6.61	6.55
	Average	26.65	10.30

Source: Field-work 1972. For explanations see text.

where E_j^w is the number of employments of wage level w at location j and E_j is the total number of employments at location j. The results are shown in Table 11.2.3. Two important observations can be made from the table. First, low-wage employment accounts for over 72 per cent of all employments in Jos while high-wage employment accounts for only 4.5 per cent. The remaining 23.4 per cent is taken by medium-wage employment. Second, the areal variation of employment shows the greatest concentrations in the major work zones of Dogon Dutse (3), Jos Prison area (7), the Market (12), Secretariat (14) and Anglo Jos (18). In terms of high-wage employment, the Secretariat (14) is the most important absolutely and relatively (see Figure 5.3.1 for the description of the zones).

The next three variables, the average household income (w), the proportion of income left after transportation and housing costs are deducted (q^w) and the out-of-pocket costs of transportation (c'_{ij}) are derived from the same source. This is the Federal Office of Statistics' Urban Consumer Surveys which since the 1950s have been spasmodically collected for some major cities of Nigeria, notably, Lagos, Ibadan and

Table 11.2.3: Employment by Wage Levels and by Workplace in Jos, 1972

Zone	Name	Low-income Employment	Middle-income Employment	Upper-income Employment	Total Employment
1	Jenta Extension	382	293	54	729
2	Jenta	414	51	24	489
3	Dogon Dutse	1,201	373	239	1,813
4	Kwararafa	670	213	23	906
5	Bauchi Road	1,192	208	25	1,425
6	Sabon Gwong	301	194	29	524
7	Prison Area	2,839	913	236	3,988
8	Stadium Area	268	189	16	473
9	Alkali Street	1,336	171	24	1,531
10	Langtang	476	393	62	931
11	Commercial	564	328	24	916
12	Market	7,393	2,174	82	9,649
13	Hill Station	413	66	22	501
14	Secretariat	2,744	1,240	487	4,471
15	Gangare	1,133	261	12	1,406
16	Mountain View	66	6	4	76
17	Reservation	211	16	45	272
18	Anglo Jos	1,818	861	167	2,846
	Jos	23,421	7,950	1,575	32,946

Sources: Column 6 comes from the following: files in the Federal Labour Office, Jos; Benue-Plateau Ministry of Trade and Industry and Economic Planning, in addition to the author's field-work. Colums 3, 4 and 5 are as calculated in the text.

Kaduna. These surveys were designed to collect information on the income and expenditure patterns of households in urban centres.

The results of the survey conducted in Kaduna in 1963 and published in 1966 had been used (Nigeria, 1966) because similar surveys had never been conducted in Jos. It was felt that the situation in Kaduna would be nearest to that in Jos. The use of these figures to represent conditions in Jos could probably not be defended except that to some extent they fill the great hiatus in the type and quality of data being collected.

The figures of 23.00 Naira ($36.51), 89.52 Naira ($142.10), 165.60 Naira ($262.86) per month (Table 11.2.4) represent the mean monthly income of the low, medium and upper groups respectively. The standard deviations and variances of these mean wages are also shown in Table 11.2.4.

The proportions of income spent by households after transportation costs have been deducted (q^w) are obtained from the same sources as Table 11.2.4, and these are 15.2, 9.4 and 4.1 per cent for the low-medium- and upper-income groups respectively. The other two variables,

Table 11.2.4: Statistical Summary of the Income Structure of Households

	Income Group	Mean Income per month (Naira)	Standard Deviation	Variance
1	Low	23.06	11.57	133.91
2	Middle	89.51	21.68	469.81
3	Upper	165.61	26.16	684.01

Source: Computed from a survey of sizes 328, 117 and 36 people in each income group. The original data are in Tables 8, 9, 22 and 23. (Nigeria 1966).

are the generalised cost of transport c_{ij} and the out-of-pocket cost of transport c'_{ij}. A method for the measurement of the generalised cost of transport, as a linear consideration of the number of variables, has been described by Wilson *et al.* (1969) but it is not possible to operationalise this in the present context. However, it was possible to measure the monthly out-of-pocket transportation costs per trip (Table 11.2.5).

These were 1.67 Naira ($2.65), 17.62 Naira ($27.97) and 23.72 Naira ($37.65) for the respective income groups. Since there must be some relationship between the generalised cost of transport c_{ij} and the out-of-pocket cost c'_{ij}, the assumption that these costs are direct multiples of the distance d_{ij} but in such a way that c'_{ij} is always less that c_{ij} was made. Thus

$$c_{ij} = wd_{ij} \tag{9}$$

$$c'_{ij} = \rho d_{ij} \; ; \; \rho \leqslant w \tag{10}$$

with ρ taking the values in column three of Table 11.2.5 for the three income groups respectively.

Table 11.2.5: Out-of-pocket Transport Costs

	Income Group	Mean c'_{ij} per month	Mean c'_{ij} per trip
1	Low	1.67	0.02
2	Middle	17.62	0.19
3	Upper	23.72	0.50
	Total	4.45	0.03

Source: Same as Table 11.2.4.

3. Calibrating and Testing the Disaggregated Residential Location Model for Jos, Nigeria

The procedure for calibrating this type of model has been outlined by Batty (1971) and Hyman (1969) and was described in Chapter 10. In the present case, six different parameters, two for each income group, are to be found using the mean trip length and the mean of the housing expenditure variance as the calibration statistics. The mean trip length $\bar{C}$ is given by

$$\bar{C}^w = \frac{\sum_i \sum_j \sum_k T_{ij}^{kw} C_{ij}}{\sum_i \sum_j \sum_k T_{ij}^{kw}} \tag{11}$$

and the mean housing expenditure variance defined as $\bar{\sigma}_w^2$ is

$$\bar{\sigma}_w^2 = \frac{\sum_i \sum_j \sum_k T_{ij}^{kw} [p_i^k - q^w(w - c_{ij})]^2}{\sum_i \sum_j \sum_k T_{ij}^{kw}} \tag{12}$$

These averages are known to be very sensitive to parameter changes during calibration. The objectives of the calibration procedure are to ensure that predicted and observed means do not differ significantly.

The calibration of spatial interaction models could often be faced with problems of data inconsistency because of variation in data sources. One such inconsistency usually concerns housing expenditure and housing costs, and is known to have led to some unacceptable results during the calibration process (Cripps and Cater, 1972). It was suggested that the consistency of these two costs may be checked by introducing a consistency factor K^w such that

$$\sum_i \sum_j \sum_k T_{ij}^{kw} P_i^k = K^w \sum_i \sum_j \sum_k T_{ij}^{kw} [q^w(w - c_{ij}')] \tag{13}$$

Another suggestion is to introduce equation 13 as a constraint on the urban system to derive a three-parameter function, two of which deal with the expenditure term (Senior and Wilson, 1973). These two are of the form

$$\exp(-\lambda^w)p_i^k \exp{ -\mu^w [p_i^k - q^w(w - c_{ij}')]^2} \tag{14}$$

Both approaches are valid, but in as much as multi-parameter models are difficult to calibrate, the first approach will be adopted. Equation 13 has thus been applied to the empirical data and the consistency factors calculated for the three income groups are 5.17, 3.25 and 4.28

Table 11.3.1: Parameter Values of the Disaggregated Residential
Location Model at Full Calibration

Income Group	Values of β	Trip Length (O)	Trip Length (P)	Values of μ	Mean variance (O)	Mean variance (P)
Low	0.36	1.92	1.91	0.86	133.91	133.24
Middle	0.27	2.13	2.04	0.52	469.81	509.16
Upper	0.52	1.87	1.83	0.28	684.01	639.98

O = Observed.
P = Predicted.

respectively. These values represent factors by which the household
expenditure patterns have been underestimated.

At full calibration, the values of the six parameters are as shown in
Table 11.3.1, while model predictions in terms of the zonal population
figures are as shown in Table 11.3.2. From Table 11.3.1 the observation
is that the middle-income group, because of its spatial disposition in the
city, makes the longest trips to work, while the upper-income group
makes the shortest trips. In some countries of America and Europe, it

Table 11.3.2: Observed and Predicted Populations by Zones in Jos

Zones	Names	Low-income Obs.	Low-income Pred.	Middle-income Obs.	Middle-income Pred	Upper-income Obs.	Upper-income Pred.
1	Jenta Extension	4,666	3,365	1,444	1,210	222	382
2	Jenta	7,825	7,368	1,191	1,113	85	297
3	Dogon Dutse	678	833	112	345	248	204
4	Kwararafa	7,301	7,447	2,686	2,023	15	334
5	Bauchi Road	6,142	6,793	1,672	1,985	14	200
6	Sabon Gwong	12,190	14,323	7,376	8,023	45	597
7	Prison Area	2,532	2,887	377	358	269	323
8	Stadium Area	4,670	3,526	2,752	2,070	500	497
9	Alkali	8,757	8,847	1,348	2,108	481	460
10	Langtang	800	3,113	2,677	1,572	75	135
11	Commercial	186	301	115	172	208	132
12	Market	9,077	9,808	1,026	1,325	63	316
13	Hill Station	900	869	66	149	347	233
14	Secretariat	188	675	470	614	611	607
15	Gangare	3,528	3,915	153	869	12	298
16	Mountain View	18	76	15	40	7	13
17	Reservation	355	1,142	50	329	949	577
18	Anglo Jos	1,105	1,406	88	242	309	423
	Jos	70,918	76,695	23,618	24,547	4,460	6,028
		R = 0.97		R = 0.96		R = 0.61	
		$R^2 = 0.95$		$R^2 = 0.93$		$R^2 = 0.37$	

has been observed that as a result of the 'movement to the suburbs', the length of the journey to work increases with increasing socio-economic status. In Jos, of course, there is no 'movement to the suburbs' as housing choice decision is constrained for the upper − and sometimes the middle-income group by the fact that housing is part of the contract between employers and of these groups.

However, of greater theoretical significance is the behaviour of the parameters. The β^w parameters confirm our theoretical interpretation as the worker's propensity to travel to work by maintaining the expected inverse relationship with the mean trip length. The μ^w parameters which govern the distribution of the behaviour of the household in residential choice decisions is governed, *inter alia,* by its ability to match its disposable income on housing with housing costs. In one study conducted for the city of Reading in Britain, Cripps and Cater (1972) report aberrant behaviour of this parameter which produced meaningless negative numbers. In another study, Senior and Wilson (1973) report that there was no systematic variation in the values of the μ^w parameters. The aberrant behaviour of the μ parameter as reported by Cripps and Cater may be corrected by using the 'consistency factor' as outlined above or by using the three-parameter location model as proposed by Senior and Wilson. On the other hand, the systematic variations between the values of μ and the housing expenditure variances for the socio-economic groups are due, as Senior and Wilson suggested, to certain deficiencies of the data base used for running the model. In the Reading example the unavailability of the interaction variable, disaggregated by house types k, was suggested as responsible for this unsystematic variation (Cripps and Cater, 1972). In the present attempt, the interaction variable has been disaggregated by both house type and income groups so that it has been possible to obviate this particular problem.

A final test of the relationship between the model's predictions and reality is the examination of the extent to which the observed and the predicted populations are similar. These are given in Table 11.3.2. which shows that the low- and the middle-income group were more accurately predicted than the upper-income group. For example, the correlations between predicted and observed populations for the low- and middle-income groups are 0.98 and 0.96 respectively (Figs. 11.3.1 and 11.3.2). On the other hand, the correlation for the upper-income group is only 0.61 (Fig. 11.3.3).

A number of reasons may be adduced for the low correlation value between observed and predicted values for the upper-income group. First, there is a fundamental issue concerning disaggregated spatial interaction

Figure 11.3.1: Low-income Group: Observed and Predicted Populations

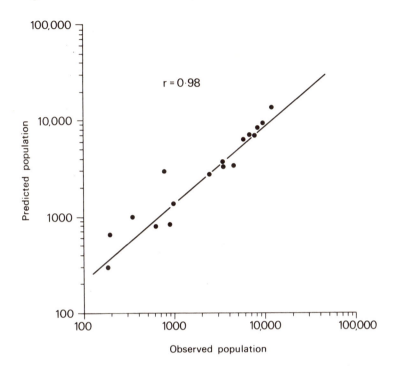

models. It has been mentioned that such models are statistical averages. The problem would seem to revolve around sample sizes of the levels of disaggregation, for if the unit being predicted is small, the model is not likely to produce a good fit. This is particularly true of the Kwararafa (4), Bauchi Road (5), Sabon Gwong (6) and Gangare (15) which, because of the smallness of the populations of the upper-income group, were rather poorly predicted (Table 11.3.2 and Fig. 11.3.3). This same reason may therefore be adduced for the overall poor performance of the model for the upper-income group which represents only 4.5 per cent of the total population. Figures 11.3.4, 11.3.5 and 11.3.6 have been drawn to show the spatial comparison of observed and predicted populations for the low-, middle- and upper-income groups respectively. It will be seen from the three maps that, where the observed populations are small, individual predictions are poor while very accurate predictions are made where populations are sizeable. In a sense, this raises the problem that if spatial interaction models were to be disaggregated, some research would be necessary into what constitutes the minimum aggregate population.

Figure 11.3.2: Middle-income Group: Observed and Predicted Populations

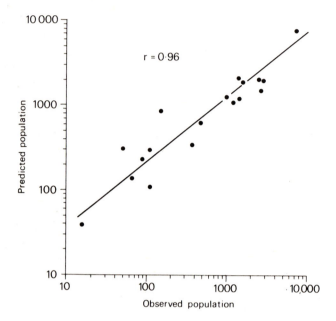

Second, there is the unique problem posed by the spatial location of the upper-income group in Jos. There is a concentration of this group in the Government Reservation Area (17) and the Secretariat (14). This concentration is neither based on consideration of accessibility to workplace nor on that of balance between income and the expenditure on houses. It is based more on status than on any other locational considerations. In many cases, houses are allocated to upper-income households by the government or by private business concerns who own the houses. Therefore considerations of house prices by types and the availability of income adequate to cover expenditure on houses hardly arise. Whether the locational behaviour of this class of people can be subject to microeconomic analysis is a point for further investigation.

(i)   Aspects of Spatial Behaviour

Although much has been said about the ability of the model to simulate reality, further hints may also be got by examining how the model simulates spatial behaviour. Consequently, for each of the three income

Figure 11.3.3: Upper-income Group: Observed and Predicted
Populations

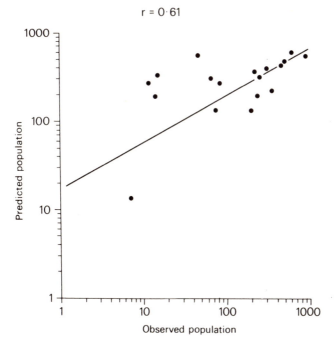

groups, three zones, each known to contain such groups in abundance,
were chosen and analysed in terms of the percentages of trips that
occurred within distance bands.

The observed and predicted percentages are shown in Figures 11.3.7,
11.3.8 and 11.3.9. In most cases the models predictions correspond with
the observed patterns of spatial behaviour.

For the low-income group, the three zones chosen are Jenta Extension (1), Prison Area (7) and Jenta (2). The patterns revealed by Jenta
Extension (1) and Prison Area (7) (Fig. 11.3.7a and c) are quite similar.
It shows that most of the people live and work between 1 and 2 kilometres with the proportion tapering very rapidly as greater distances are
approached. Jenta (2), which typifies a second pattern of spatial behaviour, shows that most people travel between 1.5 and 3 kilometres to
work (Fig. 11.3.7b). These two sets of behaviour are characteristic of the
low-income group and reflect the spatial distribution of employment in
the system. For example, Jenta Extension (1) and Prison Area (7) are
either work zones or very near to work zones. On the other hand, Jenta

Figure 11.3.4: Low-income Group: Observed and Predicted
Distributions of Population

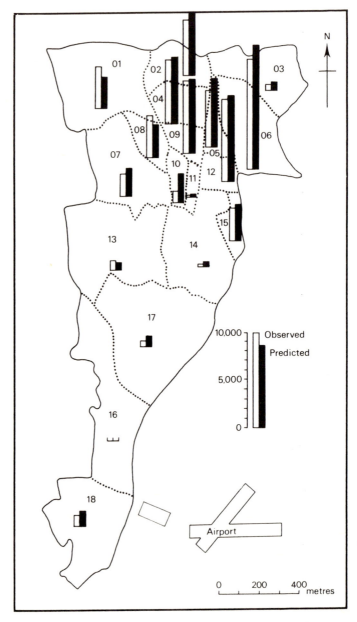

Figure 11.3.5: Middle-income Group: Observed and Predicted
Distributions of Population

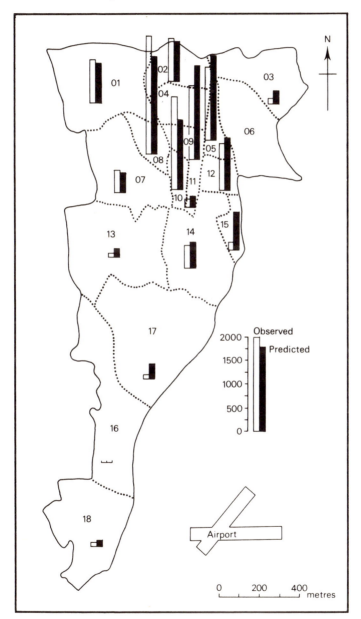

Figure 11.3.6: Upper-income Group: Observed and Predicted
Distributions of Population

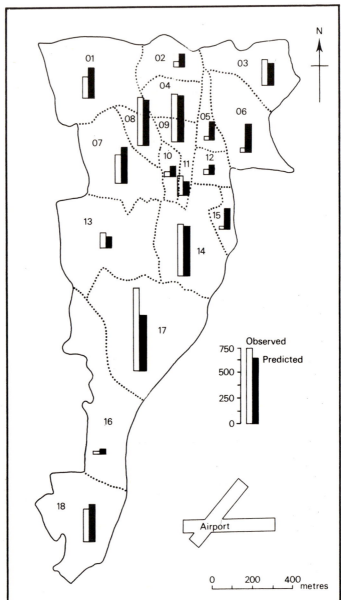

Figure 11.3.7: Travel Behaviour of the Low-income Group

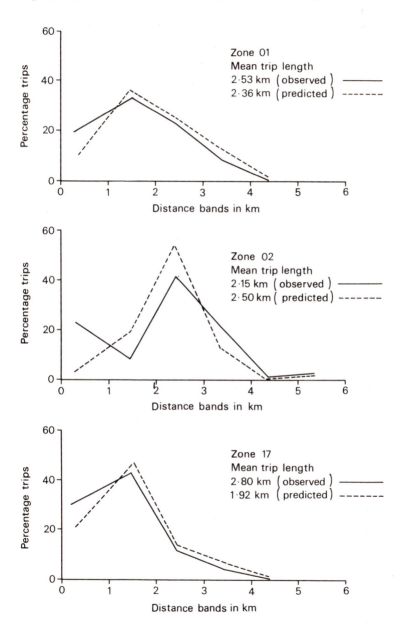

Figure 11.3.8: Travel Behaviour of the Middle-income Group

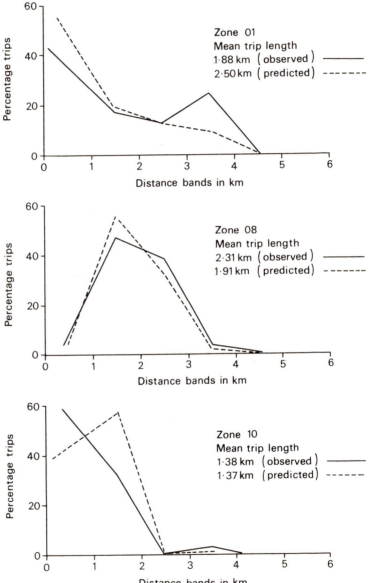

Figure 11.3.9: Travel Behaviour of the Upper-income Group

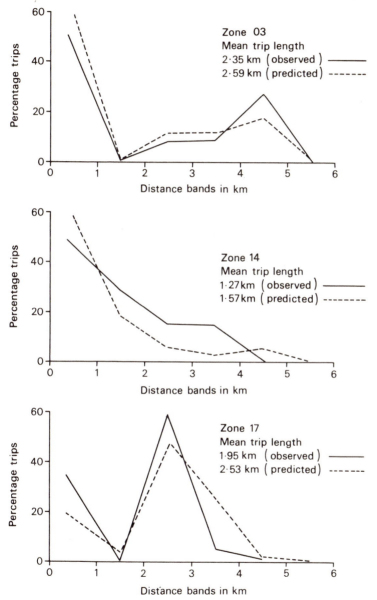

Zone 03
Mean trip length
2·35 km (observed) ————
2·59 km (predicted) --------

Zone 14
Mean trip length
1·27 km (observed) ————
1·57 km (predicted) --------

Zone 17
Mean trip length
1·95 km (observed) ————
2·53 km (predicted) --------

(2) is purely a residential zone where people have to make long trips to the Market (12), the Secretariat (14) and Anglo Jos (18) for work.

The travel behaviour of the middle-income group reveals also two major patterns. The first, typified by Jenta Extension (1) and Langtang Area (10), is one whereby most people live within a very short distance from the workplace. (Fig. 11.3.8a and c). For example, between 40 and 60 per cent of people live and work within the distance band of 0 and 1 kilometres, suggesting that some middle-income groups try to minimise the distance of their journey to work. The second type of spatial behaviour is similar to the first one of the low-income group and is typified by the Stadium Area (8). In this set most residents live and work within one to three kilometres of their homes (Figure 11.3.8b). This behaviour, it is noted, is more pronounced for the middle-income group and is a fundamental reason why the group makes longer trips to work.

The upper-income group shows a travel behaviour that suggests the growing consciousness of distance minimisation with increasing income. The situation is typified by Dogon Dutse (3) and Secretariat (14) zones where most of the people live and work within one kilometre of their home (Figure 11.3.9a and b). However the Reservation Area (17) shows a second pattern where most of the people work between one and three kilometres of their homes (Figure 11.3.9c). This observation may be due to the rather large size of the Reservation (17), which is mainly residential, and also to the fact that most of these residents commute to the Secretariat (14) and Anglo Jos (18) for work.

4. Conclusion

The disaggregation of spatial interaction models is highly desirable, especially if one wants to identify planning problems that may be peculiar to the various socio-economic groups of people in a city. Nevertheless, disaggregations should be done with care as there is a minimum size below which further disaggregation may not be carried out. This minimum size is presently not known and there are as yet few works in this direction. At present one can only hypothesise that this minimum size would be a function of both the number of zones in the system and the total population in each class grouping. The specifications of this minimum level becomes of research interest if spatial interaction models of the type we have been considering are to be used not only for large cities and metropolitan areas but also for smaller cities and towns.

Furthermore, the disaggregation of spatial interaction models should be done in such a way that the end product reflects the heterogeneity of the city population. This may be done using a number of criteria, especially the income of the household as was done in the present study. The use of wages or income to classify an urban population of a city is merely convenient. It is in no way the only criterion that can be used. For instance, a combination of social and economic variables may produce a better disaggregation. Such a combination becomes of greater relevance when it is recalled that people who are between the same wage bracket do not necessarily belong to the same socio-economic class; and hence do not usually have the same patterns of locational and spatial behaviour. This, therefore, should constitute future lines of enquiry into further development on these models.

References

Alonso, W. 1964. *Location and Land Use: Toward a General Theory of Land Rent.* Cambridge, Massachusetts: Harvard University Press

Ayeni, M.A.O. 1974. Predictive Modelling of Urban Spatial Structure: The Example of Jos, Benue Plateau State, Nigeria. Unpublished Ph.D. thesis, University of Ibadan, Nigeria

Barras, R. *et al.* 1971. An Operational Urban Development Model of Cheshire. *Environment and Planning, 13,* 115−234

Batty, M. 1971. Exploratory Calibration of a Retail Location Model, Using Search by Golden Section. *Environment and Planning, 31,* 411−32

Benue Plateau State of Nigeria. 1972. *Urban Land Use in Jos 1971−72.* Ministry of Works and Survey Jos, mime.

Cripps, E.L. and Cater, E. 1972. The Empirical Development of a Disaggregated Residential Location Model. In A.G. Wilson (ed.), *London Papers in Regional Science, Vol. 3.* London: Pion, pp. 114−45

Foley, D.L. 1964. An Approach to Metropolitan Spatial Structure. In M.M. Webber, *et. al., Explorations into Urban Structure.* Philadelphia: University of Pennsylvania Press, 1964, pp. 21−78

Hyman, G.M. 1969. The Calibration of Trip Distribution Models. *Environment and Planning, 1,* 105−12

Nigerian Government. 1966. *Urban Consumer Surveys, Kaduna, 1963* Lagos: Federal Office of Statistics

Park, R. 1915. The City: Suggestions for the Investigation of Human Behavior in the City Environment. *American Journal of Sociology, 20,* 577−612

Park, R.E., Burgess, E. and McKenzie, R.D., 1925. *The City.* Chicago: Chicago University Press

Senior, M. and Wilson A.G., 1973. Disaggregated Residential Location Models: Some Tests and Further Theoretical Developments. *Department of Geography Working Paper,* University of Leeds, England, 34 pp.

Strotz, R.H. 1957. The Implications of a Utility Tree. *Econometrica, 25,* 269−78

Strotz, R.H. 1959. The Utility Tree, a Correction and Further Appraisal. *Econometrica, 27,* 482−8

Wilson, A.G. 1967. A Statistical Theory of Spatial Distribution Models. *Transportation Research, 1,* 3, 253−69

Wilson, A.G. 1970. *Entropy in Urban and Regional Modelling.* London: Pion

Wilson, A.G. 1971. Some Recent Developments in Microeconomic Approach to Modelling Household Behaviour with Special Reference to Spatio-Temporal

Organizations. *Department of Geography Working Paper 3*. University of Leeds, England, 34 pp.

Wilson, A.G. *et al.* Calibration and Testing of the SELENEC Transportation Model. *Regional Studies, 3,* 331–50

Wingo, L. 1961. *Transportation and Urban Land*. Washington D.C.: Resources for the future, Inc., 132 pp.

12 A MODEL OF METROPOLIS

1. Introduction

The most well known and probably most well tested model of the urban structure derives from Lowry's (1964) classical model of the metropolis which had been subsequently developed and modified in recent years (Garin, 1969; Wilson, 1970). Numerous applications of this model have been made in Britain (Batty, 1970; Cripps and Foot, 1969; Echenique *et al.*, 1969; Turner, 1970) at both sub-regional and urban scales. Although other approaches do exist for modelling urban structure, as in the case of the empiric model of Hill (1965) for the Boston Region and the econometric model of the Penn-Jersey study, the Lowry model possesses the greatest appeal. This was aptly summarised by Goldner (1970) when he wrote

> Somehow, the conceptual framework of what has come to be known as the Lowry model has stimulated a population explosion of successors, each with meaningful elaborations. The development of the original model has this effect for several reasons; the promise of meaningful operationality was a prime stimulus; the simple casual structure had substantial appeal; the opportunity to enlarge and embellish the framework encourages further work.

Therefore the model developed below uses this same Lowry approach and the embellishment of the entropy-maximising methodology. It was shown in Chapter 10 that this methodology makes the equation system consistent, in addition to outlining ways of introducing planning or other constraints without violating the assumptions of the equilibrium of household behaviour.

The Lowry model is based on two principles, namely that of the urban economic base and that of spatial interaction. The economic base concept assumes that an urban economy may be divided exhaustively and exclusively into two sectors: the basic and the service (Tiebout, 1962, see also Chapter 3). Operationally the basic sector consists of industries whose products are 'exported' outside the producing city and also those industries whose locations are not population-oriented. On the other hand, the service sector produces for local consumption and the location of establishments in this category is population-oriented. It is further assumed that service employment and population are generated from basic employment through the economic base mechanism.

In the operation of the model, the location and quality of basic employment is assumed given (exogenous), but the number and location of service employment and population are generated by the model (endogenous). The allocation mechanism is the spatial interaction model which describes the urban structure in terms of residing and shopping as proxies for the two important land-use activities. These are expressed spatially as the journeys to workplaces and service centres. In Lowry's original formulation, the spatial interaction model was of the potential type but the ones used here, though of the same family, are derived using the powerful entropy-maximising methodology of Chapters 10 and 11.

The greatest contribution of Lowry is his ability to link activities and spatial interaction with the economic base concept. He thus establishes some aspects of the much talked about interdependence in urban systems (Warneryd, 1968). The immediate impact of this is the realisation that urban land-use patterns are at the same time the pre-requisite as well as the outcome of spatial interaction. Consequently urban analysis, like urban planning, shifts from a situation when land use was used to generate a traffic flow pattern (or vice versa) to the situation where this interdependence is not only recognised but also simulated. Our model of the metropolis developed in this chapter recognises this interdependence.

It is important to note that Lowry's framework has been enlarged and embellished through the entropy-maximising methodology introduced by Alan Wilson (1970). Some of these embellishments include

(i) the disaggregation of population into wage classes, and the introduction of more behavioural assumptions into spatial interaction and locational behaviour (Wilson, 1970);

(ii) the use of more consistent equations than Lowry's (1964) and Batty (1970);

(iii) interpretation of the economic base concept in terms of both export generation and locational attributes of urban activities (Goldner, 1968, Ayeni, 1975b).

Consequently, this approach to urban model-building remains the most comprehensive both in terms of its underlying theories and practical applications to solving urban problems.

2. The Mathematical Formulation of the Model

The mathematical formulation of the model is as follows. Let us assume that the urban or metropolitan area has been divided into n zones. We can then define the major variables of the urban structure in terms of a number of interaction variables between one zone and the other. Let these be T_{ij}^{kw} and S_{ij}^{mw} where T_{ij}^{kw} represents the number of people of socioeconomic class w who live in house type k in a zone i but work in zone j; and S_{ij}^{mw} is the number of employees in the service sector who belong to the socio-economic class w, sell goods in service centre type m in zone j but residing in zone i. Furthermore, let P_i^w and E_j^w be the zonal distribution of population and employment respectively for the various socio-economic groups surrogated by wage classes w.

For the journey to work-residential location model, the following constraints are defined

$$\sum_i \sum_k T_{ij}^{kw} = E_j^w \quad ; \quad i,j \in Z \tag{1}$$

$$\alpha \sum_i \sum_k T_{ij}^{kw} = P_i^w \quad ; \quad i,j \in Z_1 \tag{2}$$

$$\sum_i \sum_j \sum_k T_{ij}^{kw} (c_{ij} - W_i) + \sum_i \sum_j \sum_k T_{ij} c_{ij} = C^w \tag{3}$$
$$i \in z_2 \qquad\qquad\qquad i \in z_1$$

$$\sum_i \sum_j \sum_k T_{ij}^{kw} [p_i^k - q^w(w - c_{ij}')]^2 = \sigma_w^2 \tag{4}$$

where all terms are as defined in the last chapter. W_i is the benefit for locating a residence in zone i while Z_1 and Z_2 represent the partition of the urban system into constrainted and unconstrained set of zones respectively. Constraints may result as a result of population growth or planning requirements.

The resulting residential location model has the following equations:

$$T_{ij}^{kw} = A_i^w B_j^w E_j^w P_i^w \exp(-\beta^w c_{ij})$$
$$\exp\{-\mu_i^w [p_i^k - q^w(w - c_{ij}')]^2\}; \quad i \in Z_1 \tag{5}$$

and

$$T_{ij}^{kw} = B_j^w E_j^w \exp(-\beta^w c_{ij}) \exp(W_i)$$
$$\exp\{-\mu_i^w [p_i^k - q^w(w - c_{ij}')]^2\}; \quad i \in Z_2 \tag{6}$$

where

$$A_i = [\sum_{j \in Z_2} B_j^w E_j^w \exp(-\beta_i^w c_{ij}) \exp(W_i)$$

$$\exp\{-\mu_i^w [p_i^k - q^w(w - c_{ij}')]^2\}]^{-1} \tag{7}$$

$$B_j^w = [\sum_{i \in Z_1} A_i^w P_i^w \exp(-\beta_i^w c_{ij}) \exp\{-\mu_i^w [p_i^k - q^w(w - c_{ij}')]^2\} +$$

$$\sum_{i \in Z_2} \exp(-\beta_i^w c_{ij}) \exp(W_i) \exp\{-\mu_i^w [p_i^k - q^w(w - c_{ij}')]^2\}]^{-1} \tag{8}$$

Similarly the service centre location model component may be derived from these constraints

$$\sum_i \sum_m S_{ij}^{mw} = S_j^w \tag{9}$$

$$\sum_i \sum_j \sum_m S_{ij}^{mw}(c_{ij} - V_j) = C'^w \tag{10}$$

$$\sum_i \sum_m S_{ij}^{mw}[p_j^m - q'^w(w - c_{ij}')] = \sigma'^2_w \tag{11}$$

where the terms have interpretations similar to those of the residential location model. These are differentiated from the residential counterparts by the use of the prime superscript on the variables.

The service centre location model that results through the entropy-maximising methodology is

$$S_{ij}^{mw} = Q_j^w S_j^w \exp(-\lambda_j^w c_{ij}) \exp(v_j) \exp\{-\psi_j^w [p'_j{}^m -$$

$$q'^w(w - c_{ij}')]^2\} \tag{12}$$

where

$$Q_j^w = [\sum_i \exp(-\lambda_j^w c_{ij}) \exp(V_j) \exp\{-\psi_j^w [p''_i{}^m -$$

$$q'^w(w - c_{ij}')]^2\}]^{-1} \tag{13}$$

The above is a fully disaggregated Lowry model. It could be made more robust theoretically and mathematically but such models as this are often faced with problems of data availability and parameter estimation.

The method for solving the system of equations is as follows. We begin with the allocation of basic employment into residential zones using equation 5 or 6. During this iteration, the values of A_i^w are set equal to 1.0 and the constraints B_j^w are calculated. Next, the number of workers living in each of the zones is calculated by summing equation 5 or 6 over j, the workplaces. These figures are then scaled by the inverse of the activity rate a, which is the ratio of workers to total size of household, viz.

$$P_i^w = \alpha \sum_j \sum_k T_{ij}^{kw} \; ; \quad \alpha = \frac{1}{a} \tag{14}$$

Next, we calculate from this population, the amount of service employment demand by scaling this population by the population serving ratio γ

$$D_i^w = \gamma P_i^w \tag{15}$$

This demand is then allocated, using equations 12 and 13. This completes the first iteration.

The second iteration begins with the calculation of the total employment in each zone. This is now made up of the sum of the exogenously given employment and the service employment calculated in the first iteration. This newly calculated employment is then allocated to residences by means of equations 5a or 6a. The values of the terms A_j and B_j change accordingly but in such a way as to satisfy the constraint equations. Once the employment is allocated to residences, the associated population is found again and also the service employment as described in the first iteration. The iteration continues until the zonal simulated and observed populations do not differ by a predetermined amount, usually small enough to be disregarded. The model is then said to have converged. The final output of activities will include the matrices T_{ij}^{kw} and S_{ij}^{mw} which are the simulated patterns of interaction for the journeys to work and to services respectively, in addition to the zonal distribution of activities, that is, residential population and service employment. The solution system is described in Figure 12.2.1.

(i) Calibration Methodology for General Models of Urban Spatial Form

The calibration of spatial interaction models has increasingly assumed a central role in the design and construction of such models. Simply defined, calibration involves finding estimates of the values of parameters with which the model produces the best simulation of the real pattern. Associated with calibration procedures are the notion of 'the goodness

Figure 12.2.1: The Solution System of the Model

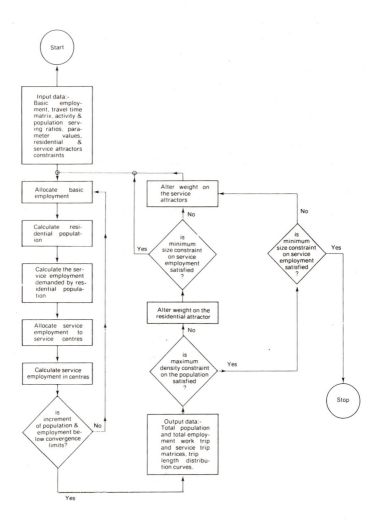

Source: After Batty (1970).

of fit' and the search for the most efficient parameters of interaction.

Several measures have been used in deciding the 'goodness of fit' of model simulation results. These include the chi-square test, the coefficient of determination between the predicted and the observed (R-squared), the RMSE (root mean square error) and even the standard deviation. These measures suffer from two weaknesses, first, their assumptions are hardly ever satisfied by the available data; and second, there is always risk of 'bogus calibration' (Cordey-Hayes, 1968). The first problem may be resolved by using non-parametric tests, but the second one is not easily removed because it deals with a fundamental concept of spatial interaction models. Bogus calibration arises when either β or μ tends to or equals zero. This is so because if β equals zero, for example, then T_{ij} in equation 5a and 6a become a simple linear function of population P_i and very good fits are obtained by R-squared statistic because of the circularity of using observed population to predict population (Batty, 1970b, 1971).

Unlike the use of statistics based on coefficients of determination between observed and predicted patterns of activities, statistics based on the interactions are known to give more useful results that obviate the problem of bogus calibration. One such statistic is the *mean* trip length or *mean* trip cost in the system. This is known also to be very sensitive to parameter changes. Another set of statistics is based on the pattern of interaction in the system, that is, the T_{ij} or S_{ij}. For example, one could compare every observed interaction with the corresponding predicted interaction and ensure that these do not differ significantly (Wilson, 1971). However, a decision as to whether one uses mean trip lengths or direct comparisons of patterns of interaction would consider the nature of the data; for if sample estimates constitute the observed patterns, it may not be worth while to compare every predicted and observed interaction, partly because the sample size may have to be nearly as big as the total population before all cells of the interaction matrix are filled, but more fundamentally because one can only meaningfully compare attributes (statistics) of a sample with those of its population and not the gross values of the sample. One is therefore left in most researches to use mean trip lengths (observed and predicted) as major calibration statistics. None the less, for purposes of comparison of results, statistics based on the distribution of activities will also be considered, but the statistic based on trip lengths is accorded some priorities during calibration processes.

Tests of the goodness of fit are usually of two types. One type tests the differences between predicted and observed mean trip lengths for each of the journeys to work and services, while the other type tests the differences between observed and predicted activities (populations and employments). The first type is represented by the well known student's 't' test of the differences of two means while the second could consist of two tests, the correlation coefficient between the observed and predicted distributional values and the powerful non-parametric Kolmogorov-Smirnov test (Siegal, 1956). While the correlation R or its square are measures of the degree of association between the observed and the predicted, the Kolmogorov-Smirnov test preserves the relative location of individual zones values and ensures that there is no directional bias in size-class distribution of these values (Morrill, 1965).

The traditional calibration procedure for gravity models is by logarithmic transformation of the equations into linear functions which are then fitted by the method of least squares (Olsson, 1965). Batty notes that models which are *intrinsically linear* can be thus transformed but models of spatial interaction as formulated above are *intrinsically non-linear* and hence require other calibration procedures (Batty, 1971). Many search techniques have been proposed for this calibration. These include Hyman's iterative solution (Hyman, 1969), the gradient search method (Turner, 1970), the Fibonnaci search method and the search by the Golden Section (Batty, 1971; Himmelbleu, 1972). All these approaches have been devised for the calibration of partial or single-parameter models. Although Batty has proposed methods of adapting the Golden Search technique to deal with cases of two-parameter models, the problem is far from solved because most of these search techniques are difficult to generalise empirically into simultaneous search framework. In the present study, Hyman's iterative method is used to run the submodels *separately* until a set of best values are obtained for each of them. These are then combined in the general model and run until the best values of the parameters β and γ are obtained. This approach is equivalent to the two-stage calibration process described by Batty (1971).

3. The Empirical Development of the Model of Metropolis in Lagos, Nigeria

The empirical development of the Lowry model requires not only easily available demographic, economic and spatial behavioural data but also an economic system that can be dichotomised into basic and service sectors. Neither such data system, nor indeed, cities are easily obtainable in Nigeria. In the former case, there is a general lack of relevant data while the low level of development does not encourage the collection of a wider body of data. For the latter case, it needs to be mentioned that the processes of urbanisation in Nigeria does not necessarily imply a corresponding process of industrialisation or vice versa, and hence it is not in all cases that the definition of the basic and service sectors, as in Western European or American textbooks, is applicable. None the less, there exists a number of cities, in particular Jos, Lagos, Kaduna and a few others, where data are not only available but also where the division of the economy into the basic and service sectors could be done with some measure of certainty. The Lowry model has been developed for both Jos and Lagos (Ayeni, 1975b; Ayeni, 1976) but Lagos is used here to provide some variety in our case studies.

For this study, Lagos, the *de facto* headquarters of the Nigerian government, was divided into 25 zones on the basis of the availability of zonally disaggregated data and the land-use characteristics of the metropolis.

A description of the 25 zones and their boundaries was given in Chapter 5 and in Figure 5.3.2.

It was shown in Chapter 3 that Lagos in 1975 provided jobs for a total of 674,160 people, 234,381 of which are in the basic sector, while the remaining 436,779 are in the service or non-basic sector. These figures were results from a survey that employed Goldner's (1968) conceptualisation of basic employment as involving not only exporting industries but also those that, even though they produce for local consumption, also generate income from local production (Table 12.3.1).

Most of the data used in the calibration of the models were derived from the author's field-work, which involved a total of 1,405 households and investigations into the socio-economic characteristics and spatial behaviour of 7,426 people. On the socio-economic characteristics, variables such as age, income, size of household and education played important roles, while the details of the travelling or spatial behaviour included such trips as the journey to school and recreational centres, the journey to work and the journey to service centres. For these trips, the average trip lengths are as shown in Table 12.3.2. The socio-economic grouping of households was on the basis of income and this was as follows. The socio-economic group is said to be low if annual incomes are less than 1,000.00 Naira; middle if between 1,000.00 and 3,000.00 Naira: while high if above 3,000.00 Naira. It is possible to infer from Table 12.3.3 that trip lengths vary by socio-economic classes — the upper socio-economic groups make longer trips.

A major component of the empirical development of the model is the operationalisation of the generalised transport cost variables. Wilson

Table 12.3.1: Schematic Classification of the Lagos Metropolitan Economy into Basic and Service Sectors*

	Locational Orientation	
Economic Base Orientation	Basic	Service
	Locate with respect to interregional transportation routes, resources and unique site features; inter-industry linkages and agglomeration economies.	Locate with respect to residential population and purchasing power, daytime population concentration.
Exports	(1) Agriculture (2) Manufacturing (3) Transportation (4) Regional administration (5) National administration (6) Finance and banking (7) Educational institutions, e.g. universities and grammar schools	
Local Consumption	(1) Wholesale trade (2) Building and construction industries	(1) Retail trade, including (2) Intra-city transportation (3) Services and service industries (8) Local government

Modified after Goldner (1968).
*Based on a similar study in Jos, Plateau State, Nigeria.

Table 12.3.2: Summary of Trip Characteristics in Lagos, 1975

Trip Types	Income Group	Mean Length (km)	Mean Cost (Naira)
Work	Low	4.89	0.115
	Middle	6.18	0.267
	Upper	8.29	0.736
Service	Low	3.45	0.079
	Middle	3.76	0.161
	Upper	5.18	0.523
Recreation	Low	4.81	n.a.
	Middle	5.86	n.a.
	Upper	7.49	n.a.
School	All groups	3.24	n.a.

Source: Field-work (Ayeni, 1976 b,p.11).

et al. (1969) noted that the generalised transportation cost c_{ij} could be made a linear combination of time-distance, t_{ij}, the distance between two points, d_{ij}, the excess time spent in travelling e_{ij}, parking or terminal costs p_j and the penalty δ paid for using a particular mode of transport, viz.

$$c_{ij} = a_1 \, t_{ij} + a_2 e_{ij} + a_3 d_{ij} + p_j + \delta \qquad (16)$$

We have used a variant of this which takes into consideration both the physical distance d_{ij}, the out-of-pocket costs of transportation and the cost of time spent in commuting. For the journey to work and service centres the mean generalised costs for the three income groups are shown in the last column of Table 12.3.2. As in the case of the mean trip lengths, trip costs increase with socio-economic class although, unlike the mean trip length, the variations are more marked as a result of the differences in the valuation of time and costs by the different classes of people.

At full calibration, the parameters of the model are as given in Table 12.3.3. In all cases the values behave in accordance with theoretical expectations that the lower the mean trip cost, the higher the value of the parameter. The same set of relationships has been observed in the United Kingdom by Senior and Wilson (1973) and in Jos, Nigeria, by Ayeni (1976b). Similar relationships also hold for the variation in the variance of the cost of housing given by the right-hand side of equation 4. In fact the variances are 70.93 Naira, 504.37 Naira and 284.70 Naira respectively.

The higher variance of the middle-income group and hence the low value of the second parameter in Table 12.3.3 is due to the larger variation that exists in the incomes of people in this group. Mean trip lengths and the variance of housing expenditures were used as principal calibration statistics to avoid the phenomenon of bogus calibration. The observed and simulated mean trip lengths do not differ significantly either for the residential location component or the journey to services – service centre location model. On the other hand, it is more difficult to accurately predict the mean variance of the housing expenditure (Table 12.3.3).

Other model outputs include six sets of interaction matrices, two for each socio-economic group, representing both the journey to work and the journey to service patterns of interaction. There were in addition the distributions of population and employment by socio-economic groupings (Tables 12.3.4, 12.3.6). This latter output compared with the

Table 12.3.3: Calibration Statistics of the Model*

(a) Residential Component

Group	1st Para.	2nd Para.	Observed Mean Trip Length	Predicted Mean Trip Length	Observed Mean Variance Housing Expenditure (Naira)	Predicted Mean Variance Housing Expenditure (Naira)
Low	0.245	0.266	4.89 km	5.11 km	70.93	77.44
Middle	0.168	0.085	6.18 km	6.10 km	504.37	285.53
Upper	0.080	0.547	8.29 km	8.95 km	284.70	234.65

(b) Service Component

Group	1st Para.	2nd Para.	Observed Mean Trip Length	Predicted Mean Trip Length	Observed Mean Variance Service Expenditure	Predicted Mean Variance Service Expenditure
Low	0.401	—	3.45 km	3.82 km	—	—
Middle	0.386	—	3.76 km	3.92 km	—	—
Upper	0.292	—	5.18 km	7.17 km	—	—

* Both mean trip length and mean trip costs were used experimentally to simulate the spatial and locational behaviour of Lagos residents. While the calibration statistics and parameters conform with theoretical expectations parameters and means based on distances rather than costs of friction were better predictors of spatial and locational behaviour.

Figure 12.3.1a: Observed and Predicted Populations: Low-income
Group, Lagos, 1975

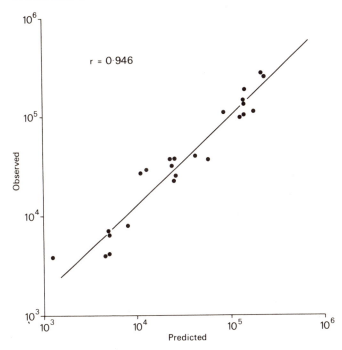

estimated distribution of people and employment in the city gives an
idea of how good the predictions or simulations are. In order to show
this, Table 12.3.4 has been prepared to give not only the product
moment correlation coefficients but also its rank counterparts. While
the product moment correlation coefficient could be expected to
measure the overall correspondence of the observed and simulated
distributions, the rank correlation coefficient should throw light on the
extent to which the two sets of distributions maintain equal ranking
and thus enables a greater evaluation of the simulation. For the distribution of population, rather good predictions were made as correlation
coefficients of 0.946 and above were recorded for the three income
classes (see Tables 12.3.4. and 12.3.5). Figure 12.3.1 also confirms that
both observed and predicted populations differ not very significantly
while Figures 12.3.2, 12.3.3 and 12.3.4 compare these distributions for
the three income groups. In general, over or under predictions do not
seem to be a serious criticism of the simulation.

For the distribution of employment, the two types of correlation

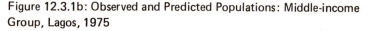

Figure 12.3.1b: Observed and Predicted Populations: Middle-income Group, Lagos, 1975

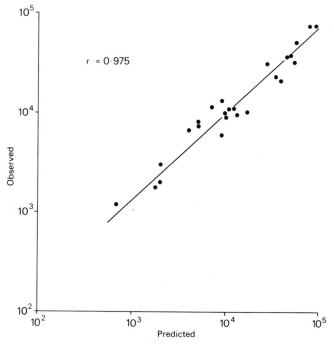

coefficients tell slightly different stories. For instance, the product moment correlation coefficients of 0.95 for the low, 0.938 for the middle and 0.942 for the upper would in general suggest a rather good prediction; but the lower rank correlation values of 0.677 for the low, 0.809 for the middle and 0.847 for the upper would suggest a lower level of accuracy in the simulation exercise (see also Table 12.3.6). While the poorer prediction could be due to some defects in the assumptions of the model, it is equally possible to attribute it to the process by which the distribution of employment opportunities in Lagos was estimated. While population distribution was based on the average housing density, housing occupancy and the number of houses in each study zone, the estimation of employment was based partly on the number of available non-residential houses as well as on the distribution of basic employment which was known. The problem then would seem to centre around the distribution of service employment. As of now, there is no reliable information on this and estimation processes of the

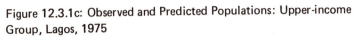

Figure 12.3.1c: Observed and Predicted Populations: Upper-income Group, Lagos, 1975

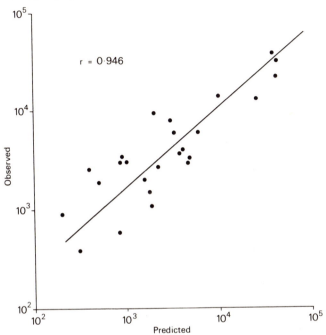

Table 12.3.4: Correlation Coefficients and Coefficients of Determination for Predicted and Observed Distributions of Population and Employment in Lagos, 1975

	(a) Population			
Income Group	Pearson's R	R-Squared	Spearman's R	R-Squared
Low	0.946	0.8956	0.945	0.900
Middle	0.975	0.9498	0.921	0.848
Upper	0.946	0.8954	0.829	0.688
	(b) Employment			
Income Group	Pearson's R	R-Squared	Spearman's R	R—Squared
Low	0.950	0.9034	0.678	0.459
Middle	0.938	0.8804	0.809	0.654
Upper	0.942	0.8874	0.847	0.717

Source: Model outputs.

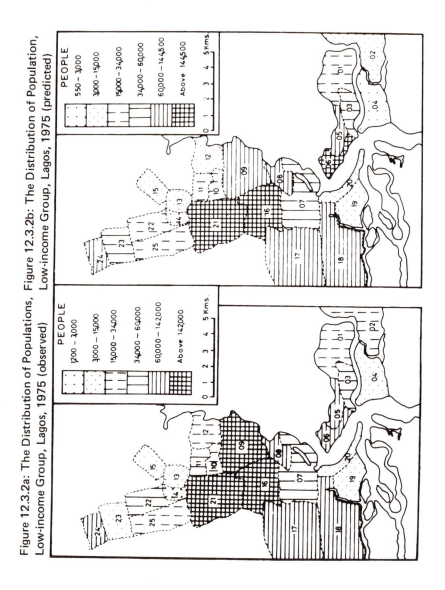

Figure 12.3.2a: The Distribution of Populations,
Low-income Group, Lagos, 1975 (observed)

Figure 12.3.2b: The Distribution of Population,
Low-income Group, Lagos, 1975 (predicted)

PEOPLE

550 – 3,000
3,000 – 15,000
15,000 – 34,000
34,000 – 60,000
60,000 – 144,500
Above 144,500

0 1 2 3 4 5 Kms.

PEOPLE

1,200 – 3,000
3,000 – 15,000
15,000 – 34,000
34,000 – 60,000
60,000 – 142,000
Above 142,000

0 1 2 3 4 5 Kms.

Figure 12.3.3a: The Distribution of Population,
Middle-income Group, Lagos, 1975 (observed)

Figure 12.3.2b: The Distribution of Population,
Middle-income Group, Lagos, 1974 (predicted)

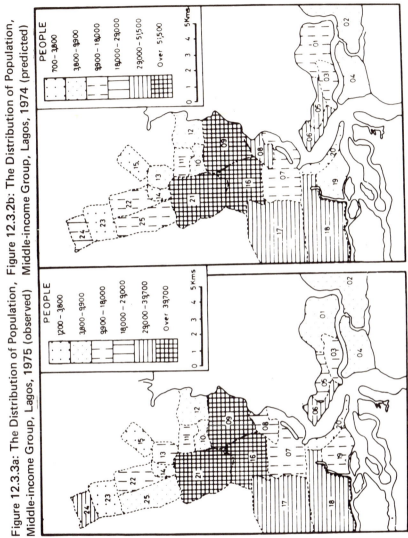

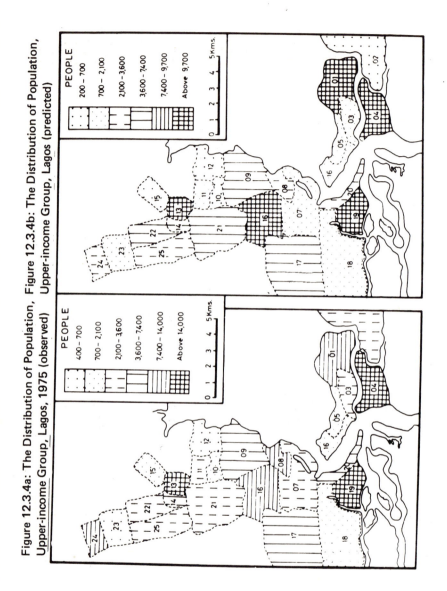

Figure 12.3.4a: The Distribution of Population, Figure 12.3.4b: The Distribution of Population, Upper-income Group, Lagos, 1975 (observed) Upper-income Group, Lagos (predicted)

Table 12.3.5: Observed and Predicted Distributions of Population in Lagos, 1975

Code	Description	Low Income Observed	Low Income Predicted	Middle Income Observed	Middle Income Predicted	Upper Income Observed	Upper Income Predicted
1	Ikoyi	24,564	26,211	9,706	13,464	13,072	24,681
2	Maroko	29,674	13,593	8,333	5,005	2,620	390
3	Ikoyi S.W.-Obalende	39,959	42,929	11,221	11,634	3,529	888
4	Victoria Is.	4,915	1,217	6,996	4,010	22,200	36,374
5	Eko	101,014	133,606	22,749	34,070	1,154	1,976
6	CBD-Marina	115,723	198,811	32,496	51,493	2,019	1,608
7	Ido-Oyingbo	36,503	59,733	10,250	17,104	3,224	1,083
8	Ebute Meta	93,755	127,599	26,327	39,343	8,279	2,662
9	Yaba	177,377	144,372	49,808	55,157	5,664	5,598
10	Igbabi-Fadeyi	22,244	25,890	6,246	9,454	1,964	507
11	Shomulu	36,559	25,196	10,366	9,905	3,228	885
12	Barriga	27,128	11,350	7,616	5,127	396	306
13	Palm Grove	4,105	4,697	11,517	5,920	38,622	36,549
14	Ilupeju Ind.	1,248	556	1,306	565	3,795	4,088
15	Ojota	4,295	5,138	3,159	2,198	993	178
16	Surulere	253,207	214,839	74,752	77,759	13,568	9,740
17	Itire-Lawanson	134,925	137,884	37,888	48,353	3,915	3,755
18	Ajegunle	141,587	141,951	39,748	44,196	1,503	1,863
19	Apapa	8,030	8,141	13,487	8,778	42,415	51,919
20	Apapa-Wharf	6,963	4,877	1,955	2,356	6,154	3,383
21	Mushin	262,341	232,099	93,667	85,330	3,167	4,772
22	Ikeja	37,434	22,767	10,512	10,655	3,306	4,938
23	Ikeja-Ind.	6,730	4,963	1,890	1,806	594	807
24	Agege	111,626	85,678	31,345	26,672	9,857	2,160
25	Oshodi	31,921	24,898	8,963	10,408	2,819	2,247
	Total	1,713,827	1,698,985	532,303	580,762	198,057	203,357

Table 12.3.6: Observed and Predicted Employment Distribution in Lagos, 1975

Code	Description	Low Income Observed	Predicted	Middle Income Observed	Predicted	Upper Income Observed	Predicted
1	Ikoyi	2,440	4,329	1,835	2,084	2,292	3,453
2	Maroko	318	1,778	89	686	28	56
3	Ikoyi S.W.-Obalente	23,289	20,513	13,441	5,769	2,710	1,439
4	Victoria Is.	5,216	2,119	1,784	1,095	4,625	5,143
5	Eko	12,331	22,016	4,219	5,922	1,478	679
6	CBD-Marina	150,215	101,751	34,245	32,944	10,863	9,318
7	Ido-Oyingbo	12,464	12,456	4,263	3,635	1,494	562
8	Ebute Meta	18,196	21,318	5,109	6,660	1,607	781
9	Yaba	23,824	20,218	1,305	7,883	458	892
10	Igbabi-Fadeyi	1,183	3,827	405	1,411	142	110
11	Shomolu	133	3,287	37	1,350	12	124
12	Bariga	250	1,486	79	702	25	45
13	Palm Grove	2,172	1,133	610	950	5,192	5,040
14	Jlupeju Ind.	818	379	280	178	98	586
15	Ojola	1,850	1,283	520	471	163	78
16	Surulere	21,084	28,354	10,370	10,658	130	1,367
17	Itire-Lawanson	10,364	17,946	5,102	6,463	32	516
18	Ajegunle	271	18,475	4,076	5,999	24	258
19	Apapa	531	1,313	149	1,261	5,047	7,116
20	Apapa-Wharf	20,303	21,588	10,919	6,204	630	2,312
21	Mushin	36,666	41,358	16,239	15,390	2,801	1,991
22	Ikeja	1,079	3,240	303	1,523	95	700
23	Ikeja-Ind.	26,537	22,397	13,068	7,686	4,110	2,718
24	Agege	10,147	11,214	4,041	3,636	13	301
25	Oshodi	180	3,250	51	1,422	16	311
Total		381,861	387,028	132,539	131,982	44,085	45,895

Figure 12.3.5a: Observed and Predicted Employment: Low-income Group, Lagos, 1975

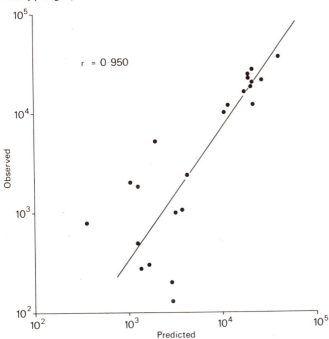

numerous street workers who may number thousands and who have no fixed locations is difficult. None the less, it is reasonable to expect that the distribution given by the model is a good reflection of the probable distribution of employment opportunities in the city, because it is based on a theory that purports to evaluate both the locational and spatial behaviour of urban residents. The correspondence between observed and predicted employment is shown in Figure 12.3.5, while the distributions are shown in Figures 12.3.6, 12.3.7 and 12.3.8 for the three income groups.

An important observation from the outputs on the distribution of population concerns those areas of the urban system where there are over or under predictions (see Table 12.3.5). It would seem that the model over-emphasises the location of employment opportunities as well as the role of housing, housing costs and accessibility or transportation costs in the residential location decision process. While it is true that these considerations are sometimes relevant to residential location decision-making in Lagos, there are a number of important constraints

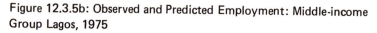

Figure 12.3.5b: Observed and Predicted Employment: Middle-income Group Lagos, 1975

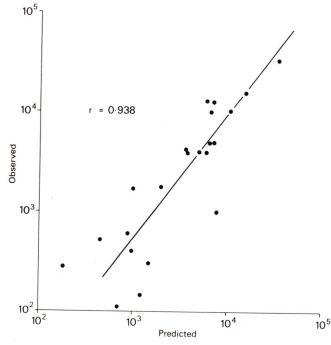

on the sort of trade-off that emerges. First, the cost of the journey to work or any other function is not always a continuous variable but rather a stepped function reflecting urban transportation pricing policy. Second, and especially for the low-income and middle-income groups, many of whom travel on motor bikes or on foot, distance rather than cost plays a significant role in the decision process.

The housing and housing costs variables are not much better. For instance, many people in central Lagos, Eko (5), CBD-Marina (6), Oba-lende (3) are indigenous to the city and hence live in rent-free family houses which are located near work centres. Added to this class is an élitist group which lives in highly subsidised, high-class houses or rent-free quarters in such zones as Ikoyi (1), Victoria Island (4) Yaba (8), Palm Grove (13) and Surulere (18). To the extent that housing was con-tractual to the terms of employment of this group of people, it is diffi-cult to say the extent to which transportation costs affect decision-making. None the less, to the extent that the rents paid in these houses are based on long-term or medium-term leases and are hence apparently

Figure 12.3.5c: Observed and Predicted Employment: Upper-income Group, Lagos, 1975

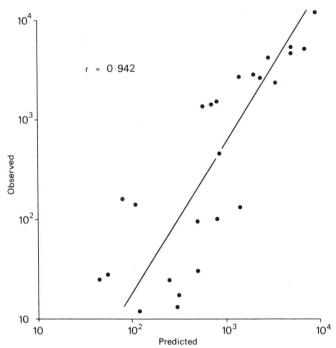

higher than those that obtain in other parts of the city, these areas have remained predominantly élitist.

The sensitivity of the model is also shown especially in the prediction of the residential distribution of the groups with low and upper income (see Table 12.3.5, especially Victoria Island (4) or Maroko (2)). The first is strictly a high-income residential area while the second is a low-income area. The situation in real life is not one of clear-cut dichotomy as housing characteristics, housing types and residential households are intricately mixed. This is to argue that, except in few cases, social segregation is not yet a distinguishing characteristic of Lagos as in the case of Jos described in the early parts of this book. All this suggests that the highly economic rationality of the model need be modified to take account of cultural and environmental factors.

An important characteristic of the spatial interaction modelling approach is the output of the patterns of interaction, outputs that are rarely available and yet very useful in understanding and planning human spatial behaviour. Therefore an important component of the

Figure 12.3.6a: The Distribution of Employment, Figure 12.3.6b: The Distribution of Employment,
Low-income Group, Lagos, 1975 (observed)   Low-income Group, Lagos, 1975 (predicted)

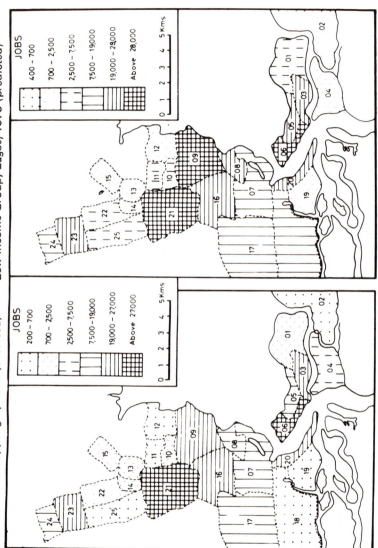

Figure 12.3.7a: The Distribution of Employment, Figure 12.3.7b: The Distribution of Employment,
Middle-income Group, Lagos, 1975 (observed)   Middle-income Group, Lagos, 1975 (predicted)

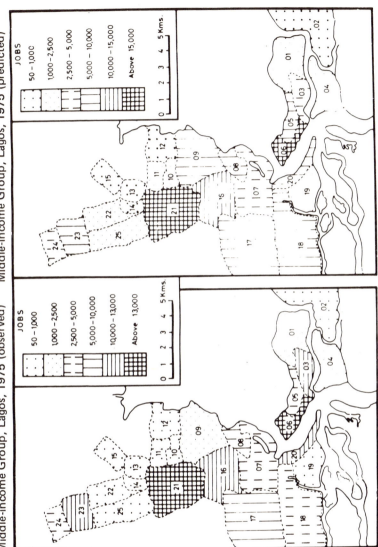

Figure 12.3.8a: The Distribution of Employment, Figure 12.3.8b: The Distribution of Employment,
Upper-income Group, Lagos, 1975 (observed)   Upper-income Group, Lagos, 1975 (predicted)

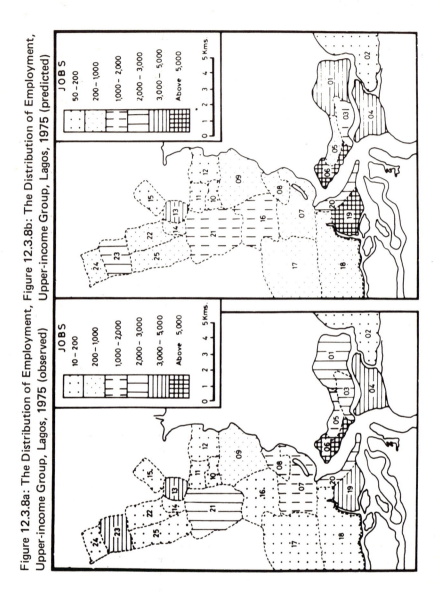

pattern of interaction is the concentration of urban activities and facilities into few areas. For instance, the areas of Isale-Eko (5), CBD-Marina (6), Ebute-Meta (8), Yaba (9), Surulere (10), Apapa Wharf (20), Mushin (21) and Ikeja Industrial Estate (23) are locations for both employment activities as well as service facilities with the first two areas accounting for about one-fifth of all activities (see Table 12.3.6). Consequently much of the interaction for the different socio-economic groups is between these and the remaining zones of the urban system. That the first two centres lie on Lagos Island is a major cause of traffic congestion and traffic hold-ups on the roads.

For the groups with low and middle incomes, much of the interaction is to three major areas of Lagos, namely Lagos Island, made up of Ikoyi (1), Ikoyi-Obalende (3), Victoria Island (4), Eko (5) and CBD-Marina (6); Apapa Region, made up of Apapa (19), Apapa Wharf (20), Ajegunle (18) and Itire-Lawanson (17); and Mushin-Ikeja area, made up of Mushin (21), Ikeja (22) and Ikeja Industrial Estate (23). For the upper-income groups, the major destinations are Lagos Island made up of the same set of zones; Apapa Area made up of only the Apapa Wharf (20) and Apapa (19) itself, and the Industrial Estate at Ikeje (23). The relatively few centres of employment for this class of people are very much scattered about the urban system and consequently contribute to the problems of traffic flow and congestion, as it may be confidently assumed that households in this class own at least one automobile.

4. Conclusion

In this chapter, we have developed a general model of the urban spatial form using the Lowry framework with the embellishments of the entropy-maximising methodology. In most of the analysis in the chapter the model has been used as an educative device both in understanding the web of interrelationships between different urban activities and also in simulating human spatial and locational behaviour. To this extent, the outputs of the model necessarily identify hiatuses that exist in our knowledge about urban processes. Consequently they provide useful inputs in designing more accurate models of the metropolis.

The Lowry framework is a useful planning device whereby the model can be used either in analysing the impacts of decisions on the spatial system or in the evaluation of strategies of growth of a city. For the former, one could experiment with changes that may take place with the distribution of basic employment and evaluate the impacts on both the distribution of people and service employment in the city as well as the impacts on the patterns of interaction. Furthermore, one could evaluate the impacts of new roads or even mass transit systems by manipulating the cost variables of the model. In these ways, the model provides a means of conducting an impact analysis on policy decisions. For the latter, on the other hand, the model would be used in a planning stage that involves extensive analysis of planning goals and objectives of the metropolitan area. It will be expected that the model generates outputs that will have to be evaluated via a cost-benefit analysis framework.

Perhaps the greatest contribution of this model lies in the ease with which it could be developed into a predictive framework. Such a development would involve the explicit incorporation of time in the equations, the evaluation of the nature of the urban stock of houses and basic employment and their conceptualisation within a predictive framework. Such a development is the aim of the next chapter.

References

Ayeni, M.A.O. 1975a. A Predictive Model of Urban Stock and Activity 1. Theoretical Considerations. *Environment and Planning, A, 7, 8*, 965–79

Ayeni, M.A.O. 1975b. A Model of the Metropolis: The Development of a Lowry Model for Jos, Benue-Plateau State, Nigeria. *Socioeconomic Planning Sciences, 9*, 273–83

Ayeni, M.A.O. 1976a. A Regional Plan of Lagos State: Planning Lagos Metropolitan Area. *Final Report Planning Studies Programme, Faculty of the Social Sciences.* University of Ibadan, Nigeria 168 pp.

Ayeni, M.A.O. 1976b. The Development of a Disaggregated Residential Location Model in Nigeria. *Annals of Regional Science, 10*, 3, 31–54

Batty, M. 1970a. Recent Developments in Land Use Modelling. Urban Systems Research Unit, Department of Geography, University of Reading

Batty, M. 1970b. An Activity Allocation Model for the Nottinghamshire–Derbyshire Subregion. *Regional Studies, 4*, 307–32

Batty, M. 1971. Exploratory Calibration of a Retail Location Model Using Search by Golden Section. *Environment and Planning, 3*, 411–32

Cordey-Hayes, M. 1968. Retail Location Models. *Centre for Environment Studies.* Working Paper 16, London

Cripps, E.L., and Foot, D., 1970. A Land Use Model for Subregional Planning. *Regional Studies, 3*, 243–68

Echenique, M., Crowther, D., and Lindsay, W. 1971. The Development of a Model of a Town. *London Papers in Regional Science, A.* Urban and Regional Planning A.G. Wilson (ed.)

Garin, R.A. 1969. A Matrix Formulation of the Lowry Model. *Journal of the American Institute of Planners, 32*, 361–4

Golder, W. 1960. The Lowry Model Heritage. *Journal of the American Institute of Planners, 31*, 2, 111–20

Goldner, W. 1968. *Projective Land Use Model (PLUM).* Berkely, California, Bay Area Transportation Study, Technical Report 219

Hill, D.M. 1965. A Growth Allocation Model for the Boston Region. *Journal of the American Institute of Planners, 31*, 2, 111–20

Himmelbleu, D.M. 1972. *Applied Nonlinear Programming.* New York: McGraw-Hill

Hyman, G.M. 1969. The Calibration of Trip Distribution Models. *Environment and Planning, 1,* 105–12

Lowry, I.S. 1964 *A Model of Metropolis.* Santa Monica, California: RAND Corporation

Morrill, W.L. 1965. *Migration and the Spread and Growth of Urban Settlement.* Lund Series in Geography, Series B, No. 26. Gleerup, Lund

Olsson, G. 1963. Distance and Human Interaction. *Geografiska Annaler, 47B,* 3–43

Siegel, S. 1958. *Non-Parametric Statistics for the Behavioural Sciences.* New McGraw Hill

Tiebout, M. 1962. *The Economic Base Study.* Washington D.C.: Committee for Economic Development, Paper No. 16

Turner, G.G. 1970. The Development of an Activity Allocation Model for the Bristol Subregion. Urban Systems Research Unit, Department of Geography, University of Reading

Warneryd, O. 1968. *Interdependence in Urban Systems.* Meddalendan Fran Goteburgs Universitets Geografiska Institutioner, Series B, No. 1

Wilson, A.G. 1970. *Entropy in Urban and Regional Modelling.* London: Pion

Wilson, A.G. 1971. Some Recent Developments in Microeconomic Approach to Modelling Household Behavior with Special Reference to Spatio-Temporal Organization. *Department of Geography Working Paper 3,* University of Leeds

Wilson, A.G. *et al.* 1969. Calibrating and Testing the SELENIC Transportation Model. *Regional Studies, 3,* 331–50

Wilson, A.G. and Senior, M.L. 1973. Explorations and Synthesis of Linear Programming and Spatial Interaction Models of Residential Location. Department of Geography Working Paper, No. 43, University of Leeds

13 PREDICTIVE MODELLING OF URBAN SPATIAL STRUCTURE

1. Introduction

Urban systems are dynamic systems and hence their analysis requires predictive models that explicitly incorporate the element of time. Consequently, the treatment of time as to whether it is discrete or continuous is fundamental in the development of predictive models. There are a number of approaches to incorporating time in urban models. One such is to recognise that change and the forces producing change may be represented in the birth, death and migration processes that are best studied at the level of the household or individual firm, and then incorporate these into the modelling framework. This involves two sets of problems: the aggregation of micro-level behaviour to produce models that posses pedagogic as well as evaluate capabilities and the incorporation of change. Wilson (1971) has shown that even when it is theoretically tractable and the incorporation of change is bound to make the situation more complex.

However it is possible to proceed from the comparative static models of previous chapters, disaggregate them and introduce dynamic or quasi-dynamic considerations in their formulation through an appropriate modelling framework. The approach obviates the theory problem of aggregation as well as retaining the modest data requirements for empirical development. In this chapter, we shall discuss major features of a predictive model and show one of the ways by which these could be integrated through the entropy-maximising framework.

2. Components of a Predictive Model of Urban Stock and Activity

The development of predictive models within the Lowry framework using the entropy-maximising methodology must take cognisance of the fact that these models 'look' at the future and hence must incorporate a number of terms and concepts not met with in models that merely simulate the urban structure. Some of these ideas and concepts are those of the 'potential mover and non-mover' in residential change (Wilson, 1970), the issue of urban stock, especially houses, employments and their growth, and a dynamic or a quasi-dynamic formulation of the economic base mechanism which constitutes the link between spatial interaction and economic growth. The incorporation of these concepts in predictive modelling requires their full development as well as their operationalisation.

Figure 13.2.1: Interdependence of the Urban Spatial System

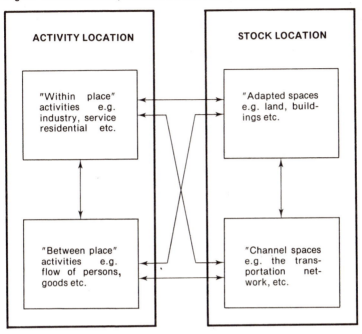

Source: Echenique *et al.* (1971).

(i) The Urban Stock

The urban stock is a major component of the spatial system. In fact the spatial structure of the city has been said to be the outcome of two interdependent elements: the locations of stock, and activities (Echenique *et al.*, 1971). The urban stock consists of adapted spaces such as land and buildings, and 'Channel spaces', such as the transportation network. The urban activities, on the other hand, comprise residing, working, shopping, recreation, and so on. Changes both in activities and stock create a demand for stock, which again constrains the location of such activities. The interaction is well known in the literature, and is schematically depicted in Figure 13.2.1.

If we interpret the supply of stock in the urban system in terms of buildings or houses, we see that the total supply consists of three major components: new houses being erected by developers on hitherto unsettled land; new houses arising from development of the central city; and old houses vacated by people who, within a time period, change their residence. If Δ represents increments in the supply of stock, then one may represent the total stock of houses in the city by the equation

$$\Delta H = \Delta H^{(1)} + \Delta H^{(2)} + \Delta H^{(3)} \tag{1}$$

where the superscripts refer to the three types of stock defined above. Equation 1 is the housing stock generation sub-model, and certain aspects of its nature are discussed in what follows.

(ii) The Concepts of 'Potential Mover' and 'Potential Non-mover' and the Measurement of $\Delta H^{(3)}$

An important sub-class of the city population changes residence between one time period and another. In the last section the house left vacant by these people were denoted by $\Delta H^{(3)}$. What this implies is the introduction of the idea of residential mobility. This problem was originally tackled by Crecine (1968) in his dynamic model of urban structure and by Goldner (1968) in his projective land-use model (PLUM), and it has been discussed in detail by Wilson (1970). What Wilson did was to construct hybrid models to denote the mobility behaviour of four types of persons: locationally unconstrained workers, that is those who can change work and residence and hence are movers; production-constrained workers, that is those with fixed residences and who are therefore non-movers; attraction-constrained workers, that is those who have fixed jobs and are therefore movers; and production- and attraction-constrained workers, that is those who have fixed residences and fixed jobs and are therefore non-movers. It is the first and third types of people who may change their residence from one time to another.

Wilson's categorisation interests us since it divides the population into movers and non-movers. As he himself observed, the term 'non-mover' is simply a convenient shorthand. Although such people are regarded as not likely to move, if they do move it is in such a way that their assignment to jobs and residences satisfies the simple gravity model. In a predictive model it is the potentiality of these two categories that is of interest. Hence, successive runs of predictive-location models should be concerned largely with the behaviour of potential movers, although the models subsequently developed are comprehensive and deal with both the potential movers and non-movers.

Two methods of estimating these sub-populations were discussed by Wilson. The first involves expressing the zonal non-mover population

as a function of a number of variables, X_i^k, which incorporate characteristics of housing supply; for example, the availability of government
houses in zone i, the occupation-age mix, the age-sex mix, and even
variables that describe occupation mix. Thus,

$$P^{(2)}_{i(t+1)} = \sum_k a^k X^k_{i(t)}, \tag{2}$$

where $P^{(2)}_{i(t+1)}$ represents the non-mover population in zone i at time
period $t + 1$ and a^k are 'dismobility' coefficients.

The formulation of this equation in terms of lags of time represents
the quasi-dynamic nature of the model. The second method is much
simpler, since it merely expresses the non-mover population at a future
period in terms of the socio-economic characteristics of the population
at a previous time period. Symbolically the equation is of the form

$$P^{(2)}_{i(t+1)} = \sum_v b^v P^v_{i(t)}, \tag{3}$$

where v represents the socio-economic characterisation of the population.
Values both for a and b are to be estimated by a least-squares procedure.
The problem of the two approaches is non-availability of relevant data
even though disaggregated data, as implied by equation 3, could be
provided by census data, whereas those for equation 2 must be specially
collected. The method that has been chosen is, in essence, a variant of
Wilson's approach, but it involves further simplifying assumptions.

Let $P^{(1)}_i$, $P^{(2)}_i$ denote the potential movers and non-movers by zone
of residence. It is obvious that

$$\left. \begin{array}{c} P^{(1)}_i \cup P^{(2)}_i = P_i \\[12pt] \text{and} \\[12pt] P^{(1)}_i \cap P^{(2)}_i = \phi \end{array} \right\} \tag{4}$$

This implies that the whole population is partitioned exclusively and
exhaustively into potential movers and potential non-movers. A simple
estimating function of $P^{(2)}_i$ is then given by

$$P^{(2)}_{i(t+1)} = a_i P_{i(t)} \tag{5}$$

where a_i are dismobility coefficients measured from cross-sectional data and assumed to be constant throughout the projection period. These dismobility coefficients are functions of some characteristics, x_i, of the zonal populations and household characteristics, that is

$$a_i = f(x_i) \tag{6}$$

Next we turn to estimating the values of a for our predictive model. From the theories of, and empirical work on, intra-urban migration processes, Bell (1968) and Moore (1972) noted four types of life-style aspirations that are capable of motivating movement decisions. These are: *consumption-oriented aspirations,* in which emphasis is placed on enjoying the material benefits of modern urban society — this style is most typical of the affluent single person or the young couple without children, *social prestige-oriented aspirations* in which the prime emphasis is placed on a life-style perceived to be appropriate to one's job and position within the community; *family-oriented aspirations* in which the provision of the right type of environment for the children is stressed — most commonly reflected in the move of the young middle-class family to the surburb, and *community-oriented aspirations,* in which the main stress is placed on the life-style which can only be achieved through interaction with others who have the same set of group-oriented values. To these we can add other motivating forces such as housing costs, accessibility characteristics, and the general condition of dwellings and neighbourhood.

On the other hand, resistance to movement may be due to house or land tenure (residential inertia), family structure, or dwellings specifically designed to accomodate the number of dependants of an individual. The significance of these variables, as factors contributing to resistance to movement, was established in an earlier study by Moore (1971). To these we can add such variables as income — people with low income being generally less mobile than those with high income — education or the lack of it, and old age. A catalogue of all these factors may not be desirable *per se,* but a combination of them may define who is a potential mover or a potential non-mover.

Considering the quality and quantity of available data and the theoretical work on intra-city migration processes discussed above, a potential non-mover can be deemed to posses the following characteristics:

X_1: This denotes that the person is in the middle- or old-age classes. An age greater than 30, or even 35, may be ideal in most cases, although this may be varied to suit local conditions.

X_2 : This denotes that the person is either married and has a family size greater that the mean for the area, or that he is single but has a large number of dependants; that is, greater than the mean for the zone.

X_3 : This denotes that the person does not experience any great congestion in his present residence; that is, his room-occupancy ratio is less than the average for the zone.

X_4 : This denotes that the person has had little or no education (and probably very low aspirations). This is perhaps the most difficult of the characteristics, and it is not easily defined quantitatively. Considering the fact that in many countries most people who have had 10 years of formal schooling are able to improve their education, for instance by in-service training, anybody with less than 10 years of formal school education is said to possess little education.

X_5 : This denotes that the person earns a rather low income, below a stated annual income.

X_6 : This denotes that the person either lives in his own house or pays a monthly rent less than the mean for the zone, or does not pay at all for the space he occupies. This is designed to capture relatives or friends who either do not pay any rent or pay a nominal rent, but are in themselves separate households.

X_7 : This denotes the the person has spent more than a stated number of years at his present residence.

This list does not pretend to be exhaustive; it represents only the most easily measured components of the factors that may prevent intra-city migration of residential households. For example, accessibility could be added, but it may be difficult to define it for every type of intra-city trip — the mean accessible distance. This also applies to other factors such as neighbourhood desirability, weakly measured by X_3, and the factors of race or ethnic relations. However, we can define a non-mover as possessing all the characteristics above, that is

$$P_i^{(2)} = f(X_1, X_2, \ldots X_n)^* \text{ for } n = 7 \tag{7}$$

---

* It is possible to conceptualise the residential migration estimation procedure in terms of entropy maximisation. It involves the development of a probability model that sees migration as an interdependent assignment of people into zones of the city. Constraint equations of the maximisation procedure would relate to

and then proceed to define a_i as

$$a_i = \frac{P_i^{(2)}}{P_i} \tag{6a}$$

(iii) The Dynamic Foundation of the Economic Base Concept

Previous attempts at urban spatial interaction modelling have tried to incorporate in one form or another the various concepts discussed above. However, recent efforts are placing greater emphasis on the introduction of quasi-dynamic or dynamic considerations into the economic base concept (Paelinck, 1970; Batty, 1972; and also Chapter 3). One of the approaches discussed in Chapter 3 would be used in developing the predictive model of this chapter.

It was shown in Chapter 3 that if it were possible to define time periods t over which the repercussions of the inputs of basic employment in an economic system may be traced, the total employment E_t, generated from annual increases E_t^B in basic employment, is given by

$$E_t = E_0 + \sum_{t=1}^{n} \delta_t \, \Delta E_0^B + \sum_{t=1}^{n-1} \delta_t \, \Delta E_1^B + \sum_{t=1}^{n-2} \delta_t \, \Delta E_2^B + \ldots +$$

$$\sum_{t=1}^{2} \delta_t \, \Delta E_{n-2}^B + \sum_{t=1} \delta_t \, E_{n-1}^B \tag{8}$$

where E_0 is the total initial employment and ΔE_t is the change in total employment between two time periods t and $t + 1$, viz.

$$\Delta E_t = E_{t+1} - E_t \tag{9}$$

---

the restraints of urban housing mechanics and the urban spatial structure as well as those arising from the life-style aspirations. The probability model has an equation of the form

$$P_{ij}(x) = \frac{[\exp\{\sum_r \lambda_j^r x\} \exp\{\sum_m \beta_{ij}^m x_{ij}^m \}]}{1 + \sum_j [\exp\{\sum_r \lambda_j^r\} \exp\{\sum_m \beta_{ij}^m x_{ij}^m \}]} \cdot P_{ij}$$

where $p_{ij}(x)$ for $x = 0$ or 1 is the probability that a household changes or does not change residence. There are two types of constraints, namely those operating at the origin or destination (but not both) and those that link origins and destinations. If there are r such constraints for the former and m for the latter, then λ_j^r are Langrangian multipliers associated with the former and β_{ij}^m are those associated with the latter and X_{ij}^m represent these latter set of constraints (Ayeni, 1977).

Further, $\delta_t \Delta E_t$ is the increase in employment generated from an increase in basic employment at time period t.

Equation 9 is obtained from the elementary economic base model (see Chapter 3) by the introduction of simple lags. It is therefore a basic employment stock-generating model which, properly calibrated, can be used to provide a trajectory of an urban system. Moreover, its data requirements are modest and this represents added advantage.

The above considerations represent ways and means by which a predictive model capable of the impact analysis of policy decisions, as well as the monitoring of an urban system, may be developed. To these one might add the issues of disaggregation of the variables to reflect various socio-economic groups of people in a city, noting in particular their distribution, the distribution of employment opportunities, also by wage levels, the different types of houses and service facilities and variations in the prices of purchasing or renting houses and structures for the service activities. A synthesis of these towards producing a predictive model is discussed in the next section.

3. The Predictive Model

The urban stock is as important as the location of urban activities. Consequently the predictive model is made up of two stock-generating and four allocation sub-models. The stock-generating sub-models are the housing generation sub-model represented by equation 1 and its subsequent amplification to include the housing stock left vacant by those who change residences — the potential movers; and the employment generation sub-model represented by equation 8. The four allocation models fall into two classes, stock allocation and activity allocation categories. The stock allocation models are designed to allocate housing and basic employment into the zones of the urban system while the activity allocation models distribute people and employment respectively. These latter are the journey to work—residential location and the journey to services—service centre location models respectively. Their equation systems are discussed further below.

As in the previous chapter the modelling framework is Lowry's, so that we assume that both population and service employment are generated by the exogenous basic employment through our dynamic formulation of the economic base concept. The resulting model and the structure of the relationships between the sub-models and the other components of the urban system are shown in Figure 13.3.1. Note the central role of transportation in the development of the model.

(i) The Basic Employment and the Stock Allocation Sub-Models

Basic employment and the urban stock of houses are exogenously generated by the systems of equations already discussed. Their allocation into the zones of the city follow the same principles and are therefore discussed together. The basic employment-location model is designed to allocate increases in basic employment within zones of the city, and it is defined as

$$\Delta E^{B\,W}_{j(t)} = \Delta E^{B\,W}_{t}\ D^{W}_{j}\ W^{w}_{j}\ \exp\left(-\phi d_{ij}\right) \tag{10}$$

where $\Delta E^{B\,W}_{t}$ is the increase in basic employment, by types (wage levels), between two consecutive time periods $t + 1$ and t. Subscript j denotes zonal distribution. W_j is the benefit derived by entrepreneurs for locating industries, and hence employment opportunities, in a zone of the city. D_j is defined as

$$D_{j} =\left[\sum_i W^{w}_{j} \exp\left(-\phi d_{ij}\right)\right]^{-1} \tag{11}$$

The surrogate for W_j may be taken as the amount and quality of basic employment already in the zone. This interpretation assumes that future locations of basic or exogenous employment will be influenced by the existing pattern of distribution of such activities. In particular, the approach identifies, albeit indirectly, the role of inter-industrial linkages and the economies of scale. Furthermore ϕ is a parameter that controls the distribution of employment facilities as a function of the intra-zonal distance d_{ij}.

The stock-location model uses as input the stock of houses generated, as indicated in the previous section. The model, following Schneider (1967) and Batty (1972), is of the form

$$\Delta H^{K}_{i(t)} = \Delta H^{K}_{t}\ A_{i} W_{i}\ \exp\left(-\theta d_{ij}\right), \tag{12}$$

where

$$A_{i} = \sum_j W_{i} \exp\left(-\theta d_{ij}\right)]^{-1} \tag{13}$$

W_i is the benefit gained by individuals and estate agents for building houses in zone i. It has as its surrogate the number of building plots that are made available in each zone. The major hypothesis in equation

12 is that developers supply houses where there are vacant plots which are accessible to employment and residential areas. Furthermore, such developments occur where similar activities had already taken place. The interpretation of θ is similar to that of ϕ.

The two models described above are simple potential models with the exponential function replacing the normal power function. The functions are the simplest that can be generated in view of the lack of relevant data to test a number of hypotheses on the behaviour of entrepreneurs and estate agents. For example, it might have seemed worth while to make the housing stock-allocation sub-model more explicit by incorporating such variables as land rents and building costs. Also, one might want to differentiate between categories of basic employment in terms of locational association with other industries. These and other embellishments can only be carried out where there is an adequate amount of data of high quality.

(ii) The Residential Location Sub-Model

The residential location model may be developed by further disaggregating the interaction variable T_{ij}^{kw} as T_{ij}^{kwn}, where $n = 1,2$ denotes for potential movers and potential non-movers respectively. The full interpretation of T_{ij}^{kwn}, therefore, is the number of people of income group w, who live in a house type k in zone i, work in zone j, and who are potential movers or non-movers, as the case may be. The following constraints are defined on it:

$$\sum_j \sum_w \Delta \, T_{ij(t)}^{kw1} = a \Delta \, H_{i(t)}^k \tag{14}$$

$$\sum_j \sum_w T_{ij(t+1)}^{kw2} = a H_{i(t)}^k \tag{15}$$

$$\sum_i \sum_k \sum_n T_{ij(t+1)}^{kwn} = E_{j(t+1)}^w \tag{16}$$

$$\sum_{\substack{i \\ i \in Z_1}} \sum_j \sum_k \sum_n T_{ij(t+1)}^{kwn} \, c_{ij(t+1)} \, +$$

$$\sum_{\substack{i \\ i \in Z_2}} \sum_j \sum_k \sum_n T_{ij(t+1)}^{kwn} \, (c_{ij(t+1)} - W_{i(t+1)}) = C_{t+1}^w \tag{17}$$

$$\sum_i \sum_j \sum_k T_{ij(t+1)}^{kw1}$$

$$[p_{i(t+1)}^k - q_{t+1}^w \, (w_{t+1} - c_{ij(t+1)}')]^{\,2} = \sigma_{w(t+1)}^2 \tag{18}$$

where as before

$$\Delta \ T^{kw1}_{ij(t)} = T^{kw1}_{ij(t+1)} - T^{kw1}_{ij(t)} \qquad (19)$$

The constraints expressed by equations 14 and 18 refer to potential movers only, equation 15 refers to potential non-movers only, and those of equations 16 and 17 refer to both classes. For a full development of the model, two sets of zones, Z_1 (constrained) and Z_2 (unconstrained) are maintained for planning purposes. For the constrained set of zones Z_1 the entropy-maximisation models are

$$\Delta T^{kw1}_{ij(t)} = A^{kw1}_{i(t+1)} \ B^{kw1}_{j(t+1)} \ \Delta H^{kw1}_{i(t)} \ \Delta E^{w}_{j(t)}$$

$$\exp\left(-\beta^{w}_{i} \, c_{ij(t+1)}\right) \times \exp\left\langle -\mu^{w}_{i} \, [p^{k}_{i(t+1)} - q^{w}_{t+1}\right.$$

$$\left.(w_{t+1} - c'_{ij(t+1)})]\right\rangle \qquad (20)$$

and

$$T^{kw2}_{ij(t+2)} = A^{kw2}_{i(t+1)} \ B^{kw2}_{j(t+1)} \ H^{kw2}_{i(t)} \ E^{w}_{j(t)}$$

$$\exp\left(-\beta^{w}_{i} \, c_{ij(t+1)}\right) \qquad (21)$$

and for the unconstrained set of zones, Z_2, the entropy-maximisation models are

$$\Delta T^{kw1}_{ij(t)} = B^{kw2}_{j(t+1)} \ \Delta H^{kw2}_{i(t)} \ \Delta E^{w}_{j(t)} \ \exp\left(-\beta^{w}_{i} \, c_{ij(t+1)}\right)$$

$$\exp\left\langle -\mu^{w}_{i} \, [p^{k}_{i(t+1)} - q^{w}_{t+1} \, (w_{t+1} - c'_{ij(t+1)})^2]\right\rangle \qquad (22)$$

and

$$T^{kw2}_{ij(t+1)} = B^{kw2}_{j(t+1)} \ E^{w}_{j(t)} \ H^{kw2}_{i(t)} \ \exp\left(-\beta^{w}_{i} \, c_{ij(t+1)}\right) \qquad (23)$$

where

$$A^{kwn}_{i} = \left[\!\left[\sum_{j} B^{kwn}_{j(t+1)} \ E^{w}_{j(t)} \ \exp\left(-\beta^{w}_{i} \, c_{ij(t+1)}\right)\right.\right.$$

$$\left.\left.\exp\left\langle -\mu^{w}_{i} \, [p^{k}_{i(t+1)} - q^{w}_{t+1} \, (w_{t+1} - c'_{ij(t+1)})]^2\right\rangle\right]\!\right]^{-1} \qquad (24)$$

and

$$B^{kwn}_{j(t+1)} = \left[\!\left[\sum_{i \in Z_1} A^{kwn}_{i(t+1)} \ H^{kwn}_{i(t)} \ \exp\left[-\beta^{w}_{i} \, c_{ij(t+1)}\right)\right.\right.$$

$$\exp \langle -\mu_i^w \; [p_{i(t+1)}^k - q_{t+1}^w \; (w_{t+1} - c_{ij(t+1)}')]^2 \rangle \; +$$

$$\underset{i \in Z_2}{\Sigma} \; H_{i(t)}^{kwn} \; \exp \left(- \beta_i^w \; c_{ij(t+1)} \right)$$

$$\exp \langle -\mu_i^w \; [p_{i(t+1)}^k - q_{t+1}^w \; (w_{t+1} - c_{ij(t+1)}')]^2 \rangle \mathbb{]}^{-1} \quad (25)$$

when the location models are given by equations 21 and 23. If the location models are given by equations 20 and 22, $E_{j(t)}^w$ is replaced by $\Delta E_{j(t)}^w$, and $H_{j(t)}^{kwn}$ is replaced by $\Delta H_{i(t)}^{kwn}$ in equations 24 and 25.

These equations represent a fully developed residential location model which incorporates research on three major fronts: the construction of disaggregated location models (Wilson, 1970); the incorporation of the mechanism of supply and demand into spatial interaction models (see also Wilson, 1970); and the introduction of dynamic considerations into urban systems modelling (Batty, 1972; Wilson, 1970).

(iii) The Service-centre Location Sub-model

We define S_{ij}^{kwn} as the journey-to-service centres interaction variable. The full meaning of S_{ij}^{kwn} is the number of people of income group w locating service facility type k at j but living in i, and who may be movers if $n = 1$ or non-movers if $n = 2$. If we assume that constraints on the zones Z_1 and Z_2 are not necessary (as it is often in practice), and that restraints on minimum size of service centres are not required, then the following constraints may be defined for this sub-model:

$$\underset{j}{\Sigma} \; \underset{k}{\Sigma} \; \underset{w}{\Sigma} \; \Delta S_{ij(t)}^{kw1} = \mu \, \Delta P_{i(t)}^{(1)} \quad (26)$$

$$\underset{j}{\Sigma} \; \underset{k}{\Sigma} \; \underset{w}{\Sigma} \; S_{ij(t+1)}^{kw2} = \mu P_{i(t+1)}^{(2)} \quad (27)$$

$$\underset{i}{\Sigma} \; \underset{j}{\Sigma} \; \underset{k}{\Sigma} \; S_{ij(t+1)}^{kwn} (c_{ij(t+1)} - v_{j(t+1)}) = C_{t+1}'^{wn} \quad (28)$$

$$n = 1 \text{ or } 2$$

$$\underset{i}{\Sigma} \; \underset{j}{\Sigma} \; \underset{k}{\Sigma} \; S_{ij(t+1)}^{kw1} \; [p_{i(t+1)}'^k - q_{t+1}'^w \; (w_{t+1} - c_{ij(t+1)}')]^2 =$$

$$\sigma_{w(t+1)}'^2 \quad (29)$$

Constraint equations 26 and 29 refer to the mover group only, where equation 27 refers to the non-mover group, and equation 28 refers to both groups. Hence for the potential movers the entropy-maximisation models are

$$\Delta S_{ij(t)}^{kw1} = K_{i(t+1)}^{kw1} \, \mu \, \Delta \, P_{i(t)}^{w} \; \Delta S_{j(t)}^{kw} \, \exp\left(-\lambda_i^w \, c_{ij(t+1)}\right)$$

$$\exp\left\langle -\rho_i^w \, [p_{i(t+1)}'^k - q_{t+1}'^w \, (w_{t+1} - c_{ij(t+1)}')]^2 \right\rangle \qquad (30)$$

where

$$K_{i(t+1)}^{kw1} = [\![\sum_j S_{ij(t)}^{kw} \, \exp\left(-\lambda_i^w c_{ij(t+1)}\right)$$

$$\exp\left\langle -\rho_i^w [p_{i(t+1)}'^k - q_{t+1}'^w \, (w_{t+1} - c_{ij(t+1)}')]^2 \right\rangle]\!]^{-1} \qquad (31)$$

and for the non-mover, the entropy maximisation models are:

$$S_{ij(t+1)}^{kw2} = K_{i(t+1)}^{kw2} \, \mu P_{i(t+1)}^{w} \; S_{i(t+1)}^{kw} \, \exp\left(-\lambda_i^w \, c_{ij(t+1)}\right) \quad (32)$$

where

$$K_{i(t+1)}^{w2} = [\sum S_{j(t)}^{kw} \, \exp\left(-\lambda_i^w \, c_{ij(t+1)}\right)]^{-1} \qquad (33)$$

If the interaction variable is summed over the residential zones i, the result is the number of service employments locating in j.

In the development of the service centre location model it has been assumed that the benefit of locating service facilities in any area of a city covaries with the available number, type and quality of service employment already existing in the particular area. This is probably the simplest assumption that can be made. The use of other variables such as floor spaces or volumes of sales, though generally desirable, is often not practicable.

(iv) Calibration and Testing

The calibration and testing of spatial interaction models involve not only the definition of the calibration statistic but also that of the 'goodness-of-fit' (Batty, 1970) and the search routine for the parameters of the system. It has been found that statistics based on patterns of interactions rather than the grouping of activities are generally more sensitive (Wilson, 1971; Batty, 1970; see also Chapter 12). Consequently the mean trip length and the variance of the mean housing expenditure have been most extensively used. The mean trip length or cost is defined as

$$\bar{c}^{wn}_{t+1} = \frac{\sum_i \sum_j \sum_k T^{kwn}_{ij(t+1)} \, c_{ij(t+1)}}{\sum_i \sum_j \sum_k T^{kwn}_{ij(t+1)}} \tag{34}$$

whereas the variance of the mean housing expenditure is

$$\sigma^2_{wn(t+1)} = \frac{\sum_i \sum_j \sum_k T^{kwn}_{ij(t+1)} \, [p^k_{i(t+1)} - q^w_{t+1} \, (w_{t+1} - c'_{ij(t+1)})]^2}{\sum_i \sum_j \sum_k T^{kwn}_{ij(t+1)}} \tag{35}$$

The object of calibration is to find approximate values of the parameters θ, ϕ, β, λ, ρ and μ such that the observed and predicted mean trip costs and housing expenditures do not differ significantly. Various search routines have been developed, which include the gradient-search method, Hyman's (1969) iterative search technique and the more sophisticated Fibonacci search (Spang, 1962) and the search by the golden section (Batty, 1971). On the other hand, 'goodness-of-fit' may involve both parametric and non-parametric (Siegel, 1956). See also the discussion in Chapter 12.

(v) The Solution of the System of Equations

Once the model has been calibrated against actual data the solution system may be discerned from model outputs. Figure 13.3.1. is a flow diagram representation of the comprehensive model, which shows the interactions of some of its components and the method of solution. The central role of transportation is evident from the figure, as it is linked to the location models (in double circles). The solution begins with the basic employment location model which uses as inputs the basic employment generated by the dynamic multiplier. The result of the operation of the basic employment location model is the distribution of basic employment which is used as inputs for the residential location model. The stock-generation model generates the stocks of houses which also form inputs for the residential model. The outputs of the residential model include the work-trip distribution and the distribution of population.

The service model uses as input the outputs of the residential model; it uses directly the distribution of population figures. The amount of service employment required at the various service centres is derived from these figures. Since there are no constraints on the service location

Figure 13.3.1: The Major Components of the Predictive Model

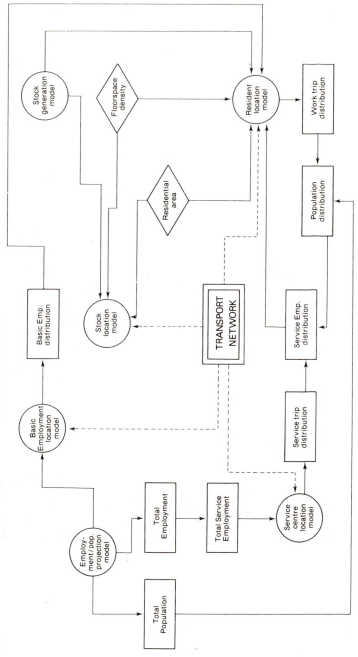

these outputs of service employment are fed back into the residential location model and the whole process is iterated again until the constraints of the systems have been satisfied.

The outputs of the model consist of two sets of information. The first deals with the behaviour of the city's sub-population designated as non-movers, whereas the second represents the behavioural patterns of the mover population. It may be rightly expected that if the model is sensitive enough, it should identify the differences in the behaviour of these two sub-populations.

Finally, it must be noted that the solution system of the model is by iteration, thus implying that for our socio-economic group characterisation, w, $w \times w$ sets of iteration, w for non-movers and w for movers must be made. Each step of iteration in virtually independent of the other; even so, the process of solution is inevitably long. Further developments of the model should concentrate on ways of making the sets of solutions dependent on one another.

An attempt has been made to amalgamate a number of thoughts and ideas that are used in the predictive modelling or urban spatial structure. The resulting model is one that should be sufficiently comprehensive so as to include the bahaviour of various sub-populations and sub-markets of urban region and, consequently, it should be one that would find applications in structural planning. Thus the model can be successfully used to provide some meaningful insights into the studies of the impact of policies as well as being of interest to those who are interested in the exploration of the behaviour of urban systems. These uses will be illustrated in the next section.

4. Empirical Development of the Predictive Model

The predictive model of the last section consists of six major submodels, two of which generate urban stock, another two allocate this stock, while the remaining two are activity allocation sub-models. The stocks are houses and basic employment while the activities are residing and shopping. It is noted that a model of this type requires both spatially and functionally disaggregated data which are easily obtained from government files or through specially commissioned surveys. The spatially disaggregated data are of two types. The first type is cross-sectional and is required for calibration, whereas the second is temporal and is required for exploring the predictive capability of the model. The most important components of the spatially disaggregated data are: the location of people by income groups of employment by type and by wage levels, and of houses and service centres by types. On the other hand, functionally disaggregated data include the rates and ratios which often link one activity with another. Such rates include the population service ratio, which is the ratio of service employment to total population, the basic service ratio, and the proportion of income spent on housing, services and transport. To these one may add the mean transportation costs and the mean housing expenditure variances which are used in the calibration process. A fuller appreciation of these data requirements should therefore emphasise the characteristics of the study. The study area itself is Jos and the study zones are shown and discussed in Figure 5.3.1.

In our attempt to develop this model empirically, it emerges that certain aspects of the system of equations have to be modified or simplified. For example, the stock generating model of equation 1 is rewritten as

$$\Delta H_t = \Delta H^{(1)} + \Delta H^{(3)} \tag{36}$$

where $\Delta H^{(1)}$, the number of new houses being put up annually, is estimated through a simple linear regression model of the form

$$\Delta H_t^{(1)} = 98.2 + 6.9t \tag{37}$$

where the temporal autocorrelation coefficient $\rho(1)$ is 0.88. $\Delta H^{(3)}$, the number of houses being left vacant by the mover, is estimated through

$$\Delta H_t^{(3)} = (1 - a_i) H_t \tag{38}$$

where a_i are the 'dismobility coefficients', and the mean of the coefficients, $\bar{a}$, is 0.68.

The growth of basic employment is studied through an examination of present trends, and it is estimated that in the city, an annual basic employment of 910 jobs is feasible, so that

$$\Delta E_t^b = 910 \tag{39}$$

The generation of total employment and subsequently service employment and total populations is given by equation 8 above.

The urban multiplier, μ, derived from cross-sectional data is 0.69. It is assumed that this is an average over the forecast period, namely,

$$\mu = \frac{1}{n} \sum_{t=1}^{n} \mu_t \tag{40}$$

and it is made up of the product of the inverse activity rate $\alpha = 3.002$ and the population-serving ratio $\beta = 0.229$.

In the disaggregation of the models it was found that houses could only be differentiated, by ownership, into owner-occupied and rented respectively. Population and employment could be differentiated into low, middle, and upper, corresponding to the wage levels of less than 600 Naira, between 600 and 1,600 Naira, and above 1600 Naira.

Very few changes were required in the allocation and activity location sub-models. These changes concern only the service location sub-model, where a disaggregation of service centres by types, and the relationship between transportation costs, the cost of locating at a centre, and proportion of income spent on services, were dropped. The resulting equations are thus

$$S^{kw1}_{ij(t+1)} = K^{w1}_{i(t+1)} \, \mu \Delta P^{w}_{i(t)} \, \Delta S^{w}_{j(t)} \exp\left(-\lambda^{w} \, c_{ij(t+1)}\right) \quad (41)$$

where

$$K^{w1}_{i(t+1)} = \left[\sum_{j} \Delta S^{w}_{j(t)} \exp\left(-\lambda^{w} \, c_{ij(t+1)}\right)\right]^{-1} \quad (42)$$

and

$$S^{w2}_{ij(t+1)} = K^{w2}_{i(t+1)} \, \mu P^{w}_{i(t+1)} \, S^{w}_{j(t)} \exp\left(-\lambda^{w} \, c_{ij(t+1)}\right) \quad (43)$$

where

$$K^{w2}_{i(t+1)} = \left[\sum_{j} S^{w}_{j(t)} \exp\left(-\lambda^{w} \, c_{ij(t+1)}\right)\right]^{-1} \quad (44)$$

(i) The Parameters of the Model

The model described above is an amalgamation of a number of sub-models, each of which requires the estimation of parameters through some calibration processes. The residential location sub-model is the most complex and has a total of six structural parameters for β^{w} and μ^{w}. On the other hand, the service component has only three parameters for λ^{w}; whereas the basic employment and stock allocation models each have one. The parameters of the residential and service location models are derived by calibrating the disaggregated model against actual data by using the mean trip length and the mean housing expenditure variance as the calibrating statistics. In both cases the inverse relationship between the statistics and the parameters confirm their relevance to residential and service centre locational decision process.

Table 13.4.1: The Parameters of the Model

Sub-model	Mean Trip Length (km)		Parameter	Mean Housing expenditure variance (Naira)		Parameter
	Observed	Predicted		Observed	Predicted	
Residential			β^w			
(1)	1.92	1.91	0.36	133.91	133.24	0.86
(2)	2.13	2.04	0.27	469.81	509.16	0.52
(3)	1.87	1.83	0.52	684.01	639.98	0.28
Service			λ^w			
(1)	1.88	—	0.39	—	—	—
(2)	1.61	—	0.54			
(3)	2.38		0.38			
Housing stock	—	—	θ 2.0	—	—	—
Basic employment	—	—	ϕ 2.0	—	—	—

The determination of the parameter values of the stock and basic employment models is less straightforward since the models could be calibrated against actual data. Inasmuch as these parameters govern the distribution of houses and job sites, and not the spatial behaviour of people, it was felt they could be made to reflect planning issues. For example, by running the sub-models against values ranging between 0.5 and 3.0, it was discovered that the higher the value, the more is the emphasis placed by the sub-model on the influence of an existing pattern of stock distribution. The value of 2.0 was assumed for the parameters. Table 13.4.1 shows the details of the calibration.

(ii) Predictions of the Model*-

The major use of the model developed in the preceding sections is to provide some means by which the trajectory of urban spatial and locational behaviour might be traced, in addition to answering questions about the impact of various changes that might take place in a city or regional system. However, in making predictions with the model, it is well to remember that there is not sufficient data with which to test

---

* Only the major features of the predictions are discussed here. For a fuller discussion, see Ayeni (1974), Chapter 11.

its full impact. Therefore the predictions that may be made are conditional, to a large extent, on the various assumptions already stated, but they allow hypotheses to be formulated and tested about the future spatial structure of Jos and the spatial behaviour of its residents. Since the aim of the research is not to draw a master plan for Jos, only two sets of predictions are made to demonstrate the uses to which the model may be put. The first set of predictions answers the following question: if present trends of growth and expansion continue, what will the effects be on the spatial and funtional structure of the city? The second set relates to the question: if growth and development are encouraged at particular zones of the city, what are the effects on the patterns of location and travel behaviour of the residents?

The answers to these two questions will provide what we have categorised as the tracing of the trajectory of urban spatial structure and the evaluation of impacts of various decisions. Since the two questions deal, in the main, with the economic and spatial growth of the city, they may be interpreted as relating directly to the increasing provision of employment opportunities and houses. They therefore focus on the two exogenous variables of the model, namely basic employment and the stock of houses. It may be noted that these are not the only aspects that can be controlled in the model. For example, one may decide to introduce changes through the network structure to examine the spatial response of people. On the other hand, one may progressively increase or decrease the values of the parameters in order to study the system's processes of adjustment over time. Answers to these questions are, however, more relevant in demonstrating the uses of the model.

In the predictions which follow, five-year time periods have been chosen, partly for convenience and partly because this interval of time is very popular with planners. Predictions are therefore made by using 1972 as base, first for 1975 and then 1980. Only two time periods are discussed since it must be recognised that the longer the forecasting period, the less accurate forecasts become.

(iii) Predicting for 1975 and 1980 if Present Trends Continue

In 1975, population would be distributed as shown in Figure 13.4.1. This figure reveals that distant zones such as Anglo Jos (18), Dogon Dutse (3), and Mountain View (16) would have attracted slightly more people than they had in 1972. The concentration of the upper-income group in Digon Dutse (3), Commercial (11), Secretariat (14), and the Reservation (17) would be further strengthened, while their relative shares in the Prison Area (7) and the Stadium Area (8) would increase. The middle-income groups would be found mainly in Langtang-Panyam zone (10), Jenta Extension (1) and Stadium (8). The relative proportions of this group in Mountain View (16) and Sabon Gwong (6) should be seen as introducing a rather drastic change in socio-economic composition of these zones. Sabon Gwong was hitherto a dormitory settlement occupied mainly by the low-income group, whereas Mountain View (16) is supposed to be a southward extension of the Government Reservation Area. The low-income group, as usual, would be found in Jenta Extension (1), Jenta (2), Kwararafa (4), Bauchi Road (5), Sabon Gwong (6), Alkali Street (9), Market Area (12) and Gangare (15). These concentrations are depicted in Figure 13.4.1.

The journey-to-work behaviour of the inhabitants of Jos in 1975 would be such that the different socio-economic groups would show different patterns of movement. For example, the low-income group would interact in a rather complex way that reveals the inefficient patterns of land-use development and spatial interaction in Jos. The volumes of interaction for the major zones are as shown in Figure 13.4.2, which also emphasises the overwhelming importance of the central zones, especially the Secretariat (14), the Commercial (11) and the Market (12) as the major areas of convergence for work trips. The middle-income group (see Figure 13.4.3) also shows a pattern of movement not much different from that of the low-income group, since movement would be towards central zones. The number of people that would be involved in the long-distance trips from the residential zones of Langtang-Panyam (10) and Sabong Gwong (6) to the work zone at Anglo Jos (18) would be relatively small. On the other hand, most of the upper-income group would work in Anglo Jos (18), Secretariat (14) and the Prison Area (7). To attend work, an increasing number of people would travel to such zones as Langtang-Panyam (10), Kwararafa (4), and Dogon Dutse (3), as shown in Figure 13.4.4.

A summary of spatial behaviour is provided by the mean trip length of the journey to work. Table 13.4.2 shows the expected mean trip lengths for 1975. Some of the observations made for 1972 would still be true in 1975. For example, the middle-income group would, on average, still make the longest trips to work, whereas the upper-income group would make the shortest. By 1975, the length of trips for both the low-income and middle-income groups would have increased by as much as 188 and 238 metres respectively over the 1972 figures, implying a corresponding increase in the out-of-pocket expenses for transportation. The effect of this increased cost of movement on family budget and on

Figure 13.4.1: The Distribution of Population in Jos, 1975

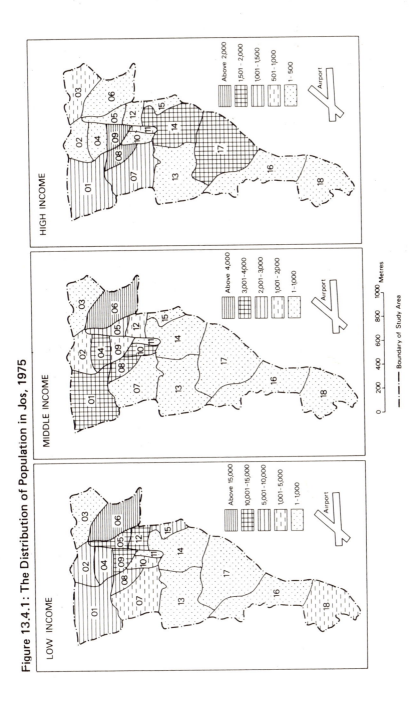

Figure 13.4.2: The Pattern of the Journey to Work,
Low-income Group, Jos, 1975

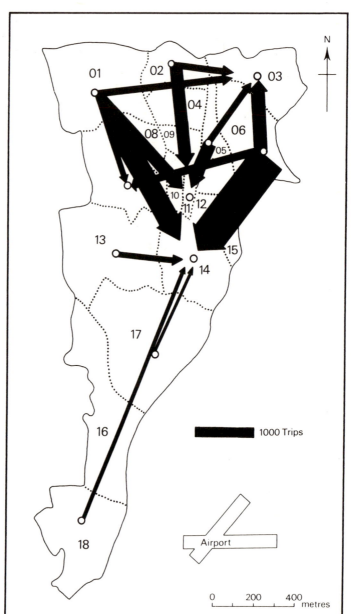

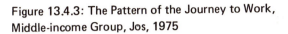

Figure 13.4.3: The Pattern of the Journey to Work,
Middle-income Group, Jos, 1975

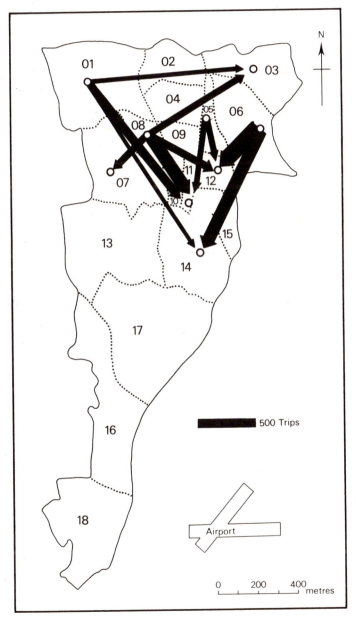

Figure 13.4.4: The Pattern of the Journey to Work, Upper-income Group, Jos, 1975

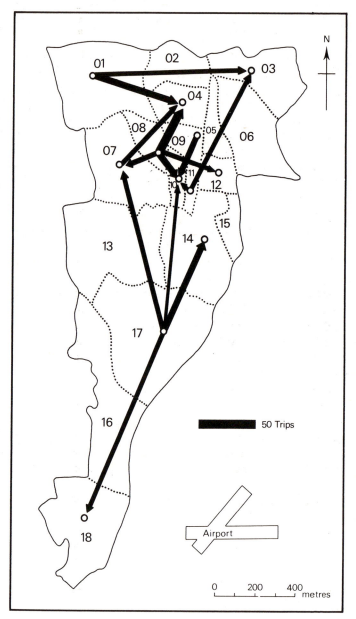

N

50 Trips

Airport

0   200   400
metres

Table 13.4.2: Spatial Behaviour for the Journey to Work:
Mean Trip Lengths (1975 Predictions for Jos)

Income Group	Mean Trip Length of Non-movers (km)	Mean Trip Length of Movers (km)
Low	2.10	1.95
Middle	2.37	2.21
Upper	1.86	1.84

welfare functions for the individual household is one that cannot be ignored in any planning considerations.

The distribution of employment in 1975 in Jos is as shown in Figure 13.4.5. In terms of gross opportunities the Market zone (12) would (as in 1972) be the largest and most important in the city, providing about 20,000 employment opportunities. However, in terms of quality of employment opportunities, Jenta Extension (1), Dogon Dutse (3), Commercial area (11), and the Secretariat (14) would particularly account for jobs that fetch higher wages. The Langtang-Payjam area (10) would provide relatively more middle-wage and high-wage employment, although the Secretariat (14) and Anglo Jos (18) would remain the most important zones for the provision of high-wage employment. On the other hand, the Market area (12) would be the largest (absolutely and relatively) centre for middle-income employment. The reservation Area (17) would remain an insignificant centre of employment, although more of the employment opportunities would be for the middle-income classes.

Associated with the distribution of employment in Jos in 1975 is the question of how the model expects people to behave in their patronage of service centres.

Table 13.4.3 summarises the journey-to-service centre behaviour through the corresponding mean trip lengths. The upper-income group, as in 1972, would make the longest trips to service centres, although

Table 13.4.3: Spatial Behaviour for the Journey to Services:
Mean Trip Lengths (1975 Predictions for Jos)

Income Group	Mean Trip Length of Non-movers (km)	Mean Trip Length of Movers (km)
Low	1.548	1.603
Middle	1.685	1.637
Upper	1.813	1.811

Figure 13.4.5: The Distribution of Employment Opportunities in Jos, 1975

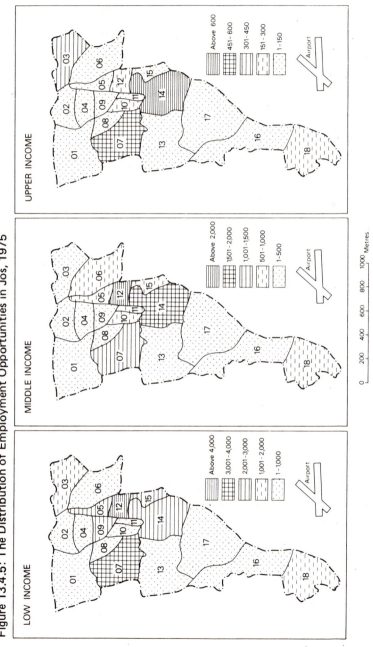

trip lengths would be shorter than in 1972. For example, the decrease may range between some 200 metres for the low-income group to some 500 for the upper-income group (there is not much difference for the middle-income group). A pertinent question, therefore, is why the inhabitants of Jos would make shorter trips to services while the length of their journeys to work increases? A possible answer is that while some people will be forced to travel many kilometres before getting to their workplace, services may be available nearby. In fact, it was in the case of the upper-income group only that something similar to loyalty to a service centre was discerned. For the other groups, in 1972, many goods and services were purchased in local or neighbourhood stores. If this is accepted, it may mean that in 1975 many more neighbourhood stores would have been established and services would be highly dispersed. Since these stores and service centres would not have been a result of any planning legislation they may further contribute to the spatial mix of activities and hence the inefficient pattern of land-use development and spatial interaction. Indeed, this is a possible trend in many unplanned towns.

If the trends noted in 1972 and seen at work in the 1975 predictions should continue until 1980, a number of interesting observations could be made. For this year the distribution of population would be as shown in Figure 13.4.6. This shows that the upper-income group would be distributed in more zones of the city than hitherto.

For instance, many more would live in Jenta Extension (1), Dogon Dutse (3), and the Prison Area (7), in addition to the traditional high-income areas of the Secretariat (14) and the Reservation (17). In addition, significant proportions of this group of people would now live in such areas as the Alkali Street Area (9), which has never been a reserve of the upper-income group. The Alkali Area (9) is more of a 'native area' and it may mean that the area would contain people who, though belonging to the upper-income group, are more local in their outlook. Such a group, usually less educated but rich, would prefer to live in their own houses or among their local people, since the present upper-class reservation areas are occupied more by highly educated 'stranger' elements and expatriates. The middle-income group would be particularly numerous in the Jenta Extension (1), Kwararafa (4), Sabon Gwong (6), Stadium (8), Langtang-Panyam (10) and the Market Area (12). This group will dominate the Langtang-Panyam Street (10) and will form an important minority in the Mountain View zone (16). Mountain View at this time would seem to have developed a mixed character, since it would contain people of all the socioeconomic groups in such a propor-

Figure 13.4.6: The Population Distribution in Jos, 1980

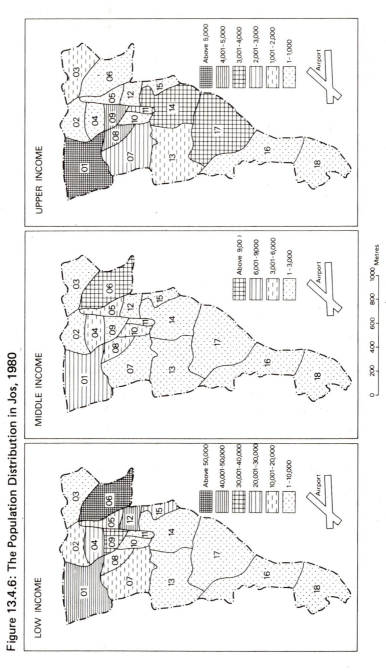

tion that the upper-income and middle-income groups combined would be slightly larger than the low-income group. The rather insignificant concentration of the middle-income group in such zones as Dogon Dutse (3), Prison Area (8), Commercial Area (11), Hill Station (13), and the Reservation (17) should also be noted, as shown in Figure 13.4.6. The major concentrations of the low-income group remain unchanged, as in Jenta Extension (1), Kwararafa (4), Bauchi Road (5), Sabon Gwong (6), Alkali (9), Market (12) and Gangare (15). It would seem, however, that this group increases rather less rapidly in zones where the upper-income group predominates. This should be expected from the budget-term constraint of the residential location model.

The patterns of spatial interaction for the journey to work are shown for the groups with low, middle and upper income in Figures 13.4.7, 13.4.8 and 13.4.9 respectively. In three cases the volumes of interaction would have increased considerably more than in the previous years. This raises an important planning question; how would the transport network accommodate the new volumes of trips generated? As shown in Figure 13.4.7, the low-income group can be seen to have increased interaction with Anglo Jos (18) although the central areas of the Market (12), Commercial (11) and the Secretariat (14) would be the principal destination zones. On the other hand, Figure 13.4.5 shows that the volume of distant trips for the middle-income group would have increased, since many people would travel from Jenta Extension (1) and Sabon Gwong (6) to Anglo Jos (18). As in the case of the low-income group, the central zones of the city, notably the Market (12) and Commercial (11), would still be the most important for the trip attractions. The upper-income group would also increase their volumes of interaction, but very long trips would be virtually absent (see Figure 13.4.9). Furthermore, it seems that the number of destination zones would increase because people would travel from the Reservation Area (17), for example, to Anglo Jos (18), the Secretariat (14), and even the Prison Area (7), or from Jenta Extension (1) to the Prison Area (7), Dogon Dutse (3) and Kwararafa (4).

Again, the spatial behaviour of the journey to work, shown in Figures 13.4.7, 13.4.8 and 13.4.9, are summarised in Table 13.4.4 by the average trip lengths. All mean trip lengths would be higher in 1980 than in the previous years, although the differential increases of the trip length are somewhat small. For example, between 1975 and 1980, the increase is only about 13 metres for the low-income group and 45 metres for the middle-income group. There is not much difference for the upper-income group. That the differential increases are small may

Figure 13.4.7: The Pattern of the Journey to Work,
Low-income Group, Jos, 1980

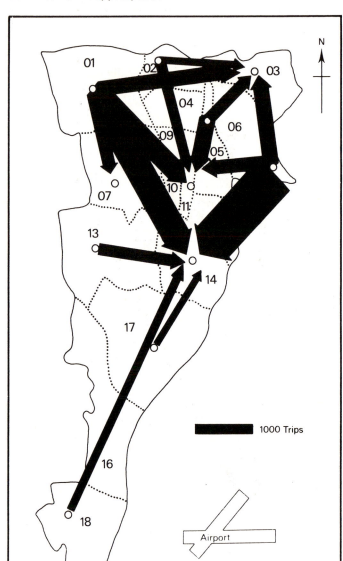

Figure 13.4.8: The Pattern of the Journey to Work, Middle-income Group, Jos, 1980

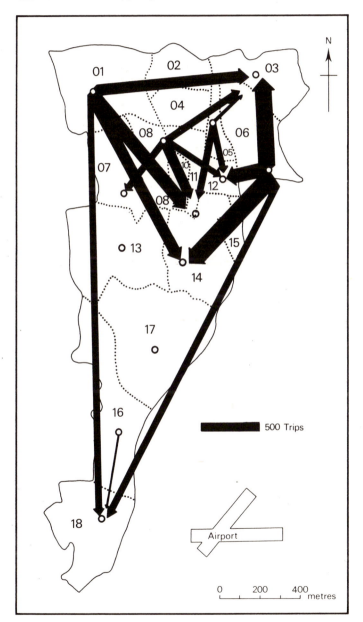

Figure 13.4.9: The Pattern of the Journey to Work, Upper-income Group, Jos, 1980

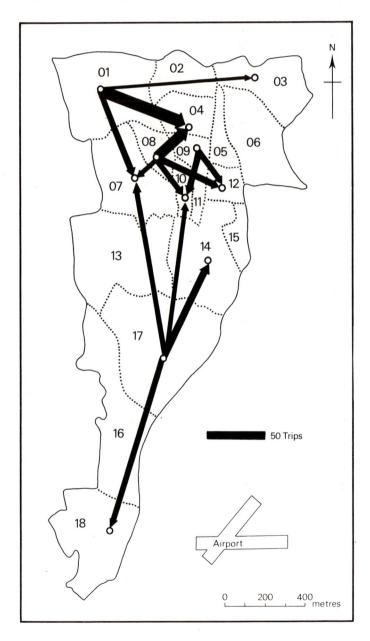

Table 13.4.4: Spatial Behaviour for the Journey to Work:
Mean Trip Lengths (1980 Predictions)

Income Group	Mean Trip Length of Non-movers (km)	Mean Trip Length of Movers (km)
Low	2.12	1.98
Middle	2.42	2.05
Upper	1.85	1.84

be due to the fact that many of the zones of the city, which by 1975 were nearing saturation, would have been fully occupied by 1980 and no new zones would have been created; hence the mean inter-zonal distances would not change. The increasing length of the journey to work should, in any case, be of concern to planners.

The distribution of employment opportunities by wage classes and by location in 1980 is shown in Figures 13.4.10. From the figure, the predominance of the Markey zone (12) as the largest and most important service centre remains undisputed, although other relatively important centres have emerged in the Prison Area (7) and Alkali Street Area (9). It should be noted that the Kwararafa area (4) remains unimportant as a provider of service employment. This observation is disturbing because the city authorities had intended to develop a new market in that zone. One can therefore say that unless very strict planning laws are made to encourage the location of service facilities in this zone, the new market may never take off successfully.

On the other hand the quality of employment, and hence the services offered at service centres, would have further accentuated the 1975 patterns, so that Jenta Extension (1), Dogon Dutse (3), Prison Area (7), Secretariat (14), and the Commercial area (11) would provide high-income service employment. More services that would attract upper-income people would, in particular, be located in the Secretariat (14) and the Reservation (17) rather than elsewhere. Low-income service employment would be as dispersed as in 1975 although the more important centres would be Alkali (9) and Gangare (15), in addition to the Market area (12). Middle-income employment would be found in the Commercial zone (11), the Secretariat (14), Anglo Jos (18), and the Market (12). Elsewhere, such employment would be relatively unimportant;

The spatial behaviour of the journey to services is summarised in Table 13.4.5, which shows the service trip lengths. There are at least two important observations that can be made. The first refers to the

Figure 13.4.10: The Distribution of Employment Opportunities in Jos, 1980

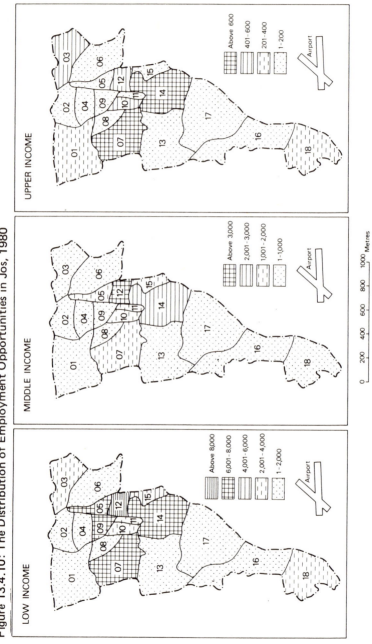

Table 13.4.5: Spatial Behaviour for the Journey to Service Centres:
Mean Trip Lengths (1980 Predictions)

Income Group	Mean Trip Length of Non-movers (km)	Mean Trip Length of Movers (km)
Low	1.69	1.75
Middle	1.79	1.58
Upper	1.96	1.88

trend in service trip lengths from 1975, whereas the second refers to the inter-group variations in trip lengths. With respect to the first observation, the mean trip lengths for 1980 are generally higher than those of 1975; for instance, the increase is about 200 metres for the low-income group, 100 metres for the middle-income group, and 145 metres for the upper-income group. As an increase in trip lengths may be undesirable from a planning point of view, it may thus be inferred that if present trends do continue, the inhabitants would spend more time and money on the journey-to-service centres. In terms of inter-socio-economic group comparisons, the upper-income group still makes the longest trips to service centres, notably the Commercial area (11) and the Secretariat (14). This behaviour has been explained in terms of loyalty to service centres by the upper-income group. Furthermore, as shown for 1972 and 1975, the low-income group makes the shortest trips to service centres and hence incurs the least costs on these trips. In general, service trips are shorter than work trips, as may be expected, since many goods and services can be obtained in almost every zone with minimum effort.

An important aspect of the model predictions is the fact that if the present trends in land use and spatial behaviour of people were to continue, there would be many more people in every zone of the city. This, no doubt, is intuitively obvious; it is the quantitative characteristics of these concentrations and movement patterns that are less obvious. And it is to this type of issue that the model has addressed itself. We feel these quantitative aspects make the model relevant to the decision-making in planning.

(iv) Predicting for 1980 if the Growth of Basic Employment is Localised

It has been noted that in the model developed so far, various growth variables such as employment, housing and route network may be controlled. Since basic employment is structurally tied to the growth of the city, one may examine the consequences that result from monitoring these sets of variables. Information concerning future basic employment opportunities gleaned from government officials suggests that a strong policy decision of the government would be the development of Makeri and Anglo Jos (18) as an industrial district. As a means of developing the district, entrepreneurs are being encouraged, through the provision of many amenities, to locate their factories there. In addition to this zone, the Jenta Extension (1) is scheduled to receive large-scale basic employment within the next few years as a result of the siting there of the permanent campus of the University of Ibadan, Jos Campus. It may therefore be expected that the growth in basic employment between 1972 and 1980 would be mainly in these two zones, namely, Anglo Jos (18) and Jenta Extension (1).

The model enables us to carry out an impact analysis of the effect of concentrating basic employment in certain zones on the rest of the city. The results show that the increase of 7,282 in basic employment between 1972 and 1980 is distributed between the two zones in the ratio of their present strengths. These are further divided into wage levels to give 1,462, 752 and 334 basic employments for the Jenta Extension (1), and 3,120, 1,308 and 259 for Anglo Jos–Makeri (18). All other inputs of the model, namely houses, the transportation network, the population-serving ratios and the activity rates remain unchanged, even though some of these may be controlled if the builder or the planner so desires.

Using the above development strategy, the distribution of population in Jos in 1980 would be shown in Figure 13.4.11. A better appreciation of the predictions emerges if this figure is compared with Figure 13.4.6. It is seen that some zones of the city, notably the Jenta Extension (1), the Secretariat (14) and Anglo Jos (18) would contain fewer people of the low-income group, whereas there would be an increase in the number of people in the upper-income and middle-income groups.

The implication here is that if growth of basic employment is localised in Jos, there may be some shift in the socio-economic composition of some zones in the city. This conclusion is further supported by a similar observation for the Jos Prison Area (7), where the number and proportion of low-income residents would have increased considerably over that given for the situation where growth was not controlled.

Furthermore, there would be more people in the peripheral zones such as the Jenta Extension (1) itself, Mountain View (16), the Reservation (17), and Anglo Jos itself (18). This is to be expected in view of the fact that the zones of economic development are located towards the periphery of the city.

Figure 13.4.11: The Alternative Distribution of Population in Jos, 1980

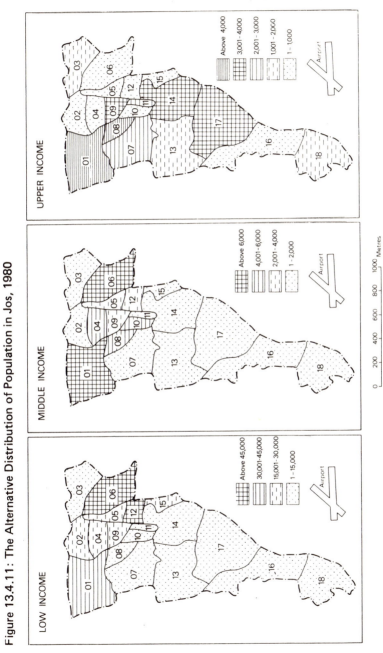

The differences between these two predictions for 1980 may be further explored by comparing the patterns of interaction and their attributes. The patterns of interaction for the low-income group for the situation where growth is localised is shown in Figure 13.4.12. When compared with Figure 13.4.7, it can be seen that, in terms of volumes of interaction, the two zones, Anglo Jos (18) and Jenta Extension (1), have not become important centres of work trips. This is partly due to the overwhelming importance of the Market (12) and Commercial area (11) as major destination zones for work trips. However, the volumes of interaction differ slightly (see Figures 13.4.7 and 13.4.12). For the middle-income group the importance of Anglo Jos (18) as a major work zone is obvious, as can be seen from Figures 13.4.8 and 13.4.13, but the volume of interaction with Anglo Jos would be greater in the case where growth is localised than where it is not. Jenta Extension (1) is not yet an important trip destination zone for this income group. For the upper-income group the interaction pattern is shown in Figure 13.4.14. When compared with Figure 13.4.9, which shows the corresponding situation where present trends are left to continue, one can observe that Anglo Jos has become important as a location centre for high-income employment opportunities alongside the traditionally important zone. The slightly insignificant nature of the Jenta Extension zone, in spite of a concentration of employment opportunities, is due, in part, to the fact that it had hitherto not been an important work centre, but rather a residential area. On the other hand its peripheral location, north-east of the city, might have been responsible for its lack of power in attracting trips in large quantities from many zones of the city.

The comparison of maps of interactions is generally difficult, although it is often easier to compare attributes of interactions. Such attributes include the mean zonal travel distances, the overall mean trip lengths for different socio-economic groups, and the volumes of trips by distance bands. The first two have been chosen in this study.

The zonal mean trip lengths for the two sets of predictions for 1980 are shown in Table 13.4.6 for three income groups. From the table, it can be seen that zonal mean trip lengths predicted for the situation when growth is localised are constantly longer than those when present trends are assumed to continue. In terms of the overall trip lengths for the socio-economic groups, the mean trip lengths for the case where growth is localised are shown in Table 13.4.7, which may be compared with Table 13.4.4. Again, these trip lengths are higher than in the alternative strategy when growth is left uncontrolled. The difference is

Figure 13.4.12: The Patterns of the Journey to Work,
Low-income Group, 1980, Alternative Predictions

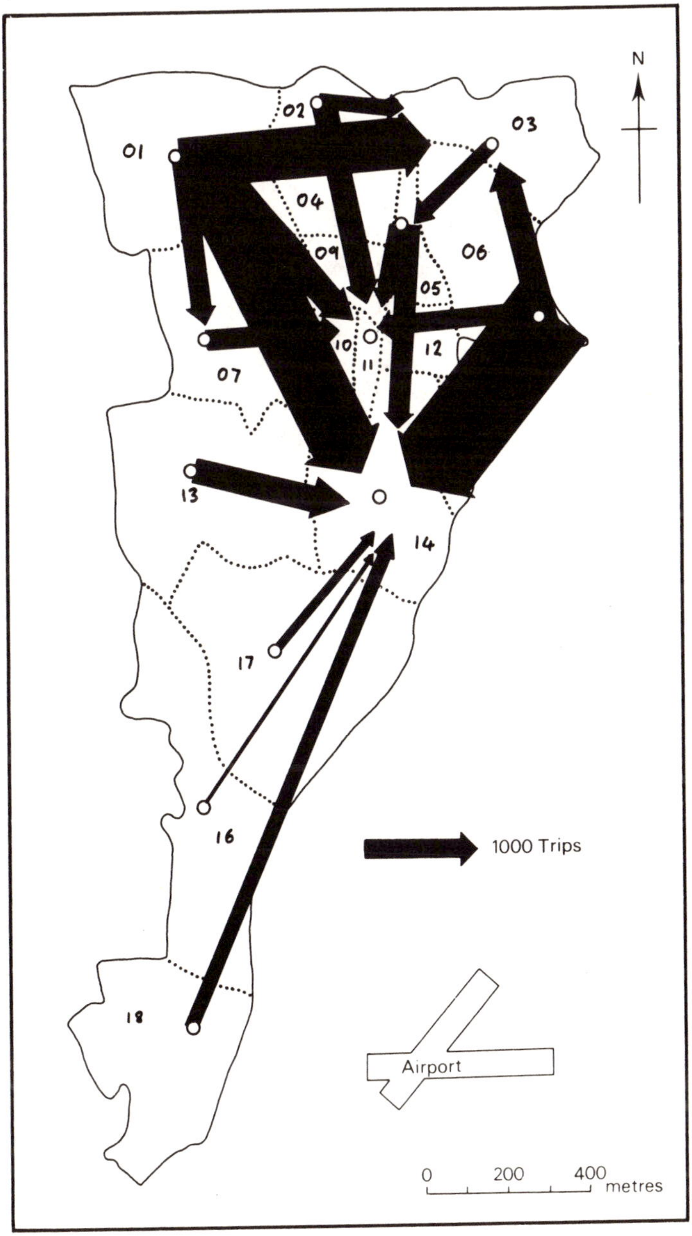

Figure 13.4.13: The Patterns of the Journey to Work, Middle-income Group, 1980, Alternative Predictions

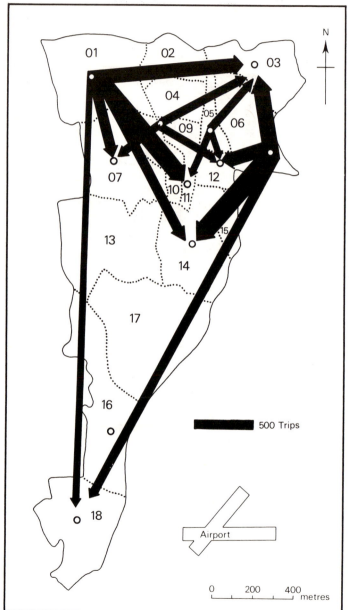

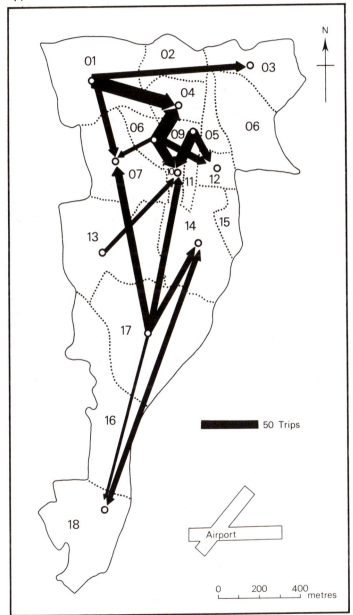

Figure 13.4.14: The Patterns of the Journey to Work, Upper-income Group, 1980, Alternative Predictions

Table 13.4.6: Zonal Mean Trip Lengths (km) for 1980

Zone	Name	Mean Trip Length*					
		Low Income I	Income II	Middle I	Income II	Upper I	Income II
1	Jenta Extension	2.77	2.96	2.78	2.91	2.01	1.80
2	Jenta	2.68	2.88	2.79	2.89	2.11	2.00
3	Dogon Dutse	2.78	2.73	2.79	3.22	2.22	2.25
4	Kwararafa	2.21	2.40	2.24	2.60	1.36	1.15
5	Bauchi Road	1.97	2.20	1.87	2.28	1.09	1.07
6	Sabon Gwong	2.31	2.53	2.11	2.57	1.54	1.55
7	Prison	1.51	1.61	1.67	2.08	1.43	1.53
8	Stadium	2.00	2.21	1.98	2.30	1.64	1.59
9	Alkali	1.65	1.81	1.70	2.09	1.30	1.33
10	Langtang-Panyam	1.13	1.28	1.32	1.72	1.00	1.07
11	Commercial	0.96	1.10	1.16	1.58	1.03	1.11
12	Market	1.40	1.59	1.40	1.84	0.94	1.02
13	Hill Station	1.47	1.40	1.98	2.28	1.95	2.06
14	Secretariat	2.69	2.93	2.33	2.20	2.17	2.15
15	Gangare	0.75	0.92	0.81	1.53	0.49	0.74
16	Mountain View	3.76	3.43	3.70	3.12	3.95	3.60
17	Reservation	2.71	2.54	2.98	2.98	3.10	3.16
18	Anglo Jos	4.93	3.85	3.43	1.50	3.00	1.16

* For each income group, the figures in the first column are expected if present trends continue; those in the second column denote that growth is localised.

of the order of 50 metres for the low-income group but much less for the others. Considering the fact that long trip lengths invariably mean higher transportation costs and more inconvenience to trip-makers, the planning issue raised by the 1980 predictions is the desirability of localising basic employment in Jos. It should be noted that such policy decisions as the localisation of growth should be tied to some set of objectives. It is really within such a framework that the two sets of predictions could be compared and contrasted for formulating plans.

An important observation from costs (Tables 13.4.4 and 13.4.7) is the fact that the trip lengths for persons in the middle-income and low-income groups are consistently longer than those of the higher-income group. Considering the fact that these two groups form over 94 per cent of the city population, it becomes an issue of policy whether this state of affairs is desirable. Unfortunately, policy considerations in planning *per se* lie mostly outside the scope of the present study. Nevertheless one could suggest that such a situation needs to be modified or reversed, but in such a way that the effects of such actions are adequately examined within a planning framework as described by Wilson (1969).

If growth of basic employment were localised in Anglo Jos (18) and

Figure 13.4.15: The Alternative Distributions of Population in Jos, 1980

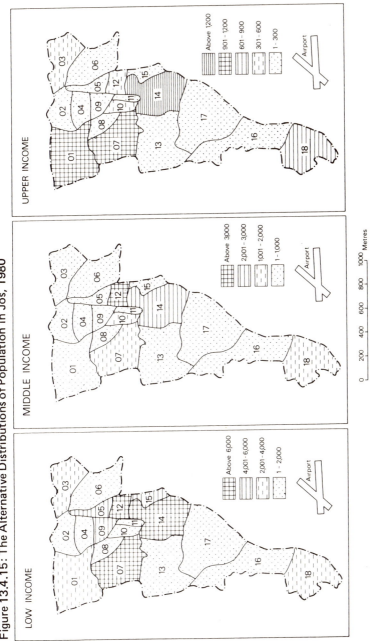

Table 13.4.7: Spatial Behaviour for the Journey to Work:
Mean Trip Lengths for 1980, Localised Growth

Income Group	Mean Trip Length of Non-movers (km)	Mean Trip Length of Movers (km)
Low	2.17	2.06
Middle	2.45	2.42
Upper	1.85	1.78

Jenta Extension (1), the distribution of employment in 1980 would be as shown in Figure 13.4.15. From these, certain observations may be made. First, there would be more employment opportunities in Jenta Extension (1), Anglo Jos (18), and also in zones immediately adjoining them. While the large employment opportunities in the two zones may be due to the localisation of new basic employment, the increases in the adjoining zones would seem to reflect the nature of the predictions of the model. Concomitant with this observation is the fact that the central zones, notably the Market (12), Commercial (11) and Bauchi Road (5) would correspondingly lose a number of employment opportunities. In Market zone (12) this would be of the order of some 4,000 while in the Bauchi Road area (5) it would be about 2,000. It may therefore be expected that the development of peripheral zones of Jos as centres of growth in basic employment may lead to a thinning out of the number of service facilities at the centre of the city.

Just as the distribution of employment changes so also does the quality. For example, the Jenta Extension zone (1) would have more low-wage and high-wage employment, at the risk of losing some middle-wage employment, whereas the Market zone (12) loses more low-wage employment to increase its share of middle-wage employment. The Secretariat (14), on the other hand, would contain more service facilities that would provide employment for the middle-income and higher-income groups at the expense of losing some low-income employment. The Reservation Area (17), though never a large employer of labour, would be able to provide more service employment that is fairly distributed between low-income and high-income groups.

The mean trip lengths for the three socio-economic groups are shown in Table 13.4.8, for the situation where growth of basic employment is localised. If the table is compared with Table 13.4.5, where predictions were made on the basis of 1972 trends continuing into 1980, one sees that there is no appreciable difference between the two sets of predictions, although the trip lengths in Table 13.4.8 are slightly higher. However,

Table 13.4.8: Spatial Behaviour for the Journey to Service Centres:
Mean Trip Lengths for 1980, Localised Growth

Income Group	Mean Trip Lengths of Non-movers (km)	Mean Trip Lengths of Movers (km)
Low	1.59	1.68
Middle	1.78	1.69
Upper	1.82	1.90

as in 1972 and in the other predictions, the mean trip length of the journey-to-service centres by the upper-income group would still be highest, whereas that of the low-income group would be lowest. This may be interpreted to mean that the localisation of basic employment would only slightly change the behaviour of the socio-economic classes as far as the service mean trip lengths are concerned. Patterns of interaction do differm but these are not examined as it is felt that the capabilities of the model have been adequately demonstrated both by the two sets of predictions and by the more detailed analyses of the journey-to-work patterns which, in any case, have been deemed as the major determinant of urban spatial structure.

5. Conclusion

At this juncture, it is appropriate to examine two major themes that arose from the predictions of the model: namely, the empirical verification of certain aspects of the theory behind the construction of the model and the use to which these predictions can be put in terms of urban or regional planning. On the former, a major point concerns the categorisation of the city's population into mover and non-mover classes. It will be recalled that this categorisation results from the realisation that residential location cannot be studied without residential mobility. There is no doubt that those who change residences are those who are aware of various opportunities of maximising accessibility to urban facilities and welfare services. On account of this, such people would be expected to adjust their locational and spatial behaviour in such a way that their transportation costs to workplaces and service centres are minimised. This is exactly the situation in Jos. For example, for the journey to work, the potential movers' mean trip length is clearly shown in Tables 13.4.2, 13.4.4, and 13.4.7. In Table 13.4.2, which shows the predictions for 1975, the movers' mean trip length is on average lower by 150 metres, 160 metres and 20 metres for the low-income, middle-income and upper-income groups respectively, whereas for the first set of predictions for 1980 these differentials are 150, 370 and 10 metres respectively for these same income groups. For the situation where growth is localised, the differentials are 170, 30 and 80 metres. This no doubt lends further strength and justification to out conceptualisation of locational and spatial behaviour.

On the second theme, namely the use or relevance of these predictions, it should be remembered that only a few of the many planning and policy questions which can be posed have in fact been indicated. As mentioned earlier, these questions, as well as the predictions and outputs, relate to the analysis stage of the planning process. Answers to many more questions can be derived from the model and can be evaluated and costed within the set of objectives and goals of a planning authority. Consequently, neither the sets of predictions in this section not the maps may be taken as constituting plans or master plans for Jos. They are only a few of the many 'scenarios' of the future which the model can provide as basis for structural planning at either the urban or the regional scale. The introduction of this type of model-building operation is bound to result in a productive revolution in urban and regional planning.

References

Ayeni, M.A.O. 1974. Predictive Modelling of Urban Spatial Structure: The Example of Jos, Benue Plateau State, Nigeria. Ph.D. thesis, University of Ibadan, Nigeria

Ayeni, M.A.O. 1977. Intra-urban Residential Migration: An Entropy Maximizing Approach. Department of Geography, University of Ibadan, Nigeria, mimeo.

Barrass, R., Broadbent T., Cordey-Hayes, M., Massey, D.B., Robinson, K. and Willis, J. 1971. An Operational Urban Development Model of Cheshire. *Environment and Planning, 3*, 115–234

Batty, N. 1970. An Activity Allocation Model for the Nottinghamshire–Derbyshire Subregion. *Regional Studies, 4*, 307–32

Batty, M. 1971. Exploratory Calibration of a Retail Locational Model Using Search by Golden Section. *Environment and Planning, 3*, 411–32

Batty, M. 1972. Dynamic Simulation of an Urban System. In A.G. Wilson (ed.), *London Papers in Regional Science, 3. Patterns and Processes in Urban and Regional Systems.* London: Pion

Bell, W. 1968. Social Change, Life Styles and Suburban Residence. In W.M. Dobriner (ed.), *The Suburban Community.* New York: Putnam

Crecine, J.P. 1968. *A Dynamic Model of Urban Structure.* Rand Corporation, Santa Monica, California: RAND Corporation, P3803

Cripps, E.L., and Foot, D.H.S. 1971. A Land Use Model for Subregional Planning. *Regional Studies, 3*, 243–68

Czamanski, S. 1965. A Method of Forecasting Urban Growth by Distributed Lag Analysis. *Journal of Regional Science, 4*, 15–20

Echenique, M. Crowther, D., and Lindsay, W. 1971. The Development of a Model of a Town. In A.G. Wilson (ed.), *London Papers in Regional Science, 2. Urban and Regional Planning.* London: Pion

Garin, R.A. 1969. A Matrix Formulation of the Lowry Model. *Journal of the American Institute of Planners, 32,* 361–4

Goldner, W. 1968. *Projective Land Use Model (PLUM)*, Berkeley, California: Bay Area Transportation Study, Technical Report 219

Hill, D.M. 1965. A Growth Allocation Model for the Boston Region. *Journal of the American Institute of Planners, 31,* 2, 111–20

Hyman, G.M. 1969. The Calibration of Trip Distribution Models. *Environment and Planning, 1,* 105–12

Lee, D.D., Jr. 1969. *Models and Techniques for Urban Planning.* Ithaca, New York: Cornell Aeronautical Laboratory, Inc.

Lowry, I.S. 1964. *A Model of Metropolis.* Santa Monica, California: RAND Corporation

Moore, E.G. 1971. Comments on the use of Ecological Models in the Study of Residential Mobility in the City. *Economic Geography, 47,* 1, 73–85

Moore, E.G. 1972. Residential Mobility in the City. *Resource Paper 133.* Washington, D.C.: Association of American Geographers

Paelinck, J. 1970. Dynamic Urban Growth Models. *Papers Regional Science Association, 24,* 25–38

Schneider, M. 1967. Access and Land Development. In G.C. Hemmens (ed.), *Urban Development Models*, Report Number 97. Washington D.C.: Highway Research Board

Seigel, S. 1956. *Non-parametric Statistics for the Behavioural Sciences* New York: McGraw-Hill

Spang, H.A. 1962. A Review of Minimization Techniques for Nonlinear Functions. *SIAM Review, 4,* 343–65

Strotz, R.H. 1957. The Implications of a Utility Tree. *Econometrica, 25,* 269–318

Strotz, R.H. 1959. The Utility Tree: A Correction and Further Appraisal. *Econometrica, 27,* 482–8

Warneryd, O. 1968. *Interdependence in Urban Systems.* Meddelanden Fran Goteburgs Universitets Geografiska Institutioner, Series B, No. 1

Wilson, A.G. 1968. Models in Urban Planning: A Synoptic Review of Recent Literature. *Urban Studies, 3,* 2, 249–76

Wilson, A.G. 1969 Forecasting Planning. *Urban Studies, 6,* 347–67

Wilson, A.G. 1970. *Entropy in Urban and Regional Modelling.* London: Pion

Wilson, A.G. 1971. Some Recent Developments in Microeconomic Approach to Modelling Household Behaviour With Special Reference to Spatio-temporal Organization. WP-3, Department of Geography, University of Leeds, Leeds, England

13 CONCLUSION

1. Introduction

> Throughout history, men have employed elaborate rituals to help them reach a decision. They have poured libations, sacrificed animals, read the stars and watched the flight of birds. They have put faith in proverbs and rules of thumb devised to take some of the guesswork out of living (Himmelblau, 1972, p. 3).

Urban studies have not been left out. Rather, it has over the years continuously perfected its rules of thumb through an embrace and greater utilisation of methods of scientific enquiry in order to understand human spatial organisation and human spatial behaviour. During this process, the field has responded to what Harvey (1973) described as 'outside pressures to discover the means for manipulation and control' of human activities and other social phenomena within an urban system.

The book therefore has shown some of the various approaches to understanding this very important phenomenon, the city: neither by sacrificing animals nor putting faith in the flight of birds but through a theoretical and methodological framework bequeathed to us by the quantitative revolution. To this end, statistical and mathematical models, whose use has been facilitated by developments in computer hardware and software systems have provided the tools of analysis. It is realised that statistical and mathematical models *per se* are nothing more than representations and simplifications of a phenomenon of interest. Consequently they cannot be substitutes for theory, although they aid understanding and theory formulation. They could also identify gaps which exist in our thinking. In the same vein, they need not be technocratic if they are based on widely tested and used concepts that constitute their theoretical base. They are therefore crucial in discerning urban spatial structure as they constitute a prelude to the study of the dynamics of urban systems.

Although the book concentrates on the search for, and the illustration of, appropriate concepts, methods and techniques for investigating the complexities of an urban system, it in no way sees these techniques as an end but rather as a means to an end. The rapid rates at which cities grow, coupled with attendant socio-economic and spatial problems, constitute some of the 'pressures from outside' which force urban analysis to relate the spatial organisation of societies. Indeed, these outside pressures are causing the social sciences as a whole to examine their role within a policy-making and executing framework (Lerner and Lasswell, 1959). In order to be meaningful to the society, urban analysis must see itself within the framework of a policy science. It must be concerned with decision-making and the development of criteria that are evaluative of societal problems and strategies for the solution of these problems, as well as the development of criteria that are evaluative of the strategies and objectives of urban development. Urban analysis would play these roles within a suitable planning framework.

2. Concepts, Models, Techniques and the Planning Process

Planning is a process of human thought and action about the future. It consists of a set of activities and interventions in processes carried out to achieve a set of goals for a society. By emphasising interventions in processes, such a definition involves a procedure that heightens the understanding of the set of problems which require examination as well as producing a set of possible alternative solutions, the relative merits of which are judged by the needs, goals and objectives of the society. Consequently, planning within any society cannot be divorced from the role of values and the societal system. In this latter sense, the issue of distribution of income, for instance, may be resolved in a number of ways ranging from enlightened capitalism through welfare socialism to Marxist socialism. While each of these would involve different forms of manipulation and control of the system, it is clear that an understanding of how particular systems work is crucial. None the less, while these forms of manipulation describe some elements of human action involved in the planning process, it is possible to provide a general framework for conceptualising or thinking about the future. This latter aspect is fundamental and hence will be discussed further.

Berry (1973) provides a rather broad but very useful four-fold categorisation of the ways urban planners conceptualise the future. These he called reactive of ameliorative problem-solving; allocative trend-modifying; exploitive opportunity-seeking and development leadership; and normative goal orientation. The first style involves the natural tendency to do nothing until there are problems, or undesirable trends are seen to exist in such a magnitude as to require correction. For instance, with this mode of planning more roads and overhead bridges are unnecessary until traffic jam becomes unbearable and the urban system becomes grossly inefficient. This process of planning therefore involves continuous reacting to processes that have already worked themselves out. Consequently it is past-oriented.

The allocative trend-modifying approach is a slight improvement on the first. In fact, it is the future-oriented version of the reactive problem-solving mode (Berry, 1973). It involves the projection of present trends to the future and the forecast of likely problems. The planning procedure involves devising regulatory mechanisms to modify the trends in ways that preserve existing values into the future while avoiding predicted future problems. Most metropolitan areas that develop by the conventional master-plan technique, which is a static representation of a dynamic situation, utilise this approach. An important criticism of the allocative trend-modifying approach is its lack of mechanism for identifying and focusing on specific problems of the present as well as a mechanism for evolving a city of the future that is compatible with societal goals and welfare (Table 14.2.1).

The exploitive opportunity-seeking and de/elopmental leadership approach is one whereby analysis is performed not to identify future problems but to seek out new growth opportunities for investment. This is the approach of the real estate developer, the industrialist or the corporate planner. In its extremity it does not consider problems that may arise as a result of actions or investments but concentrates on those opportunities that are most feasible and less risky. It is indeed a form of planning without specific aims and goals for the welfare of a society as a whole but rather for the investors (see Table 14.2.1).

The fourth planning style involves explicit normative goal orientation. For instance, goals must be set based on images of the desired future. Then policies are designed and plans are made to guide the system towards the goals or change the existing system if it cannot achieve the goals. The distinguishing characteristic of this style of planning is the way it views the future. Consequently, its long-term results differ considerably from those of the other approaches, even though short-term results may be similar (see Table 14.2.1). Furthermore, it could be more demanding in time and costs since its successful adoption would involve not only a deep understanding of the system being planned, how to monitor and control it, but also an appreciation of the range of problems that need be solved. None the less the benefits are as rewarding as the style is challenging.

It is obvious from the above considerations that planning in general and urban planning in particular should be essentially future-oriented, and should be of the normative goal orientation variety. In particular, it must be seen as neither an accidental nor a random set of activities

Table 14.2.1: Modes of Planning

	Planning for Present Concerns	Planning for the Future		
	Reacting to Past Problems	Responding to Predicted Futures	Exploitive Opportunity-seeking	Creating Desired Future
	Ameliorative Problem-solving	Allocative Trend-modifying		Normative Goal-orientated
Planning	Planning for the present	Planning towards the future	Planning with the future	Planning from the future
Technique	Analyse problems, design intervention, allocate resources accordingly	Determine and make the *best* of trends and allocate resources in accordance with desires to promote or alter them	Determine and make the *most* of trends and allocate resources so as to take advantage of what is to come	Decide on the *future desired* and allocate resources so that trends are changed or created accordingly; desired future may be based on present, predicted, or new values
Short-term Results	Ameliorate present problems	A sense of hope New allocations shift activities	A sense of triumphing over fate New allocations shift activities	A sense of creating destiny New allocations shift activities
Long-term Results	Haphazardly modifying the future by reducing the future burden and sequelae of present problems	Gently balance and modify the future by avoiding predicted problems and achieving a 'balanced' progress to avoid creating major bottle-necks and new problems	Unbalance and modify the future by taking advantage of predicted happenings, avoiding some problems and cashing in on others without major concern for emergence of new problems	Extensively modify the future by aiming for what could be; 'change the predictions' by changing values or goals, outcomes to desires, avoid or change problems to ones easier to handle or tolerate

Source: B.J.L. Berry (1973), p. 174, Table 8.

but rather as a set of activities which should be continuous, 'having no definitive beginning and no definitive end'. In addition, it should enable us to proceed towards new solutions as new problems arise.

There are various formulations of such a planning process (Boyce *et al.*, 1970; Lichfield *et al.*, 1975; Harris, 1965). There is, however, a consensus that these should include the following steps:

(i) the formulation of objectives in relation to the general goals, problems and the regional context;

(ii) the provision of an outline of alternative strategies of growth;

(iii) the testing and evaluation of alternative strategies;

(iv) decision-making.

An underlying theme of this approach is that the deliberate control of a metropolitan system must be based on a point of view whereby there is a continuous interaction between one level and the other of these steps in a cyclic way (see Figure 14.2.1). The formulation of goals and objectives is crucial, as other aspects of the planning process depend on what these are. Goals could be formulated in slightly vague ways but it is the duty of the planner to translate them into well-designed and operational sets of objectives. For instance, prevention of traffic congestion is a goal, while a corresponding objective may be a reduction of the travelling time for the journey to work by half, for example.

Possible courses or strategies of growth arise as a result of preferences and tastes of people and also as a result of variations that exist in the various factors of the production process. An enumeration of these courses is facilitated through controls that can be exercised on some 'policy variables'. In a metropolitan area, for instance, such variables may include employment, houses and even the transportation networks. These are the same variables that were used extensively in many of the models described in this book.

Evaluation occurs throughout the planning process in an implicit way as well as explicitly in a formal way. Explicitly it involves the description, testing and analysis of individual plans as well as a comparison of alternative plans. The first may be achieved through some techniques of model-building, while the latter will involve a development of an evaluative criteria (Lichfield *et al.*, 1975) on selecting which plans meet the interests of the people. Inasmuch as the analysis stage of the planning framework generates, from a set of alternative strategies (see Figure 14.2.1), the plans that are subsequently evaluated, one can see that it is the prop of the planning process. In practice it should involve

Figure 14.2.1: A Cyclic View of the Planning Process

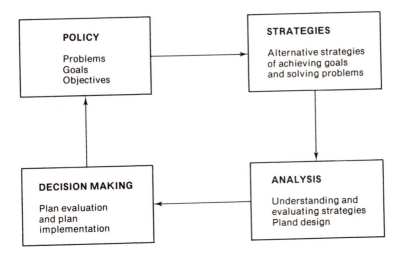

a sound understanding of the mechanisms of the urban growth process, their interactions and interrelationships; and it should be capable of predicting the impacts of the different strategies of solving the problems (i.e. the possible courses of action) to the fullest account.

An important attribute of the planning process described in Figure 14.2.1 is the way each level is linked to the other. This ensures that the planning process is constantly being exposed to new information that may arise either from change in policies or strategies of urban growth in response to changing concepts of the future. Because of this lack of a definitive beginning and a definitive end, this style of planning is flexible, and in this way differs from the old concept of master plans which are essentially maps of land allocation that neither explore the symbiotic relationship between urban land use and transportation development, nor leave room for an exploration of the socio-economic consequences of the plans. The new approach has been described in British planning context as structure planning. A structure plan is

a written statement of broad strategy, with the effects of the strategy discussed in relation to alternatives. Structure plans are to be concerned with long range policies (20–30 years) and therefore detailed allocation and site definition cannot be made in map form although diagrams may be a useful supplement to the written text (Massey and Cordey-Hayes, 1971).

Structure itself is used to mean the social, economic and physical systems of an area in so far as they are subject to planning control or influence. It thus includes such things as the distribution of population, activities and the relationships between them, the pattern of land uses and the development of activities that give rise to them; together with the network of communications and the system of utility services (Massey and Cordey-Hayes, 1971).

Critical aspects of our categorisation of the planning task therefore (Figure 14.2.1) are the analysis and decision-making stages and it is at these stages that many of the techniques, concepts and models discussed in this book could be useful and evaluative of societal needs, goals and objectives. All these become necessary not only if the planner wants to intervene in processes but also if he wants to move away from the concept of producing final answers to such a thing as urbanisation, urbanism or even the complexities of an urban system; but rather to find spatial forms which will achieve goals and objectives in the best way. While a discussion of how to use these techniques, concepts and models within the analysis stage of the planning task does not lie within the ambit of this book, it needs to be mentioned that their utilisation has been one of the important consequences of the quantitative revolution in planning.

It is obvious from our view of planning that a quantitative assessment of the role of the various compenents of the city is as crucial as the evaluation of plans and alternative strategies of urban development. Concepts, models and techniques provide systematic statements of relationships between the different elements of the urban structure. The analytic framework within which these are evaluated provides better understanding and increasing rigour in the thinking process. Although techniques and models *per se* are not likely to become the end-all of the planning process, they will remain very useful as tools for the identification, articulation and solution of some of the spatial problems of the city.

None the less, it is wise at this stage of our knowledge to treat many of these concepts, models and techniques as explorative methods whose theoretical bases would need to be expanded and restructured in the

continuing understanding process. In this context, one cannot but agree
with Ira S. Lowry that

> Above all, the process of model-building [or urban analysis] is
> educational. The participants invariably find their perceptions
> sharpened, their horizons expanded, their professional skills aug-
> mented. The mere necessity of framing questions carefully does
> much to dispel the fog of sloppy thinking that surrounds our efforts
> at civic betterment (Lowry, 1965; words in brackets are my inter-
> pretation).

Urban analysis can therefore be seen as not only playing increasingly
important role in planning, but also in improving general understanding
of urban systems. The years ahead should be more eventful. Our
theoretical understanding of city systems should be greatly improved
through a modification and improvement of present techniques and the
generation of new ones. Furthermore, urban planning systems should
evolve in such a way that planning is seen as a means of creating a desired
future rather than of projecting present trends. Urban analysis would
emerge with tools and techniques that are neither mechanistic nor
technocratic in their application to solving urban problems.

3. Prospects and Perspectives of Urban Analysis

In a field as dynamic as urban studies, it may be presumptuous to talk
about the future. None the less, the present rates of world urbanisation,
especially the rather unprecedented rates of urbanisation in the developing countries of the world, compel us to make some prognostication for
urban analysis.

Reviewing the growth of cities in this century, Lefebvre describes
the twentieth century as the age of the urban revolution (Lefebvre,
1970, pp. 13, 25). According to him, this urban revolution represents

> the total ensemble of transformations which run through contem-
> porary society and which serve to bring about the change from a
> period in which questions of economic growth and industrialisation
> predominate to the period in which the urban problematic becomes
> decisive, when research into the solutions and forms appropriate
> to urban society takes precedence (quoted from Harvey, 1973,
> p. 306).

Although Lefebvre's definition may not be totally correct when applied to the world as a whole, because the developing countries of the world still show as much concern for issues of economic growth and industrialisation as for urbanisation, the twentieth century undoubtedly could be described as one of urban revolution. For instance, many developing countries witness large-scale rural—urban and urban—urban migrations which result in the growth of what McGee (1967) describes as a premature metropolis. The premature metropolis has developed without a strong industrial base and hence fails to provide residents continuously with employment, housing, transportation and the basic infrastructural needs of a society. The problems generated by such metropolises are many and complex. To the extent that these problems are of much concern to developing countries, and inasmuch as it believed that the location of cities as well as their hierarchical distribution could be utilised to speed economic development (Friedman, 1969), the present century could be characterised as one of world-wide urban revolution.

In the years ahead, concern would be shown for the growth of individual cities as much as for the development of a system of cities. Although the latter has not been as of great concern for the present study, it might be expected that future years would produce critical evaluations of the roles of concepts such as the central place and growth pole theories (Perroux, 1950) in regional development. It would, however, be expected that urban analysis in the years ahead would strive to show the links between what Lefebvre describes as the ensemble of transformations and their relationships to urban economic growth. Furthermore, it will recognise the fact that urban 'space and the political organization of space express social relationships but also react back upon them' (Lefebvre, 1970, p. 25; see also Harvey, 1973, p. 306). In this context, it might be expected that the issues of values, value systems and the socio-cultural environments (Buttimer, 1973) would be a crucial issue.

The role of values in urban analysis has often been neglected in many theoretical formulations whilw it is treated as a residual variable in others. Here again, it needs to be noted that the relationship between social values and social space is symbotic, a point recognised by Buttimer (1969) and Sorre (1957). According to them, social space is

> a mosaic of areas, each homogeneous in terms of the space perceptions of its inhabitants. Within each of the areas, a network of points and lines radiating from certain 'points privilégié' (theaters, schools, churches and other foci of social movement) could be identified.

> Each group tended to have its own specific social space, which reflected its particular values, preferences and aspirations. The density of social space reflected the complementarity, and consequently the degree of interaction between groups (M. Sorre, 1957, pp. 87–114; quoted from Buttimer, 1969, p. 419).

The pertinent question therefore should concern how human activities create these interactions and hence how daily social practices solve the relationship between social processes and spatial form. One way of doing this is to probe more deeply into the integration of the theoretical basis of human spatial behaviour and currently available models of urban spatial structure.

Current operational models and techniques in urban analysis are aggregative and usually generate good results in terms of conventional 'goodness-of-fit' tests, especially when zonal data are used. Such good results are not only deceptive, since there is much loss of information arising from grouping; they are also bad predictors of human spatial behaviour. It would seem that urban models should be constructed out of micro-level considerations if they are to improve their goodness of fit and provide better explanatory and predictive capabilities.

In principle, operational urban models may be developed by constructing a model at the micro-level and performing some aggregation using the concept of the utility tree (Strotz, 1957, 1959). As interesting as such a procedure is, the inherent analytical problems involved (Wilson, 1971; Cesario and Smith, 1975) are prohibitive. None the less, it might be expected that urban analysis would not only want to solve this aggregation issue but would also emphasise more the operationalisation of the concept of the utility tree.

Associated with the concept of the utility tree is the role of utility maximisation and the probability basis of human spatial behaviour. For instance, the desire to make a trip to a shopping centre is based not only on the relative location of opportunities, the choice attributes of decision-making and the socio-economic characteristics of the decision-maker, but also on the notion that the decision-maker selects that alternative that offers him maximum net utility or surplus. Since the costs and benefits of each opportunity are perceived differently by members of a population, their valuation will be non-uniform and it is possible to expect that some uncertainty will be involved in the decision processes.

Recent studies (see Williams, 1977, for example) are showing that it is feasible to construct operational models of human spatial behaviour within a probabilistic choice theory and random utility framework. Such models generally assume a rational assessment of choice alternatives in which the probabilistic component of the theory arises because of the different perception of utility associated with any alternative (Williams, 1977). Since the approach is essentially behavioural, although the models are similar to those developed through conventional techniques, it possesses the added advantage of providing explanations of the variability in human spatial behaviour at the micro-level in terms of economic rationality. It might therefore be expected that this approach will not only solve the aggregation problem but will also lead to the construction of valid and consistent urban models that recognise the symbiotic relationship between spatial processes and urban form.

It is feasible to expect that urban analysis would proceed into more detailed investigation of processes and undoubtedly would find itself relying more on techniques of systems analysis. Thus, it will provide a clear understanding and viewing of individual components of the urban system through an explanation of the structure of their interrelationships within both their vertical and horizontal dimensions. While the former will relate to the aggregation problem and its level of organisation, the latter will relate to the optimum relationship which each element of the system of interest maintains (Beer, 1966). In this context much reliance is likely to be placed on the methods of operations research as well as cybernetics, which Wierner defines as the science of control and communications in the animal and the machine. It must, however, be noted that successes in this endeavour will not be as rapid as in the case of physical or biological systems because it is yet to be proved that the main quantities affecting the society are statistical. Even if this is true, the large statistical runs which are required for calibration and theory development in physical systems are as yet unavailable for social systems. None the less urban analysis would be expected continuously to perfect present tools and develop more appropriate techniques on the lines suggested above.

4. Conclusion

In spite of the apparent successes in modelling urban spatial form, there is still a rather poor understanding of this phenomenon. Its geometry is as little understood as its dynamics, though an understanding of one could be the much-needed key to the other. Spatial form is a consequence of spatial processes which in turn result from the utilisation of energy in a system. Couldn't one then expect that developments in the physical sciences such as mathematics and physics would increasingly affect our conception of the problem? For instance, couldn't it be that the space-time concepts of Minkowski would be applicable to the understanding of the geometry of the urban form? Or shouldn't we expect some correspondence between the physical sciences' concept of energy and work and some of the mechanisms that underly the growth of urban systems? It may therefore be expected that a clarification of many of these issues would constitute valuable researches which could make the role of urban analysis more relevant to the articulation and solution of some of the problems of the society.

There is now a deeper need on the part of urban analysts to bridge the apparent disparity between their theoretical orientations and what is known about the phenomenon of interest, just as there is an urgent need to clarify basic postulates. This is not an unattainable task and the next few years could be decisive in our attempts.

References

Beer, S. 1966. *Decision and Control*. New York: John Wiley

Berry, B.S.L. 1964. Cities as Systems within Systems of Cities. *Papers Regional Science Association, 13*, 147–63

Berry, B.J.L. 1973. *The Human Consequences of Urbanization*. London: Macmillan Papermac

Boyce, D., Day, N. and McDonald, C. 1970. *Metropolitan Plan Making*. Monograph No. 4, Regional Science Research Institute, University of Pennsylvania, Philadelphia

Buttimer, A. 1969. Social Space in Interdisplinary Perspective. *Geographical Review, 59*, 417–26

Buttimer, A.1973. *Values in Geography*. Washington D.C.: Association of American Geographers

Cesario, F.J., and Smith, T.E. 1975. Direction for Future Research in Spatial Interaction Modelling. *Papers Regional Science Association, 35*, 57–72

Friedman, J. 1969. The Role of Cities in National Development. *American Behavioural Scientist, 22*, 5, 13–31

Harvey, D. 1973. *Social Justice and the City*. Baltimore, Maryland: The Johns Hopkins University Press

Himmelblau, D.M. 1972. *Applied Non-Linear Programming*. New York: McGraw-Hill

Lefebvre, H. 1970. *Le Revolution Urbaine*. Paris

Lerner, D., and Lasswell, H.D. (eds.). 1959. *Policy Sciences: Recent Development in Scope and Method*. Stanford, California: Stanford University Press

Lichfield, N., Kettle, P., and Whitbread, M. 1975. *Evaluation in the Planning Process*. London: Pergamon Press

Lowry, I.S. 1965. A Short Course in Model Design. *Journal of the Planners*, May, 158–65

McGee, T.G. 1967. *The Southeast Asian City*. London: Bell, pp. 204

Massey, D.B., and Cordey-Hayes, M. 1971. The Use of Models in Structure Planning. *Town Planning Review, 42*, 28–44

Perroux, F. 1950. Economic Space, Theory and Applications. *Quarterly Journal of Economics, 64*, 89–104

Sorre, M. 1957. L'espace du geographe et du sociologue. In *Recontres de la Sociologie*. Paris, pp. 87–114

Strotz, R.E. 1957. The Implications of a Utility Tree. *Econometrica,25*, 269–318

Strotz, R.E. 1959. The Utility Tree: A Correction and Further Appraisal. *Econometrica, 27*, 482–8

Williams, H.C.W.L. 1977. On the formations of travel demand models and economic evaluation measures of user benefit. *Environment and Planning A, 9*, 285–344

Wilson, A.G. 1969. Forecasting Planning. *Urban Studies, 6*, 248–369

Wilson, A.G. 1971. Some Recent Developments in Microeconomic Approach to Modelling Household Behaviour with Special Reference to Spatio-temporal Organization. Department of Geography Working Paper No. 3, University of Leeds

INDEX